Introduction to Computers and C Programming

(THIRD EDITION)

AF653865

S K BAJPAI
Formaly Professor & Head
Department of Computer Science
Institute of Engineering & Technology
Lucknow (UP)

D S YADAV
Formaly Professor
Department of Computer Science
Institute of Engineering & Technology
Lucknow (UP)

Publishing Globally

NEW AGE INTERNATIONAL (P) LIMITED, PUBLISHERS
LONDON • NEW DELHI • NAIROBI
Bangalore • Chennai • Cochin • Guwahati • Hyderabad • Kolkata • Lucknow • Mumbai
Visit us at www.newagepublishers.com

Published by New Age International (P) Ltd., Publishers
Third Edition: 2002
Reprint: 2017

GLOBAL OFFICES

- **New Delhi** — **NEW AGE INTERNATIONAL (P) LIMITED, PUBLISHERS**
  7/30 A, Daryaganj, New Delhi-110002, (INDIA)
  Tel.: (011) 23253771, 23253472, **Telefax:** 23267437, 43551305
  E-mail: contactus@newagepublishers.com • Visit us at www.newagepublishers.com
- **London** — **NEW AGE INTERNATIONAL (UK) LTD.**
  27 Old Gloucester Street, London, WC1N 3AX, UK
  E-mail: info@newacademicscience.co.uk • Visit us at www.newacademicscience.co.uk
- **Nairobi** — **NEW AGE GOLDEN (EAST AFRICA) LTD.**
  Ground Floor, Westlands Arcade, Chiromo Road (Next to Naivas Supermarket)
  Westlands, Nairobi, KENYA, **Tel.:** 00-254-713848772, 00-254-725700286
  E-mail: kenya@newagepublishers.com

BRANCHES

- **Bangalore** — 37/10, 8th Cross (Near Hanuman Temple), Azad Nagar, Chamarajpet, Bangalore- 560 018
  Tel.: (080) 26756823, **Telefax:** 26756820, **E-mail: bangalore@newagepublishers.com**
- **Chennai** — 26, Damodaran Street, T. Nagar, Chennai-600 017, **Tel.:** (044) 24353401
  Telefax: 24351463, **E-mail: chennai@newagepublishers.com**
- **Cochin** — CC-39/1016, Carrier Station Road, Ernakulam South, Cochin-682 016
  Tel.: (0484) 2377303, **Telefax:** 4051304, **E-mail: cochin@newagepublishers.com**
- **Guwahati** — Hemsen Complex, Mohd. Shah Road, Paltan Bazar, Near Starline Hotel
  Guwahati-781 008, **Tel.:** (0361) 2513881, **Telefax:** 2543669
  E-mail: guwahati@newagepublishers.com
- **Hyderabad** — 105, 1st Floor, Madhiray Kaveri Tower, 3-2-19, Azam Jahi Road, Near Kumar Theater
  Nimboliadda Kachiguda, Hyderabad-500 027, **Tel.:** (040) 24652456, **Telefax:** 24652457
  E-mail: hyderabad@newagepublishers.com
- **Kolkata** — RDB Chambers (Formerly Lotus Cinema) 106A, 1st Floor, S N Banerjee Road
  Kolkata-700 014, **Tel.:** (033) 22273773, **Telefax:** 22275247
  E-mail: kolkata@newagepublishers.com
- **Lucknow** — 16-A, Jopling Road, Lucknow-226 001, **Tel.:** (0522) 2209578, 4045297, **Telefax:** 2204098
  E-mail: lucknow@newagepublishers.com
- **Mumbai** — 142C, Victor House, Ground Floor, N.M. Joshi Marg, Lower Parel, Mumbai-400 013
  Tel.: (022) 24927869, **Telefax:** 24915415, **E-mail: mumbai@newagepublishers.com**
- **New Delhi** — 22, Golden House, Daryaganj, New Delhi-110 002, **Tel.:** (011) 23262368, 23262370
  Telefax: 43551305, **E-mail: sales@newagepublishers.com**

ISBN: 978-81-224-1379-3

C-16-11-9776

Printed in India at Kanishik Printing Press, Delhi.

NEW AGE INTERNATIONAL (P) LIMITED, PUBLISHERS
7/30 A, Daryaganj, New Delhi-110002
Visit us at **www.newagepublishers.com**
(CIN: U74899DL1966PTC004618)

Preface to the Third Edition

The third edition of "Introduction to Computers and C Programming" is fully revised and enlarged edition. All attempts have been made to clarify the concepts with the help of diagrams and illustrations.

The book exhaustively explains the basic concepts in computer software and hardware as well as the features of operating systems like DOS, UNIX and Windows. Internet and C programming have also been explained. We hope that this book will serve as sufficient study material to first year students of B.Tech of UP Technical University as well as to the beginners in the field.

S K Bajpai
D S Yadav

Acknowledgements

Authors would like to put on the record the effort of Mr. S K Shuka, Registrar, UP Technical University, which has paved the way for improvement in the contents. Authors are also thankful to him for providing an excellent working environment for writing this text.

Authors express their sincere thanks to Mr. S S Yadav, DGM (Telephones) Ghaziabad, who provided the details of various internet services offered by MTNL/DOT. Authors are thankful to Dr. A K. Majumdar, IIT Kharagpur, Prof. O P Singhal, Prof. V S Yadav BIET, Jhansi, Prof. Girish Chandra, Prof. M H Khan, Prof. S P Tripathi of IET, Lucknow and Mr. Gaurav Bajpai for their suggestions for improvement of text.

Authors deeply acknowledge Mr. L N Mistra of New Age International for his deep involvement in this project and the help provided by him to prepare the manuscript in such a short time.

S K Bajpai would like to thank his son Vaibhav Bajpai, who helped in reading the manuscript. He would also like to thank his wife Shoba for her cooperation, daughter Garima Bajpai and son Gaurav Bajpai, both students of B.Tech (Computer Engineering) for their full cooperation and critical suggestions. Lastly, he would like to thank his spiritual guruji Shri Gopal Chand Lahiri for his blessings.

D S Yadav is grateful to his daughters Ankita and Surabhi for giving time to prepare the manuscript of this book. He would also like to thank his wife Gayatri for her active cooperation in preparing the manuscript. His thanks are also due to Mr. K P Singh Yadav and Mrs. Malti Yadav for their blessings.

S K Bajpai
D S Yadav

Contents

1 Introduction to Computers

1.0 INTRODUCTION

In today's world, the term Information Technology (IT) is probably the most talked about and discussed term. This has become a must for the growth of every business sector. In the past few years, a tremendous growth in this sector has been witnessed. Rapid advancements in the technologies for communication media like television, computer, internet, printing and publishing of newspapers has allowed us to get prompt access to required information. Computer is the most versatile machine man has ever made. The use of computers at home has become a reality and use of computers at work is quite common. Now almost all the government departments and private organizations have accepted the computer as a major tool to renovate their style of functioning. Computers are being used in multiple areas ranging from solving most intricate scientific problems to art, cultural, historical, accounting, financial, medical, and other disciplines' problems. Truly, with IT, the computer has revolutionized our life and has made a significant impact on all dimensions of our day-to-day activities e.g. reservation of air and railway ticket, buying and selling items on internet, electronics market, inquiry of various departments, bank transactions on net, entertainment, education, communication, hotel reservations, tourism have become a reality. IT has replaced the conventional methods to solve technical and operational problems by introducing much faster and more convenient way by accessing a large and complex pool of data.

The computer is considered as a basic ingredient for application of IT. This electronic equipment is able to store, process and communicate the information at a much faster rate. This chapter discusses the basic details of digital computer, which is referred in this text as computer.

1.1 WHAT IS A COMPUTER?

The concept of computer evolution is not recent. With gradual research in the past it has acquired the status of today. With the advent of computers all sciences, art, cultural, historical, accounting, financial, medical, and other disciplines are required to change with the base of computing environment. Engineering education in this environment is required to change its base from science to computers. Mathematics as mentioned earlier was mother of all sciences; similarly computing may be mentioned as brain for all kinds of education.

The development of computer machinery is not one-day research. In fact it began with the civilization and first computing instrument known by name ABACUS was developed in 400 B.C. Napier's bones, Pascal, Leibnitz, Babbage's "Difference Engine" etc. were developed in the past that gave birth to the present-day computers, which are versatile to be used in many different forms. The advent of present-day computer may be thought to have started from MARK-1 computer (1939-44), ENIAC Computer (1946), IBM-602-603 (1946). Then came the revolution in this area by introduction of UNIVAC-1 (1950), IBM-360 (1964). This was the period when mini-computer also saw its dawn (1964). Varieties of computer for variety of users were introduced. Super markets also saw the applicability of the machines. From 1980-90 PC's captured all small/large application as main frame computers were doing because of down trend in their costs and affordability of people in their homes.

British Mathematician Augusta Ada Byron became the first programmer in the history who programmed Babbage's Analytical Engine (1836-1852). BASIC was introduced by John Kemeny and Thomas Kurtz at Dartmouth College in 1965. IBM PC was introduced in 1981, First Macintosh computer, "MAC" with graphic interface came in 1984. Windows 1.01 by Microsoft was founded in 1985. Windows 3.1 was introduced in 1992.

A computer is a general-purpose machine that processes data according to a set of instructions that is stored internally. In other words, it is a programmable computing machine. Computer may be considered as an electronic machine which takes the data from the outside world. Upon processing, this data is produced in the form of output or result to the outside world. Initially this machine was used for scientific and engineering computation but now it is used for all kinds of jobs at school, university and college, offices, hospitals, bank, railway, agriculture, recreation etc. In fact, there are three types of processing, namely, calculating, comparing and copying which are performed by a computer. By the word copy we mean that the computer can move data around to create any kind of report or listing of any order. Thus a computer accomplishes all forms of data processing by calculating, comparing and copying.

1.2 FUNCTIONAL UNITS OF COMPUTER

Every computer comprises four basic components known as basic functional units, as shown below in figure 1.1. These basic components are Input, Output, CPU and Auxiliary Storage.

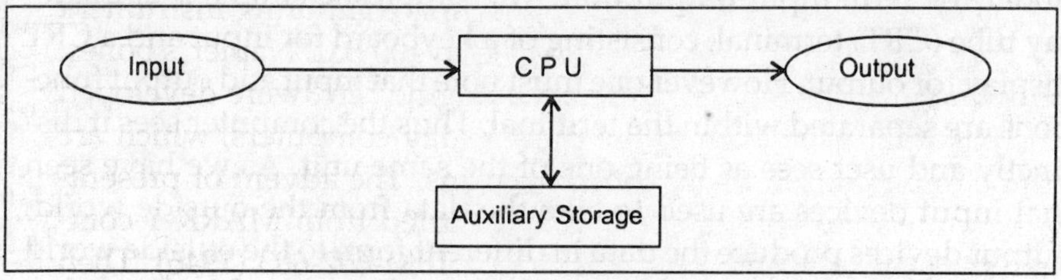

Fig 1.1 Functional units

Input Unit

The component "Input Unit" refers to the devices, which convert the data or signals from outside/real world into the form of data which is understandable in the computer system. The function of input unit is to accept coded information from human operator or from electromechanical device or from other computer connected to it or from internet or by any other media. These are devices by which a programmer or computer operator interacts with the computer system. These devices allow the user to feed the data and program the computer to do specific task. The most popular input device is *Keyboard*. This device allows the user to enter the data and program to the computer by pressing the appropriate keys. Whenever a key or combination of keys is pressed, it generates the electrical signals which may be understood and processed by the computer. Another popular input device is *Mouse*. This device is used to position the cursor on the monitor. By just a click of a button on the mouse several tasks or programs may be executed. *Scanner* is another input device which allows the user to scan images or photographs to feed into the computer. After scanning, digital image of the photograph or the document is created, which can be stored and processed in a Computer. *Digital Camera* is another input device, which can be used to capture the videos (visuals) and store them into the computer system in electronic formats. These stored videos may be processed and produced again by the computer. Therefore, Input devices are those devices which takes the data from outside world and it can be stored and processed in the computers.

Output Unit

Output Unit refers to the device which is used to present the data processed by the computer to the outside world. The function of the output unit is to store the processed information as and when required by the user. In fact, input and output equipment, is usually combined under the term input-output unit. The simplest example is cathode-ray tube (CRT) terminal, consisting of a keyboard for input and a CRT display for output. However one must note that input and output functions are separated within the terminal. Thus the computer sees it distinctly and user sees as being one of the same unit. As we have seen that input devices are used to take the data from the outside world, output devices produce the data in different form to the outside world or users. The most popular output device is known as *Monitor*. It is a Video Display Unit, which shows the status of your work on the computer. For example, whatever you type in through the keyboard, it may be verified on the monitor. It also gives an impression, as if you are typing on the screen. It may be used to present the text, document, graphics or video to the users. Another important output device is known as *Printer*. This device is used by the user to print the different types of data in different formats. Nowadays, with the help of colour printers, it is also possible to produce the different colours to your documents while printing.

Central Processing Unit (CPU)

The Central Processing Unit (CPU) is considered as the brain of the computer. It is the place where all kinds of processing are done. This carries out fundamental computing operation called calculation, comparison and copying. This unit also controls the operation of all other functional units of a computer such as memory, input and output devices.

The CPU is composed of following three parts

1. Arithmetic and Logical Unit (ALU)
2. Control Unit (CU)
3. General Purpose Register/Register Array

The Arithmetic and Logic Unit (ALU) is also called Number Crunching Unit. The data gathered from outside world through input devices are processed in arithmetic and logical unit. The function of arithmetic and logical unit is to perform arithmetical operations on data by adding, subtracting, multiplying and dividing one set with another and logical operations, often known by using AND, OR, NOT and Exclusive OR operation, which is done by analyzing and evaluating data by matching it with a set of known data that is included in the program or called from memory. This unit also performs increment, decrement, shift and clearance operations as well. This unit mainly performs arithmetic and logical operations on the set of data. Most common arithmetic operations are addition, subtraction, multiplication, division, square, square root etc. The logical operations like comparison, equality, ordering etc. on alphanumeric data are also performed by this unit. Some of the important arithmetic and logical operations are listed in following table.

Table 1.2

Arithmetic Operations		Logical Operations	
+	Addition	=	Equal
–	Subtraction	>	Greater Than
×	Multiplication	<	Less than
/	Division	<>	Not Equal
√	Square Root		

Control Unit (CU)

Control Unit is another important unit of CPU which works in close association with other units. This unit is used to control other devices and units by issuing appropriate control and timing signals. Control unit generates control and timing signals necessary for the processing of an instruction. It controls all the operations of the computer. The program, a set of instructions, is required to be executed in order to process the data. The program is stored in the memory. CPU fetches the instructions of the program one by one and executes them in order. These instructions are executed by issuing appropriate timing and control signals by Control Unit at the same time the arithmetic/logic operations are performed by the Arithmetic and Logical Unit. CPU also communicates with the I/O or peripheral devices to read or write the data. It also controls the timing while communicating the data with other devices. The timing signals in communication process are also issued by Control Unit.

General Purpose Register/Register Array

Central Processing Unit also possesses the memory to hold the data temporarily during the execution of an instruction. This memory is called Register Memory. It is a very small memory in comparison to Main Memory or Auxiliary Memory. The register memory may be logically thought of a stack or array of registers. The register is the basic unit or smallest unit of storing the data. The total number of registers available in the CPU varies from processor to processor. These registers are programmable, i.e. a programmer may use them to load the data or result by writing program. Out of these registers, some registers are used for specific purposes. Accumulator is a special register used for specific purpose, holding the result of current operation temporarily.

CPU can be shown schematically as follows

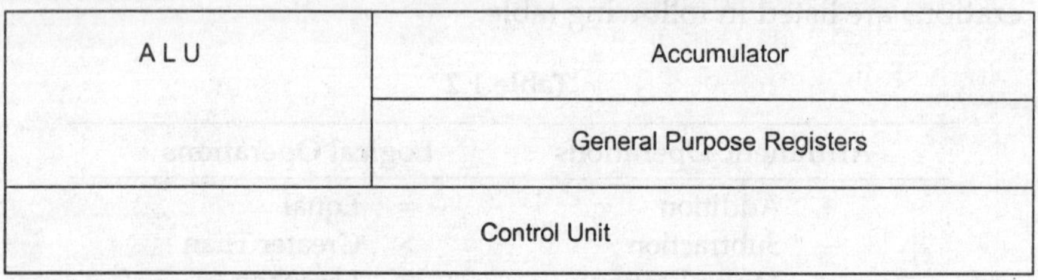

Fig 1.3 Schematic of CPU

Auxiliary Storage Unit

Auxiliary storage unit is another important unit of a computer. The auxiliary storage devices or secondary memory is used to hold the output, data or program for future use. Magnetic Tape, Magnetic Disk, CD ROMs, Floppy Disks are examples of auxiliary storage devices. The auxiliary storage devices are much larger in capacity than main memory but they are generally slower than main memory. The contents of these devices are not directly transferred to the CPU for processing. Auxiliary storage data is first transferred to main memory and then CPU fetches the data from main memory. We will discuss this in details in Memory Hierarchy in the following sections.

1.3 MICRO COMPUTER

During last three decades, there has been tremendous improvement in semiconductor technologies. Improvement in these technologies resulted in lesser space requirement for hardware and consistently increasing speed of processing. After the invention of transistors in

1960's, Integrated Circuits (IC) came into existence. With Integrated Circuits, it has become possible to put several transistors on a single chip. The technology of putting number of logic gates onto a single chip was named Small Scale Integration (SSI). In SSI, it was possible to put 50-100 gates on a single chip. With further advancements in semiconductor technology, it has become possible to put 100-1000 logic gates on one chip. It was called Medium Scale Integration. With Large Scale Integration (LSI), more than one thousand gates may be fabricated on a single chip. Slowly through Very Large Scale Integration (VLSI), we have entered into the era of Ultra Large Scale Integration (ULSI). Journey from SSI to ULSI has changed the size of electronic circuits with rapid advancement in the processing speed. Nowadays it is possible to fabricate the electronic circuitry required for a Central Processing Unit into single piece of chip. This Chip is known as Microprocessor.

Therefore, a Microprocessor is nothing but a CPU fabricated into a single piece of a chip. A computer system built around Microprocessor is called Micro Computer. Schematic of a Micro Computer is shown in the following figure.

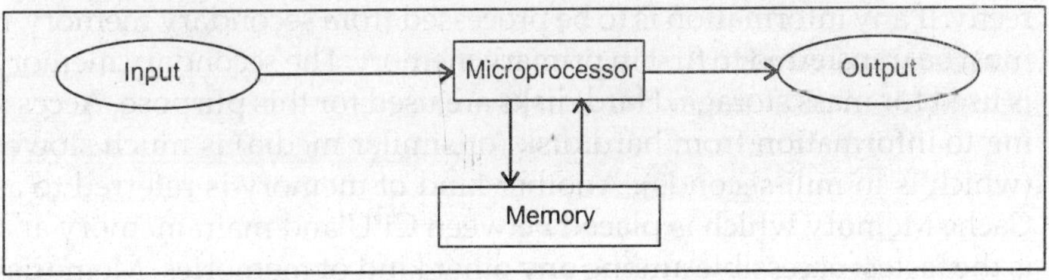

Fig 1.4 Functional Units of Micro Computer

Fig 1.4 remains unaltered even for this representation but for CPU replaced by microprocessor. The word Central in CPU is used to indicate that most of the control functions in the computer are centralized in a single unit. Another point the reader must note that a computer, though, shown above into functional units consists of five functional independent main parts, namely, input, memory, arithmetic and logical unit, output and control units as shown below:

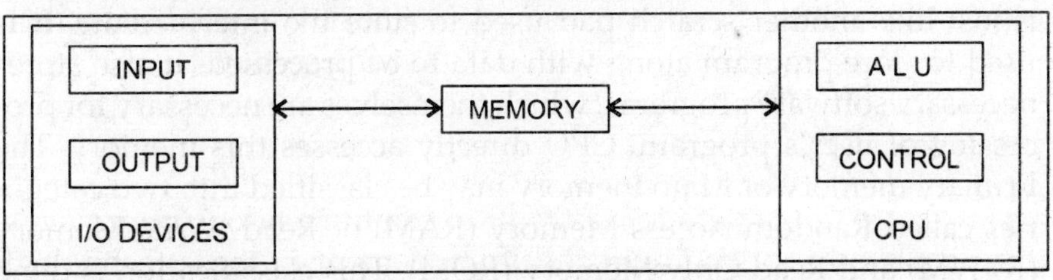

Fig. 1.5 Main Functional Units of a Computer

1.4 MEMORY

The Memory is also known by the term storage. Its function is to store coded form of information from human operator, from input devices, from other computers connected to it. The information stored may be used immediately or for later reference for processing by CPU. Two or three levels of memory are provided in a computer. Main memory, also known as primary memory is a fast memory. It is used to store program along with data to be processed. It also stores necessary software programs, which themselves are necessary for processing of user's program. This memory is directly accessed by CPU. The accessing of data from this memory takes randomly and thus referred as Random Access Memory (RAM). Its access time is in nano second (ns). This memory does not store data/program permanently and RAM is therefore called volatile memory, and volatile with switching off the computer or by replacement of information in it. Secondary memory or auxiliary memory is used to store operating system, compiler, assembler, application programs, data files etc. and are not read by CPU directly. If any information is to be processed from secondary memory, it must be transferred to first in primary memory. The secondary memory is used for mass storage. Hard disks are used for this purpose. Accessing to information from hard disk (or similar media) is much slower (which is in mili-seconds). Another kind of memory is referred to as Cache Memory which is placed between CPU and main memory and is the fastest accessible among any other kind of memories. Memories become costlier from secondary to primary and become fastest accessible in reverse order.

The memory can be classified into following categories.

1. Main or Primary Memory
2. Auxiliary or Secondary Memory

Primary or Main Memory is the fastest memory of a digital computer system. This memory is primarily used to store the data and program temporarily during the execution of a program. This memory is just like another scratch pad used to store the intermediate. It is used to store program along with data to be processed. It also stores necessary software programs, which themselves are necessary for processing of user's program. CPU directly accesses this memory. The Primary memory or Main memory may be classified into two categories called Random Access Memory (RAM) or Read/Write Memory (R/WM) and Read Only Memory (ROM). This classification is done on the basis of temporary or permanent storage of data.

Random Access Memory (RAM) is a part of Primary Memory and called Volatile Memory. The volatile memory means that it holds the data temporarily and when the power is switched off, all the data stored in this memory is washed. This memory is also called Read Write Memory because it is used by the CPU to temporarily load the program instruction and intermediate results. The program instruction and data keeps on changing by the process of reading and writing to it therefore it is also called read/write memory. The accessing of data from this memory takes randomly and thus referred as Random Access Memory (RAM). Its access time is in nano second (ns). This memory does not store data/program permanently and RAM is therefore called volatile memory, and volatile with switching off the computer or by replacement of information in it. Secondary memory or auxiliary memory is used to store Operating System, Compiler, assembler, application programs, data files etc. are not read by CPU directly. If any information is needed to be processed from secondary memory, must be transferred to first in primary memory. The secondary memory is used for mass storage hard disks are used for this purpose. Accessing of information from hard disk (or similar media) is much slower (which is in mili-seconds). The Random Access Memory may be classified into two categories as shown below.

1. Static RAM
2. Dynamic RAM

Static RAM is made up of Flip Flops, an electronic device, which stores a bit as a voltage. Static RAM are fast but the disadvantage is packing of Flip Flops. A comparatively less number of Flip Flops are packed on a memory chip therefore the memory density of Static RAM is low.

Dynamic RAM is based on technology called MOS transistor gates. Advantage of MOS transistor gates is that more number of MOS gates may be packed on memory chip, therefore the memory density of Dynamic RAM is high. The drawback of Dynamic Memory is that its flip-flop based on MOS transistor gates use charge as a bit. This charge is stored across the capacitor. The property of a capacitor is that the charge leaks with the time. Therefore a special circuit called refreshing circuit is also placed with the dynamic RAM to refresh the memory.

Read Only Memory (ROM) is also a part of primary memory and it is called Non Volatile memory. As the name indicates the ROM can be used only for reading or fetching data from it. The data or program are written into ROM only once and once written, it cannot be modified or altered. It is used to contain the programs or data, which are critical and used frequently. Here the non-volatile means that even if the power is switched off the data or program stored on it is not destroyed. Whenever the power comes, the same data appears once again. This so happens because of permanent hardware pattern are used to store the data on ROM. One important use of ROM is to store the Basic Input Output Software (BIOS). This program is very important and is used by operating system at the time of starting up or booting of the system. Since this program is used every time the computer is turned on, it must be stored in the ROM.

Why is ROM Non-Volatile?

The data stored in the ROM are of permanent nature. Even when the power to ROM is switched off, data is not deleted. When the power is switched on, it retains the data stored in the memory. The ROM is based on the fact that there is a mesh of diodes or fuses placed in a matrix form. The selective fuses are burnt as per the data to be stored in the ROM. Similarly the presence or absence of the diode or fuse denotes whether bit 1 or 0 is stored. Since the pattern of placing diode or fuses is decided by the manufacturer of ROM, it becomes a permanent pattern.

There are four types of ROM, namely, Masked ROM, Programmable ROM, Erasable Programmable ROM and Electrically erasable programmable ROM.

Masked ROM is manufactured by masking and metalization process. The pattern or matrix once created is permanent and no change or alteration is permissible afterwards.

Programmable ROM (PROM) may be programmed by the programmer. Manufacturer of PROM produces PROM by placing a fuse at all the positions. A special device called PROM Programmer is used to store the desired pattern by selectively burning the fuses. Those fuses are burnt wherever a bit 0 has to be stored. The presence of fuse represents a presence of bit 1. After this process the pattern stored is permanent in nature.

Erasable PROM is the programmable ROM which may be programmed again and again. This so happens because the pattern stored on EPROM is semi-permanent. Electrically Erasable PROM (EEPROM) is same as EPROM; the only difference is that electrical signals are used to programme the ROM.

1.5 VON NEUMAN ARCHITECTURE

A Digital Computer may be defined as a programmable electronic machine that takes the data and program from the Input Devices in binary form, processes it according to the program instruction and produces the output on Output devices. The Digital Computers are different from Analog Computers in the sense that Analog Computers process the analog Data. Here the word analog represents the continuous data or real world data. Analog computer may process the real world data like Current, Voltage, Speed in the real time frame. The Digital Computer takes the binary data at input, processes according to the set of instructions called program and produces the digital output. Most of the computer systems have been developed on the basis of Von Neuman computer architecture. Von Neuman has developed preliminary concepts for the execution of program on a computer. Von Neuman computer system uses stored program concept. It means that both the data and programs are stored in the same memory unit. Each memory unit of Von Neuman machine may be addressed independently. General Architecture of Digital computer based on Von Neuman principles is shown in the figure 1.6.

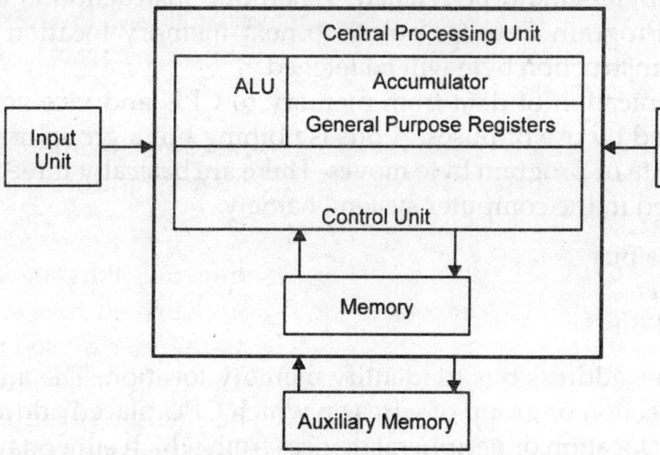

Fig. 1.6 Functional Units of a Digital Computer

The term Programming a computer means that the computer system may be provided with a set of instructions. When these instructions are executed in sequential order they perform specific task for which the instructions were written. A collection of such instructions is known as computer program. Von Neuman had proposed that there should be a separate unit in central processing unit which does all arithmetic and logical operations. It was named as Arithmetic and Logical Unit. The control unit is another section of CPU from where timing signals are generated to synchronize all activities in order to execute a Instruction or Program.

In order to execute a program, the program and required data are supplied by the user through Input devices. The data and program are first placed in the memory. The program which is a collection of several instructions begins when CPU fetches the instruction from the memory. These instructions or instruction bytes are fetched from the memory in sequential order and are placed in special register called Instruction Register located in CPU. The instruction bytes placed in the Instruction Register are decoded and appropriate timing and control signals are generated by the control unit. All the activities required to complete the execution of instruction are synchronized with the clock of computer system.

The fetching of the program instruction from memory in sequential order is established by use of special register in the memory called Program Counter. The Program Counter is a specialized register which contains the address of the memory, location from where the next instruction byte should be fetched. When one instruction is under execution, Program Counter points to next memory location from where next instruction byte will be fetched.

Communication of data from memory to CPU and vice versa is accomplished by use of Buses. A Bus is nothing but a group of wires on which data or program byte moves. There are basically three types of buses used in the computer system, namely,

1. Address Bus
2. Data Bus
3. Control Bus

CPU uses address bus to identify memory location. The address bus is a collection or group of wires on which CPU placed address of the memory location or peripheral devices from which either data has to be fetched or data needs to be written. This is done by placing the address on the address bus. The memory location, whose address is transmitted by CPU on address bus, is selected by Memory Decoder. Once the memory location is selected, data may be read from or write to that memory. The data bus is another selected group of wires which are used to transport the data bytes from memory to CPU and vice versa. Control Bus is a group of independent wires on which the Control Unit (CU) of Central Processing Unit generates control and timing signals. The control and timing signals are required to execute the instructions and synchronize various activities required for execution of instruction or program.

1.6 HISTORY OF COMPUTER

Usually, history of computer and generations of computer are dealt together. In this book, we will deal with them separately, as these are two different notions. History of computer is a study of past development of computers, whereas generation of computer may be defined as an average time or a period of time in which old computer technology may be replaced by newer technology.

History of computer begins with the counting number, essentially this states the discovery of ZERO by Indians in 200 A.D., which gave computation a new era. Gradually in due course of time Napier's bones (1600), Pascal's first computer (1642), Leibnitz's mechanical calculator (1971), Babbage's difference engine (1822) were few discoveries that gave birth to a new horizon in computation. This work ultimately, led to the discovery of computer. First computer, named MARK-1 was created, which marked the beginning of computer developments and generation of computer. A brief history of computers, which is not exhaustive, follows as under.

Year	Origin of computer	Produced by
1939-44	Mark-1	IBM used mechanical relays to store data
1943-45	ENIAC	Physicist John W. Mauchly and Electrical Engg. J. Presper Eckert who used Vacuum technology, officially released in 1946
1946	IBM 602 and IBM 603	IBM, used transistor technology
1950	UNIVAC-1	Remington Rand (used transistor technology). This development took place from the discovery of transistor by Nobel Prize winner John Burdeen, W.H. Brattain and W.B. Shockley)
1963	IBM- 7040	IBM (G. Amdhahl)
1964	IBM- 360	IBM (G. Amdhal) used transistor and Integrated Circuit Technology
1974	Commercial MicroComputer ALTAIR	Ed. Robert used chips
1976	Apple Computer	Apple Computer Inc used chips
1981	IBM PC	IBM used chips

1984	MAC	Macintosh Computer (Steven and Steves)

- This era gave birth to the PC revolution whose generation will be dealt in next sections.

1985	TEXT	Apple Computer Inc (Steve Jobs)

- This era gave revolution in software and various other interfaces with computer.

1987	PC – Windows / 286 / 386	Microsoft GUI upgrade for PC.
Imac	Macintosh Computer	

- This is an era in Computer software and in Computer communication. This may be marked the beginning of Information Technology.

1.7 GENERATION OF COMPUTERS

Generation of computer may be described by taking several factors into considerations.

1.7.1 Technological Considerations

Base technology for the generation of computers begins with the electrical computers, which used electrical relay and switching circuits. Then came electronic digital computers, whose generation is characterized by the type of switching circuit used in designing of these computers This is explained in the table below.

Generation	Technology used	Periodical life
First	Vacuum tube	1945-1955
Second	Transistors (flip-flop)	1955-1963
Third	Integrated Circuits	1963-1975
Fourth	Large scale integrated Circuit on chip	1975 till date
Fifth	Parallel Processing Circuit	Under developing stage

1.7.2 The Stored Program Concept

Abilities of a computer to call in instruction and process them or follow them are known as stored program concept. This concept was introduced by John Von Neuman, a great mathematician who designed the Electronic Discrete Variable Automatic Computer (EDVAC in 1947) with a memory having ability to store both instruction and data. This gave birth to those computers, which possess greater versatility in computer programming.

1.7.3 Computer's Copying Ability into its Memory

Ability of a computer of copying instructions into memory from a disc, tape, other sources before any data can be processed is referred as computer's copying ability. This copying concept allowed computers to direct to start the processing of first instruction in the program. By program we mean the set of instructions that are to be followed in a sequence one after the another. Under this copying concept computer possessed the ability to hold the instruction in its memory from where, first instruction is copied from memory to control unit circuit and matches against the built-in set of instructions. Once matching is found, correct processing is done, otherwise, it comes to an abnormal end. This ability allowed computer to execute instruction of a program sequentially until it finds GOTO instruction that tells it to go to different place(s) in the program. This helped computer to execute millions of instructions over and over again on same set of data or new set of data.

1.7.4 Size Consideration

When we deal with the classification of generation of computers technology that allows the miniaturizing of computers is also one of the considerations. The technological innovation in the IC technology has also triggered considerable size reduction. From Small Scale Integration (SSI) to Super Large Scale Integration (SLSI), the size of computer has been reduced by factor of thousands. Today, it is possible to fabricate thousands of transistors on a single chip.

1.7.5 Speed Consideration

Computer generations may be classified on the basis of speed of computer to process set of instructions per second. With contribution to knowledge in architectural design like parallel processing, vector processing and super computers, the overall speed of operations has been changed dramatically. It is the reason many persons choose speed as a basis for elaborating computer generation.

1.7.6 Overlapping of Operations

While one program is waiting for input from one user, the operating system in this case directs the computer to process other program from which data is available. Large computer is usually designed to allow input and output to occur simultaneously with the processing. While one user's data is being processed, data from next user in queue can be retrieved into the computer.

1.8 COMPUTER GENERATIONS

In this section we will discuss the development and improvement that took place in the computer technology.

1.8.1 First Generation of Computers

This generation may be marked with the incoming of UNIVAC-1 in 1950 where vacuum tubes were used, and their memory was made of thin tube of liquid mercury and magnetic drums.

1.8.2 Second Generation of Computers (1955-1963)

This is a highly revolutionized period in which a new technology of transistors (1959) replaced vacuum tube technology, and used magnetic core of memory. In this generation size of computer was reduced. These computers were more reliable than their predecessor. Computers like IBM – 1401 and Honey well – 800 were produced.

1.8.3 Third Generation of Computers (1963-1975)

Integrated circuits, first Operating system and DBMS marked the beginning of third generation of computer. IBM – 360 and CDC6400 computer are well known examples of this generation. In this generation most processing was batch oriented using punch cards and magnetic tape, however on line systems were also developed in this period. The beginning of this generation is usually varies from 1963-1975.

1.8.4 Fourth Generation of Computers (1975-1994)

In this generation chip replaced integrated circuit. Microprocessor and PC covered most of development. Office automation and distributed processing were introduced. Query languages, Report writers and spread sheet becomes the main part of a computer in the period ranging from 1975 to 1994 and revolutionized the life in advance countries. Computers of this generation made an impact and revolutionized the development of computer and generation of PC took the existence.

1.8.5 Fifth Generation of Computers (1994-2000)

Voice recognition, Natural Language Processing (NLP), language translation, speech processing, other multimedia application, video databases, optical discs and fiber tec and Artificial Intelligence capabilities in computer formed fifth generation computer.

Generation of computers is categorized in the following table:

Generation	First	Second	Third	Forth	Fifth
Average age	1945-1955	1955-1963	1963-1975	1975-1994	1994-2000
Use of technology	Vacuum Tube Technology	Transistor Technology	IC's Technology and multiprogramming	Use of large Scale very large IC on chips	Chips, Microprocessor
Average storage capacity	Nil	Tape, limited storage	Increased storage	Much more increased storage	Any level of storage
Average speed of computer	Slowest	Fast	Faster speed	Much faster	Any speed up to 10^6 Mhz or more
Average size of computer	Enormous size, filling up entire rooms with 10000 vacuum tubes	Enormous but smaller than first generation	Small size and better performance	Highly small and better performance	Desktop and PC/AT, Pentium era
Language used	Absolute machine language not even machine or programming language was known	Fortran or assembly language	Fortran, BASIC and more high level languages	All popular programming language / 4 GL	All popular programming languages with graphical facilities
Data Base used	Unknown entity	Unknown entity	Yes, low level data bases/file system	Yes, High level data bases	Oracle and other high level data bases

Work done	Straight forward numerical calculation were available	Scientific calculations such as solving differential equation	Different kind of calculation with commercial use	All scientific, engineering and commercial application	All scientific/commercial/educational/invasion in all fields
Commercial availability	No possibility	Manufactured and sold	Yes Banks and other organization include military and other installation used	Most of organization computerized	World computerization a phenominon
Reliability	Nil initially but later improved with punch card	Reliable	High reliability	Very high reliability	Reliability of high order
Operating system	Unknown	Batch Processing Fortran Monitor system (FMS)-operating system IBSYS for 7094	UNIX/Time sharing	UNIX/Time sharing	UNIX, DOS, LINUX, WINDOWS etc.
Cost	Very costly	Multi million dollar cost	Expensive	Expensive	Cheap, affordable
Computer	MARK-1	IBM-1401, IBM-7094, CDC-1604, ATLAS	IBM360, 370, P II	PC's Origin, Motorola 68000	PC generation, CRAY-XMPIG, PARAM-2000

1.9 PC GENERATIONS

Personal Computer made a revolutionary change in our culture. PC's have become common in public and offices; they replaced typewriter of any kind. Personal memories were replaced by stored memories of computers. Paper technology is in threat; paper currency is also on the verge of being replaced by credit cards. PC's entered from offices to homes to kitchens and to any place one can think of. Functioning of all machines from home to factories, villages to cities, from secrets of atomic plants to any warfare and other places have become dependent on microprocessor-based computer technology. This all means that PC's define our culture. The personal computer is the most logical, scientific and engineering modern machine that is an aid to human mind. This leads us to think that PC's are an extension of human abilities. What human beings can perform? PC's can perform 100 thousand times faster. There are the tools that are not bound by limitations of mechanical rules. In this chapter we will discuss how some recent developments took place till this technology is replaced by newer and finer one.

1.9.1 Development in the Area of Computing

The first PC was designed by IBM with the name IBM personal computer and was introduced in 1981. In general any machine that was compatible with IBM PC, which used a microprocessor and understood the same programs and languages at least as in the PC qualified this term and IBM design was accepted by industry and became Industry standard (1981-1987). After 1987, the term IBM compatible was abandoned. Later on, none of the PC's fulfilled the standards as laid down by ANSI (American National Standards Institute), IEEE (Institute of Electrical and Electronics) or neither ISO (International Standards Organizations) nor any government made them mandatory. Two major organizations Multimedia PC (MPC) marketing council and Microsoft Corporation have promoted PC certified standards. In fact Multimedia PC marketing council developed the first certification of PC standard for assuring that it can run Multimedia software and so the concept of multimedia PC was floated. Such a computer was supposed to be equipped with all peripherals necessary for producing sound and images. A committee of software publishers association superseded these. Similarly when Windows-95 was developed, Microsoft set a minimum requirements on PC that could run it. This set of requirements later were known by PC-95 with next generation of windows 95/98 etc. Based on the above, PC generation can be put in comparative form. Major PC comparison based on above discussion is listed below.

1.9.2 Comparison of PC's Standards

Standard	MPC-1	MPC-2	MPC-3	PC95	PC97
Year	1990	1993	1995	1995	1997
Personal computer	386 SX	486 SX	Pentium	No requirement	Pentium
Speed	16 MHz	25 MHz	75 MHz	No requirement	120 MHz
Memory	2 MB	4 MB	8 MB	4 MB	16 MB
Floppy disc	1.44 MB	1.44 MB	1.44 MB	Not required	Not required
Hard disc	30 MB	160 MB	540 MB	Not required	Not required

1.10 HISTORY OF PC FROM 1981-1990

The PC's discovered in 1981 gave PC culture and the world saw new kinds of computer capable of doing the human work from office to house and to all places on affordable price. Though one time revolutionary system that are obsolete now, gave the birth to Pentium, a high speed computer, which can be used individually or in group with on cost effective price. A brief comparison of these systems should give the idea to the reader how these computers are gradually improved and came into existence. The real development on architectural ground is not in our scope and will be dealt in separately.

1.10.1 Comparison of PC's

Name of PC Generation	Year of origin	Speed of computer	Processor used and Bus Size	RAM	HDD	OS
IBM PC	1981	4.77 MHz	8088 8 bit	16 KB	NA	DRDOS
IBM PC-XT	1983	16 MHz	8088 16 bit	256 KB to 640KB	10 or 20 MB	DOS
IBM PC-AT-286	1984	25 MHz	80286 16 bit	1 to 4 MB	20 or 30 MB	DOS WINDOWS
IBM PC –AT-386	1987	33 MHz	80386 32 bit	2 to 8 MB	60 or 200	DRDOS DOS WINDOWS
IBM PC–AT-486	1989	66 MHz	80486 323 bit	4 to 12 MB		DOS /2 WINDOWS

Note that PCs listed from IBM were not the only PCs available, other companies were also in race but they all produced PC's which were IBM compatible. This compatibility in later race of development was not maintained. Looking at the Table beside the architectural difference, speed of computer and storage capacity of the computer became real distinctive features for any ordinary user. In the time ahead, one more factor added to this distinctive feature was whether softwares and multimedia can run on these computers. Thus, focus from specialized features was extended to software application and INTERNET and Time-Sharing concept on one hand and databases use capabilities on the other hand. On these considerations new PC generation named Pentium was introduced successfully. The development of Pentium, which is recorded, will give real comparison from PC's to Pentium.

1.10.2 Pentium Comparison Table

Name of computer	Year of Origin	Speed of processor	Processor used and Bus size	HDD	OS
Pentium (80586)	1993	60-200 MHz	MMX Pentium 64bit or 128 bit	500MB – 4 GB	DOS WIN presently used DBMS
Pentium II	1997	233-333 MHz	MMX Pentium-II	500MB – 40GB	DOS WINDOWS LINUX
Pentium III	1999	500MHz-1GB	MMX (Multimedia extension) Pentium III	500MB –40 GB	DOS WINDOWS LINUX
Pentium IV	Expected in 2000	1.4 GB	Net Burst (Three times faster than P-II)	–	–

It will be worthwhile to note that PC revolution which was continuously carried out could be distinguished on the basis of unique feature of microprocessor chip sets from 8088, 286-486 to Pentium-Pentium-4. Giving three generations of the PC's, it is expected that this technology may saturate and something new will enter on the basis of more storage and on revolutionary speed breaking all barriers.

1.11 VARIATIONS IN COMPUTING MACHINE

Another mode of classification of computers is the work that is to be carried out by them. Some of these are:

1.11.1 Workstation

By Workstation, we refer to powerful, specialized computer that will be worked upon by a single individual. Weather forecasting workstation is one such example of specialized work. Similarly, graphic workstation is used for manipulating technical drawing and video or satellite images at a very high speed. Workstations are expensive and powerful computers, supposed to operate on much higher speed than PC's and could carry sophisticated works for which they are designed and should be capable of supporting networking links with computers. Now a days with so much in Pentium, it could be used as a workstation.

1.11.2 Network Computer

The Network Computer, commonly abbreviated as NC, is one, which satisfies standards developed by Apple, IBM, Oracle, Netscape, and Sun Micro systems introduced the first NC in 1996. Net PC on the other hand was created by INTEL and Microsoft assisted by Compaq, Dell and Hewlett Packard companies computers qualifying for Net PC or NC reference profile. They are required to comply with many languages and protocols, namely, for Java, HTML (HyperText Make up Language), HTTP E-mail protocol, Multimedia formats, Internet Protocols, Transmission Protocols, File Transfer, protocols along with several management and security standards.

1.11.3 Personal Digital Assistants

These are palm size computers, which have limitation in programming and hardware capabilities and were designed for limited number of application. These are designed to work with PC but these themselves do not run as PC's.

1.11.4 Laptops and Notebooks

It is a portable PC with specialized packing, which is entirely self-contained. A single pack contains all processing power and memory, the keyboard, battery. As name indicates, it could work in very small space, space of size of a lap.

Journalists usually prefer notebook computers. This computer usually fits into a briefcase. These have external floppy disk drive, monitor and small keyboards with battery. Toshiba Protégé is one such note-book computer.

1.11.5 Mainframes

Computers which can process several million program instruction per second may qualify this name. Large organizations such as banks, air-lines, railways, use mainframe computers. IBM S1390 is one such main-frame computer. These days capabilities of Pentium are quite high and they may also qualify to be used as mainframe computers.

1.11.6 Mini Computers

Mid range Mainframe computers on cost effective basis were developed for the organization called Mini-Computers, which range application of computers. Today it is difficult to distinguish between mini computer and Pentium computers.

1.11.7 Super Computers

C-DEC'S Param is a super computer produced by our country. Usually such computers are Parallel Processors and their speed is measured in nano–seconds or in Pico seconds. Some examples of super computer are CRAY Y-MP/C – 90 (1991), CRAYT3D (1993), Fujitsu VP-2600/10 (1991), CRAY T3E-900 with 1.8 tera flops (Max) at 450 MHz, IBM's Supercomputer (1998) can perform 3.9 trillion mathematics calculation/second and is fully operational and used in US nuclear weapon testing. Param 10,000 is an Indian supercomputer whose computing power goes up to 100 G flops. SGI corporation produced origin TM – 2000 Super Computer which can load 35 trillion and 200 billion instructions/sec.

1.12 COMPUTER STORAGE MEASURING UNITS

Typewriter used 26 English alphabets (or characters), 10 numbers and enough number of punctuation marks for English language that make entire English speaking population occupied by this and any human stored information in him/ her by remembering complex symbols on composed of typewriter characters, numerals and punctuation marks. Computers use them differently. Computer engineers converted all typewriter symbols to binary (i.e., in 0 or 1) numbers. It was found by them, if all alphabets, numbers, special characters and punctuation marks are converted into codes by using only binary digits 0 and 1 in the lowest power of 2 that would be 128 in all. This let them use eight bit code for alphabets, numbers, special characters and punctuation symbols that give capacity of coding 256 symbols are shown below for understanding, where each 0 or 1 is called bits (i.e. binary digits).

English Alphabets Numerals Symbols	8 bit code Extended Binary coded Decimal Interchange code EBCDIC
A	1100 0001
B	1100 0010
C	1100 0011
D	1100 0100
E	1100 0101
F	1100 0011
.	
.	
.	
X	1110 0111
Y	1110 1000
Z	1110 1001
0	1111 0000
1	1111 0001
2	1111 0010
9	1111 1001
(blank or space)	0100 0000
<	0100 1100

The utility of this eight bit code really made eight bits the standard unit of computer storage. All information in computer is therefore consists of this EBCDIC System. The most recent Intel processors are designed to handle data in large groups. For improving performance of computer they used wider internal buses between their integral cache memory and process circuitry. Thus the size of primary storage units, as are now standards, are summarized below.

Units	Bits	Bytes
Bit	1	0.125
½ byte	4	0.5
Byte	8	1
Word	16	2
Double word	32	4
Quad word	64	8
Line (for PC-AT 486)	128	16

The names bit, ½ byte, byte, word, double word are standard ones, whereas line or quad word concept is an architectural concept may vary from computer to computer, company or in MMX, may add some measuring unit of this information. Large scale measuring units are described by the following:

Unit	Abbreviation	In unit	In bytes
Byte	B	8 bits	1
Kilobyte	KB or K	1024 bytes	1024
Megabyte	MB or M	1024 KB	1048576
Gigagyte	GB	1024MB	1073741824
Terabyte	TB	1024GB	too big to display
Pentabyte	PB	1024TB	- do -
Exabyte	EB	1024PB	- do –
Zetabye	ZB	1024EB	- do -
Yottabye	YB	1024YB	- do -

1.13 SPEED OF COMPUTERS

There are several units, which are used to judge the speed of a processor. Although none of them is a perfect indication to judge the performance of a processor. It is measured by the number of instruction executed per unit time, such as the use of million instructions per second (MIPS) in case of a super scalar architecture processors whereas for a vector processor, the speed is measured in the Million Floating Point Instruction per unit time such as the use of Mega Floating Point Instruction per Second (Mega FLOPs).

Most popular notation for judging the performance of a computer is the unit Hertz. It is the frequency of system clock and this clock is used to synchronize various operations, a processor performs. Simplest or earliest processor was 8085 microprocessor. It was an 8 bit processor and supports 64 KB of memory space. This processor was a

40 pin chip and used to operate on single phase clock. The phase at which this used to operate is 3 MHz. Advanced version of this processor works in 5 MHz. Nowadays the Pentium processor are many times faster and works at 750 MHz.

1.14 NUMBER SYSTEM

We use decimal number system in our day-to-day work. This system uses digits 0,1,2,3,4,5,6,7,8 and 9. The normal day-to-day work is carried out by using decimal number system. This is called decimal because it uses total ten digits and any number is represented as a string of these ten digits. Computer cannot use this number. Instead, a computer works on binary digits. A binary system has only two digits—0 and 1. This is because of this reason that computers use integrated circuits with thousands of transistors and process the work submitted by the outside world with the electronic pulses.

1.14.1 Decimal Number System

Decimal number system uses ten digits (0,1,2,3,4,5,6,7,8,9). Since decimal number system uses total ten digits to compose a number, this number system is said to have a base of ten. Using the different digits in different positions we can express any number. For example, the base in decimal number system is 10, the number 4563 is written as $4563/_{10}$

The digit used to represent a number carries a weight, when it is used at a specific position. For example, the decimal number 4563 may be represented as

4563 = 4 * 10^3 + 5 * 10^2 + 6 * 10^1 + 3 * 10 ^0

1.14.2 Binary Number System

This number system uses only two digits, thus it is known as binary number system. These numbers are 0 and 1. Any number to be represented in binary number system is a string of 0 and 1's, hence binary number system has base 2. The abbreviation of binary digit is bit. A string of 8 bit is known as byte. Byte is the basic unit of computer. In most of computers, the data processed in the string of 8 bits or some multiple of 8bits. As in the decimal system the binary number system is position weighted. For example, the binary number 1001 may be represented as

1001 = 1* 2^3 + 0 * 2^2 + 0 * 2^1 + 1 *2^0

1.14.3 Octal Number System

Octal number system uses eight digits (0,1,2,3,4,5,6,7). Since octal number system uses total eight digits to compose a number this number system is said to have a base of eight. Using the different digits in different positions we can express any number. Since the base in octal number system is 8, the number 4563 is written as $4563/_8$.

The digit used to represent a number carry a weight when it is used at a specific position. For example, the octal number 4563 may be represented as

4564 = 4 * 8^3 + 5 * 8^2 + 6 * 8^1 + 3 * 8 ^0

1.14.4 Hexadecimal Number System

Hexadecimal number system uses sixteen digits (0, 1, 2, 3, 4, 5, 6, 7, 8, 9, A, B, C, D, E, F). Since hexadecimal number system uses total sixteen digits to compose a number this number system is said to have a base of sixteen. Using the different digits in different positions we can express any number. Since the base in hexadecimal number system is 16, the number 4563 is written as $4563/_{16}$.

The digit used to represent a number carry a weight when it is used at a specific position. For example, the hexadecimal number 45AB may be represented as

45AB = 4 * 16^3 + 5 * 16^2 + 10 * 16^1 + 11 * 16 ^0

Following table presents four bit equivalent binary numbers of hexadecimal digit.

Hexadecimal Digit	Four digit Binary Equivalent
0	0000
1	0001
2	0010
3	0011
4	0100
5	0101
6	0110
7	0111
8	1000
9	1001
A	1010
B	1011
C	1100
D	1101
E	1110
F	1111

1.14.5 Binary to Decimal Conversion

A binary number may be converted into a decimal number using the following process.

Example: Convert 11001 to decimal number system.

Since each position has a weight, first bit (Least Significant Bit) has a weight 2^0, if the position is nth from the LSB, position has a weight 2^(n-1).

Thus

11001 = 1* 2^4 + 1 * 2^3 +0 * 2^2 + 0 * 2^1 + 1 * 2^0
= 1 * 16 + 1* 8 + 0 * 4 + 0 * 2 + 1 * 1
= 16 + 8+ 0 +0 + 1
= 25

Hence equivalent decimal number is 25.

1.14.6 Decimal to Binary Conversion

To convert decimal into binary, a method of successive multiplication by 2 is used. After each multiplication, the integer part is noted and the fraction is again multiplied by 2 till the remainder becomes zero. Sometimes, it is possible that the remainder doesn't become zero even after many stages. In such a case approximation is made and the result is taken up to a certain number of bit after the binary point. A similar procedure is adopted for a number having both integer and fraction. Binary fraction is added and subtracted as the decimal numbers.

Thus this method involves successive division by 2 and recording the remainder (the remainder will always be 0 or 1). The division will be stopped when we get a quotient of 0 with remainder of 1. The remainders when read upward give the equivalent binary number.

Example : Convert decimal number 25 to binary number

		remainder
2	25	
2	12	1
2	6	0
2	3	0
2	1	1
		1

Procedure begins with the successive division by 2. Keep noting the remainder of division until '1' comes as quotient. The string of remainder obtained from the successive division constitutes the equivalent binary number. Binary equivalent to decimal number 25 is 11001.

1.14.7 Hexadecimal to Binary Conversion

The hexadecimal number system is very convenient and extensively used because hexadecimal numbers are very short as compared to binary numbers.

Hexadecimal means 16. Thus the hexadecimal system has a base of 16. It uses 16 digits to represent all numbers. The digits are 0,1,2,3,4,5,6,7,8,9,A, B, C, D, E and F.

Hexadecimal digits are converted to binary number by obtaining its 4-bit equivalent as per conversion table.

Example: Convert 45A4 to binary equivalent.

Hexadecimal Number	4	5	A	4
Each digit Equivalent	0100	0101	1100	0100
Equivalent Binary Number		0100010111000100		

1.14.8 Binary to Hexadecimal Conversion

Convert each 4-bit binary into an equivalent hexadecimal.

Example: Convert 0001010001001101 to equivalent hexadecimal number.

Binary Number :	0001	0100	0100	1101
	1	4	4	D
Equivalent Hexanumber	144D			

1.14.9 Addition of Binary Number

The rules for addition of Binary number are as under:

0 + 0	1
0 + 1	1
1 + 0	1
1 + 1	10

It may be noted that 1+1 is represented as 10 i.e. sum is 0 and carry is 1.

Example: Add two binary numbers 111010 and 1001.

Carry			1	1			
First Number			1	1	1	0	1	0
Second Number	+				1	0	0	1
		1	0	0	0	0	1	1

1.14.10 Binary Subtraction

The rules for subtraction of Binary number are as under:

0-0	0
1-0	1
1-1	0
10-1	1

In both the operations of addition and subtraction, we start with the least significant bit (L.S.B) i.e. the bit on the extreme right side and proceed to the left.

Example: **Subtract 10001 from 110001.**

First Number		1	1	0	0	0	1
Second Number	–		1	0	0	0	1
		1	0	0	0	0	0

1.14.11 Multiplication of Binary Numbers

The four basic rules for multiplication of Binary numbers are as under:

- 0 x 0 = 0
- 0 x 1 = 0
- 1 x 0 = 0
- 1 x 1 = 1

The method of binary multiplication is similar to that of decimal multiplication. The method involves forming partial products, shift-

ing successive partial product left one place and adding all the partial products.

Example: Multiply 10001 by 101

			1	0	0	0	1
X					1	0	1
			1	0	0	0	1
		0	0	0	0	0	
	1	0	0	0	1		
	1	0	1	0	1	0	1

1.14.12 Signed Binary Number

Negative numbers in binary number system are represented by using digit 0 which is used for the +ve sign and 1 for the –ve sign at the Most Significant Digit. The most significant bit is the sign bit followed by the magnitude bits numbers expressed in this form are known as signed binary numbers. The number may be written in 4 bits, 8 bits, 16 bits etc. In every case the most leading bit represent the sign bit and remaining bits represent magnitude.

1'S COMPLEMENT

The 1's complement of a binary number is obtained by complementing each bit.

Example: Obtain the 1's Complement of 100001.

Number	1	0	0	0	0	1
	0	1	1	1	1	0

2'S COMPLEMENT

The signed binary number require too much electronic circuit for addition and subtraction. Therefore, positive decimal numbers are expressed in signed-magnitude form but negative decimal numbers are expressed in 2's complements.

2's complement of a number may be obtained by adding a binary digit '1' to the 1's complement of a number.

Example: Obtain the 2's Complement of 100001.

Number	1	0	0	0	0	1
1's Complement	0	1	1	1	1	0
+						1
2's complement	0	1	1	1	1	1

2'S COMPLEMENT ADDITION, SUBTRACTION

The use of 2's complement representation has simplified the computer hardware for arithmetic operation. When A and B are added, the B bit are not inverted so we get,

$$S = A + B$$

When B is to be subtracted from A, the computer hardware form's the two's complement and then add to it to A. Thus

$$S = A + B' = A + (-B) = A - B$$

Conversion of Hexadecimal to Decimal

One method to convert a hexadecimal into a decimal equivalent is to first convert hexadecimal to binary and then convert binary to decimal. A direct conversion of hexadecimal into decimal is also possible. Since the base of a hexadecimal is 16, the weight of different bits are 160,161,162, etc. starting with the bit on the extreme right. The decimal equivalent of a hexadecimal number equals the sum of all digits multiplied by their weights.

Decimal to Hexadecimal Conversion

One method is to convert the decimal to binary and then convert binary to hexadecimal.

The direct method is successive division by 16 and to write the hexadecimal equivalent of remainder.

1.14.13 Binary Coded Decimal (BCD)

In Computer world the numbers are represented as binary numbers and the outside world deals with decimal. The BCD codes are used to represent decimal number to binary. A weighted binary code is one in which a number carries certain weight. As string of 4 bit is known as nibble. BCD means that each decimal digit is represented by a nibble (binary code of 4 digits). 8421 code is the most predominant BCD code. The designation 8421 indicates the weight of the 4 bits. When one refers to BCD code it always means 8421 code. Though 16 number (24) can be represented by 4 bits only 10 of them are used. The remaining 6 are invalid in 8421 BCD code. To represent any number in BCD code each decimal number is replaced by the appropriate 4-bit code. BCD code is used in pocket calculator, electronic counter, digital voltammeter, and digital clock. Early version of computer used BCD code. However BCD code was discarded for computer because this code is slow and more complicated then binary.

BCD ADDITION

Addition is the most important arithmetic operation. Subtraction,

Multiplication, Division can be done by using addition. The rule of BCD addition is:

1. Add the two numbers using binary addition. If the four-bit sum is equal or less than 9, it is a valid BCD number.
2. If the four-bit sum is more than 9 or carry is generated from the group of four bits, the result is invalid. In such a case add carry to next four-bit group.

1.15 ALPHANUMERIC CODE

For the proper communication we need to represent number, letter and symbols. Alphanumeric code can represent all these three.

ASCII CODE (American Standard Code for Information Interchange) It is seven-bit code used extensively for printers and terminals of small computer system. Many large computer systems also accommodate this code. The characters are assigned in the ascending binary numbers. Some time an 8 bit is also added and this bit is either 0 or 1 or used as parity bit.

EBCDIC Code (Extended Binary Coded Decimal Interchange Code)

EBCDIC is used in most of the large computer for communication. It is eight bit code and uses BCD.

Error Detection Codes

Every digit if a digital system must be correct. An error in any digit can cause a problem because the computer may recognize it is something else. Many methods have been devised to detect such errors.

Parity

Parity refers to the number of 1s in the binary word. When the number of 1s in the binary world is odd. It is said to have odd parity. When the number of 1s in word is even, it is said to have even parity. One method for error detection is to use 7 bits for data and 8th bit for parity. The parity can be 1 or 0. At the receiving end the parity is checked, if the error has been committed and the data is required to be transmitted again. In some computer systems even parity is used.

Check Sums

The parity check cannot detect two errors in the same word. One method to check such cases is the check sums. As each word is transmitted, it is added to the previous words and the sum is retained at the sending end. Each successive word is added to the sum of the previous words. At the end of transmission, the sum is also sent and is checked at the receiving point. Check sum method is commonly used in Tele processing.

1.16 PHYSICAL STORAGE MEDIA

Several types of data storage exit in most computer systems. These storage media are classified by the speed with which data can be accessed, by the cost per unit of memory and by how "reliable" they are. Among the media typically available are:

Memory Hierarchy

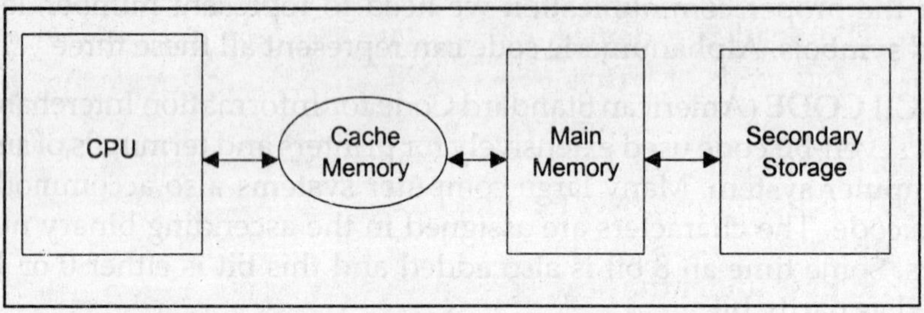

Above diagram shows the memory hierarchy.

- **Cache Memory**
  Cache is the fastest and the most costly form of storage. The size of cache memory is very small and use of the cache is managed by operation system. Since the CPU works much faster than Main Memory, thus most frequently accessed data are kept on Cache Memory, so that it can be made available to CPU on demand without time delays.

- **Main Memory**
  Main Memory is the storage media used for data that is available to be operated on. The general-purpose machine instruction operates on main memory. Although main memory may contain several mega byte of data, main memory is generally too small to store the entire database. Main memory is sometimes referred to as core memory, a reference to technology used in 1960s and early 1970s to implement main memory. The contents of main memory are usually lost if a power failure in system crash occur.

- **Secondary Storage**
  Secondary or Disk Storage this is the primary medium for the long-term storage of data. Typically the entire database is stored on disk. Data must be moved from disk to main memory in order to the data to be operated on. After operations are performed the data

must be returned to disk. It is referred to as direct access storage because it is possible to read data on disk in any order (unlike sequentially access- storage.) Disk storage devices themselves may fail and destroy data but such failure are significantly less frequent than system crashes.

- **Tape Storage:** This storage is used primarily for back up and archival data. Although tape is much cheaper than disk, access to data is much slower; tape storage is referred to as sequential access storage and is used primarily for recovery from disk failure.

The disk storage is of central importance in data base implementation. The head is a device, which stays close to the surface of the platter and reads or writes information encoded magnetically on the platter. The platter is organized concentric track of data. The arm can be positioned over any one of the tracks. To read or write information, the arm is positioned over the correct track. Since the platter rotates at a high speed it does not take very long for the content of an entire track to pass under the head. This amount of time is referred to as the disk latency time. Relative to the latency time, it takes a long time to reposition the arm. The time for repositioning thc arm, the seek time, grows as the distance that the arm must move increases. Multi-platter disks are called disk packs when we wish to distinguish them from single platter disk. We use the term disk; we shall be referring to multiple platter disks.

All the disk arms are used as the unit actuator. Each arm has two heads: one to read and another to write. Data is transferred between disk and main memory in units called block. A block is a contiguous sequence of bytes from a single track of one platter. Block size ranges from 512 bytes to several thousand bytes. The simplest way to optimize block access time is to organize the block on disk in a way that corresponds closely to the manner in which we expect data to be accessed.

1.17 FILE ORGANIZATION

A file is organized logically as a sequence of record. These records are mapped on to disk block. Files are provided as a basic construct in operating systems. Files of fixed length record are easier to implement than files of variable length records.

1.17.1 Organization of Records into Blocks

A file may be viewed as a collection of records. Since data is transferred between disks storage and main memory in unit of a block, it is worthwhile to assign record to blocks in such a way i.e. single block contains related record. If we assign record to block randomly, it will usually be the case that a different block must be accessed for each record accessed. On the other hand, if we can access several of the records desired using only one block access, we have saved some disk accesses. Since disk access is usually the bottleneck in the performance of a database system, careful assignment of record to block can pay significant performance dividends.

1.17.2 Sequential File

A sequential file is designed for efficient processing of records in stored other on some search key. To permit pointers chain fast retrievals of records in search-key order, records together. The pointer in each record points to the next record in search key order. Further more, in order to minimize the number of block accesses in sequential file processing, records are stored physically in search key order, or as close to search-key order as possible.

1.17.3 Indexed File

An index for a file works in much the same way as does a catalog in library. As an alternative to indexing, techniques using hash functions may be used. We shall consider several techniques for both hashing and indexing. No one technique is best. Rather, each technique is best suited to particular database applications. Each technique must be evaluated on the basis of:

- **Access time**: The time it takes to find a particular data item, using the technique in question.
- **Insertion time**: The time it takes to insert a new data item. This includes the time it takes to find the correct place to insert the new data item as well as the time it takes to update the index structure.
- **Deletion time**: The time it takes to delete a data item. This includes the time it takes to find the item to be deleted as well as the time it takes to update the index structure.
- **Space overhead**: The additional space occupied by an index structure provided that the amount of additional space is moderate, it

is usually worthwhile to sacrifice the space to achieve the improved performances

It is often the case that we desire to have more than one index or hash function for a file. The attribute or set of attributes used to look up record in a file is called a search key.

In order to allow fast random access to record in a file, an indexed structure is used. Each indexed structure is associated with a particular search key. If the file is sequentially ordered, and it choose to include several indices on different search keys, the index whose search key specified the sequential order of the file is the primary index. The other indices are called the secondary indices. The search key of a primary index is usually the primary key.

SELECT EXERCISES

Q. 1. What is a Computer? Explain its functional units?

Q. 2. Explain types of electronic devices that are revolutionizing the low – cost and low performance computer market, whether, it will be correct to say that they are low performance, if so in what comparison?

Q. 3. What is Central Processing Unit (CPU)? Explain the role of Arithmetic and Logical Unit (LU) and Control Unit (CU).

Q. 4. What is memory? What is the difference between Register Memory and Main Memory? Which is faster and why?

Q. 5. Differenciate between static and dynamic RAM? Which one is faster and compact?

Q. 6. What do you mean by Von Neuman computer machine? Explain the important features of Von Neuman's principles.

Q. 7. Explain the major differences that allow saying that some computers are qualified to mini or micro or mainframe computer?

Q. 8. When is a computer said to be general-purpose or special purpose? Explain with concrete footing.

Q. 9. Differentiate between the primary and secondary memory?

Q. 10. What do you mean by Volatile and Non Volatile memory? Why ROM is Non Volatile? Explain with examples.

Q. 11. Name few 16 bit microprocessor families?

Q. 12. Give generations of computers based on software application?

Q. 13. Why should the Pentium generation of computer be dealt separately? What are the ways these could be classified in a distinctive basis?

Q. 14. How the technological advances have made an impact on deciding computer generations.

Q. 15. Give a brief account of development computing with respect to PC Generations.

Q. 16. Differentiate between a multi chip microcomputer and single chip computer, first by explaining them?

Q. 17. What is the difference between a micro-computer and a micro-processor?

Q. 18. Differentiate between a parallel interface and a serial interface?

Q. 19. Why computers are said to be more versatile machines, man has ever made?

Q. 20. What are the functional units of a computer? Whether these units could be located in different places and can be accessed? If so explain how?

Q. 21. 4 bit wide data was processed by first microprocessor introduced in 1970, 8 bit wide data was processed by Intel microprocessor introduced in 1973-1974, 16 bit microprocessor were introduced in 1977 so on, based on similar facts categorise microprocessor on generations of computers based on the number of bits microprocessor can process and complete the following table.

Microprocessor Generation	Year of origin	Bit of data can process	Performance
First	1970	4	Low
Second	1974	8	Low

Q. 22. Give a brief account for storing measuring units of computers. Give examples of those computers with name, who produced, in what year it was produced, and how much RAM capacity varying from 2MB to 1.2 GB it had?

Q. 23. Define Hertz. How this unit is used in computers for measuring their processing speed?

Q. 24. What are the parameters on which the speed of a processor is judged?

Q. 25. How many applications in home are found to be computer run or possibly they may be run through computer by making some changes in them? Give your own account.

Q. 26. Convert following decimal numbers to Binary, Octal and Hexadecimal Numbers.

- 1000, 22, 556, 229

Q. 27. Write down the rules to add two binary numbers. Compute the addition of following binary numbers.

- (1001 + 10 + 11010), (1 + 1111), (10101 + 11100 + 10101)

Q. 28. Do the following operations on binary numbers.

- Subtract 1001 from 110001
- Multiply 1001 by 110001

Q. 29. What are signed binary numbers? How the addition is performed using signed numbers.

Q. 30. What are BCD Codes? Explain.

Q. 31. What are Alphanumeric Code? How are they used?

Q. 32. What do you mean by Physical Storage Media? Explain the Memory Hierarchy in brief.

Q. 33. What is Cache Memory? What is the role of Cache? What happens if the size of Cache is more than Main Memory?

Q. 34. What are files? How they are represented?

Q. 35. What is the difference between Sequential File and Indexed File?

2 Computer Software & Hardware

2.0 INTRODUCTION

Computer is the most versatile machine man has ever made. Now-a-days, computers are being used for day-to-day work, may it be home or office. Past decade had witnessed an exponential growth and development in various areas of computer both in fields of hardware and software. Computers, like any other machine are made up various functional items, working together to ensure the impressive performance one normally associates with them. One may think of computer as a mysterious thing just because of unawareness about the main functional components. If one understands the basic working of each of these components, computers would not be mysterious for them.

One who uses the computer at home or at work must know about the basic hardware that are normally associated with this machine. A computer can be thought of combination of two parts, namely, hardware and software. As discussed in chapter 1 a computer is an electronic device that accepts digital information and processes it in a predefined fashion, according to the set or sequence of instructions provided to it and produces the desired binary output. The computer works with the help of support circuits which are constantly providing the signals that microprocessor needs to work. It also provides signal to PC and to its other peripherals.

A computer requires a whole lot of support circuits and devices to co-ordinate its operations and to help control the signals that enable it to run. Inspite of growth and progress of other components like microprocessors, which are now designed to handle most of the computers tasks themselves, support devices have not lost their importance. The functions performed by support devices remain as vital as ever.

Every computer requires the same necessary elements to function. In this chapter we will discuss computer software, hardware components and storage devices.

2.1 COMPUTER SOFTWARE

Computer Software is considered as a set of programs or instructions which when executed perform specific task. A program may be defined as a set of instructions written in a computer language, which when executed by the computer generates the required output after processing the data. The operations which need to be performed on the data are coded into the program instructions. For example, computations of salary of employee, generation of salary slip for employee database; preparation of electricity, telephone bill, reservation chart according to the rule and regulations of an organization, it is necessary to code the requirements and objective in the form of computer program. The computer produces required results after execution of the program. There exists another class of programs, which are required to interact with the computer system for the purpose of execution of programs, which solves any real world problem. The operating system and compilers are the softwares which are required to execute or run a program for real world computation. On the basis of utility the software can be divided into the following two broad categories:

1. Application Software/Programs
2. System Software/Programs

2.1.1 Application Software/Program

The application programs are written by the programmer to solve a real world problem. For example, writing a program for report generation, queries, preparation of reports are all application programs. Application programs or software are designed and developed for specific real world computer application. For writing an application program, a programmer does not require to control the basic hardware or electronic circuitry of the computer. A programmer requires familiarity with any programming language skillfully. He may then code the requirement of data processing in specific manner, storage and retrieval of data in programming language. These programs are written in either High Level Languages or using 4GLs. The application program may be altered, modified as per the change in the requirement by the programmer.

The application program may further be divided into two broad categories according to the nature of application. The application program written for scientific computations are called Scientific application programs and applications written to solve business application are called business application programs. Although both the types of program may be developed and written in any general purpose high level language but some of the programming languages are suitable for specific type of application. For example, Pascal and Fortran languages provide good construct and features for writing scientific application programs. Cobol language is suitable for developing business application program as it provides easy and simple construct to code business applications.

2.1.2 System Software/Program

The System Programs are those programs, which are generally used to create the environment for development and execution of application programs. These programs or software are written to make the computer easier to use. Most of the system programs are written and developed by the manufacturers. Operating Systems, Compilers are the example of system program or system software. Just think, how difficult it would be to execute the application programs, if the operating systems are not there. The Operating System allows the user to interact with the hardware in most simple way. It manages the systems resources and hardware, controls the execution of application programs, usage of main memory etc. Operating System is a collection of several system programs and OS facilitate the user to interact with the hardware. The application program written in any programming language needs to be translated to machine level language before the execution. This translation is required because a computer is able to execute and process only machine level code. The Language Translators are the programs which do the translation of programs written in high level programming language to machine level language. The compiler is a language translator, which is used to convert the application program written in high level language to machine language program.

Another category of system softwares are Utility programs. These softwares are different from Operating System and Compilers. The utility programs are those system programs which are used either on programmers request or helps managing the hardware resources. All accessories or hardware required to be attached to the computer system for upgrading its performance are usually supplied along with their software, popularly known as driver programs or device drivers. For example, attaching a modem or printer or mouse or sound card to your computer requires the device driver. These driver programs are used to configure your existing system to cope with new hardware being attached to your system. There can be more utility programs like copying bulk data transfer from disk to tape or tape to disk, sorting and merging huge volume of data etc.

2.2 PROGRAMMING LANGUAGE

Programming Language provides the environment and syntax to code the real world requirement in such a way that they can be executed on the computer system. Programming language provides the set of rules/syntax/instruction format in which various instructions are written. The computer program is a set of instructions which when executed does a specific task. The Microprocessor or CPU processes the data as per the instructions given to it. These instructions are written using various syntax and rules. A sequential collection of instructions is called program. A program can be written in many languages. The programming language may be divided into three following categories.

1. High Level Language
2. Assembly Language
3. Machine Language

2.2.1 High Level Language

The program written in high-level language needs to be translated into the language which a machine understands. The Processor or Machine understands the code written in assembly language or machine language. The programmer may write and solve the real world application program in High Level Language (HLL) without knowing the machine or hardware details. HLLs are machine independent. It provides the basic constructs and syntax to code the requirement of any real world application. It is not required for the programmer to know the rigorous detail of architecture of a processor to write the programs. COBOL, BASIC, PASCAL, ADA, C are all high level languages. Each language provides its own construct/syntax and set of statement and the program written in any of these languages may be executed on any machine. Writing programs in High Level Languages are more convenient as it provides the construct and set of statements, which are easy to use and meaningful. Consider the following program written in high level language BASIC, which adds two numbers.

```
10    LET A= 200
```

```
20   LET B = 300
30   C= A *B
40   PRINT C
50   END
```

Each statement is coded with the meaningful construct. The first statement initialises the variable A with 200, second initialises variable B with 300, third multiples the number A and B and stores result in to C and next statement prints the value of C. Writing a program for a problem in high level language is quite easier than machine and assembly language. The program development time in high level languages is considerably low.

2.2.2 Translation of High Level Language (HLL) Program

The program written in high-level language needs to be translated in to the language which a machine understands. The processor or machine understands the code written in assembly language or machine language. Therefore, all the programs developed in high level language has to be translated into lower level language before they are executed. This translation of program written in high level language to low level language is done by the software called Compiler. This process is shown in figure 2.1. As shown in the figure the program written in high level language is translated into object code by the compiler. The processor or machine executes the object code.

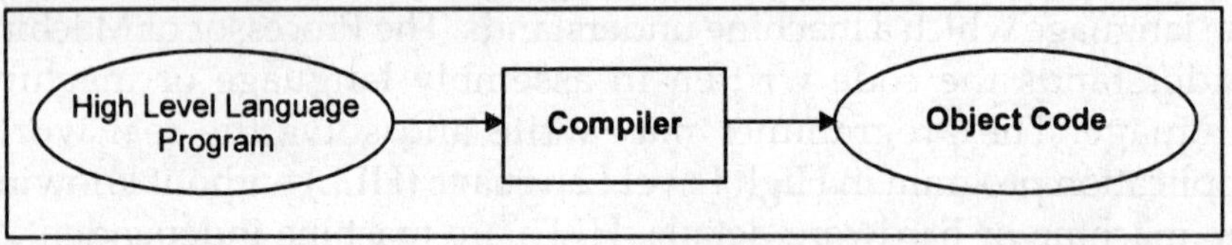

Fig. 2.1 Compiler

2.2.3 Compiler Vs Interpreter

The compiler and interpreter are softwares which translate the code written in high level language. The difference in the compilation and interpretation is on the methodology of translation. The Compiler takes the whole program and generates the object code and the Interpreter executes the program line by line. In the compilation process the whole program is scanned for the syntax, the compiler lists errors all at a time. In the interpreter, translation is done line by line, only one line is checked for the syntax error. Execution time of the compiled code or object code is faster than the interpreter. The debugging of a program is difficult in compilation process because all the errors are listed at every compilation attempt. However, the interpreter is best suited for debugging process because the errors are reported line by line.

2.2.4 Machine Language

Each processor or CPU has its own set of instructions. These instructions are binary instructions and are written in a sequence of 0's and 1's. The program written using these binary instructions is said to have written in Machine Language. The Machine Language for every processor is different. A Machine level instruction may be divided into two parts. First part is called operation Code or Op Code and second part present the binary data or list of operands. Consider following machine language instruction of microprocessor 8085. This program adds two hexadecimal numbers 20H and 30H stored in register A and B. The result is stored in register C.

Sl.No	Hexadecimal Code	Binary Code	Remarks
1.	3E	00111110	; Instruction 3E moves the data 20 to register A
2.	20	00100000	
3.	06	00000110	; Instruction 06 moves the data 30 to register B
4.	30	00110000	
5.	80	10000000	; Instruction Code 80 adds the contents of Register A and B
6.	4F	01001111	; Instruction Code 4F moves the result to Register C from Accumulator

As shown above this machine code corresponds to following set of operation.

Load Data byte 20H in Register A	:	3E	20
Load Data byte 30 H in register B	;	06	30
Add register A to B	;	80	—
Move result to Register C	;	4F	—

We can see that first two instructions has two parts, '3E', '06' are operation code and '20', '30' are operand for the first two instructions respectively. The next instruction '80' has only operation code and the operands are implicitly known.

Earlier, the programs used to be written in machine language and it is the language which a processor understands and executes only those programs written in this language. Writing a program in machine language is very cumbersome and difficult as for every task the machine codes are to be searched or remembered. Since machine language of all the processors are different, this prevents the programmer to use the code written for one machine and execute it on other machine. Advantage of the machine language code is that a processor can execute it without any translation but the disadvantage is that it is difficult to write program and understand it.

2.2.5 Assembly Language

Consider the program written for the addition of two numbers in the machine language. The programming may be easier and it is slightly better to understand the code, the code may be represented using letters and digits and carry some meaningful identifier. The assembly language uses mnemonic, a meaningful name and assembly language program is written. Consider the following:

Sl.No	Assembly Code	Hexadecimal Code	Binary Code	Remarks
1.	MVI A,20h	3E	00111110	; Instruction 3E moves the data 20 to register A
2.		20	00100000	
3.	MVI B, 30h	06	00000110	; Instruction 06 moves the data 30 to register B
4.		30	00110000	
5.	ADD B	80	10000000	; Instruction Code 80 adds the contents of Register A and B
6.	MVI C,A	4F	01001111	; Instruction Code 4F moves the result to Register C from Accumulator

In the above program, the assembly code is written, which are substitute for the machine code. Instruction code MVI A, 20h transfers the data '20' to register A.

2.2.6 Assembler

The assembly codes are easier to write but the processor still executes the machine code. Therefore a translator is required to translate the assembly language program into machine language program. The assembler is a program which converts the assembly language program into machine code (Object Code) which may be executed by processor. This is shown in figure 2.2.

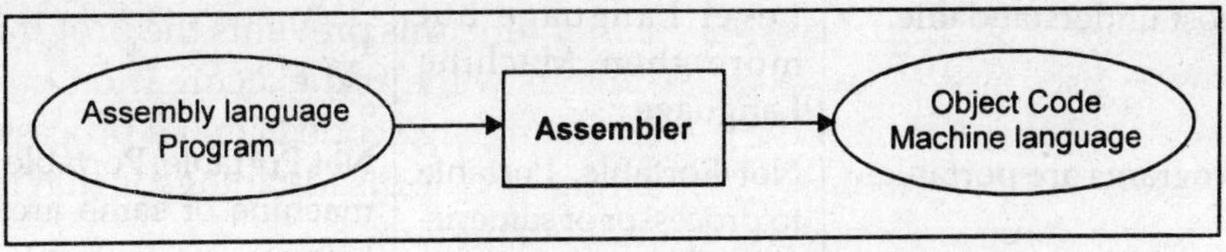

Fig. 2.2 Assembler

Assembly language and machine language are also known as lower level languages. These languages are dependent on the processor or processor specific. The advantage of assembly language over machine language is that it is more convenient for the programmer to write programs in assembly language. The disadvantage of assembly language is that this language is machine or processor specific. Therefore it is not possible to execute the assembly language program written for a processor to execute it on another one if the architecture of processor is different. This requires another programming language which is not machine dependent and the program code written for one processor could be executed on another the processor without requiring to know the details of the processor. These languages are called High Level Languages (HLL).

2.3 COMPARISON OF HIGH, ASSEMBLY, MACHINE LEVEL LANGUAGES

The comparative analysis of various languages are shown in the following Table 2.3.

2.4 FOURTH GENERATION LANGUAGES (4GL)

High level languages are considered to be third generation languages. Examples of third generation languages are BASIC, COBOL, PASCAL, FORTRAN etc. These all languages are procedural languages. Programmer who is writing a program to solve any real world problem must specify the procedure in the program. This procedure is reflected in the program in which the executions of the statement are done in a sequential order. These languages deal with the textual interface and programs are executed after writing a textual command on

Table 2.3

High Level Language	Assembly Language	Machine Language
Program developed in High Level language are most understandable.	Program are less understandable then High Level Language but more then Machine Language	Programs are less understandable
Programs are portable	Not Portable, Portable to processor of same architecture	Not Portable, Portable to machine of same architecture.
Debugging is easier.	Debugging is more complex than High Level Language	Debugging is most difficult.
Most suited for Software development	Not good for large programs	Difficult to write large programs
Programs are not machine dependent	Programs are machine dependent	Programs are machine dependent
Provides flexible construct for program development	Does not provide flexible construct for program development.	Not good
Programs are translated using Compiler and assembler to generate object code	Uses assembler to generate object code.	No translation is required.

the operating system prompt. The machine and assembly language are considered to be first and second generation languages. It has become very easy to write the program in high level language in comparison to assembly and machine language. With the gradual development in IT sector, the need for the graphical interfaces was realized, where the user has to type minimum number of textual commands. Several operating systems and other softwares were developed, which requires minimum entry of textual command. The database is one of the areas of information technology, which is most widely used. Database is the repository of data, in which data are organized in a structured fashion.

Consider a case of preparation of results of a large competitive examination. Suppose one lakh students appear in this examination. The organization, who conducts this examination would require several operations to be done on the data bank of students, starting from the data entry, preparation of roll list, allotment to the different centers, merit list preparation, preparation of mark sheets, admit card etc.

All these activities are required to be done in order to get successful conclusion of examination. Writing programs for all these activities and managing such a huge data bank is a challenging job. Writing programs for a huge database in high level language also requires lot of efforts.

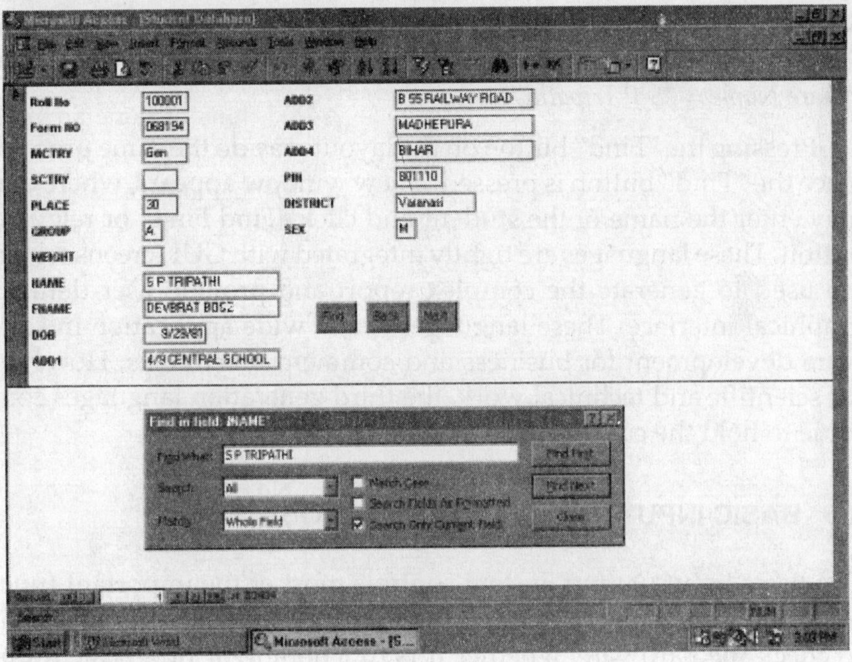

Fig. 2.4

After the introduction of graphical user interface, the people have started for alternative solutions, which will ease handling the large databases, and do not require excessive programming in high level language. The answer was fourth generation languages.

Structured Query Language (SQL), Query by Example (QBE) is considered as fourth generation languages. These languages are used to gather data from the database with visual interface like Visual Basic (VB), Developer for Oracle, Application Program Tools (APT) for Sybase works well and requires minimum amount of efforts to query the database. Most of the fourth generation languages are used for developing the large and complex software systems. These languages use automated report generator, menus etc. Most of the time, various visual objects are to be placed on the canvas and a routine has to be written to specify the task. In the figure, a record of a student is shown. The format in which various attributes like name, father's name etc are shown appears to be more user friendly. Simple queries to search the record for a particular student etc may be served by pressing a button or clicking a mouse.

Following is the query written in SQL to print the roll Number, name and father's name of a student whose name is "S P Tripathi". The data of all students are stored in file 'Student'.

Select *Rno, Name, Fname*
From *student*
Where *Name = "S P Tripathi"*

Pressing the "Find" button on the layout may do the same process. Once the "Find" button is pressed, a new window appears, where one may enter the name of the student and click "Find First" or relevant button. These languages are tightly integrated with GUI screens which are used to generate the complex report and provide user defined graphical interface. These languages find a wide application in software development for business and commercial activities. However for scientific and technical work, the third generation languages continue to hold the command.

2.5 BASIC INPUT OUTPUT SYSTEM (BIOS)

The Basic Input Output System controls most of the important function, which are required to be done at booting. It enables the processor to check the hardware, whether it is functioning or not. Basic Input Output Software is a combination of several softwares, which are stored in the read only memory. These softwares are invoked at the time of booting of the system. The BIOS controls many of the most important functions of the PC, like how it interprets keystrokes, communication through the computer ports etc. It also has the job of testing the computer every time it is turned on. In fact it is also responsible for the allocation of system resources. The BIOS serves as a link between the hardware and software of the computer system. The BIOS routines are written on the chip which is nothing but a read only memory (ROM). BIOS one installed onto the computer system is permanent. Since BIOS software routines are softwares and it is permanently coded on to the chip, it gives an impression that it is an hardware. Whether it is a software or hardware is difficult to answer. The BIOS cannot be treated as only software or only hardware. In fact, BIOS is both. The fact that BIOS coded onto the chip gives it the hardware classification. In fact, a correct term something like the BIOS is Firmware. The BIOS code of most PCs has to take care of a wide variety of functions. Typically it comprises program routines that test the computer. It also does the task of letting software take over control of the computer's hardware, so that the programs can run more smoothly.

BIOS also includes a complete system for determining the peripheral devices or I/O devices, which are attached to the computer system. It also ensures not to conflict in their requests for input/output ports and memory assignment. In most cases the first thing the BIOS tells the microprocessor to do is to run through all the hardware of the computer system and test if they are working properly. Booting process is followed afterwards. The booting process of a computer is triggered only after every aspect is found to be in proper running condition by the BIOS. During the Boot process, the BIOS code instructs the microprocessor to go to a particular section of code, that tells the chip how to read the first sector of your hard disk. The program code then takes over from the BIOS and tells the processor how to load the operating system to get your machine up and running. This, however, does not mean that the BIOS's work is done; it then carries out the normal routine tasks like reading keystrokes, timing events etc. that enable the smooth running of your machine.

2.6 INTEGRATED CIRCUITS AND MOTHER BOARD

As we have mentioned earlier, that major breakthrough in the third generation of computers was the introduction of Integrated Circuit (IC). Prior to that electronic components and computing equipments were used to build different electronic components like transistors, capacitors etc. These components were manufactured separately and assembled on a circuit board by soldering. This process of making a computing machine was quite complex as most often thousands of such components were required to manufacture a minimal computing machine. With the invention of ICs, it has become possible to fabricate thousands of such components on a single chip made up of semiconductor material. This has resulted in huge reduction in the space requirement and cost of production of such ICs was also small. An integrated circuit is constructed on a thin wafer of silicon. Whole area on the wafer is divided into several small segments and logic gates, transistors etc are packaged onto these segments by the process called Fabrication. With the advancement in the technology, nowadays using Super Large Scale Integration (SLSI), it is possible to put more than a million components on a single chip. Motherboard is probably one of the most important parts of a computer and is considered as basic building block.

The motherboard is considered as the backbone of the entire computer system. The circuitry or the components on the motherboard define capabilities and limitations of a computer. Motherboard is responsible for the characteristics in a computer. All computers contain a single, large printed circuit board popularly known as PCB. The PCB contains all the important components that define the computer system: microprocessor, circuitry and memory. Microprocessor is known as the heart of the computer system. It is fabricated on a small chip made up of silicon material. Motherboard also has provisions to plug in additions that may be required like graphic, sound and network cards, peripherals, etc. Most manufacturers found that designing a single component motherboard was the best design for computers especially since it was cheaper than designing several individual components. They also added sockets into which you could plug in additional circuits to add additional capabilities to the computer.

The motherboard is the basic foundation of a computer. It holds all the various cards, lets you attach connections to external elements as well as it provides the base to support the central electronics of the computer. Latest Pentium processor launched by the Intel are complex and require a supporting chip so that it may interact to various Input/Output devices. The provisions are made on the motherboard itself to accommodate and connect to various peripheral devices. While a computer can be defined by its motherboard, its circuits and components define the motherboard. The most important devices may be required to get connected with the processor or motherboard is discussed in the following sections of this chapter.

2.7 MICROPROCESSOR

The Microprocessor is known as the heart of a computer. It has all the capabilities of a central processing unit (CPU). Since memory requirements are increasing day by day, therefore microprocessor chip is kept on the motherboard of the computer system and memory chips are separately placed in the specified slots on motherboard. Microprocessor contains ALU (Arithmetic and Logical Unit) and Control Unit. ALU does all Arithmetic and Logical computation and controls unit issues basic control sequences or control signals to synchronize various operations which a computer has to perform. Microprocessors, as the name implies, determines the processing power of the computer. There are several units, which determine the processing power of the microprocessor. Most popular unit is the clock speed, which is measured in Hertz as frequency. Nowadays the processor also determines what software languages the computer understands, and therefore what software it runs. A microprocessor handles most, if not all, the data processing done by the machine.

The microprocessor is the brain of a computer, but it still needs the help of other components to be of any real use. Support circuitry does just that—it provides support to the main processor. Each of these individual support circuits has its respective job and thus helps to determine how the computer works. A microprocessor is made up of silicon, which is nothing but an extremely pure crystal. This silicon is cut into extremely thin slices, which are then baked in ovens at a high temperature to change their electrical properties. Microprocessor hardware is designed to carry out specific functions for which purpose silicon technology has been equipped for work.

First generation computers were made of mechanical components like gears, levers and other such movable parts to replicate the functions of today's microprocessors. These mechanical components, in earlier computers carried out the logical functions in the same way. The advantage, a silicon microprocessor has over older gear and lever microprocessors is the speed. Electrical signals travel at the speed of light, which make microprocessors allow us, elaborate programs which could never have been written. Microprocessors therefore make computers what they are to us today.

2.8 MEMORY

Memory is just like a piece of paper where one can write and rub the contents. Memory is used to hold the data that needs to be processed, as well as the intermediate result of computations. Memory also plays the role of a channel for communication between the microprocessor and the peripheral devices. A processor is of no practical use without a place at hand to instantly store data for future retrieval. A processor by itself can hardly store a couple of bytes, which are not enough for the smooth running of a program. Memory allows the microprocessor to store millions of bytes, enough to hold a whole load of program instructions or even blocks of data. The Memory can broadly be classified into two categories called Primary and Secondary Memory. Primary Memory or Main Memory is used to hold the temporarily during the execution, while secondary memory or auxiliary memory is used to hold data permanently outside the computer. These are defined as under.

2.8.1 Main Memory

Main Memory is volatile memory of the computer. Contents of this memory are erased as the power to machine is turned off. This memory is faster than the auxiliary memory and speed of this memory must match with the speed of microprocessor to get the best performance of your computer. It is easily accessible and ready to be used by the processor but is limited in capacity when compared to other storage media. Main Memory is relatively costlier than secondary memory. This form of memory could be called online memory because it is always connected to the computer.

The Main Memory can be classified into two categories as follows

RAM (Random Access Memory) or R/W Memory

This memory is also called read write memory because it is volatile. The bits of information are stored in the primary memory of the computer, and can be randomly accessed by the processor to be worked on. This type of memory is called Random Access Memory (RAM). At present, 64 MB/128 MB RAM are being used in the PCs.

Read Only Memory (ROM)

Contents of this memory are permanent and are not erased when the power is turned off. This memory is used to keep the program or data, which are used frequently without modification. The best example is the BIOS (Basic Input Output Software) which lies in the ROM. This program is recalled every time you start your computer.

2.9 AUXILIARY MEMORY

The Main memory is capable of holding the data and programs as long as the programs are executed. The current requirement for warehousing of large amount of data requires that different programs, softwares and huge database should be stored at different places. With gradual development in application of computing machines to solve real world problems, it has become almost impossible to store all the applications and the files in one place. This requirement has triggered the scientists to develop separate memory/storage devices space which was called Auxiliary storage devices or secondary memory. It is now not necessary to store all the programs and data to the fixed size memory available with the computer system e.g. hard disks. The programs and data file which are to be used frequently may be kept in the hard disk and rest of the files containing the data and program may be stored in auxiliary storage devices. Therefore, program and data file, which are required in the later stage may be stored and fetched from the auxiliary storage devices. Bit is the smallest unit of information that a computer can work with. All the information it works with is in the form of bits. A byte is a set of eight bits. Most computers use one byte to represent each character.

It is worth mentioning here that auxiliary memory includes storage devices like the hard disk, tape or any other magnetic device which are used to store huge amount of data or programs. These memory devices are for long term storage. This form of memory is maintained for a long time, hence it is non-volatile. It is only erased, as and when the user wants to delete it. The data on secondary storage mediums is stored offline and is not directly accessible to the computer. For secondary storage data to be used by the processor has to be transferred to the primary memory.

It can be therefore said that the primary memory is important due to the quick accessing speed that it provides to the processor, whereas secondary memory is important for the capacity it offers as storage space in the computer. Since computers process a huge amount of data on a daily basis, they require some sort of storage space to store all the data. This is where the mass storage system comes into the picture. Storage systems are supposed to make data and applications available to users when they need it. That will happen only if you make sure that enough storage is available and that it is not overburdened by useless or unnecessary data. Some of the external storage devices are magnetic disks (hard disks and floppy disks), optical disks (CD-ROMs and WORMs), and tape storage systems (tapes, tape drives and tape cartridges). All these storage media work on the line of an audiocassette on which you can record and erase music, and also store.

2.10 ONLINE/NEAR LINE/OFFLINE DATA STORAGE

As per the nature of requirement for keeping or storing the data, there exist three types of data storage method in which the data may be kept. These are called Online, Near Line and Off Line data storage. Magnetic disks and optical disks provide direct access to data, while tape systems provide slower sequential access. By arranging these systems in a hierarchical structure, it is possible to support three different data storage models, Online, Near-line and Offline Storage.

When the data needs to be stored and fetched quickly by the processor, online storage is preferred. Magnetic and optical storage devices like CD, Floppy Disk etc. These devices prompt access of data to processor. On online storage data is stored on high-speed magnetic disk drives that can provide the highest response to user's queries. On near line storage data is stored on high-volume optical disks, which have slower read and write times than magnetic disks. On offline storage data is stored on tapes for archival purposes.

2.11 MAGNETIC STORAGE DEVICES

Based on the technology used for storing the data on secondary storage, various devices may be categorized into two categories called Magnetic Storage Devices and Optical Storage Devices. The magnetic storage devices use magnetic material for storing the data or information. The optical storage devices use different technology for storing the data or programs. These devices differ from the conventional storage device in such a way that conventional storage device uses the magnetic material to store the information. The data onto the optical storage devices are written using the optical rays. CDROM (Compact Disk - Read Only Memory) is any example of optical storage devices. Examples of magnetic storage devices include floppy disk, magnetic tape, magnetic disks. In the next section we will study some of the important magnetic storage devices.

2.11.1 Hard Disk Drive (HDD)

The hard disks are similar to the floppy disk but contain a number of platters. The hard disk is used to provide storage for high amount of data. The data storage and retrieval onto the hard disk is faster in comparison to the floppy disk. A hard disk stores and provides relatively quick access to large amounts of data on an electro-magnetically-charged surface or set of surfaces. Today's computers typically come with a hard disk that contains several gigabytes (GB) of storage space. A hard disk is really a set of stacked 'disks', each of which like phonograph records has data recorded electro-magnetically in concentric circles or 'tracks' on the disk. A 'head' (something like a phonograph arm but in a relatively fixed position) records (writes) or reads the information on the tracks. Two heads, one on each side of a disk, read or write the data as the disk spins. Each 'read' or 'write' operation requires that data to be located, which is an operation called 'seek'. A hard disk/drive unit comes with a set rotation speed varying from 5400 to 7200 rpm. Disk access time is measured in milliseconds. Being a very precisely engineered device, the HDD must operate in a totally clean, sealed chamber.

The hard disk may logically be thought of a collection of several magnetic disks. These magnetic disks are placed in such a way that they form a stack of magnetic disks. The stack of these disks may contain as many as 5 to 10 magnetic disks. The storage capacity of a hard disk is much higher than a floppy disk. Nowadays, hard disk are available with the storage capacity of 10 GB to 40 GB. The data is written to the hard disk using the Hard Disk head.

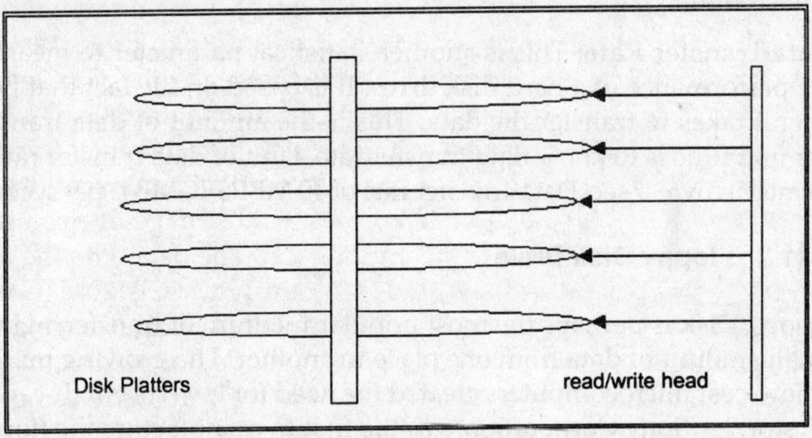

Fig. 2.5 Magnetic Disk

As shown in figure 2.5, the head is placed over the track to read or write the data. The magnetic disk is divided into several tracks and a track is divided into several sectors. Whenever the data is to be written onto disk, the track and sectors are selected and are positioned according to the position of head. The head which remains in a fixed position writes or reads the data on the tracks. Two heads, one on each side of a disk, read or write the data as the disk spins. A hard disk/ drive unit comes with a set rotation speed varying from 5400 to 7200 rpm. Disk access time is measured in milliseconds. Hard disks provide the required performance to support online data access.

Hard disks provide the required performance to support online data access. A typical server that supports hundreds of users at a time will require high-performance disk interfaces and drives.

Performance Parameter of Hard Disk Drive

Following are the performance parameters by which you may evaluate the performance of any hard disk drive:

Rotation Speed: This is the speed at which the disk platters spin. Spin rates are typically 5400 rpm and 7200 rpm. The newest and fastest drives run at 10000 rpm. Higher spin rate allows the access the data in minimum time.

Seek Time: This is the amount of time it takes for the read/write head to move one-third of the way across the disk. It is important in such a way that Seek time should be measured on average because of distance between heads actual position to their destinations. Average Seek time of most hard disk drives varies but it should be between 8 and 12 milliseconds.

Data Transfer Rate: This is another statistical parameter to measure the performance of a hard disk drive. It is based on the fact that how long it takes to transfer the data. This is the amount of data transfer per unit time is to know data transfer rate. Unit of data transfer rate is termed in bytes/sec. Data Transfer rate of 10 MBPS 10 MB is per second.

2.11.2 Floppy Disk Drive

Floppy Disk is perhaps the most popular medium of transferring the small amount of data from one place to another. The growing market of low-cost microcomputers created the need for low-cost high-capacity storage. Sony Corporation was the first to manufacture the floppy disk and has introduced floppy disk drive way back in 70's. Floppy disk is a soft magnetic disk. It is made up of magnetic oxide-coated tape material. It is called floppy because it flops if you wave it (at least, the 5.25" disk does). These are often called floppies or diskettes. Unlike most hard disks, floppy disks are portable, because you can remove them from a disk drive. Disk drives for floppy disks are called floppy drives.

In comparison to the hard disk, the floppy disks are slower and have less storage capacity, but are less expensive. The floppy disks are highly portable and data/programs written to it may be moved easily from one place to another. Initially the floppy disk of size 5.25" was very popular but soon after it was replaced by smaller size (3.5") which had higher capacity for data storage. 5.25" size was common for PCs made before 1987. It is generally capable of storing between 100 KB and 1.2 MB of data. The most common sizes are 360 KB and 1.2 MB. 3.5" floppy is a better choice over 5.25" disk as they are covered in a rigid envelope. The flexible tape material is cut into circular pieces of 3.5" in diameter. Newer 3.5" floppy disks are packaged in a thick, hard-plastic cartridge with an opening for the read-write head. These openings remain closed until the cartridge is inserted into a floppy drive. These are opened when the disk starts spinning. Read/write head reads the contents of the disk through this opening. For reading and writing on the disk, the head has to be in contact with the disk surface. Thus disk and head wear takes place. Despite their small size, 3.5" disks have a large storage capacity as compared to 5.25" floppies. It ranges from 400 KB to 1.44 MB of data. Data is stored along concentric tracks. Each track is divided into sectors.

Nowadays floppies are available which allow recording on both sides and a recording density up to 14000 bits per inch along each track. The commonly used sizes for PCs are 720 KB (double-density) and 1.44 MB (high-density). Some of the technology used in hard disks such as non-contact recording, light weight heads driven by voice coils (similar to the ones used in loudspeakers) and effective sealing of the disk are being used in the design of floppy disk drives. It is predicted that normal 3.5″ floppies will store close to 20 MB in the next 3-4 years.

2.11.3 Magnetic Tape

The magnetic tape is similar to the tape of music cassette. It is a long tape having the length between 2000-3000 feet. Tape provides offline storage for backing up and archiving data. The tape is an electromagnetic storage medium that is both readable and writeable. A tape drive is the device that positions, writes from, and reads to the tape. A tape cartridge is a protectively encashed tape that is portable. Tape storage is inexpensive and provides high capacities. In early computers, the tape was a primary storage medium and computer system operators spent a lot of time mounting and unmounting tapes for different jobs at different times of the day. The tape contain the magnetic material capable of storing the digital data. The Data and programs are written on the magnetic tape using a device called head and the tape is rolled over the head as shown in the figure 2.6.

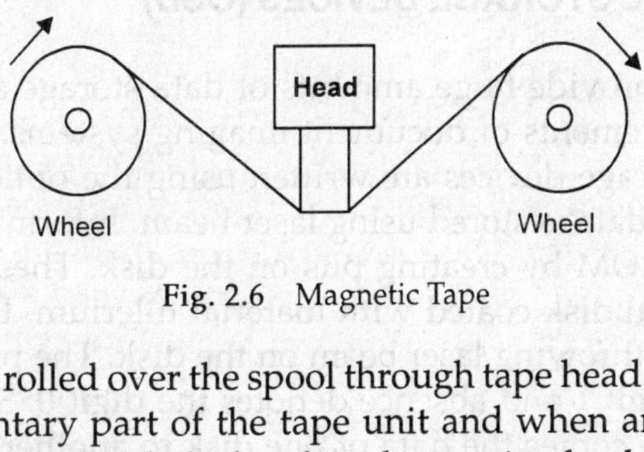

Fig. 2.6 Magnetic Tape

The tape is rolled over the spool through tape head. Tape reader or head is elementary part of the tape unit and when any part of tape passes through the head, the head reads or write the data. The storage capacity of the magnetic tapes is measured in bytes per inch. This indicates the data density on the tape. A 10 feet long tape having the density 200 bytes per inch will be able to save 24000 bytes. The data may be written and erased number of times in the magnetic tape. The magnetic tapes are sequential access device.

With the development of the magnetic disk, tape became a medium for backing up the large amounts of data on mainframes. Major drawback of tape is that it can only be accessed, only by starting at the beginning, and rolling through the tape until the desired data is located. For this reason, its main application use has been for batch processing of large amounts of data, for example, payroll. Today, tape is still sometimes used on mainframes for archiving purposes. New forms of tape are being used for automatic backup. Automated tape devices provide a way to make archived data on tape available to network users. On personal computers, a tape is also used for backup although Iomega's Zip drive and disk is much more popular. A variety of tape formats and drive technologies are available.

2.11.4 Redundant Array of Inexpensive Disks (RAID)

Redundant Array of Inexpensive Disks (RAID) systems is the best option against a disk's fastest rotational speed. They provide large amounts of storage, fast access, and fault tolerance at a reasonable price. Some operating systems, such as Windows NT, let you configure your own disk array configurations. You don't need a RAID configuration to take advantage of fault tolerance features. Most network operating systems support *mirroring* of data on one disk to another disk. Mirroring protects against disk failures by continuously duplicating data on a primary drive or set of drives to secondary drives. If a drive fails, the matching secondary drive set can take its place.

2.12 OPTICAL STORAGE DEVICES (OSD)

Optical disks provide huge amounts of data storage and easily support the requirements of document imaging systems. The data onto the optical storage devices are written using the optical rays. In the CD-ROM, the data is stored using laser beam. Information is written onto the CD-ROM by creating pits on the disk. These optical disks consist of metal disk coated with material tillerium. Pits on the disk are created by throwing laser beam on the disk. The presence of a pit denotes the digit 1 and absence denotes the digit 0. Stamping is the process, which copies the data of one disk to another. The stamping process produces the CD-ROM in the bulk quantity. A laser head moves radically in and out to the specified position.

Three types of optical diskettes are available nowadays, which are known as CD-ROM, WORM (Write Once, Read Many) and re-writeable. It is not possible to write *WORM* disks again after first write. WORM disks are also known as called CD-R (Compact Disk-Recordable). As the name indicates the re writable disk may be written again and again. CD-E (Compact Disk-Erasable) or CD-RW (Compact Disk-Read Writeable) format is in the making. Unfortunately these three types of optical disk are not compatible to each other and each requires different disk drives and technology to access the content of disk.

2.12.1 CD-ROM (Compact Disk- Read Only Memory)

Nowadays, CD-ROM, an optical data disc has emerged as replacement for audio and video tape/cassette. Audio/Video Compact Disks are not only cheaper but also provide high density storage. Since the CD being an optical device, the quality of data stored in the CD remains same even after a long time as opposite to magnetic tapes or cassettes. Computer CD-ROM drives can play audio compact discs. Like audio CDs, CD-ROMs come with data already encoded onto them. The data is permanent and can be read any number of times, but CD-ROMs cannot be modified. The most used technology for high-capacity portable storage is the CD-ROM. This technology has evolved out of the entertainment electronics, where cassette tapes and long playing (LP) records are being replaced by CDs. In the similar ways CDs are being preferred over magnetic tape/disk for storing volumes of data. The disks used to data storage are known as Compact Disk Read Only memory (CD-ROM). The CD-ROM disk also known as a LASER disk. The disk made of a shiny metal whose size in diameter is 5.25 inches. The traditional CD-ROM stores around 650 MB of information, which is equivalent to approximately thirty thousand pages of information. The major application of the CD-ROM is in distributing large amounts of data.

It is not possible to pack the material contained in thirty to fifty books in one CD-ROM. This material can be transported from one place to another as it is highly portable and cost economic. With CD-ROM images, sound, graphics, video can also be stored. Currently every computer reseller is selling multimedia CD-ROMs in which text, audio and video are stored. These CD-ROMs can be used for education and entertainment. Another major application is in the field of music. Audio CDs use the same technology as CD-ROM. Pieces of soundtrack, be it speech or music, are converted into sound files and are written on a CD using the same technology. A normal CD of size 650 MB should have a soundtrack of about 75 minutes. Information is written on to the CD-ROM by creating pits on the disk surface by shining a laser beam. As the disk rotates, the laser beam traces out a continuous spiral, the sharply focused beam creates a circular pit wherever a '1' is to be written and no pit (land), if a zero has to be written. From a master disk, a disk can reproduce many copies in a process called Stamping. The CD-ROM with pre-recorded information is read by a CD-ROM reader, which uses a laser beam for reading. The CD-ROM is inserted into a drive. A laser head moves radially in and out to the specified position. As the disk rotates, the laser beam and the sensing head translate the pits and lands to 0's and 1's by the electronic interface. The rate of reading data ranges from 150 kilobytes/sec (KB/s) and the time taken to access a specified file is about 100 milliseconds.

2.12.2 Recordable CD ROM

Recordable compact disk are generally used by the publisher to news paper/magazines/books where the data stored into used for mass distribution. In this method, the disk is written only once i.e. at the time of beginning and it can be read/accessed number of times. CD manufacturer accept the data stored on magnetic tape or disk from the party and they create a CD-ROM called master CD-ROM. By the process, popularly known as stamping, CD manufacturer create the CDs for public distribution. The master is used to stamp multiple copies, which are tested and labelled. This is economical for reproducing a large number of copies. Any standard CD-ROM player can read this CD-ROM. Until recently, CD-R drives were quite expensive, but now prices have dropped dramatically. To create CD-ROMs and audio CDs, you need not only a CD-R drive, but also a CD-R software package. Often, it is the software package, not the drive itself that determines how easy or difficult it is to create CD-ROMs.

Most of the CD-R drives support the concept of multi-session recording. This means that data may be recorded to the CD over a length of time. This feature is important if the CD-R drive has to be used for creating backup CD-ROMs. CD-ROMs are read-only, but nowadays recordable CD technologies have become quite popular, and many organizations are using the medium to record and distribute catalogues, price sheets, and other information. They are also used at Web sites to provide information for Web users that is safe from corruption, since hackers cannot destroy data on CD-ROMs. With a Write Once Read Many (WORM) disk drive, you can write data onto a WORM disk using a CD-writer, but only once. After that, the CD-ROM behaves just like a CD-ROM. Recordable CD drive is a type of disk drive that can create CD-ROMs and audio CDs. Recordable CD drives can also read CD-ROMs and play audio CDs.

2.12.3 DVD (Digital Versatile/Video Disks)

Both the digital versatile disk and compact disk appears to be the same but in fact they are different in several aspects. The DVD technology provides a storage capacity that is at least 6 to 7 times greater than a CD, in the same space. A movie, that is 90 minutes to longer than two hours can be stored on a DVD with very high quality video. Additionally, there is an equivalent increase in audio quality. In addition to the high quality audio and video experience, the DVD format defines a way to have multiple languages on movies plus subtitles. Not all movies have this feature, but the capability for them to do so exists. When compared to a VCR, the advantage is even greater. Unlike a tape playing on a VCR player, the DVD disc is not touched by any mechanical part. Thus, the DVD has no wear and tear. A DVD can also be used for data storage for use in your computer, using a DVD-ROM drive. DVD provides all the benefits of the WORM/CD-ROM technology, but supports many times the storage capacity of any previous technology.

A DVD can store up to 17 Gigabytes (GB) of data as compared to a CD-ROM disc, which stores about 650 Megabytes (MB) of data. This greatly increased storage capacity is accomplished by using both sides and by storing two layers of data on each side. A single later DVD holds 4.7 GB of data. For technical considerations a single sided, dual layer disc will hold 8.5 GB of data. The transfer rate of data from a DVD can be sustained at more than 1 MB per second. DVD-ROM drives are also backward compatible with CD-ROM. Thus DVD-ROM drive plays CD-ROM's and audio CDs also. DVD technologies consist of DVD-ROM (a high-capacity storage medium), DVD-video, DVD-audio, DVD-R (Recordable), and DVD-RAM (an erasable format).

2.13 JAZ DRIVES AND SUPERDISK

Jaz drives are capable of storing high amount of data in comparison to other drives but they are quite expensive. The removable cartridges used in Jaz drive may hold up to 1 GB of data on each disk. The cartridge may be used again and again and more amounts of data may be written using more number of cartridges similar to the other disks. There is no limitation to the number of disks to be used. Jaz drives are faster than most of the hard drives. The Jaz drive has a 12 millisecond seek time and a transfer rate of 5.5 MBPS. Like Zip drives, they are portable and make transporting information easier. A drive weighs less than 1 kilogram. Jaz drives are commercially available in two forms, external (portable) and internal. A Jaz insider drive fits into any available 3.5-inch drive may and will be cheaper Jaz drives and disks are the ideal solution for storing, transporting and playing multimedia applications. It even can handle full screen, full motion video. With a Jaz drive, you can backup a 1 GB hard disk in as little as 5 minutes. With the Jaz drive's speed and the Jaz disk's capacity even large system backups are easy. A Jaz drive will supplement the existing hard disk on computers with expandable storage. The fast data rates and large storage capacity make it a viable alternative for backup storage as well as for everyday use.

SuperDisks are similar to other drives in concept and they are very high-density diskettes. SuperDisk diskettes are etched with a servo pattern at the factory. This pattern is then read by the SuperDisk drive to precisely align the read/write head. This results into SuperDisk having 2490 tracks, as compared to 135 tracks in conventional 3.5" 1.44 MB diskettes. They have storage capacity of 120 MB per diskette. SuperDisk is backward compatible with older diskettes, i.e., they can read and write the older 1.44 Mb diskettes as well as the new 120 Mb SuperDisk diskettes.

2.14 INPUT /OUTPUT DEVICES (I/O)

Input-Output (I/O) devices enable interaction with the computer. They allow the user to submit data from outside world and display the output to outside world. They serve as medium l of communication between the user and the computer.

2.14.1 Keyboard

The most common and basic input device for computers, is the keyboard. Since the keyboard technology is almost standard the world over, keyboards pose no problems for a person buying a computer. Probably the only difference in working is how keyboards convert the input into signals to be transmitted to the computer.

QWERTY Keyboard: Any beginner of the computer may find it difficult to understand the key layout on the keyboard. The standard that people have used for years is the QWERTY key arrangement. It is widely believed that this arrangement came into use, since the time typewriters were in use. The alphabetical position of the keys, made typing very quick. This led to jammed keys on the typewriters. To avoid this problem, this arrangement of keys was decided upon. The jamming of keys has nothing to do with computer keyboards, but the arrangement continues.

Dvorak Keyboard: The Dvorak key board has been named after its inventors, August Dvorak and Williams L. Dealey. The basic principle behind the arrangement is to promote ease of use, by placing the keys in such a fashion, that the typist using both his hands alternates between the two, while typing. According to them, this would speed up typing.

Ergonomic Keyboard: It has been a common complaint by several persons that most of the keyboards cause stress and pain while working on them. This has resulted in the development of ergonomic keyboards. The keyboard is split into two, and though it looks odd, the arrangement is supposed to lessen the pain while typing continuously. The most common ailment is the carpal tunnel syndrome, which is caused due to the stress suffered by the ligaments in the wrist, because of keeping them bent in a fixed position while typing. Hands assume the natural position of hanging down at the sides of te body, thus resulting in a relaxed action. Of course, the layout of ergonomic keyboards require a little getting used to, and the choice of regular or ergonomic, depends on personal comfort levels.

Cordless Keyboards: Keeping with the trends, keyboards too are going cordless. They are, of course more expensive than the regular ones, use batteries, and are used mainly for presentations in halls, etc. to reduce the tangle of wires, and enable greater mobility for the user.

2.14.2 Mouse

The most common and most widely used input device after the keyboard is the mouse. After introduction of Graphical User Interface (GUI) for several applications the utility of mouse increased extensively and programmers/operators use mouse for most of the time while sitting on a computer. Using a keyboard appears to be tough task for the beginners as they have not only to type in commands but also to remember them. Mouse with GUI application offers lot of flexibility and several tasks can be done at the click of a mouse. The array of keys, and the need to learn typing, often deters many users. The mouse, on the other hand, poses no such problems. The palm size peripheral, with a long wire, has become an indespensible tool for computer users today. The mouse was conceived to supplement the keyboard with a more flexible device to make complex visual operations easier. The pointing device became extremely popular because of the emergence of the GUI, and the end of DOS based screens on desktops. Click and drag has changed the way millions interact with their computers. Mouse is generally of two types: 2-button mouse and the 3-button mouse. In a 2-button mouse, the left button is used for the regular clicking operations whereas the right button, is used to generally bring up short cut menus, in various applications. Many applications do not use the third button of the three-button mouse. However some applications like MS word use the centre button as a scrolling tool. Now the cordless mouse is rapidly becoming popular.

2.14.3 Scanner

Scanner is an input device used to input the images to computer. It is very helpful to feed in large amounts of data without typing. Scanners are also effective in detecting codes at supermarkets, thus speeding up the whole process at the payment counter. It is not yet as popular as the other two input devices. Scanners convert images as well as text, so they can be viewed on computer screens, and then reproduced in print. Scanners differ in their ability to distinguish colours, just black and white, or also greys.

Scanners can broadly be divided by the method of operation as Sheet Feed Scanner, Flatbed Scanner and Handheld Scanner. Sheet Feed Scanner moves the paper past the scan head with the help of mechanical rollers. The limitation is that only single regular size sheets can be scanned, but the image is captured very accurately. Flatbed Scanner moves the scan head past the stationary paper. It uses a series of mirrors to keep the image focused on the lens. The lens gives feedback to a number of sensors. With each reflection, the quality of the image deteriorates. It can scan documents of any size. Handheld Scanners are held in the hand and moved over the paper. The output depends on the steadiness of the hand. These are generally less expensive than the others, since no mechanism is required to move the scan head or the paper.

2.14.4 Monitor

The pixel (picture element) is the smallest display element of any picture. In a Cathode Ray Tube (CRT) display, the smallest possible pixel, is the trio of a red, green and blue (RGB) phosphor dots set. An electron gun shoots out a stream of electrons, one for each of the three primary colours. The holes (or dots) are arranged on a metal plate, called the shadow mask. Dot pitch is the shortest distance between two dots of the same colour. It determines the precision and sharpness of a picture. Thus, the smaller the dot pitch, the better is the picture. Normally, display units support dot pitches from 0.39 to 0.22 mm.

Smaller dot pitches are possible, but would result in more expensive display devices. Sony's Trinitron (Aperture grille) technology makes brighter and sharper images, but also costs more. This difference arises since other CRTs use dots arranged in the shape of a triangle, while Trinitron CRTs use a set of strips, parallel to each other.

The dot pitch is still measured the same way, i.e. the shortest distance between two colour strips. Due to the difference in shape of the strips and the dots, the result is superior in the Trinitron CRTs. The screen refresh rate of a monitor is essential to eliminate screen flicker. A high refresh rate demands a correspondingly high performance requirement on the display adapter and its memory. Today, for 15 or 17-inch monitors the screen refresh rate of 75 Hz, (or 75 times per second), is generally acceptable to all, as against the 50-60 Hz rates of earlier PCs. But with screen sizes bigger than 17 inches, a rate as high as 80-100 Hz might be required.

Energy Star compliant monitor saves power. Other options like standby and sleep modes, are also a big help. In the standby mode, the electron beam and gun in the monitor shut down, and there is about 74 per cent reduction in power consumption. In the sleep mode, the monitor components shut down to cool the gun and the components, resulting to nearly zero watt consumption. The latter takes unto several seconds to return to working mode, compared to the few seconds of the former.

2.14.5 Printer

The printers are output devices that produce the hard copy (on paper) of the result which can be procured for long time. With the advent of color printers, desktop publishing has become a roaring business. The different types of printers are Dot Matrix printers, Color Ink-Jet printers and Laser printers.

Dot Matrix Printers (DMP): The Dot Matrix printer is still most widely used and most economical printer against the maintenance and running cost. The technology used is very basic, and so the costs involved are low since a new ribbon hardly costs much. Maintenance is also easy. The Dot Matrix printer has a ribbon that is coated with ink. A moving pin strikes it, and its impact on the ribbon, transfers the ink onto the paper behind the ribbon.

As the name indicates, Dot Matrix Printer print the character, which is made up of various vertical dot patterns. Some printers pass the print head (the pin), over the paper a second time, slightly offset from the first print. This improves the quality of the output. The noise made while printing is very loud, but with advances in technology, manufacturers have tried coming up with quieter, faster and smaller Dot Matrix printers.

Color Ink-Jet Printers: These printers are smaller in size as compared to the Dot Matrix printers. The noise level is much lower and almost non-existent in the colour ink jet printers. The working is very much similar to the Dot matrix printer. The Ink-Jet printer also has a printer head that moves over the page, printing an entire line with each pass. The only difference is that the head spews out the ink onto the paper, making it a non-impact printer. The print head contains four ink cartridges (one each for cyan, magenta, yellow and black).

Most of the Ink Jet cartridges are available with two-cartridge option. One of the cartridges is filled with black ink and other filled with color inks. The size of the dots printed by the Ink-Jet is smaller than the Dot matrix printer. This results in greater clarity of the output. Color Ink-Jet printers have become popular because they offer the best of both the dot matrix and the laser printers.

Laser Printers: Laser printers have become very popular nowadays and are replacing dot matrix printer. These printers are being used extensively in the offices and perhaps produce best quality print output. Laser printers create lesser sound than dot matrix printers and the sound produced by them at the time of printing is almost comparable to ink jet printers. They are commonly found in large offices. The prohibitive costs involved deter their wide usage. The laser printer produces 4-16 pages per minute. As the name indicates, Laser is used as main mechanism for printing. There is a small processor built into the laser printer which interprets the data received from the computer. The concept is almost similar to the most of the photocopiers who produce output.

2.15 OTHER IMPORTANT HARDWARE DEVICES

2.15.1 Sound Cards

Music has been the source of inspiration, relaxation and enjoyment for many years. Music is an essential part of the life. Your mail program may play music, whenever you get new mail. You may talk over the net with a mike and headphone. You may play soulful music.

Multimedia computers enrich your computing experience. Playing/recording/sequencing of music, telephony over the Internet, sound effects in games are all made possible by the little piece of hardware called the sound card. Initially, computers did not have any sound cards. In fact, they did not have any sound at all. As time went by, computers started to get voice, i.e., just beeps. By the mid-seventies, computers acquired beeps to alert the user to errors during boot-up. New computers had tiny internal speakers, which had different types of beeps in its collection of music. Sound still was not considered important enough to warrant a separate board/card. However, music companies had woken up to the possibilities of synthesized music, that is music by electronic simulation. Musicians could get a reasonable simulation of trumpets, guitars or drums using a keyboard.

When a company called Creative Labs (makers of SoundBlaster) burst in on the scene with a card that could record human voices, the sound card industry really took off. The mid-eighties were witness to the competition with Advanced Gravis' card being the first one to incorporate Wave-table synthesis. Soon Creative Labs introduced a more advanced version (16 bit) of SoundBlaster.

2.15.2 MIDI (Musical Instrument Digital Interface)

Playing back stored data does not create all music that can be generated by a computer. Music is actually made by using a synthesizer, an electronic musical instrument with attached keyboard that creates sounds. Mimicking any instrument in an orchestra or creating sounds otherwise is difficult or impossible to make. If you connect two MIDI keyboards with a cable, the note you play on one keyboard (the master) is mimicked on the other (the slave).

If you have seen musicians attach synthesizers to computers, then you have seen MIDI at work. A commercial music is a blend of actual or traditional musicians and sound engineers, creating effects on the synthesizers. MIDI is a protocol (language used by devices to 'talk' to each other), that enables various musical instruments and computers to connect to each other to play/record/synthesise/manipulate music. In fact, good synthesisers can be connected to your sound card to allow you to compose MIDI files using the synthesiser. There are synthesisers that make the strings of a guitar sound like the tone of a trumpet.

MIDI doesn't tell the card what frequencies of sound to reproduce, rather it tells the card to behave as a musical instrument. MIDI files store the commands that are sent to MIDI devices to reproduce the desired sound. You can think of MIDI music as a page with musical notes on it, and digitised audio music as a finished recording of that page of music. When MIDI instruments are connected to a computer loaded with the right software, you can store, compose, arrange, edit, playback and even print your music. Since there is no actual sound encoded (stored) in a MIDI file, unlike WAVE files, they are much smaller than digitized audio files. These files have the extension '.mid'. To standardise communication among computers and electronic musical instruments such as synthesisers, MIDI devices are used. To enable MIDI manufacturers' equipment (synthesisers and other digital equipment) to 'talk' to each other, a common standard General MIDI (GM) has evolved.

2.15.3 Modem

The Modem has slowly but surely become one of the most vital components of a computer. Due to the popularity of the Internet, the average computer buyer's list is sure to include the modem, despite the hidden cost of telephone, involved in using the Internet. In the early days, there was not too much you could do with a modem, except maybe logging on to a Bulletin Board Service, which was not exactly what the masses were demanding. But once VSNL (Videsh Sanchar Nigam Limited) started its TCP/IP services, and e-mail become popular. You can send any amount of e-mail without being charged, a modem became a part of almost every PC. Today, with private ISPs (Internet Service Providers) popping up, it is high time you add a modem to your list of essentials.

Modems are used for e-mail purpose or for browsing the Internet. You can also use your modem to send and receive faxes, record incoming voice calls, or even page you when there is an incoming call. Today's modems are generally either 33.6 or 56 KBPS. The minimum features to look for in today's modems are voice support and user friendly software. Most modems today, are usually plug-n-play and are fairly easy to set up and configure. Quality, appearance and vendor support, are the other essential features one should look out for, while purchasing a modem.

There are high-end modems for ISDN and leased lines but most PC users will be dealing with the dialup models. Internal modems match external modems in terms of performance and robustness, but the machine needs to be rebooted, if it crashes. The performance of a modem is highly dependent on the quality of your telephone line and the ISP.

2.16 UNINTERRUPTED POWER SUPPLY (UPS)

UPS is a device that improves the quality of the Alternating Current (AC) in order to allow uninterrupted operation of AC power equipment. The UPS device thus takes in poor quality power from the mains as input and provides enhanced quality power as output. In case of a power failure, it provides enough power to keep your system running for several minutes, enabling you to save data and prevent file corruption. An UPS device consists of a battery, a transformer and an inverter. It protects your system against sudden changes in power, which can damage your system.

2.16.1 UPS Protection

The UPS protects your system from the following type of threats which may emerge because of faulty power supply.

Spikes: Sudden and brief surges of very high voltage. These momentary highs can cause irreparable damage to the components of your computer and cause premature failure of devices.

Blackouts: A blackout is the total loss of power, whereas a brownout is a short drop in the power line. While blackouts can cause loss of data in RAM and at times corrupt hard drives, brownouts usually result in frozen keyboards and system crashes.

Fluctuations: During summer you may have noticed that the lights in your room dim every time you turn on the air conditioner. This is because the air conditioner draws a substantial amount of power from the mains, leaving less power for the lights causing them to dim. Computers require a constant flow of power. Any fluctuations in the supply could damage the fine soldering on the motherboard and other components of your computer.

2.16.2 Types of UPS

UPS can be classified into the following three categories.

Offline UPS: An offline UPS provides an alternative source of power in the case of a power failure or fluctuation. By default, power is supplied directly from the mains to the system. Any drop in the voltage or current is detected by the UPS, which automatically switches the battery into the circuit, cutting off the main power line – thus allowing the battery to supply the required power. The time taken for this changeover is noteworthy.

Ideally, the change should not take more than 4 milliseconds, as this is the tolerance limit of a typical computer power unit. If it does not happen within this timeframe, the system detects the change in power condition and reboots. When the power condition returns to normal, the UPS automatically switches the PC back to the power mains again. This also means that if there are frequent power fluctuations, the UPS will be rapidly switching 'on' and 'off'. In the offline mode, when the battery is not being used, the main power supply keeps on constantly charging it.

On-line UPS: In on-line UPS, power for the system is supplied by the battery, which in turn is powered by the mains. This type of 'on-line' power eliminates any interruptions in the flow of electricity. Since it uses more electronic circuitry than offline UPS, it is priced higher. Besides the high price tag, on-line UPS also has the disadvantage of high running costs and temperature. Since the battery acts as the primary power source to the system, an on-line UPS battery charger has to be powerful enough to generate enough power to compensate for the battery's power drain.

The conversion from AC mains to DC for the battery and back to AC through the inverter results in a 25 to 30 percent power loss. The heat generated as a consequence of the power loss shortens the life of electrical components and reduces battery life. In contrast, offline UPS has a power loss of a mere 1 to 2 per cent, which means a longer life span.

2.16.3 Constant Voltage Transformer (CVT)

The CVT ensures that the output voltage (the voltage that leaves the unit) stays within a specified range and that it does not fluctuate. It consists of a saturating transformer that chops off the top of a sine wave, thereby producing a near-square wave with constant amplitude. This voltage is then converted into a constant amplitude sine wave using a resonating circuit using external capacitors. These devices are useful in areas that face regular and high voltage fluctuations. To protect the computer from fluctuations, plug your computer system into a separate power line that does not have any other power-consuming heavy machinery like air conditioners or motors plugged on it. In addition, keep all devices such as printers or modems plugged to the same outlet. This will minimize the chance of devices having different voltages and affecting each other.

SELECT EXERCISES

Q. 1. What are Peripheral Devices? Explain the role of peripheral devices in reference to computers.

Q. 2. Differentiate between computer hardware and software. Support your answer with examples

Q. 3. Enlist some of the input and output devices that are used in a computer.

Q. 4. Describe motherboard and enlist those items that it contains or those items that can be plugged into it?

Q. 5. Distinguish between RAM and ROM and auxiliary memory?

Q. 6. Differentiate between computer hardware and software. Explain how firmware is different from Software and Hardware. Support your answer with a suitable example.

Q. 7. What do you mean by Computer Generations? List the major achievements in each generation which have revolutionised the age of computer.

Q. 8. What do you mean by Personal Computing? Comment on the era of personal computing.

Q. 9. What are I/O devices? List some of the important I/O devices..

Q. 10. What is a Microprocessor? What are the basic differences between Microprocessor and Microcomputer?

Q. 11. Explain the differences between a Microprocessor and CPU?

Q. 12. What is a Microprocessor? What are the differences between a Microprocessor and CPU?

Q. 13. What is BIOS? Whether BIOS is hardware or software? Justify your answer.

Q. 14. Distinguish between Online/near line and offline data storage?

Q. 15. What are the performance parameter's of HDD? Which HDD is used for what kind of work, describe in detail.

Q. 16. What are RAID? What are the advantages of using RAID?

Q. 17. What is a floppy disk? Of what sizes and capacity floppy disk are available now?

Q. 18. How many kinds of driver are available in computer? Enlist them.

Q. 19. Give the description of floppy disk drive, CDROM and DVD's?

Q. 20. What is a recordable CD-ROM? Explain how recording is done to CD-ROM.

Q. 21. What is BIOS? Whether BIOS is hardware or software? Justify your answer.

Q. 22. What is the function of Control Unit?

Q. 23. What are Static RAM? How they are different from Dynamic RAM? Explain the functions of Refreshing Circuit used in Dynamic RAM.

Q. 24. What are Auxiliary Storage Devices? Can Hard Disk be categorized as Auxiliary Storage Device? What are the performance parameters of HDD.

Q. 25. What is a floppy disk? Of what sizes and capacity floppy disk are available now a days?

Q. 26. What is ROM? Why the data stored in the ROM are not erased even after the power is switched off. Justify your answer with a example.

Q. 27. What is a Jaz Drive? How it is different than ZIP drive?

Q. 28. What are Superdisk? What are the advantages of Superdisk?

Q. 29. What are the multimedia elements available? In what kind of computer they may be used?

Q. 30. What kind of device is a keyboard? How many type of keyboards are available for use in computers?

Q. 31. Classify printer and describe them for the purpose they are made?

Q. 32. What are the advantages of using Ergonomic Keyboard?

Q. 33. What is a Monitor? Explain how the color graphics is displayed on the monitor?

Q. 34. What are Optical Storage Devices? How the data recording is done on the optical storage device? Explain what are the differences between the CD-ROM and Digital Versatile Disk? How the DVDs are being used in day-to-day life?

Q. 35. What is Modem? Is it necessary to have a modem to connect to internet? Describe the specification of a modem.

Q. 36. What is the main function of UPS? How many types of UPS are available?

Q. 37. If you intend to buy a computer, how would you decide which computer should be purchased and what peripherals it should have?

Q. 38. Give a comparative analysis of High Level Language, Assembly Language, and Machine language.

Q. 39. What are Fourth generation languages (4GL)? Explain where these languages are used and how they are different from third generation languages?

Q. 40. What are Application programs? What are differences between a application program and system program? Cite any two examples of each.

Q. 41. What do you understand with the memory hierarchy? What is cache memory and why cache is used?

Q. 42. What are programming languages? Explain the difference between Machine, Assembly and High Level language? Give some examples of High level Language?

Q. 43. Explain the drawbacks and difficulties in writing programs in low level languages? Why a large software product is not written in low level language?

Q. 44. Explain with example, which language is more suitable to write a program; an assembly or a machine language? Justify your answer.

Q. 45. Why a program written in High Level Language or Assembly Language are translated before execution?

Q. 46. What are Compilers? How are they different from Interpreters? Compare the features of Compiler and Interpreter.

Q. 47. What are assemblers? Explain the difference in assemblers and compilers.

Q. 48. What is the difference between a UPS and a CVT?

3 Concepts in Operating System

3.0 INTRODUCTION

The Operating System may be considered as a collection of software programs which allow a user to interact with the hardware. Computer System consists of several hardware devices like, processor, memory, peripheral devices. The operating system provides several routines which control the hardware and provide an environment for any user to execute their application program without worrying for the details of hardware. Working with computers, without an Operating System (OS), would be a difficult task because the task like loading an application program from disk to primary memory, allocation of memory, scheduling etc would require hours of work. Application programs themselves would be longer, more complicated and more expensive than they are now. This will result in writing complicated application program which not only deals with the logical details of program logic but also include other functions which allow the application program to use hardware. Apart from that different softwares would be required for different configurations (processors) to be written. Luckily, the availability of standard operating systems has prevented all sorts of problems and more. It may be emphasised that Operating System, therefore, is a collection of programs which act as a interface between user and hardware and provides an environment for executing application programs. An abstract of computer system alongwith hardware, operating system, application software and users are shown in the figure 3.1.

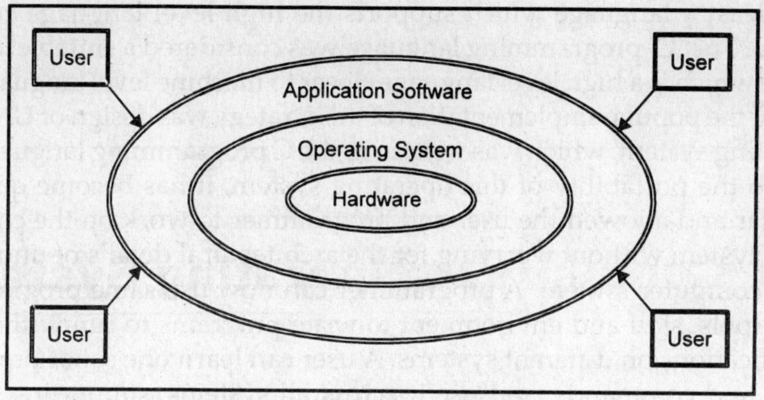

Fig. 3.1 View of Computer System

3.1 EVOLUTION OF OPERATING SYSTEMS (OS)

In the early stages of computing, operating systems were developed for specific computer systems. VM and CMS operating systems were developed for IBM 360 and IBM 370 computers. CP/M was developed for the microprocessor system Z80 of Zilog Corporation. Microsoft developed MS-DOS for the Intel 80x86 range of processors. This approach of developing operating system proved to be ineffective when the two or more than two computers used to be integrated. Since each computer system running its own operating system, it was difficult to transfer file, use the resource available at different computers was difficult to achieve due to compatibility problems. Sometimes, it is also not possible to run same application program or software on different computer systems. In all such cases, significant amount of work used to be redone. Extreme cases were those where all the application program used to be rewritten. Many of the operating systems used support only a subset of programming language and many programming languages were supported by only few of them. Therefore, in the early days due to the problem of compatibility of file formats and other simple jobs, the strategy of developing different operating system for different processor did not last long and people started developing operating systems which were not machine dependent.

Due to the problem of compatibility raised initially, operating systems were developed that could be easily transferred across different computer systems. This has become possible by development and design of operating system which were not dependent on architecture of the underlying computer system. This is probably the reason when attempts were made to write operating systems in high level language or at least a language which supports the high level language constructs. The 'C' programming language was considered a suitable language which is a high level language closer to machine level language. First of the popular implementation of this strategy was design of UNIX operating system, which was written in the C programming language. Due to the portability of this operating system, it has become quite popular and allowed the user and programmer to work on the computer system without worrying for the architectural details of underlying computer system. A programmer can now use same programming tools, skill and environment to write programs to run without modifications on different systems. A user can learn one set of procedures and commands, and use it across all systems, supporting his chosen OS.

The first effort towards writing whole set of program required for operating system was the development of CP/M. The Control Program for Microprocessor (CP/M) was developed by Gary Kildall in 1973. He first of all developed the programming language called PL/M, (Programming Language for Microcomputers) and then has written the operating system CP/M in the programming language PL/M. CP/M later was adopted by personal computer based on Z80 based computer system and supported floppies and hard disk drives. After the introduction of CP/M, the small computer built around microprocessor became very popular because not only they were available at affordable price but also this operating system allowed the user to handle hardware more effectively. In 80's, after the introduction of Microsoft's Disk Operating System(DOS), IBM Personal Computer has revolutionised the personal computer market. IBM PC loaded with MS DOS has become a choice for the independent programmer and they found it very useful. At the time when MS DOS emerged as a choice for personal computer, UNIX had established itself as platform for larger mainframe computers.

Biggest problem with the Disk Operating System (DOS) and UNIX was that they had textual interface. This problem was more acute with the users of personal computer running with MS DOS. Since the low cost PCs were targeted at general audience, remembering the commands and syntax of DOS were not easy to remember. Microsoft realised it and they came up with their solution called Windows in 90s, which was introduced as a replacement of DOS. Earlier version of Windows used to run on top of DOS. Later with the introduction of Windows 95/98 with fully functional graphical user interface, it has become very easy for general users to work with PCs and get their task done by few clicks of mouse. Windows NT was introduced for the network of a computer and it is very easy to frequent tasks like sharing of file/folders, transfer of data with single click of mouse. Main advantage of GUI based operating system like windows were that users can get rid of typing and remembering the command of DOS.

3.2 FUNCTIONS OF OPERATING SYSTEM

An operating system is perhaps the most important program which creates any user friendly environment for an user to interact with the machine. It co-ordinates and controls the operation of computer hardware and software resources. These resources are mainly processors, main memory, secondary memory, input-output devices and files. The operating systems functions can broadly be categorised into two categories called Resource Management and providing friendly interaction of user with hardware by allowing him to write command to do specific tasks. The major function of an operating system is therefore to bridge the gap between the hardware and user. The operating system not only manages the hardware but also provides services to application programs by allocating the hardware resources which are essential for execution of the program. These services and resource include file systems, memory management, process management, process communication, and networking. Whenever an application program is written and executed by an user, it accesses several software and hardware resources. These resources are processors, main memory, secondary memory, input-output devices and files. Major role of an operating system is to allocate these resources to application program efficiently and effectively. The operating system lies between the applications program and the computer hardware. Operating systems also resolve conflicts, attempt to optimise performance and simplify the effective use of the system.

Let us understand how an operating system makes the life of an user simple by providing him easy access to hardware. Early days operating systems used to provide a textual interface. This means that a user may access the functionalities of an operating system by writing textual commands. The operating system interprets these commands and translates them into sequences of further instructions to the hardware. For example, if you have to create a file, the user may submit a command for creation of a file and operating system does rest of the task. It will find the free space on the disk, is responsible for saving your work as long as user wants to keep his file on the disk. These files may be copied, edited, deleted at the wish of the user. The only thing required by the user is to type in an appropriate command using key board. Therefore, an operating system performs tasks, such as recognising input from the keyboard, sending output to the display screen, keeping track of files and directories on the disk, and controlling peripheral devices such as disk drives and printers. User interacts with the OS through a set of commands.

The user's command are submitted by user through keyboard. The Command Interpreter, which is a subset of operating systems software routine, reads the command entered by the user and converts it into a stream of electronic pulses. These commands are executed by the operating system on the hardware and the required task is done without forcing user to learn rigorous details of hardware. For example, a copy command submitted to the operating system may copy the file from hard disk to floppy, or vice versa without letting the user to know the details or working principle of either floppy disk drive to hard disk drive.

The textual interface to the operating system at the later stage is found to be little more cumbersome and started proving difficult to operate. The main reason to this was that users used to remember the lengthy command, their syntax etc. This has paved the way to design and develop the operating system where the user need not to remember large and complex commands. The Microsoft was the first who came with their operating system called Windows. The windows have proved to be an alternative to textual interfaces to operating system. Windows has provided Graphical User Interface (GUI) which allows user to enter commands by pointing and clicking at objects and icon displayed on the monitor by mouse. Windows hides the internal details of hardware components and presents a simple, usable working environment. Example of textual interfaces are Disk Operating System (DOS), UNIX etc. Windows 95/98/NT are graphical user interface based operating systems. The operating system is therefore system software, which is loaded in the memory of the computer at the time of booting process. It remains their all the time and provides a platform on top of which application programs may run. The operating system apart from allowing the user to run their command and application program also helps the user for housekeeping activities in the computer system. This includes maintenance of files, allocation of resource, etc. Every general-purpose computer must have an OS to run other programs, and provide the base upon which application programs can be written.

3.3 MANAGEMENT OF RESOURCES

The operating systems are in two modes, single user mode and multi user mode. In single user mode, it is assumed that only one user will have access to all the resources of computer system. These resources are mainly Memory, Processor, I/O and Files. In the multi user mode, the operating system is designed to allow several users at a time. Most of the large computer systems work in multi user mode. Microsoft Disk Operating System (DOS) is considered as a single user operating system and all of the resources available are at the disposal of the user. In this environment, an user may submit only one task at a time. If he wish to run another application, in that case he needs to terminate the previous one. This feature excludes the DOS being multitasking or multiprocessing operating system. The UNIX is considered as multi user operating system, which allows more than one user to work at a time. In the conventional UNIX based system, the multiple user sitting at their terminal may send request to the CPU and these requests are served by the CPU one by one. The requirement and methodologies of management of resources (memory, processor, I/O devices and files) varies in single and multi user operating system. Based on the resources, chiefly operating system perform following four management functions.

- Memory Management
- Processor Management
- Device Management
- File Management

3.3.1 Memory Management

The memory management function finds all available free space in memory and allocates it to the processes. The process is program/task under execution stage. The operating system manages whole memory by dividing it into several blocks and partitions. Every job under execution stage requires memory. If there exists two or more than two processes then the operating system allocates the memory segments as per the requirement of the job. In case any job execution has to be suspended or it has been terminated, the operation system combines the memory freed by the process and allocates the memory to other process. The operating system, therefore, decides which process gets memory, when and how much and then allocates the memory when that process requires it. It finally frees the allocated memory space as and when the process is executed completely. Memory Management is the important function carried out by operation system. It is also the responsibility of the operating system that memory should be allocated in such a way that the utilisation is maximum.

3.3.2 Processor Management

The processor management function of operating is related with allocation of process or job to processor. The speed of processor or CPU is much faster than peripheral devices. Every process is completed only after its processor and I/O requirement. Since the speed of CPU is much faster then I/O devices, the scheduling is done in such a way that CPU remains idle for minimum amount of time. When a process waits for I/O to be completed, during that wait time, the CPU may be allocated to other process waiting for processor. There exists several scheduling techniques which maximise CPU utilisation.

3.3.3 Device Management

This function of operating system deals with allocation of devices to process. Operating system schedule the I/O devices, I/O channel to process, whenever it requires. For managing the different request arising from different process for grant of devices, scheduling of I/O devices are done according to some strategies. In I/O scheduling, after finding the status of device, channels, a schedule is prepared which states which device is allocated to the process.

3.3.4 File Management

The file management of operating system is related with management of files stored onto secondary storage. The file is considered as collection of logically related data item which are organised in records. These files may contain a set of commands, executable code or reports. Purpose of file management is to hide the complex details of device specific aspects from the user. Users wish to rely on a uniform set of file manipulation services which are independent of details of devices from user's perspective. File Management of operating system keeps track of all information on files. It finds and records the following for all files: location, size, usage (attribute), status etc. It also finds as to which process, which file is required, checks through the protection routine, opens the file if allowed, and allocates it to the process. It essentially does the task of mapping the request of file from process to physical disk, swapping the file contents between primary and secondary memory, keeping track of allocation and de-allocation of space and support for protection and sharing of files.

3.4 OPERATING SYSTEMS CLASSIFICATION

The operating systems provide software layers between user and hardware, which creates an environment for user to run his application and control hardware without knowing the rigorous details of hardware. Users submit their jobs to the operating system and operating system schedule their jobs. The job may be handled by the operating system serially or concurrently. The serial-processing means that the resources of the computer system are allocated to single job and remain allocated until job is finished. In concurrent processing the resources may be dynamically allocated to the jobs as and when required. Current application requires the distributed operating system, which co-ordinates the allocation of resources located at different sites or computer system. For the job requiring the resources located at different computer systems, all of them have to follow a common set of protocol. These types of requirement are being served by distributed operating system.

Based on the nature of application and functionalities, the operating system may be classified into several categories. We will discuss some of thc modes of operating system and different types of operating system in this section.

3.4.1 Batch Operating System

One major design issue for the operating system is to increase the resource utilisation. It also includes the reduction in CPU idle time by removing the manual or programmers intervention during the execution of program. Batch operating systems are based on the concept that if the several programs are batched together on input, they can be executed one after another without programmer's intervention. This reduces the overhead for each program, as the program does not need require human intervention. The batch processing is suitable in programs with large computation time with no need of user interaction or involvement. For example, payroll, forecasting, statistical analysis and large scientific number crunching programs. Users need not wait while the job is being processed. The instructions are provided by embedding the commands in a batch stream. These commands are written in a language called Job Control Language (JCL). JCL commands are required to mark the beginning and end of the job, to announce their resource need and memory requirements.

Batch Monitor, a part of batch operating system, reads and interprets the command written in JCL. The total time from submission of job into the queue till it gets completed is called Turn Around Time. The major disadvantage of batch operating systems are non-interactive environment. It also imposes several drawbacks from programmers' point of view e.g. the programmer is bound to do off-line debugging. The time taken between job submission and job completion is generally very high although the time lapsed in actual execution of program may be quite less. Since the programmer does not have any control over intermediate results of a program, batch operating systems are considered quite inflexible in software development. Off-line debugging also does not permit the programmer to correct the bugs whenever they occur, but has to correct them at later stage.

3.4.2 Multiprogramming Operating Systems

In batch operating system, the jobs are submitted in the batch and all the resources are reserved to one job at a time. This practice improves the turn around time but shorter length jobs suffer adversely because they have to wait for a longer time for their turn. Another disadvantage of batch operating system is that it does not maximise the resource utilisation. This drawback of batch operating system may be overcome by Multiprogramming Operating Systems. The multiprogramming allows the interleaved execution of two or more than two programs. Multiprogramming operating systems are fairly sophisticated as compared to batch operating systems.

Multiprogramming improves both system throughput and resource utilisation. The job submitted to the operating system requires CPU for computation and I/O for their I/O needs. During the serial execution of program when CPU completes the computation, it remains idle for the time when I/O operations of the job are under progress. This idle time of CPU poses heavy penalty on the jobs waiting for CPU intervention. Multiprogramming operating system allows concurrent execution of two or more than two jobs and schedules them in such a way that whenever computation work of one job is completed and it goes for I/O, this idle time of CPU may be utilised by allocating another job to the CPU. This improves throughput of operating system. The number of jobs active in the system are known as degree of multiprogramming. Higher degree of multiprogramming ensures higher resource utilisation. Concept of multiprogramming is illustrated in the following schematic diagram.

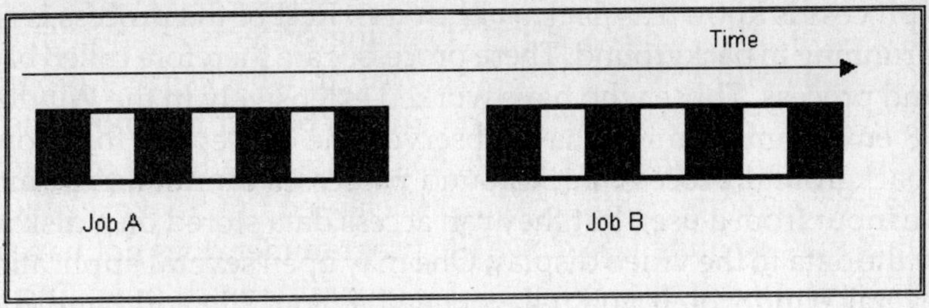

Fig. 3.2(a) Sequential Execution of Job A and B

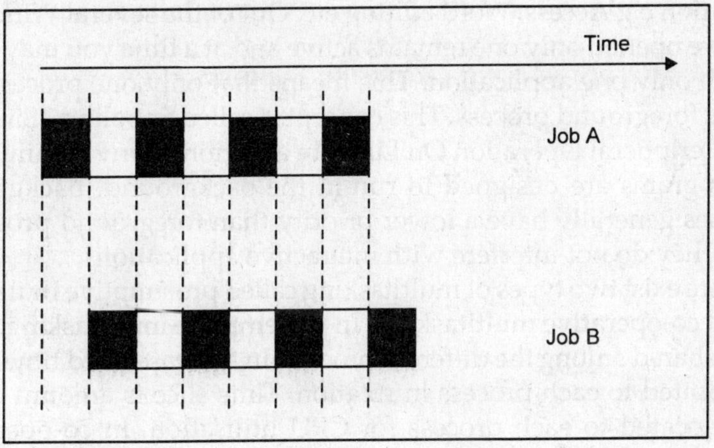

Fig 3.2(b) Concurrent Execution of Job A & Job B

Figure 3.2 (a) shows the sequential execution of two jobs A and B. Their time requirement for CPU is shown as shaded box. Fig 3.2 (b), shows the interleaved or concurrent execution of both jobs in such a way the when Job A does its I/O bound work, the CPU is utilised for computation work of Job B.

3.4.3 Multitasking Operating Systems

A multitasking operating system allows two or more than two active processes. The instance of a program execution is known as process. Multitasking is implemented by maintaining code and data of several processes simultaneously in the memory. Multitasking is often coupled with hardware and software support. During execution of more than two processes, it is the responsibility of the operating system to protect the memory space reserved for one process from other process. Most of the multitasking systems, out of multiple processes only process accept the input from keyboard, mouse or other input devices.

This process is known as *foreground process*. Rest of the process is said to be running in background. These processes are therefore called background process. Those who have worked extensively in the Windows 95/98 environment might have observed the concept of foreground and background process. Background processes cannot accept interactive input from a user, but they can access data stored on a disk and write the data to the video display. One may open several applications in several Windows. If you have opened a word file and have given print order. The computer will keep printing the document in background and Windows allow you to work at the same time in another application e.g Access, Word editing etc. Out of the several Windows, you have opened only one remains active and at a time you may interact with only one application. This means that only one process will work as foreground process. This concept is called Spooling. (Simultaneous Peripheral Operation On Line). In addition, many communication programs are designed to run in the background. Background processes generally have a lower priority than foreground processes so that they do not interfere with interactive applications.

There exist two types of multitasking called pre-emptive multitasking and co-operative multitasking. In pre-emptive multitasking, CPU time is shared among the different process. In this case fixed time slices are allocated to each process in rotation. Time slice is amount of the time allocated to each process for CPU utilisation. In co-operative multitasking, each process may hold the CPU for the duration it wants. A process not utilising the CPU may allow others to process program to use it temporarily. Windows 95, Windows NT, and UNIX operating system are examples of pre-emptive multitasking operating system.

Windows 95/98 are considered as multitasking operating system but DOS does not qualify as multi tasking operating system. Although DOS allows some of the tasks to be done in background like printing in the background. MS Windows 95/98, Mac OS, UNIX are the example of operating system which are complete multitasking operating system.

3.4.4 Multiprocessing Operating Systems

A multiprocessing or multiprocessor operating system is that which manages operations of a computer system having two or more than two (multiprocessor) processors. The multiprocessor operating systems are also multitasking operating system because they allow multiple process to be executed at a time on different processors. Here it must be noted that multitasking may not be allowed on different processors. The multiprocessor operating system provides all features of operating system along with the management of multiple processor. Multiprocessing can be done in two ways called Symmetric and Asymmetric multiprocessing. In Asymmetric multiprocessing, different jobs may be allocated to different processors. The disadvantage in asymmetric multiprocessing is that one processor may be overloaded while the other processor remains idle. In symmetric multiprocessing same job may be executed simultaneously at different processors. Through this model all processors share memory and I/O.

3.4.5 Multi-user Operating System

A multi-user OS allows two or more users to work simultaneously. It is achieved by allowing two or more users to connect to the computer system from different terminals. Multiuser operating system does not guarantee that multiprogramming or multitasking will be done. The general purpose time sharing system incorporates features of both multiuser and multiprocessing operating system.

3.4.6 Multithreading

Threads, a comparatively new concept, are used to increase the performance of operating system by reducing the context switching time. Threads are a good mechanism for achieving high degree of concurrency. Each thread represents a process and they are also called light weight processes. Each thread corresponds to exactly one process and no thread can exist. Each thread represents a flow of control and have its own state. Concept of threads have been implemented in operating system Mach OS and OS/2. Threads are individual processes that execute simultaneously in multitasking operating systems. The programmer must carefully design the program in such a way that all the threads can run at the same time without interfering with each other. Programmers writing programs for multitasking operating systems can design processes that can be split into threads. These threads may be executed simultaneously. It is always beneficial to do multitasking with threads on multiprocessor system. Even in case of Uni. Processor system, each thread is executed in turn, one after the other. A single thread does not dominate the processor, but instead is given a short period of time to complete some or all of its tasks.

3.4.7 Time Sharing System

Time-sharing is extension of multiprogramming where multiple jobs are executed simultaneously by the CPU. The switching between the processes occurs so frequently that its users may interact with each job in execution state. It is a form of multi-programmed OS that operates in an interactive mode with a quick response time. The user types a request to the computer through a keyboard. The computer processes it and a response, if any is displayed on the user's terminal. A time sharing system allows many users to simultaneously share the computer resources. Since each action or command takes a small fraction of time, only a little CPU time is needed for each user. The CPU switches so rapidly from one user to another, that each user is given impression that he has his own computer, while actually it is one computer being shared among many users.

3.4.8 Real-time Systems

Real time systems are used in the environment where most of the inputs or events are accepted from the environment external to computer systems. These jobs must be processed meeting their deadline. In real time system meeting the deadline of job is a must. Thus Real Time systems are defined as those systems in which the correctness of the systems depends not only on the logical result of computation but also on the time in which the results are produced. Real Time operating system intends to complete the submitted job within the time limit. The job is said to have served successfully only if the job has met the deadline. Real Time System is deployed in mission critical application, flight control, simulation, military operation where meeting the deadline is as important as job completion. Primary objective of real time system are therefore to meet the deadline. Example of real time operating system are Maruti II, VRTX (Virtual Real Time Executive) and HART OS (Hexagonal Architecture for real time operating system). The deadlines in the real time operating system are met by maintaining the calendar management. A resource allocation chart for a job is prepared first before the execution of the job. All the resources are made available to the job so that it completes the execution meeting the deadline. General overview of a real time system is presented in following schematic diagram.

As shown in figure 3.3, typically a real-time system consists of a controlling system and controlled system. The controlled system can also be viewed as the environment with which the computer interacts.

The controlling system interacts with its environment based on the information available about the environment from various sensors. The state of the environment, as perceived by the controlling system, should be consistent with the actual state of the environment. Otherwise the effects of the controlling system activities may be

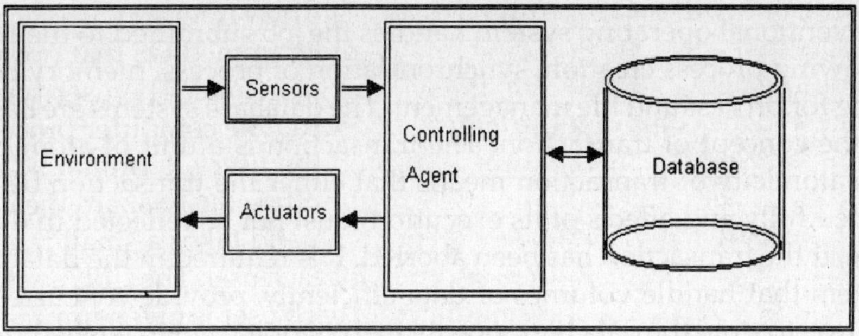

Fig. 3.3 Real Time System

disastrous. Hence periodic monitoring of the environment as well as timely processing of the censored information is necessary. Timely processing of the information in real-time system is necessary because of the physical impact of the controlling system's activities. For example, if the computer controlling a robot does not command it to stop or to run on time, the robot might collide with another object on the factory floor possibly causing serious damage.

There can be two types of the task which may be submitted to Real Time System. These are called periodic and aperiodic.

- **Periodic task:** A periodic task is one that is activated at regular time intervals (T). The deadline for each activated instance may be less than, equal to, or greater than the period T. For example a radar that tracks the flights produces data at a fixed rate.
- **Aperiodic task:** An aperiodic task is activated at unpredictable times, e.g. an object falling in front of a moving robot.

3.4.9 Database Operating System

Database Management System provides the set of programs for creating and processing database. Conventional database management system e.g Oracle, Sybase etc run on top of the operating system. With growing demand of heavy data processing, it has been found that some of the operating systems do not yield good performance for database management system because of incompatibility in the configurations. The database management system performance remains under-utilised as operating system does not provide sufficient functionality to the database implementation. Database operating system are those which are designed for supporting the function needed by database management system. Development of such operating system is a costly affair, therefore the existing operating system may be modified whenever interface to the underlying database management system is changed.

Conventional operating system handles the job submitted to them by following process creation, synchronisation of process, memory handling for process and file management. The database systems are based on the concept of transaction. The transaction is a unit of atomicity. The atomicity of transaction means that either the transaction be executed fully and effects of its execution must not be reflected in database, if the transaction has been aborted. It is required in the database system that handle volumes of data efficiently, provide concurrency control, to store the data temporarily in the storage when fetched from the secondary storage. This all has to be done without sacrificing the integrity of data. The operating system designed by emphasising the database systems need is called database operating system.

3.4.10 Network Operating System (NOS)

Computer Network refers to the collection of several computing machines, peripheral devices, storage unit. The computer systems may communicate with computer network and share the resources. These networks enable the computer to communicate a remote computer where the remote computer may be located as a distance of few meters to several thousand kilometers. The users of a computer system on network are able to share the software resources such as programs, databases, and program utilities. These computers may communicate the data to each other, participate in solving a problem collectively, and share the resources available. A computer network installed in a very small area e.g. a room or building is known as Local Area Network (LAN). Network Operating Systems provide features for controlling Local Area Networks. Network operating system is designed and developed towards the need of computer user on network e.g. the users may transfer or copy files from one machine to another machine, and can log into remote machines on network. A network operating system may provide a shared file system and a set of security features to control user access to network resources. Some typical characteristics of network operating systems are as follows.

- All computer systems have their own operating system which provides an environment for an user to use that computer system as stand alone system.
- Instead of providing a whole network wide operating system which controls all of the machines on the network. Network Operating System provides an environment where for certain application user of one computer may interact with another computer for sharing resources. Most of the time the user works on his system and

whenever he wants to use the resources available at another system, NOS allows him to do it by means of transfer of files, remote log-in etc.

- Network Operating System allows all the users aware of the locations of the different files and resources on the network. Users are also allowed to transfer file from one computer to another by means of File Transfer Protocols.

In NOS, many operating systems provide point to point resource sharing e.g file/printer sharing similar to the services offered by full-featured network operating systems. These environments usually lack the security and access controls. Most of these systems are not fault tolerant.

Salient features of the network operating systems are summarised below.

- NOS allows the multiple users to share the resources available on the network.
- It also provides location transparency. It means the user at one system may access the resources available at other system. NOS provides authorisation and authentication features.
- NOS also controls and restricts access of the resources by adopting the security features like password etc. at other systems without worrying for the location of resource.
- NOS also provides some fault tolerance using clustering and back-up services.
- It includes the common services like documentation of activities in network, software and hardware inventory, replication of data and file etc.

Novell Netware, Windows NT are popular network operating systems being used for management of local area network. They support one or other features of network operating system. All the network operating systems available today have their own set of functions and provide features, which may or may not exist in other NOS. Nowadays, the NOS are using some of the standard protocol to implement the common services e.g TCP/IP protocol for internetworking.

3.4.11 Distributed Operating Systems

A distributed system is defined as a collection of co-operating computer system which does not share either memory or clock. These computer systems may be geographically located. Each computer in a distributed system has its local memory and its own operating system.

Whenever the users on different computer system work, they generally realise the need of sharing the resources like data file etc and other costly resources. The distributed system allows the users to share the resources over a communication network. Distributed operating system appears to its users like a centralised operating system but it runs on multiple independent processors. The user views the system as virtually single processor but not as a collection of distinct machines. This is known as transparency. The resources located at different computer systems are so managed that users are not even aware of where their programs are being actually run or where their files are. All these activities are handled by distributed operating system. The major limitations of distributed systems are:

- Absence of global clock
- Absence of shared memory

Major issue in the design of distributed operating system is the lack of global knowledge. This problem occurs because different computers not only have their own operating system but also they do not share the memory and clock. In scheduling the job in distributed system, it is required to know the upto date status of the system resources. Other important issues in design of distributed operating system are related with the scalability, naming conventions, processes synchronisation, mutual exclusion and deadlock detection. Distributed operating systems allow the job to be executed on different processors at the same time. They also require to deploy complex scheduling algorithms as compared to centralised operating system.

The different computer systems co-operate towards execution of a job which requires the resources available at different sites. The only method of obtaining the knowledge of other site or computer system is by exchange of messages. These messages are often time stamped and delivered at destination after arbitrary time delays. This also imposes serious restriction over the distributed operating system. Fault tolerance is another area in which distributed operating systems are different from centralised operating system. Fault tolerance on distributed system is quite stronger in the sense that most of the time the system has ability to recover from the failure of job, data link or malfunctioning of hardware.

We may therefore define distributed system as a pool of many computer systems located geographically and they do not share memory or clock. Inter-process communication among the processes running on different computer systems is established by exchange of messages over communication channel.

Advantages of distributed operating system may be summarised as below.

- **Price /Performance advantage**
  It has been noticed that if less powerful computer systems are interconnected and are used as collective resource, then their computing power is enormous. Therefore for high end application, instead of going for costly and powerful processor like main frame computer, it is always a better option to interconnect low cost, less powerful computer systems. Collective computing power of these cheaper, less powerful computer systems is enormous. Therefore distributed systems clearly have a price/performance advantage over more traditional systems.
- **Resource Sharing**
  In a distributed system, a computer may request for a service or resource located at another computer system. These requests are sent in the form of messages over the communication network. This allows other computer system to use the hardware and software resources and the power of over all distributed system is increased many times.
- **Reliability**
  The distributed operating system provides high reliability as few components of the system may fail without affecting the rest of the system. The services, files and data are still accessible even if a computer system fails. This so achieved by replication of data and services.

3.5 SOME COMMERCIALLY AVAILABLE OPERATING SYSTEMS

3.5.1 CP/M (Control Program for Microcomputers)

CP/M was the first OS to win widespread popularity. Gary Kildall wrote its direct predecessor in 1975. It was a program to control the input and output signals of a paper tape reader connected to an 8-bit Intel 8080 microprocessor chip. No general purpose OS existed for the 8080 at that time, so after finishing his control program, Kildall set out to write one. He formed Digital Research, which now writes and markets all the operating systems in the CP/M family. Sometimes the title CP/M-80 is given to regular 8-bit CP/M, version 2.2 or 3.

Over the years, piece by piece, CP/M was written and improved. It played a pivotal role in the history of microprocessors for a simple reason: many companies manufacturing 8-bit computers found that customising CP/M was cheaper, smarter, and easier than writing a proprietary system.

Previously, before CP/M was really established, Apple Computer, Commodore, and Tandy (Radio Shack) all developed proprietary operating systems for their personal computers. All three have continued in that tradition and have even been rather protective of their proprietary rights. That is, they have not encouraged other manufacturers to develop compatible machines. Consequently, while Apple-DOS, TRS-DOS and Commodore's BASIC operating systems are still pushed, CP/M has become the 8-bit OS for almost everyone else. Microsoft developed a card for the Apple II that allows it to run CP/M.

An unprecedented amount of software was written to run under CP/M in the late seventies and the early eighties. Fortunately, most programmers stayed within the bounds of the system, so compatibility flourished. But CP/M and 8-bit computers are now under heavy challenge from 16-bit and 32-bit machines. While a certain amount of good software is still being written under CP/M, the speed, power, and primary memory capacities of 16-bit and 32-bit computers make them more suitable for the kinds of complicated software now demanded.

In addition to programs for editing, debugging, and assembling, many other housekeeping utilities are included on all CP/M distribution diskettes and are available through the system. Some people consider CP/M an antiquated, unwieldy OS. Its basic design has been criticised as inelegant, having been written in fragments. Because the way the system evolved, unforeseen functions had to be accomplished, as they were found undesirable. Nevertheless, CP/M is and will continue to be the only sensible OS choice for buying 8-bit portables. For all practical purposes, it is the only 8-bit OS made available at least till Apple-DOS and TRS-DOS remain isolated to Apple and Radio Shack machines.

3.5.2 Microsoft Products

Microsoft has a family of OS products, designed to fully utilise the range of PC hardware available in the market today, while providing a consistent user interface for end users and a programming environment for developers. Windows 3.x and Windows for Workgroups 3.x on MS-DOS are designed for mainstream portable and desktop PC platforms. Windows 95 and 98 are successors of the aforementioned products running atop the same or improved hardware configuration. Windows NT 3.x and 4.0 and Windows NT 2000 (Windows NT5) are designed for the high-end business and technical workstation platforms and Windows NT Advanced Server is designed as a server platform.

➢ MS-DOS

Tim Patterson originally developed MS-DOS in 1980. From the very beginning it was designed to be a full-fledged OS for 16-bit personal computers built around the 8086 microprocessor. Patterson originally christened it 'QDOS' for 'Quick and Dirty Operating System'. The initial versions of DOS were very simple and resembled CP/M. Work began on MS-DOS because, Digital Research was very slow to release a CP/M based OS to go with the new 8086 chip. Eventually they did, but by then MS-DOS was well established. In 1981, IBM (International Business Machines) released its Personal Computer (PC). At the same time, it announced that MS-DOS (renamed PC-DOS) was the OS of the choice for the new machine. Practically overnight MS-DOS became the standard OS for virtually all 16-bit microcomputers, not just the PC.

Although CP/M and MS-DOS differ significantly, IBM persuaded Microsoft to create some similarities, making it easier for the people familiar with CP/M to move to MS-DOS. Since IBM's selection of MS-DOS, many programs originally written for CP/M have been rewritten in 16-bit versions to run under MS-DOS or PC-DOS. A great deal of new software has been written under it as well. Subsequent versions have become increasingly sophisticated as they incorporated features of minicomputer operating systems. However, DOS is still a 16-bit operating system and does not support multiple users or multitasking.

➢ Microsoft Interface Manager and Windows 1.0

According to an estimate Windows dominates 90% of the personal computers. Windows provides a Graphical User Interface (GUI), virtual memory management, multitasking, and support for many peripheral devices. Microsoft first began development of the Interface Manager (subsequently renamed as Microsoft Windows) in 1981. Microsoft finally announced Windows in 1993. Windows promised an easy-to-use graphical interface, device-independent graphics and multitasking support. However, the development was delayed several times, and the first version came in the market, after 55 programmer-years of development in November 1985. However, the selection of applications was inadequate and Windows sales were moderate. The major features of Windows 1.0 were a GUI with drop-down menus, tiled windows, support for mouse, device-independent screen and printer graphics, and co-operative multitasking of Windows applications.

➢ Windows 2.0

Windows 2.0, introduced in 1987, provided significant usability improvements to Windows. With the addition of icons and overlapping windows, Windows became a viable environment for development of major applications such as Excel, Word for Windows, CorelDraw!, PageMaker, etc.

➢ Windows/386

In late 1987, Microsoft introduced Windows/386. While it was functionally equivalent to its associate, Windows/286, in running Windows applications simultaneously in the extended memory.

➢ Windows 3.0

Microsoft Windows 3.0, released in 1990, was a complete overhaul of the Windows environment. With the capability to address memory beyond 640 K and a much more powerful user interface, independent software vendors started developing Windows applications vigorously. The powerful new applications helped Microsoft sell more than 10 million copies of Windows, making it the best-selling GUI in the history of computing.

➢ Windows 3.1

Microsoft Windows 3.1, released in April 1992 provided significant improvements to Windows 3.0. In its first two months in the market, it sold over 3 million copies, including upgrades from Windows 3.0. It continued to sell at a rate of over 10 lakh copies per month. The major change from Windows 3.0 was multimedia capability. 'Mouse Trails' were incorporated for easier mouse use with Liquid Crystal Display (LCD) devices, better inter-application protection and better error diagnostics. It has an additional OS interface that emulated some 32-bit functions, called Win32s. Win32s is a set of libraries for Windows 3.1, which enable users to run most Windows NT 32-bit applications on Windows 3.1.

➢ Multimedia Windows

Multimedia Windows is a package with Windows 3.0 and the Multimedia extensions. These extensions were included in Windows 3.1, and thus Multimedia Windows was no longer sold as a separate product.

➢ Windows 3.11

Windows 3.11 added no new features but corrected some existing, mostly network-related problems. It replaced Windows 3.1 at the retail and OEM (Original Equipment Manufacturer) levels, and the upgrade was available free from the Microsoft site.

➢ Windows for Workgroups 3.1 & 3.11

The Windows for Workgroups 3.1 package, released in 1992, was the first integrated Windows and networking package offered by Microsoft. The simple to use and install networking allowed the user to specify which files on the user's machine should be made accessible to others. The files could then be accessed from other machines running either Windows or DOS. Windows for Workgroups also included two other applications: Microsoft Mail, a network mails package, and Schedule+, a workgroup scheduler. Windows for Workgroups 3.11, added 32-bit file access, fax capabilities and higher performance to Windows for Workgroups 3.1. Most of the Windows 3.x operating systems ran on Intel-based machines.

➢ Windows for Pen Computing 3.1

Microsoft developed Windows for Pen Computing for use on pen-based systems. In most aspects, it is equivalent to Windows 3.1 with extensions for pen support. These extensions include the use of a pen as a pointing device as well as handwriting recognition and conversion. Pen Windows was first shipped in 1992.

➢ Windows 95

It was a major release of the Microsoft Windows OS in 1995, and the successor to Windows 3.x and Windows for Workgroups 3.11. Windows 95 represented a significant advance over its precursors, Windows 3.1 and Windows for Workgroups 3.11. It is a pre-emptive, multithread, multitasking, networking 32-bit OS, with advanced file systems, running on Intel-based machines. For customers, Windows 95 presented a major step forward in functionality on mainstream desktop platforms by providing a system that is easy to use, offering responsive multitasking performance, and providing a great platform for communications. Ease of use is delivered through the Plug and Play architecture and an improved, intuitive user interface.

Windows 95 is a complete, integrated protect-mode OS that does not require or use a separate version of MS-DOS. In addition to wearing a new user interface, Windows 95 also included a number of important internal improvements, implementing the Win32 API (Application Programming Interface), providing pre-emptive multitasking and multiple threads of execution for 32-bit applications, which meant that applications written specifically for this OS would run much faster.

It has essentially removed DOS as the underlying platform. It included MS-DOS 7.0, but took over from DOS completely after starting. This means, removal of many of the old DOS limitations, such as 640 KB of main memory and 8-character file names. The communications capabilities of Windows are enhanced with integrated, high-performance networking, built-in messaging, and features such as Remote Network Access and File Synchronisation, designed for mobile and remote computer users. Windows 95 implements new working set management technologies that optimise the use of memory on low-configuration systems. Windows 95 runs most of the current applications for Windows and MS-DOS. Windows 95's new shell provides a complete set of services that is tightly integrated with the OS components. It allows full access to hardware, hence it is useful for older games. Home users prefer it, as games run unobstructed.

The Windows 95 user interface offers dramatic gains in ease of learning and of use for the broad range of people using PCs today. Instead of mastering different tools to work with different resources on their computers, users will be able to browse and access all resources in a consistent fashion with a single tool. This is much easier than learning separate applications such as Program Manager, File Manager, Print Manager, Control Panel, etc. as users of Windows must do. Windows 95's smart set-up technology uses the current system settings to present an initial configuration that is familiar for the current Windows-based user. And for corporate customers and individuals who may not want to make any user interface changes initially, Windows 95 enables them to continue running their current Program Manager and File Manager configurations. A system toolbar that is always accessible makes it much easier to start and switch between full-screen tasks. The direct manipulation of data through drag-and-drop in the user interface makes working with documents easier ands more intuitive.

The set-up program enables customers to uninstall Windows 95, assuring customers a way to remove it if they are in any way unhappy with it, and have provided tools for system administrators to customise the configuration of Windows 95.

➤ Windows NT (New Technology)

It is a robust, pre-emptive, multitasking, 32-bit OS, with symmetric multiprocessor support. It is intended for use in network servers, workstations and software development machines. Windows NT Workstation 4.0 version has come a long way since its inception in 1996. So much so, that the mainstream desktop PCs and laptops now come with Windows NT Workstation preinstalled, and has now become a great solution for all business users, not just power users, engineers, and developers. Windows NT 4.0 comes in two versions, as Windows NT Server, designed to act as a server in networks and Windows NT Workstation for stand-alone or client workstations. Corporations prefer this version and a lot of business establishments are standardising their desktops and laptops on Windows NT workstation because it is cheaper, fast, reliable, efficient, and powerful.

The Windows NT's user interface is very similar to that of Windows 3.1 and Windows 95, internally it is totally different from either of them. Windows NT ensured fully protected applications, wherein all programs are protected from each other, with virtualised hardware access. Windows NT does not allow access to hardware like UNIX. The Windows NT file system, NTFS (New Technology File System) provides a lot of security and reliability.

➢ Windows 98

The successor to Windows 95 was released in 1998. Originally it was called Memphis, and then Windows 97, but Microsoft changed the name when it realised that it was going to miss its target 1997-release date. Windows 98 offers support for a number of new technologies, including AGP (Accelerated Graphics Port), MMX (Multimedia Extensions), USB (Universal Serial Bus), DVD (Digital Video Disk, etc. Its most visible feature is the Active Desktop, which integrates the Web browser Internet Explorer, with the OS. The Microsoft Windows 98 (Second Edition) is downloadable from the Internet. It consists of two parts: Microsoft Internet Explorer & and revised core components of the OS, called Windows 98 Service Pack 1. The only new feature that is not available for downloading is Internet Connection Sharing (ICS), which lets networked Windows 98 systems share a single user connection. To get ICS, one needs to buy a new CD-ROM containing the complete Second Edition. Users who already have Internet Explorer 5 installed over an existing Windows 98 setup will see no obvious differences. The Desktop, Start Menu, and Explorer windows look the same. Windows' built-in applications look and act exactly as before. The Windows 98-Second Edition, is more stable than the original, reflecting many bug fixes in the core Windows files, but performance seems identical. The most obvious change is Internet Connection Sharing, which adds a feature previously available in Windows 98 only through third-party networking software. When ICS is installed on a home or small-office network, all networked client computers can access the Internet through a single host computer. The host can use any existing Internet connection. The Second Edition does smarter networking.

Windows 98 Second Edition is desirable but not a crucial upgrade. If your Windows system is already stable and you do not need the new security features, you may prefer not to bother with the long download.

➢ Windows 2000

Microsoft is continually enhancing its Windows OS product line. There is a great deal of interest in and speculation about the Windows 2000 project, the technology development effort which will deliver the next major release of Windows for the mainstream desktop and portable PC. Windows 2000 is advertised as the state of the art OS that uses the latest hardware. It is supposed to be a major upgrade aimed at the OS market, which is largely dominated by the different features and variants of UNIX.

Windows 2000 uses a new security protocol with an encryption facility to authenticate users logging into the network. It maintains encrypted passwords in the active directory and ensures that user connections are secure.

The interface of Windows 2000 is similar to that of Windows 98, with a lot of hidden features waiting to be discovered. All Explorer windows have customisable toolbars. In the previous versions (both of Windows NT and Windows 9x), you could view or hide various toolbars. In this, you have control over the buttons to view in the toolbar. For example, you can open My Computer, and add the Map network drive button in the toolbar, or add buttons necessary for Internet activity (like home page, refresh, stop, etc.). The display properties have also been changed in the new addition. You can view all the display modes and refresh rates for your display adapter. There is also a colour management option built in.

3.5.3 OS/2

OS/2 is an OS for PCs developed originally by Microsoft Corporation and IBM, but sold and managed solely by IBM. OS/2 is compatible with DOS and Windows, which means that it can run all DOS and Windows programs. However, programs written specifically to run under OS/2 will not run under DOS or Windows.

Since its introduction in the late eighties, OS/2 has travelled a particularly rocky road. The first releases were hindered by a number of technical and marketing problems. Then Microsoft abandoned the project in favour of its own OS solution, Windows. This break generated a feud between the two computer giants, which is still being played out in many areas.

3.5.4 MAC OS—The Macintosh Operating System

Earlier versions were called System x.x, where x.x were the version numbers. With its earlier release, Mac OS 8, however, Apple has dropped the System moniker. It is the system of choice for more than 20 million users around the world. With PowerPC processor-inherent multitasking, a thoroughly updated desktop, and an integrated suite of Internet services, Mac OS continues as the undisputed leader in Web authoring and browsing, multimedia, and ease of use. The latest release from Apple is the Mac OS 8.6.

The Mac OS 8.6 is the free upgrade of the Mac OS 8.5 and the Mac OS 8.5.1. It improves the indispensable OS upgrade of Mac OS 8.5 with better performance, additional convenience and more power. Leading the powerful new features in Mac OS 8.6 are the expanded capabilities of Apple's Sherlock – the personal search engine, which searches the Internet and finds the information you need, faster and easily. It saves valuable time, by querying multiple search engines simultaneously. It can send your query to more than 20 leading search engines with a single click. It also provides search results summaries – giving you a one- or two-paragraph summary of an entire document.

A Mac OS 8.6 copy files over a network faster than with Windows NT and moves files to removable disks faster than ever. Mac OS 8.6 provides efficient network usage by taking greater advantage of the network bandwidth. The network browser speeds your navigation across network file servers.

It also allows you to save your favourite URLs as desktop icons. You can double-click on them to go directly to any site. Mac OS 8.6 provides free 30-day Internet access. Mac OS's Internet date and time services checks and synchronises the date and time with Internet time servers based on the world's atomic clocks. Mac OS 8.6 lets you enjoy Web sites from all over the world with the latest versions of the most popular browsers – Microsoft Internet Explorer and Netscape Communicator software. An improved installer allows you to install new system software in minutes. It makes custom installations as simple as easy installations and lets you save custom configurations for later reuse. It checks the system for problems, and fixes them without requiring you to boot from a CD-ROM.

3.5.5 UNIX

UNIX is a powerful, flexible and manageable OS with good utilities, communication abilities and GUIs. The UNIX project was justified to the management, as a vehicle for document preparation—the first users of UNIX were in the Bell patent department, which used the system's document preparation software. Dennis Ritchie wrote a C compiler under UNIX, and in 1973 Thompson and Ritchie rewrote the UNIX kernel in C.

➢ Linux

Linux is a free, powerful, UNIX-like OS. It is a 32-bit OS that runs on a variety of platforms, including Intel, SPARC, PowerPC, and DEC Alpha processors as well as multiprocessing systems. A young computer science student, Linus Torvalds, at the University of Helsinki in Finland initially created it as a hobby. He developed the original OS as a college project. When he realised that the lack of UNIX programming facilities was hampering its work, he decided to rectify it, by writing his own UNIX-like micro-kernel on a 386 machine. Linus had an interest in Minix, a small UNIX system, and decided to develop a system that exceeded the Minix standards. He began his work in 1991 when he released version 0.02, including all the source code of the software. Source code is the exact specifications by which a computer makes an executable program.

With the help of literally thousands of volunteers, Linux grew dramatically. Linux is a 'user-developed' product, meaning that users around the world who ran the OS for their own use have developed many of its components and drivers. Linux worked steadily with the assistance of developers around the world, and in 1994, version 1.0 of the Linux Kernel was released. Torvalds remained the co-ordinator of the project, and determined which of several competing designs for feature implementations would make the next distribution, often combining the best of several implementations to make a tool far better than any of the original designer's intentions. The current full-featured version is 2.2, released on 25 January 1999, and the development continues. Linux is now well-supported and gaining ground as a respectable OS despite its homegrown roots. Linux also has an official mascot, the Linux Penguin, which was selected by Linux Torvalds to represent the image, he associates with the operating system he created.

The Linux OS is available free of cost. Its source code is freely available to everyone. This however, does not mean that Linux and its various distributions are free; companies and developers may charge money as long as the source code remains available. Thereby, a number of companies have developed their own 'distribution' of Linux, so there are many different Linux distributions, or versions available in the market. A 'distribution' is the compiled Linux source code, usually combined with extra features and software, and some are equipped towards specific types of computer systems. You can download Linux from the Web. Some distributions are available for download at no charge while others are available at affordable price on CD-ROM from Linux retailers world-wide, the top commercial Linux vendors today being Caldera and Red Hat. Other options include purchasing Linux pre-installed on a computer, or purchasing a book or magazine containing a complimentary CD-ROM. You can purchase a book that includes a CD-ROM with the entire OS. In India, PC-Quest magazine has recently issued several versions of Linux Red Hat distributions in its CD-ROMs. Each distribution has its own purpose and a number of factors should go into deciding which distribution is best for each user. Some distributions are better suited to home users, others are excellent for commercial settings. Some are better suited for Intel or Macintosh PCs, other are excellent for use on high-performance computers. The only problem with this approach is that drivers and fixes are only available if some user decides to develop them. Support is another issue since you cannot call any particular vendor. Anyone that plans to use this OS for production use should first make sure that applications run on the OS and that appropriate drivers are available to support hardware and software.

Linux 2.0 provides a cross-platform, 64-bit kernel that supports SMP (Symmetrical Multiprocessing). It confirms to the X/Open and POSIX (Portable Operating System Interface for UNIX) standards for UNIX-like operating systems, and programs intended for the SCO (Santa Cruz Operations) and SVR4 (System V Release 4) UNIX systems will run unaltered. Linux also supports standard UNIX and Internet protocols and supports Java. It can also be used as an Internet server and an Internet firewall. Documentation is provided in HOWTO files, which are written by users and developers and freely available on some of the Web sites listed in the Bibliography at the end of this book.

Computer software vendor organisations are now selling the easy-to-install SuSE distribution of Linux, which comes with a manual and other support, for a nominal price. New distributions such as the Caldera's OpenLinux 2.2, which is a novice-friendly version of Linux, have an installation procedure that starts within Windows. It lets the user install and run Linux without ever seeing the confusing command line interface and also helps in overcoming the fear that a new user will have. Corel also has plans for an easy-to-use, consumer-specific version of Linux. Nowadays, Linux has a group of people following it as popular fashion or a particular interest. What is still leading forcefully the development and increasing world-wide popularity of Linux is the very nature of Linux's functionality and availability. The availability of the source code of Linux in the public domain has enabled a vast number of software programmers to take its source code and adapt it to meet their individual needs. At the same time, hundreds of developers eagerly start to work continuously to develop Linux – not for monetary gain, but literally for the love of it. At a given time, there are dozens of ongoing projects for importing Linux to various hardware configurations and purposes.

➢ BSD (Berkeley Standard Distribution) UNIX

BSD is a family of open-source UNIX variants based on the 4.4BSDLite Berkeley Standard Distribution: FreeBSD, NetBSD and OpenBSD. Although BSD and Linux are similar in function, one could say that BSD has a much more rigorous development process. Rather than have a single developer leading the group, each of the BSD variants has a steering committee to shape how the system operates. Like Linux, the BSD systems are rock-solid server and workstation operating systems, and like Linux, it tends to have more user-configurable settings than Mac OS or Windows. The functional differences between BSD systems and Linux are almost non-existent to the end user. The various BSD characteristics are widely used in Internet Service Provider (ISP) facilities for e-mail routing and handling, and as graphics workstations by game companies.

➢ Sun Microsystems Solaris

The Solaris operating environment is based on industry standard UNIX System V Release 4. It has been optimised for distributed network environments and performance enhanced for running database and Web applications. The system is also Java-enabled and includes support for the Java VM (Virtual Machine). The HotJava browser is also included. Centralised administration features allow administrators to control the OS remotely. The latest release includes CDE (Common Desktop Environment) as the default desktop. CDE is based on the X Window System Motif desktop and provides a consistent look and feel across UNIX platforms. The OS is designed for Web networking

(Intranets) and enterprise networking. It includes WebNFS, a version of the popular Network File System that is designed for use on the Web and intranets.

Network computing features in Solaris include ONC (Open Network Computing) technology—a TCP/IP-based set of services, facilities, and APIs that include file and printer sharing, data exchange, RPC (Remote Procedure Call), and distributed naming services. NIS+ Global Directory Services provides a secure, high-performance, distributed data repository for network and system management information. The OS also includes DCE (Distributed Computing Environment). Solaris runs on SPARC (Scalable Performance ARChitecture) and Intel platforms and will be available on PowerPC platforms. Multiprocessor systems are supported, and Solaris uses symmetrical multiprocessing techniques to take full advantage of these systems. Multithreading is supported, which allows applications to be broken into segments that execute simultaneously on each processor.

3.5.6 BeOS

It is developed by Be Incorporated, and runs on the PowerPC platform and Intel x86 processors. Despite being smaller than modern operating systems, such as the Mac OS and Windows, BeOS nevertheless wears a modern GUI, pre-emptive multitasking, multithreading, and built-in support for SMP, and is designed to handle multimedia. It is positioned for multimedia production. The original plan was to ensure backward compatibility and take complete advantage of the new hardware in the market. BeOS is, unequivocally, one of the most technically advanced operating systems for personal computers in the market. It is multithreaded widely through every part; i.e. all tasks are broken down into very small sections of instructions, which can be processed more efficiently. It is multiprocessor aware, so it runs well with two or more CPUs.

BeOS handles multimedia so well, that one software vendor for BeOS has used the same technology for navigating 3-D graphs for its spreadsheet application. This means that the BeOS gets out or forces work of every processing power out of one's system, and makes it available for use. Commercial deployment of the BeOS is limited. Currently, Be Inc states that its OS is aimed at persons who have habitually strong feeling of interest and admiration about it, and its current release is not meant for mass consumption. The latest release has substantially improved hardware support, while some of the core services are optimised for the Intel platform. This has not prevented a number of developers from releasing software for the platform in its nascent state, with an industry leader Maxon announcing its Cinema 4D product for BeOS. Using the BeOS reveals a lot of forethought and planning in its user interface. There are some aspects, which are Mac-like, others that were borrowed from Windows, and still others taken from NeXT, plus a lot of indigenous innovation. The BeOS is responsive. The file system has a built-in searchable database, and the windows one uses to navigate in one's hard disk, are live queries, automatically updated as one modifies files.

3.6 OPERATING SYSTEM ALTERNATIVES TO WINDOWS

Alternative operating systems are not hard to install. Most computer users buy machines with Windows pre-installed. Installing Windows 98 on a new machine and getting everything to work can take as little as 30 minutes, or as long as several days depending on factors such as correctly interpreting and following the installation instructions. There is also lack of familiarity with alternative operating systems. Many of the installer tools are not as familiar as the Windows hardware Setup Wizards. BSD and BeOS, and a number of Linux distributions, come with extensive installation help to get you through the process, and in many cases and in BeOS in particular, it is easier to install than it is to upgrade to Windows 98.

Of course there is maximum software for Windows, but it does not mean that there is no software on other operating systems. Linux, if you are willing to compile the code yourself, rivals Windows in its depth of software. BSD can use 90% of the software written for Linux with no changes. BeOS has a strong developer's support movement going for it and is starting to attract commercial vendors, as is Linux. Many of the networkable games, such as Doom and Quake 2, are ported to all of these platforms.

You do not have to give up Windows, if you were to use some other OS. Each of these operating systems will reside on its own hard disk partition independently and will co-exist with Windows with no real problems. All of them have drivers to allow read access to Windows files, and Linux has a fully functional read-write driver for Windows files. You may find that as you use these operating systems, your tolerance for many of the things you take for granted will diminish, and you would be able to extract more productivity out of your tools.

3.7 FUTURE TRENDS

A number of clear trends are emerging which will point the way the future operating systems will be designed. These are:

- Multiprocessing feature will be much more common because of development of VLSI (Very Large Scale Integration) chips and the decline in the cost of hardware.
- Micro-code will support all the functions of operating system integrated into it, currently performed by software, therefore, the execution will be faster.
- The trend is towards distributed control among the localised processors in place of centralised system. Therefore the use of distributed operating system will increase.
- The concurrency is becoming an important feature of programming language. Hardware and operating systems are being designed to execute concurrent programs more efficiently.
- Developments in software engineering will result in operating systems that will be easily maintainable, more reliable and simpler.
- Lot of developments are taking place in computer networking. The data transmission rate is also increasing. Therefore, the use of networking operating systems will also increase.
- Practically all operating systems (especially desktop operating systems) will be supporting multimedia (video and graphics) applications in the near future.

SELECT EXERCISES

Q. 1. What do you mean by operating system? Why an operating system is required?

Q. 2. Explain the hierarchy of application programs and operating system? What do you mean by the statement that all application programs run on top of operating system?

Q. 3. Explain the functions of operating system in brief.

Q. 4. What do you mean by the command interpreter? How do they execute the command entered by the user?

Q. 5. What do mean by the management of resources in operating system? Explain the different types of resource managed by the operating system.

Q. 6. What do you mean by the memory management in an operating system? Explain the issues in memory management.

Q. 7. What is file management? Explain how the data from the secondary memory are brought to the processor for execution?

Q. 8. Explain the salient features of Batch Operating System?

Q. 9. What are Time-Sharing System?

Q. 10. What do you mean by multiprogramming? Explain the term degree of multiprogramming? Explain how multiprogramming affects throughput?

Q. 11. Explain in the brief, how turn around time is affected in Batch Operating System?
Q. 12. What is different between Multiprogramming Operating System and Multitasking operating system? What are the similarities in multiprogramming and multitasking operating system?
Q. 13. What are threads? Explain the advantages of multithreading operating systems?
Q. 14. Explain Real Time System?
Q. 15. What are the two main functions of Operating Systems? Describe them in detail?
Q. 16. Give type of Operating Systems came into existence. Describe the most popular operating Systems that are in wide use.
Q. 17. What are multiprocessing operating systems? Explain weather multiprogramming may be done on uniprocessor system? If yes then justify your answer.
Q. 18. What do you mean by Multi User operating system? List any two multi user operating system.
Q. 19. Describe the components of any operating system along with their functions?
Q. 20. Enlist the functions of an Operating System?
Q. 21. Give brief details how Operating System manages various components of a computer?
Q. 22. Give a classification of Operating Systems and indicate their merit and demerits if they are used?
Q. 23. What are the differences between Network operating system and distributed operating system?
Q. 24. Discuss the role of Command Interpreter in brief.
Q. 25. Write a short note on the Process Management in a operating system.
Q. 26. Discuss the salient features of Controlled program for Microcomputers (CP/M).
Q. 27. What do you mean by time sharing operating system? Explain how the time sharing improves the performance of operating system.
Q. 28. What are the main advantages of distributed system? Explain in brief, why distributed system offer better price/performance ratio?
Q. 29. Draw a comparative chart to explain the gradual improvement in the Windows product of Microsoft.
Q. 30. What is real time system? Under what circumstances it is necessary to meet the deadline of job?
Q. 31. What do you mean by periodic and aperiodic jobs?
Q. 32. Write a short note on operating system of Microsoft family.
Q. 33. How Window NT is different from Windows 98?
Q. 34. List the important features of MAC OS.
Q. 35. How LINUX is different from UNIX?
Q. 36. Discuss the Operating System product of Sun Microsystems.

4 MS DOS (Principles & Practice)

4.0 INTRODUCTION

DOS (Disk Operating System) refers to any operating system but in practice we use Microsoft Disk Operating System (MS DOS). This operating system was originally written for the IBM PC by the Microsoft Corporation. The first release of the DOS came in 1981. Remarkable development took place when Microsoft released MS DOS 2.11 and MS DOS 3.25 in the year 1984 and 1986. MS DOS 6.0 was released in the year 1993. Initial version of the DOS did not support multitasking. Keeping the advanced application in the mind Microsoft released MS Windows, an GUI based which used to run on the top of Disk Operating system. The Windows 95 and Windows 98 were full operating system, which were least dependent on the DOS services. However, DOS services and commands may be used in Windows. MS DOS is a single user operation system, which allows the user to enter command using textual interface.

4.1 HOW TO START DOS

To start DOS while working in Windows, go step by step as shown in figure 4.1.

- Go to Start
- Click Program -> MS DOS Prompt

After clicking MS DOS prompt following DOS Prompt will appear on the screen. Now you may type in any DOS Command as under.

Microsoft(R) Windows 98
(C)Copyright Microsoft Corp 1981-1998.
C:\WINDOWS> DIR

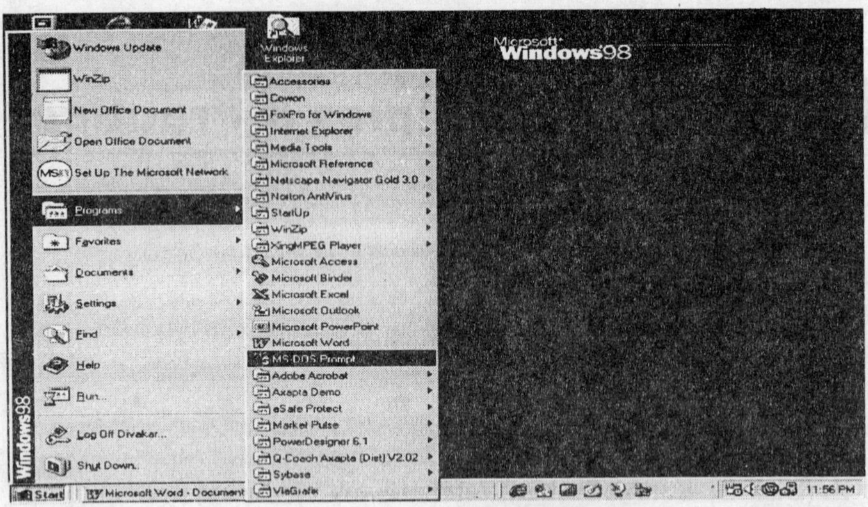

Fig. 4.1

4.2 INTERNAL & EXTERNAL DOS COMMANDS

Internal Commands are most simple and frequently used. These commands are contained in the file command.com, which is loaded into the memory at the booting of the computer system. The internal commands are not visible in the sense that they are not listed as file in any directory. All these commands are contained in command.com.

Copy, Delete, Dir etc are the example of Internal DOS commands.

External commands are contained in separate files, which usually have extension .com or .exe or .bat. The external commands are contained in file whose name is similar to that of command. For example, the external command 'format' will be contained in the file ' format.com'. All external commands are listed in the C:\windows\command directory. When you see the directory, these files are listed with the command name and followed by their extension. SYS, TREE, XCOPY, FORMAT, DISKCOPY are the examples of external DOS Commands. Since all External commands are contained in the files, it is also possible for you to create a new command and add it to DOS. You should also note that if you have more than one external command with the same name then DOS will run only one of them in the following order i.e, .COM, .EXE, .BAT.

When you attempt to run the external command it checks with the present directory for the file. If it is not there then you must specify the path. It means that while executing a DOS command, it is necessary to specify the path of the file.

4.3 MANAGING THE FILES & DIRECTORIES

In this section we will discuss how to display the files stored in a directory, change, and delete any directory. You will also learn how to create directories and subdirectories.

4.3.1 Directories and Sub-Directories

A directory is a place in the computer system, where the file which contains data and programs may be placed. It is the responsibility of DOS to create and allocate the space on the disk. These directories and files can be managed by the user by issuing the command. The DOS interprets these commands and does the function as requested by the user. The directories may be created by the users as well as by application. It may be observed that by installing a software on the computer, it creates several directories and file on the disk. Directories in DOS are similar to the folders in Windows 95/98.

A directory may contain other directories. These directories contained in other directory is known as sub-directory. In fact, all the directories are sub-directories, except one called root directory. The root directory is the starting place from where all the directories are rooted. The root directory does not have any specific name. The overall structure showing the organization of directory is known as directory tree. Consider the following directory tree as shown in figure 4.2

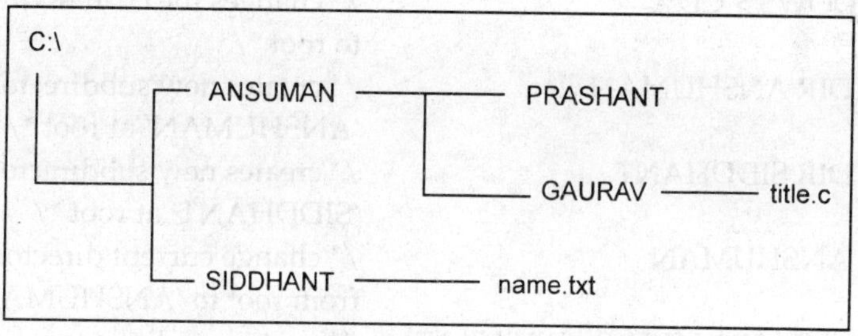

Fig. 4.2

As shown in the figure, C:\ is the root directory, which is created on the disk drive C:. The root directory contains two directory 'ANSHUMAN' and 'SIDDHANT'. The 'ANSHUMAN' directory contain the sub directory 'PRASHANT' and 'GAURAV'. The 'GAURAV' directory contains the file 'title.c ' AND 'SIDDHANT' directory contains the file ' name.txt '.

Whenever you are in root directory, the command prompt in DOS appears as

C:\ >
You may type in following command to check the current working directory.
C:\ > CD
C:\ *ANSHUMAN* will be displayed on the terminal, if you are working in the subdirectory 'ANSHUMAN' at root.

Path in the directory structure indicates the path from root to the file you want to use. For example if you want to delete the file title.c, then the path of the file should be mentioned. The DOS command to delete the file title.c would be,
del C:\ ANSHUMAN \ GAURAV \ title.c

➢ CREATING A DIRECTORY (MKDIR Command)

This command creates a subdirectory in your working directory. For example to create a new directory named XYZ under your working directory (say WINDOWS), enter following command.
C:\WINDOWS > MKDIR XYZ

Example:

Suppose your current working directory is WINDOWS. Create the directory structure as shown in the figure 4.2.

Issue following command at DOS prompt to create the directory structure shown in the figure 4.2.

C:\WINDOWS > CD \	/* changes the current directory to root */
C:\>MKDIR ANSHUMAN	/* creates new subdirectory 'ANSHUMAN' at root */
C:\>MKDIR SIDDHANT	/* creates new subdirectory 'SIDDHANT' at root */
C:\>CD ANSHUMAN	/* change current directory from root to 'ANSHUMAN' */
C:\ANSHUMAN>MKDIR PRASHANT	/*creates subdirectory 'PRASHANT' in 'ANSHUMAN" */
C:\ ANSHUMAN > MKDIR GAURAV	/*creates subdirectory 'GAURAV in 'ANSHUMAN" */

Example

Suppose your current working directory is WINDOWS and you have to create a subdirectory XYZ at root. Write the following commands.

```
Microsoft(R) Windows 98
 (C)Copyright Microsoft Corp 1981-1998.
C:\WINDOWS>cd \           /* This command changes your cur-
                          rent directory to root */
C:\>mkdir xyz             /* This command creates directory
                          XYZ at root */
C:\>cd xyz                /* This command change your current
                          directory to XYZ */
C:\xyz> dir /p            /* This command displays the files of
                          current working directory */.
Volume in drive C is DIVAKAR
Volume Serial Number is 3623-1CE8
Directory of C:\xyz
.        <DIR>      10-13-00 9:56p.
..       <DIR>      10-13-00 9:56p..
   0 file(s)     0 bytes
   2 dir(s)      103,690,240 bytes free
C:\xyz>
```

➢ HOW TO CHANGE WORKING DIRECTORY (CHDIR)

It is quite easy to change from your present working directory to a different directory. DOS allows you to do it by CHDIR (Change Directory) command followed by a path. You may also do the changes in the current working directory by typing only CD command. For example to change the working directory to XYZ, enter following command.

CHDIR \XYZ

Example

You may change from two directories either by entering the command CHDIR or by specifying the path. In the following, the current working directory is changed from WINDOWS to XYZ and vice versa.

```
Microsoft(R) Windows 98
 (C)Copyright Microsoft Corp 1981-1998.
C:\WINDOWS>chdir\xyz        /* Changes current working
                            directory to XYZ */
C:\xyz>chdir \windows       /* Changes current working
                            directory to WINDOWS */
C:\WINDOWS>cd c:\xyz        /*Changes current working
                            directory to XYZ */
C:\xyz>cd c:\windows        /* Changes current working
                            directory to WINDOWS */
C:\WINDOWS>
```

You can also specify any path after the command so that you can travel around the directory structure. The following command, for example, puts you in the parent directory of your working directory:

C:\Windows> cd.

C:\

➢ HOW TO DELETE A DIRECTORY

If you create a directory and decide later that you don't want it any more, you can delete it with the MS.DIS RMDIR (remove directory) command.

The RMDIR command lets you delete any directory by specifying its path, but the directory must be empty. This prevents you from accidentally deleting files and directories. For example, if you want to delete the directory PRASHANT as shown in figure 4.2, enter following command.

C:\>RMDIR C:\ ANSHUMAN\PRASHANT

It will delete PRASHANT directory if it is empty.

To remove all the files in a directory enter del followed by the path of the directory. For example, to delete all files in the \xyz\ abc directory, all the files in directory will be deleted.

del \ xyz\ abc

MS.DOS prompts you with the following message :

Are you sure(Y/N) ?

If you really want to delete all the files in the directory, type Y (for Yes). If not, type N(for No) to stop the command.

Now you can use the rmdir command to delete the \XYZ\ABC directory by typing the following command :

RMDIR \XYZ\ABC

Example

Write command to delete all the file in directory \xyz\abc and then delete the directory \xyz\abc. Following is the sequence of commands in DOS.

```
Microsoft(R) Windows 98
   (C)Copyright Microsoft Corp 1981-1998.
C:\WINDOWS>del \xyz\abc
All files in directory will be deleted!
Are you sure (Y/N)?y
C:\WINDOWS>rmdir \xyz\abc
C:\WINDOWS>
```

➢ HOW TO COPY FILES TO ANOTHER DIRECTORY

You may copy the files of one directory to another directory using COPY command. For this you have to specify the path of both the directories.

Example

Command copy c:\dbase*.dbf c:\xyz copies all the file with extension.DBF from the directory c:\dbase to c:\xyz.

```
C:\>copy c:\dbase\*.dbf  c:\xyz
c:\dbase\FINAL.DBF
c:\dbase\RAA.DBF
c:\dbase\RAC.DBF
c:\dbase\raf.dbf
c:\dbase\RAF1.DBF
c:\dbase\RAF2.DBF
c:\dbase\SIR1.DBF
   7 file(s) copied
C:\>
```

Example

Write the DOS command to do following for the directory structure shown in the figure 4.2.

1 Copy the file name.txt from present location to PRASHANT.
2 Copy the file title.c to the root.
3 Copy the file title.c to SIDDHANT.

DOS command to do above jobs are written below.

1. C:\ > COPY C:\SIDDHANT\NAME.TXT C:\ANSHUMAN\PRASHANT\
2. C:\> COPY C:\ANSHUMAN\GAURAV\TITLE.C C:\
3. C:\> COPY C:\ANSHUMAN\GAURAV\TITLE.C C:\SIDDHANT\

4.4 WILD CARDS

If you want to carry out a task for group of file or with the file whose name are not clearly known, the DOS allows the user to use the wild card. A wild card is a character which allows you to group one or more file. DOS allows two types of wild card '*' (asterisk) and '?' (question mark).

? (Question Mark) : Use of this wild card allows the user to group the files with single character.

* (Asterisk) : Use of this wild card allows the user to group the file which represent one or more character.

Example

1. *. COM represents files which has same extension.COM but they may have different name of any character. This binds ABC.COM, FORMAT.COM, B.COM, START.COM etc.
2. ABC.* represents the files, which has the file name REPORT but they may have any extension. Examples are ABC.TXT, ABC.COM, ABC.EXE etc.
3. AB*.* represents the files which begin with string AB followed by any character and any extension. Examples are ABC.TXT, ABCD.TXT, AB.COM, ABCD.EXE.
4. AB?.TXT represent files which begins with string AB followed by any one character and extension is.TXT. Examples are ABC.TXT, ABM.TXT,ABP.TXT.
5. AB??.* represents the files which begins with string AB followed by any two characters and any extension. Examples are ABCD.TXT, ABCD.COM,ABGH.EXE, ABMN.PRG.

These wild cards may be used in the commands. For example, to print all the files in the directory is as given below,

C:\> DIR *.*

4.5 DOS COMMAND

In this section, the frequently used DOS commands are explained with their syntax and switches.

4.5.1 DIR Command

This command displays a list of files and subdirectories in a directory.

Syntax of DIR Command

DIR [drive:][path][filename] [/P] [/W] [/A[[:]attributes]] [/O[[:]sortorder]] [/S] [/B] [/L] [/V] [/4]

[drive:][path][filename]	Specifies drive, directory, and/or files to list.
/P	Pauses after each screenful of information.
/W	Uses wide list format.

/A	Displays files with specified attributes.
Attributes	
D Directories	R Read-only files
H Hidden files	A Files ready for archiving
S System files	
/O	List by files in sorted order.
Sortorder	
N By name (alphabetic)	S By size (smallest first)
E By extension (alphabetic)	D By date & time
G Group directories first	
/S	Displays files in specified directory and all subdirectories.
/B	Uses bare format.
/L	Uses lowercase.
/V	Verbose mode.
/4	Displays year with 4 digits

4.5.2 DEL Command

This command deletes one or more files in a directory.

Syntax of DEL Command
DEL [drive:][path]filename [/P]
ERASE [drive:][path]filename [/P]

[drive:][path]filename, specifies the file(s) to delete.
/P prompts for confirmation before deleting each file.

4.5.3 PROMPT Command

Changes the Windows command prompt.

Syntax of Prompt command
PROMPT [text]

Here text specifies a new command prompt. Prompt can be made up of normal characters and the following special codes:

$Q	= (equal sign)
$$	$ (dollar sign)
$T	Current time
$D	Current date
$P	Current drive and path
$V	Windows version number

$N	Current drive
$G	> (greater-than sign)
$L	< (less-than sign)
$B	| (pipe)
$H	Backspace (erases previous character)
$E	Escape code (ASCII code 27)
$_	Carriage return and linefeed

Example

```
C:\WINDOWS>prompt $q $d
= Fri 10-13-2000
```

Type PROMPT without parameters to reset the prompt to the default setting.

4.5.4 COPY Command

This command copies one or more files from a source to defined destination.

Syntax of COPY Command:
COPY [/A | /B] source [/A | /B] [+ source [/A | /B] [+ ...]] [destination [/A | /B]] [/V] [/Y | /-Y]

source	Specifies the file or files to be copied.
/A	Indicates an ASCII text file.
/B	Indicates a binary file.
destination	Specifies the directory and/or file name for the new file(s).
/V	Verifies that new files are written correctly.
/Y	Suppresses prompting to confirm you want to overwrite an existing destination file.
/-Y	Causes prompting to confirm you want to overwrite an existing destination file.

Example

Following command copies all files from \xyz directory to \abc directory.

Copy c:\xyz*.* c:\abc*.*

4.5.5 MORE Command

Displays output one screen at a time.

Syntax of MORE command

MORE [drive:][path]filename
MORE < [drive:][path]filename
command-name | MORE [drive:][path][filename]

[drive:][path]filename	Specifies file(s) to display one screen at a time
command-name	Specifies a command whose output will be displayed.

Example

Suppose you want to display the contents of a huge file (data.txt) to view it on the screen. You may use following command.

More < data.txt
Or
Type data.txt | more

4.5.6 SYS Command

The SYS Command copies MS-DOS system files and command interpreter to a disk specified by you.

Syntax of SYS Command

SYS [drive1:][path] drive2:

[drive1:][path]	Specifies the location of the system files.
drive2:	Specifies the drive the files are to be copied to.

The SYS command updates your system files on a disk. The files that are copied also contain hidden files IO.SYS and MSDOS.SYS. These files are not listed using DIR command. This command does not transfer command.com file. These files have to be copied to target disk using copy command.

Example

SYS A:
This command copies MSDOS system files to disk in drive A.

4.5.7 DISKCOPY Command

This command copies the contents of one floppy disk to another disk.This command works only with floppy disk not with hard disk.

Syntax of Diskcopy command
DISKCOPY [drive1: [drive2:]] [/1] [/V] [/M]

/1 Copies only the first side of the disk.
/V Verifies that the information is copied correctly.
/M Force multi-pass copy using memory only.

The two floppy disks must be of the same type. You may specify the same drive for drive1 and drive2. Diskcopy command destroys the contents of target disk.

Example

Diskcopy a: b:
This command copies contents of disk a: to disk b:

4.5.8 XCOPY Command

This command copies files and directory, including lower level directories, if it exists.

Syntax of XCOPY command
XCOPY source [destination] [/A | /M] [/D[:date]] [/P] [/S [/E]] [/W]
[/C] [/I] [/Q] [/F] [/L] [/H] [/R] [/T] [/U] [/K] [/N]

Source	Specifies the file(s) to copy. It must have a pathname
Destination	Specifies the location and/or name of new files. It must also have pathname. If the pathname is not specified then XCOPY uses the default directory with default filename, *.*.
/A	Copies files with the archive attribute set, doesn't change the attribute.
/M	Copies files with the archive attribute set, turns off the archive attribute.
/D:date	Copies files changed on or after the specified date. If no date is given, copies only those files whose source time is newer than the destination time.
/P	Prompts you before creating each destination file.
/S	Copies directories and subdirectories except empty ones.
/E	Copies directories and subdirectories, including empty ones.
/W	Prompts you to press a key before copying.
/C	Continues copying even if errors occur.
/I	If destination does not exist and copying more than one file, assumes that destination must be a directory.
/Q	Does not display file names while copying.

/F	Displays full source and destination file names while copying.
/L	Displays files that would be copied.
/H	Copies hidden and system files also.
/R	Overwrites read-only files.
/T	Creates directory structure, but does not copy files. Does not include empty directories or sub-directories. /T /E includes empty directories and subdirectories.
/U	Updates the files that already exist in destination.
/K	Copies attributes. Normal Xcopy will reset read-only attributes.
/Y	Overwrites existing files without prompting.
/-Y	Prompts you before overwriting existing files.
/N	Copy using the generated short names.

4.5.9 FORMAT Command

This command is used to format a disk for use with MS-DOS.An unformatted disk must be formatted before you use it for saving your files.

Syntax of FORMAT command :

FORMAT drive: [/V[:label]] [/Q] [/F:size] [/B | /S] [/C]
FORMAT drive: [/V[:label]] [/Q] [/T:tracks /N:sectors] [/B | /S] [/C]
FORMAT drive: [/V[:label]] [/Q] [/1] [/4] [/B | /S] [/C]
FORMAT drive: [/Q] [/1] [/4] [/8] [/B | /S] [/C]

/V[:label]	Specifies the volume label.
/Q	Performs a quick format.
/F:size	Specifies the size of the floppy disk to format (such as 160, 180, 320, 360, 720, 1.2, 1.44, 2.88).
/B	Allocates space on the formatted disk for system files.
/S	Copies system files to the formatted disk.
/T:tracks	Specifies the number of tracks per disk side.
/N:sectors	Specifies the number of sectors per track.
/1	Formats a single side of a floppy disk.
/4	Formats a 5.25-inch 360K floppy disk in a high-density drive.
/8	Formats eight sectors per track.
/C	Tests clusters that are currently marked "bad."

Example

To format a floppy disk in drive A and copying operating system in it.Enter following command.

Format a: /s

Or

To format a floppy disk for storage of your file, enter following

Format a: /v

4.5.10 CHKDSK Command

This command checks a disk and displays a status report. This command also checks for errors if any.

Syntax of CHKDSK command

CHKDSK [drive:][[path]filename] [/F] [/V]

[drive:][path]	Specifies the drive and directory to check.
filename	Specifies the file(s) to check for fragmentation.
/F	Fixes errors on the disk.
/V	Displays the full path and name of every file on the disk.

Type CHKDSK without parameters to check the current disk. Instead of using CHKDSK, try using SCANDISK. SCANDISK can reliably detect and fix a much wider range of disk problems.

Example

Enter the following command to check disk C.

```
C:\>chkdsk c:
CHKDSK has NOT checked this drive for errors.
You must use SCANDISK to detect and fix errors on this drive.
Volume DIVAKAR created 03-04-1999 9:26p
Volume Serial Number is 3623-1CE8

2,585,858,048 bytes total disk space
  102,993,920 bytes available on disk

        4,096 bytes in each allocation unit
      631,313 total allocation units on disk
       25,145 available allocation units on disk

      655,360 total bytes memory
      594,608 bytes free

Instead of using CHKDSK, try using SCANDISK. SCANDISK
can reliably detect and fix a much wider range of disk problems.
C:\>
```

4.5.11 FDISK Command

This command is used to configure a hard disk for use with MS-DOS. Using this command you can DOS partition, you may create more than one DOS partition, create extended DOS partition, logical drive etc. This command must be used with proper care.

Syntax of FDISK command
FDISK [/STATUS] /X

/STATUS	Displays partition information.
/X	Ignores extended disk-access support. Use this switch if you receive disk access or stack overflow messages. After running this command on dos prompt, a menu is displayed on the screen. You may choose the appropriate option.

Example

Enter following at DOS prompt

FDISK

Microsoft Windows 98
Fixed Disk Setup Program
(C)Copyright Microsoft Corp. 1983 - 1998
FDISK Options

Current fixed disk drive: 1

Choose one of the following:

1. Create DOS partition or Logical DOS Drive
2. Set active partition
3. Delete partition or Logical DOS Drive
4. Display partition information

Enter choice: [1]

Press Esc to exit FDISK

4.5.12 CHDIR Command

This command displays the name of or changes the current directory.

Syntax of CHDIR command
CHDIR [drive:][path]
CHDIR[..]
CD [drive:][path]
CD[..]

Here '..' specifies that you want to change to the parent directory.

Examples

CHDIR \ XYZ
CD.

4.5.13 CLS COMMAND

This command is used to clear the screen. This will leave your screen with dos prompt and cursor.

Syntax of CLS command
CLS
C:\>CLS

4.5.14 PATH Command

This command displays or sets a search path for executable files.

Syntax of PATH command

PATH [[drive:]path[;...]]
PATH ;

Example

The following command will be able to execute the external commands with a search in the three directories. The three paths can be provided in a single string.

Path c:\xyz\dbase;a:\new ; \usr

4.5.15 VERIFY Command

This command tells DOS whether to verify that your files are written correctly to a disk. You can use this command to verify that your files are written correctly to the disk. You will receive an error message if the file has not been written successfully.

Syntax of VERIFY command :
syntax of VERIFY command

VERIFY [ON | OFF]
You may enter VERIFY command without a parameter to display the current VERIFY setting.

4.5.16 DOSKEY Command

This command is used to edit command lines and recalls command lines.

Example

Enter following at dos prompt.

Once the dos key is installed, you may use following keys to do specified function.

UP,DOWN arrows recall commands
Esc clears current command
F7 displays command history
Alt+F7 clears command history
[chars]F8 searches for command beginning with [chars]
F9 selects a command by number

4.5.17 FIND Command

This command is used to search for a text string in a file or files.

Syntax of FIND command

FIND [/V] [/C] [/N] [/I] "string" [[drive:][path]filename[...]]

/V	Displays all lines NOT containing the specified string.
/C	Displays only the count of lines containing the string.
/N	Displays line numbers with the displayed lines.
/I	Ignores the case of characters when searching for the string.
"string"	Specifies the text string to find.
[drive:][path]filename	Specifies a file or files to search.

If a pathname is not specified, FIND searches the text typed at the prompt or piped from another command.

Example

Following command displays all the lines which contain string "hello world " from the file xyz.txt.

Find "hello world" xyz.txt

4.5.18 MEM

This command displays the amount of used and free memory in your system.

Syntax of MEM command

MEM [/CLASSIFY | /DEBUG | /FREE | /MODULE modulename] [/PAGE]

/CLASSIFY or /C	Classifies programs by memory usage. Lists the size of programs, provides a summary of memory in use, and lists largest memory block available.
/DEBUG or /D	Displays status of all modules in memory, internal drivers, and other information.
/FREE or /F	Displays information about the amount of free memory left in both conventional and upper memory.
/MODULE or /M	Displays a detailed listing of a module's memory use. This option must be followed by the name of a module, optionally separated from /M by a colon.
/PAGE or /P	Pauses after each screenful of information.

Example

Enter MEM command at dos prompt.

```
C:\WINDOWS>mem
Memory Type          Total      Used     Free
----------------------------------------------------
Conventional         640K       60K      580K
Upper                0K         0K       0K
Reserved             384K       384K     0K
Extended (XMS)       31,744K    184K     31,560K
----------------------------------------------------
Total memory         32,768K    628K     32,140K
Total under 1 MB     640K       60K      580K
Total Expanded (EMS)            32M (33,030,144 bytes)
Free Expanded (EMS)             16M (16,777,216 bytes)

Largest executable program size      580K (594,288 bytes)
Largest free upper memory block      0K   (0 bytes)
MS-DOS is resident in the high memory area.
C:\WINDOWS>
```

4.5.19 DATE Command

This command displays current date and set the date. This command sets the internal clock of the computer.

Syntax of date command

Date [mm-dd-yy]

Example

Enter date command at MSDOS prompt.

```
C:\WINDOWS>date
Current date is Sat 10-14-2000
Enter new date (mm-dd-yy):
```

4.5.20 DISKCOMP command

This command compares the contents of the disk in the source drive to the disk in the target disk drive. This command performs a track by track comparison of the disk.

Syntax of diskcomp command
Diskcomp [drive1:][drive2:][\1][\8]

[drive1]	source drive
[drive2:]	target drive
[\1]	compare the one side of disk.
[\8]	compare first 8 sectors of the track.

4.5.21 TYPE command

This command displays the contents of a file to the screen. Type command may be used to display the contents of.txt file.

Syntax of type command
Type [drive :] filename

Example

To direct the contents of xyz.txt file, enter following command.

Type a:xyz.txt

SELECT EXERCISES

Q. 1. What is the difference between Internal and External DOS commands. List any two examples of each.

Q. 2. Explain in brief why DOS was named as Disk Operating System ? What is the significance of the term Disk?

Q. 3. What are the basic differences between MS-DOS and WINDOWS.

Q. 4. Given both MSDOS and WINDOWS 98 in your computer which would you prefer to use and why?

Q. 5. What is a file? How does it differ from a directory? Explain the meaning of directory structure in brief.

Q. 6. What do you mean by the PATH of a file? How is it different from relative path?

Q. 7. Distinguish between the internal and external DOS command. Illustrate your answer by examples?

Q. 8. Explain the following MS DOS command with example.
DIR, DISKCOPY, MKDIR

Q. 9. Explain the meaning of C:\WINDOWS>CD\, C:\>MKDIR xym, C:\>cd lmn, and C:\xyz >dir/p?

Q. 10. Give DOS command for changing your working directory to a different directory?

Q. 11. Give complete procedure for copying files from one directory to another directory?

Q. 12. Enlist the meaning of P,W,A,O,S,B,L,V 4 in a syntax of DIR command. Explain at least one by one demonstrating in actual working?

Q. 13. When PROMPT command is used? Illustrate it by an example.

Q. 14. Give full syntax of XCOPY command and explains the meaning of all terms in it?

Q. 15. Give command which enables you to display memory used free memory in your system?

Q. 16. What is a FDISK Command and how it is used?

Q. 17. What do you mean by a boot record? Where the boot record is stored? Explain the process of booting of a computer system.

Q. 18. What are wild cards? When they are used? Explain with suitable example.

5 Introduction to Windows 98

5.0 INTRODUCTION

Windows 98, a product of Microsoft is an operating system that manages scheduling of work and hardware accessories. The entire task performed in an operating system can be accomplished in Windows 95 environment. Unlike previous operating system DOS (disk operating system), it is a Graphical User Interface (GUI) based operating system. You may enter the command by clicking desired objects using mouse. Windows 98, a successor of DOS removed the major limitation of Disk Operating System. Main features of Windows 98 are as follows.

- Windows is Graphical User Interface (GUI) based system, while DOS was based on the textual interfaces.
- While working with Windows, it is not necessary to remember the lengthy DOS command and with syntax.
- Windows allows the user to get rid of typing commands and all major operations are performed by a few clicks of mouse.
- Basic operating system services, file and folders are shown in the graphical form as Icon and using the mouse pointer to those Icons and clicking on top of them invoke the services.
- Management of file and folder like Copy, Delete, Create operation may be performed by mouse and it also allows drag and drop operation.
- Windows allows the multitasking while DOS is not a multitasking system. It is possible to open several applications in windows at the same time.
- Windows exhibit a better mechanism to show and remove the error occurred in different operation.

Windows allows the user to control the hardware in the most simple way. It allows the user to add new hardware, configure the system and enable them to work together. It allows users to run different program or application in windows. Microsoft Office package which includes MS Word, MS Access, MS Excel etc. are compatible with the Windows. It also allows the ease of the organizing users information in form of files and folders. It provides the user all the tools and services to copy, delete, sort, move the files and folders.

When any computer which runs windows 98 operating system is turned on, after few seconds it displays a screen as shown in the figure 5.1. This area is called desktop, which contains various objects such as task bar, mouse pointer and several icons.

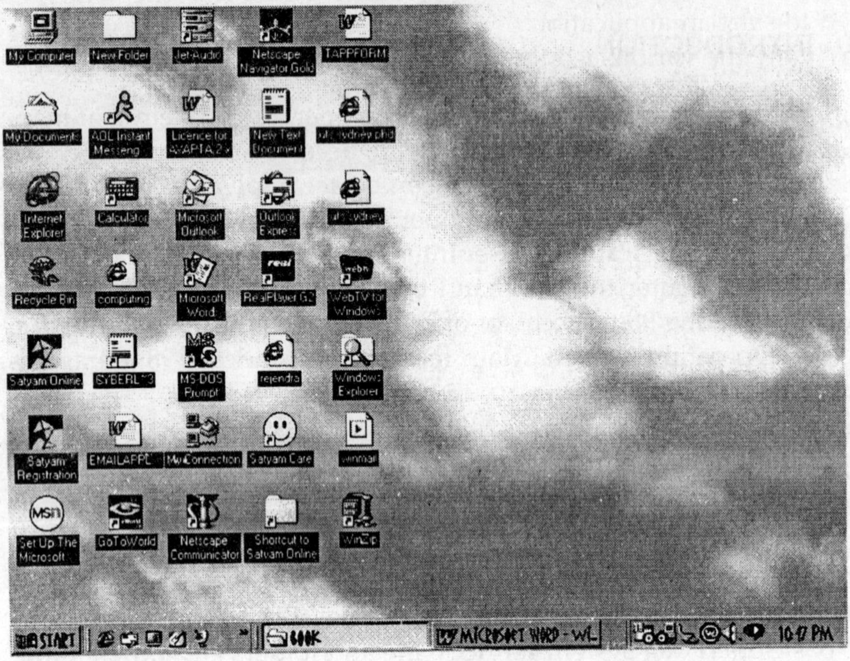

Fig. 5.1 Desktop

5.1 KNOWING OBJECTS OF WINDOWS

5.1.1 The Desktop

Total visible area on the screen, which you get immediately after turning on your computer, is called Desktop area. You may keep your important folders on desktop or you may create shortcut to the program that you use very frequently. You may customize the desktop according to your requirements and ease by adding the shortcut to program, folders or documents. You may also change the setting such as desktop color, screen saver, size, background, appearance and other effects. For this you have to right click the mouse button on the desktop, and select the properties. The desktop may contain many items like My Computer, Network neighborhood, My Documents, Recycle Bin along with the items which a user creates. The Desk Top is shown in the figure 5.1.

5.1.2 Task Bar

At the bottom of the screen a horizontal strip is seen which is called taskbar. It contain the Start button on the extreme left side, which is used to start an application or program. On the right hand side you may view the various icon which represent various process running by the system. To know about the programs or process under active condition, you may move mouse pointer to them and see their name. At the extreme right side you can see the clock running.

Fig. 5.2 Task Bar

5.1.3 Start Button

You may click on the start button to start various programs or applications. When you click on the start button the screen as shown in the figure 5.1 appears. By navigating the mouse pointer you may select & click on the appropriate icon. This will start your application. For example, going through program-accessories-entertainment-CD player, you may start CD player application. You have to use this button if you want to change in the setting or to find a file or folder on your disk.

5.1.4 My Computer

You can use My Computer to see everything stored on your computer. All you need to do is to double click on My Computer icon on the desktop to browse through files and folder stored onto your disk. It will show you all the accessories attached to the computer. As shown in figure 5.3, My Computer lists Floppy Drive A, Disk Drive C & D, CD Drive, Control Panel etc. On clicking to the drive icon like A, C, D or CD Drive, you may explore the contents of either floppy, disk or CD.

If you want to the find out the current amount of space available / used on hard disk, floppy disk, CD etc, then point to the corresponding disk icon and right click the mouse select properties. This will show you the total disk space available and used in graphical form as shown in the figure 5.4.

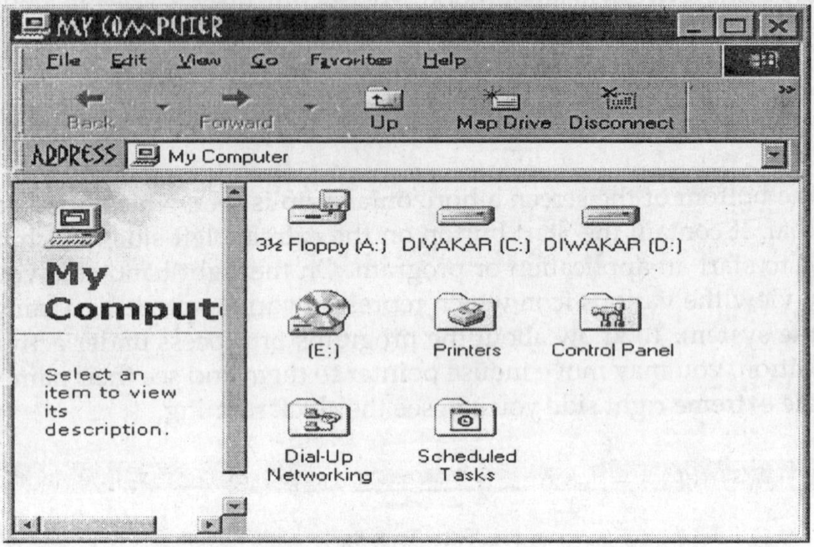

Fig. 5.3 My Computer

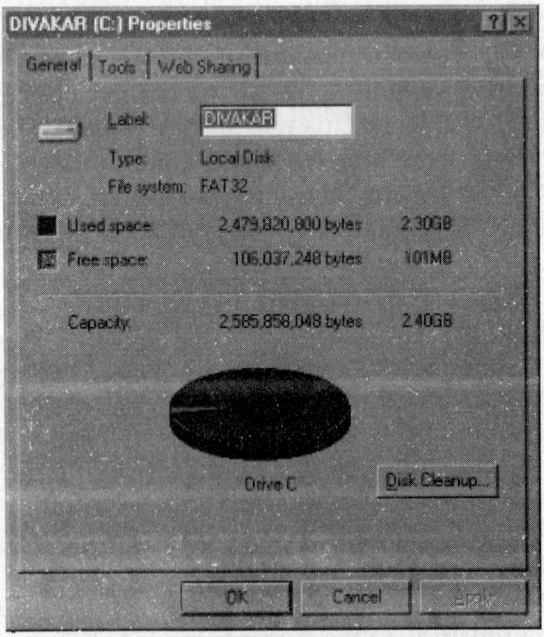

Fig: 5.4 Display of Disk Space

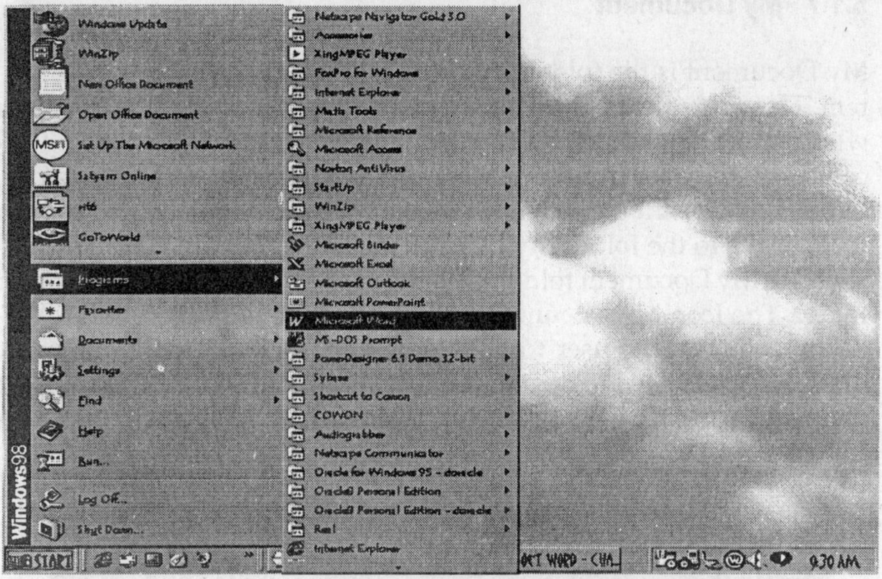

Fig 5.5 Starting an application

5.1.5 Recycle Bin

You may delete any file or folder or program or shortcut etc. After deleting any object, it is not actually deleted but it is sent to the recycle bin. This avoids the possibility of accidental deletes. If any point of time, you feel that a file has been deleted accidentally, you may restore it to the original location by right clicking the mouse on that object in the recycle bin. If you run short of space on the disk, you should first delete the item in recycle bin. Here you should remember that any item deleted from recycle bin cannot be restored i.e. it is finally deleted.

5.1.6 Starting an Application

Various other icons present on the desktop are graphical representation of files or programs or applications. Any icon on the desktop represents an application, file, folder or the shortcut. You can start a program or application or open a folder by double clicking on the icon. It will then start the application or open the file/folder. For example you may start Internet Explorer application by double clicking the icon. Another way of starting an application is to select program from start menu. It will present you a list of applications available on your system. You may select the application of your choice which you want to start. This procedure is shown in figure 5.5.

5.1.7 My Document

My Document is the folder provided by the Windows operating system. This folder is the utility provided by the Windows. It is the place where user may keep the files, documents etc which needs to be accessed by the user in future. Most of the applications like MS Word, Excel, PowerPoint etc attempt to save the work done by the user in form of file to the folder My Document. These files are automatically saved in My Document folder until the user deliberately saves in other folder. The Icon My Document is placed on the desk top by the Windows. It allows the user to have quick access to the previous work done. All users need to do it to double click on the Icon My Document on the desk top. The view of file and folder in My Document is shown in figure 5.6.

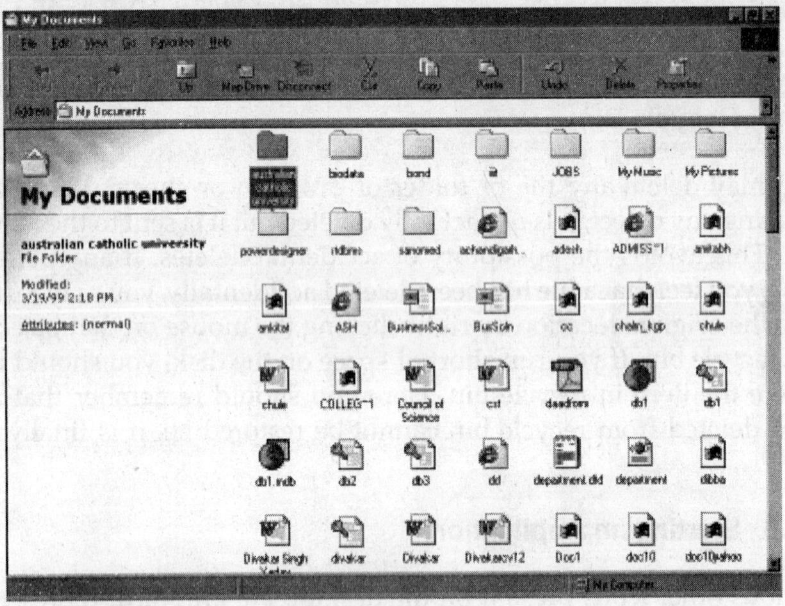

Fig 5.6 My Document

The documents, files and folders contained in My Document may be customized according to users requirements like size of icon, arranging the file/folders in order of their size, alphabetically etc.

5.1.8 My Briefcase

My Briefcase is another utility provided by windows. The Icon for My Briefcase folder is placed by the windows on the desktop. This utility is very useful to those persons who travel very frequently with the electronic documents. Frequent travellers carry the documents electronically in the form of files and folders. These files and folders may be kept in floppy disk or laptop while travelling. Major advantages of this folder is that the user may get rid of subsequent changes in the documents. For example, if the user have saved one document in the My Briefcase for the purpose of transportation. If any change has occurred in the document, you may select the utility of 'Update All ' of My Briefcase contained in briefcase menu for subsequent changes in the file.

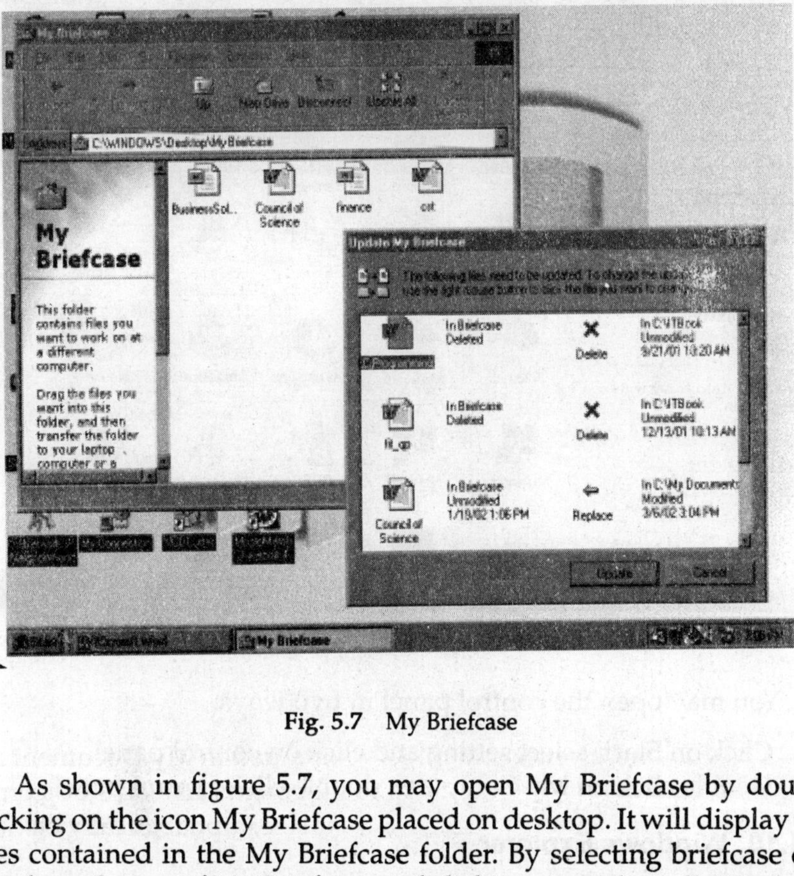

Fig. 5.7 My Briefcase

As shown in figure 5.7, you may open My Briefcase by double clicking on the icon My Briefcase placed on desktop. It will display the files contained in the My Briefcase folder. By selecting briefcase option from the top of My Briefcase and clicking on update all, Windows will open a new screen (Update My Briefcase) which will display the file which have been deleted from My Briefcase and the files which have been modified outside my briefcase. You may choose the action accordingly to modify the contents of My Briefcase.

5.1.9 Control Panel

Control Panel is one of the most important utility provided by MS Windows 95/98. It allows you to change the parameters and setting. In fact, Control Panel contains a number of small utilities. You may change the setting of the desk top, printer, mouse, screen savers, keyboard and other hardware devices. A view of contents of the control panel are shown in figure 5.8. All the facilities are provided at one point from which user may customize the setting or windows environment according to his choice.

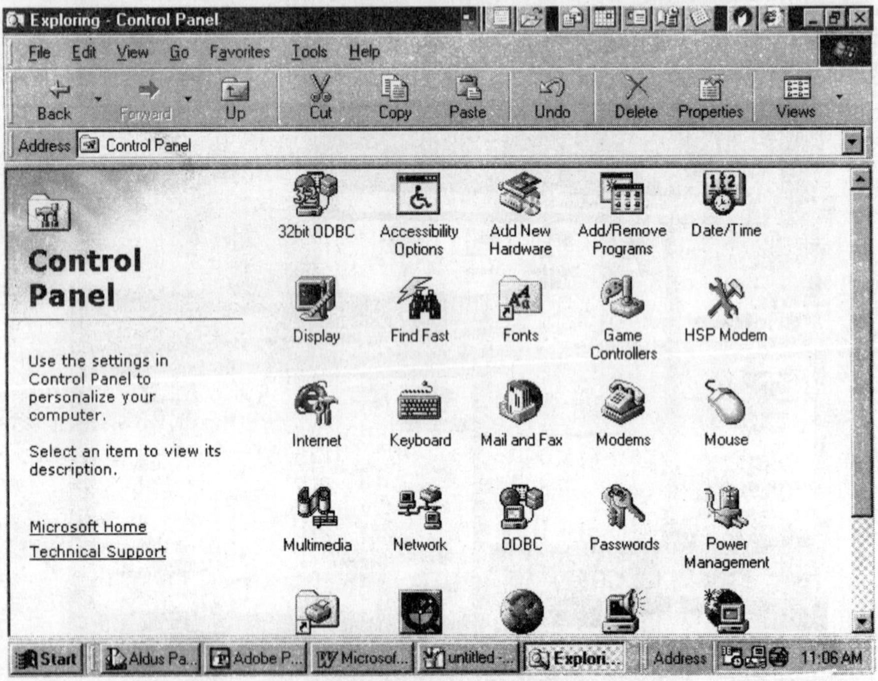

Fig 5.8 Control Panel

You may open the control panel in two ways:

1. Click on Start, select setting and click on control panel.
2. Double click on My Computer, double click control panel.

5.1.10 Windows Explorer

Windows Explorer is one of the most important utilities provided in the windows which allows you to view various files and folders placed on floppy disk, hard disk and CD. It can also be used to locate the file and folder on your computer system. Windows explorer is two pane window, when any element in left pane is clicked, right pane displays the contents of that folder. Windows explorer can be started from start menu, program and windows explorer. Typical snap shot of windows explorer is shown in figure 5.9.

Fig. 5.9 Windows Explorer

As shown in figure 5.9, windows explorer displays the contents of all hard drives, CD and floppy disk. In the left pane, if you click on to any item e.g. Floppy, the contents of floppy disk will be displayed in right pane. You may use drag and drop operation to copy the files and folders from one place to another in windows explorer.

5.2 IMPORTANT FUNCTIONS

In this section, the tips for doing some important function in the windows are given.

5.2.1 To Open a File or Folder

1. Double-click My Computer on the desktop.

2. Double-click the drive that contains the file.
3. Double-click the file or folder you want to open.

It will then open the file for you.

5.2.2 To Open a File You've Used Recently

1. Click Start, and then point to Documents.
2. Click the document you want to open.

5.2.3 To Copy a File or Folder from One Disk/Folder to Another

1. In My Computer or Windows Explorer, click the file or folder you want to copy.
2. On the Edit menu, click Copy.
3. Open the folder or disk where you want to put the copy.
4. On the Edit menu, click Paste.

5.2.4 To Change the Name of a File or Folder

1. In My Computer or Windows Explorer, click the file or folder you want to rename.
2. On the File menu, click Rename.
3. Type the new name, and then press ENTER.

5.2.5 To Delete a File or Folder

1. In My Computer or Windows Explorer, click the file or folder you want to delete.
2. On the File menu, click Delete.
3. You can also drag file or folder icons into the Recycle Bin. If you press SHIFT key while dragging, the item will be deleted from your computer without being stored in the Recycle Bin.

5.2.6 To Find a File or Folder

1. Click Start, point to find, and then click files or folders.
2. In Named, type all or part of the file name.
   Enter a word or phrase in dialogue box if you do not know the name of a file but know a distinctive word or phrase it contains.
   If you want to specify the location to start the search, click Browse.
3. Click on Find Now.

5.2.7 To See What's on Your Computer

1. Double-click My Computer.
2. Double-click the icon of the drive you want to see.
   Windows displays the files and folders on the drive. Folders can contain files, programs, and other folders.
3. To open a file or folder, or to start a program, double-click it.

5.2.8 To Change the Background of the Desktop

1. Go to start - setting -control panel and double click on display icon.
2. Alternatively you may right click the mouse and select properties.
3. In Wallpaper, click the background you want to use or click Pattern to choose or modify the background.
4. Click Apply to see the changes before you close the dialog box, or click OK to accept the changes and close the dialog box.

5.2.9 To Set up a Screen Saver

1. Go to start - setting -control panel and double click on display icon.
2. Alternatively you may right click the mouse and select properties
3. To open the Display Properties dialog box at the Screen Saver tab.
4. In Screen Saver, click the screen saver you want to use.
5. To customize the screen saver, click Settings

Display properties are shown in figure 5.10.

5.2.10 To Adjust the Rate at which the Cursor Blinks

1. Go to start - setting -control panel and double click on keyboard icon
2. On the Speed tab, drag the Cursor blink rate slider.

The test cursor to the left of the slider area blinks at the new rate.

5.2.11 To Send a File or Folder to a Disk

1. If you are copying a file or folder to a floppy disk, insert the disk in the disk drive.

2. In My Computer or Windows Explorer, click the file or folder you want to copy.
3. On the File menu, point to Send To, and then click the drive you want to copy the file or folder to.
4. After selecting a file or folder to copy, right click the mouse and select Send To Floppy Disk.

5.2.12 To Move a File or Folder

1. In My Computer or Windows Explorer, click the file or folder you want to move.
2. On the Edit menu, click Cut or Copy
3. Open the folder where you want to put the file or folder.
4. On the Edit menu, click Paste.

5.2.13 Creating a Shortcut

A shortcut is a quick way to start a program or open a file or folder without going to its permanent location in Windows Explorer. Shortcuts are especially useful for programs, files, and folders you use frequently. There are three ways you can create a shortcut

5.2.14 To Put a Shortcut on the Desktop

1. In My Computer or Windows Explorer, click the item, such as a file, program, folder, printer, or computer, for which you want to create a shortcut.
2. On the File menu, click Create Shortcut.
3. Drag the shortcut icon onto the desktop.

5.2.15 To Create a Folder

1. Click the drive in Windows Explorer where you want to create the new folder.
2. On the File menu, point to New, and then click Folder.
   The new folder appears with a temporary name.
3. Type a name for the new folder, and then press ENTER.

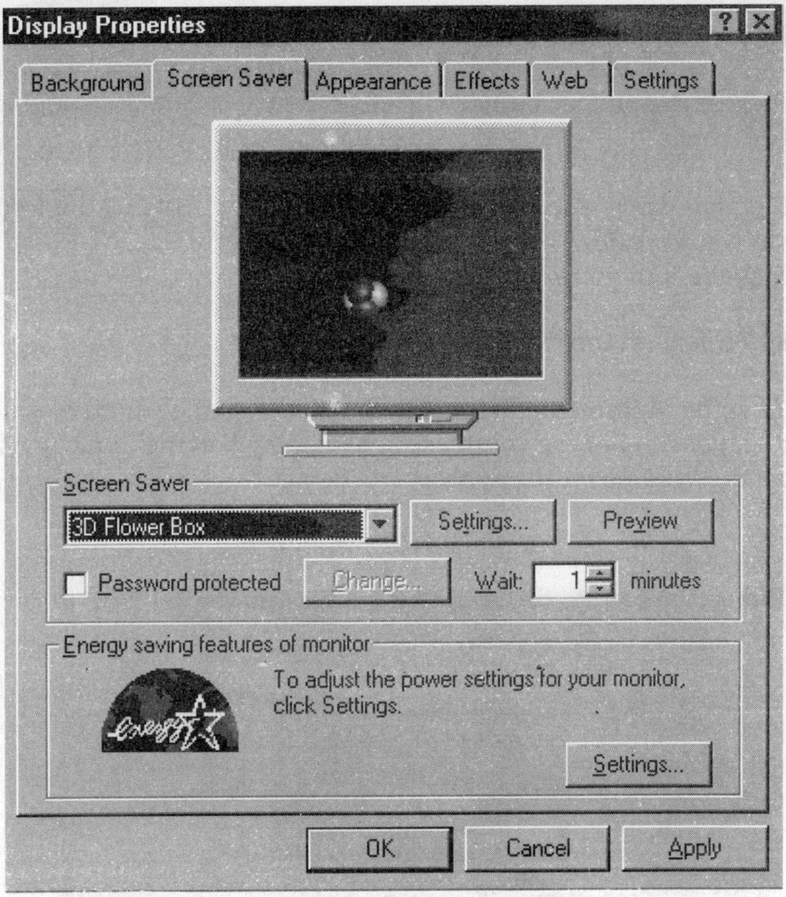

Fig 5.10 Setting your screen saver

5.2.16 To Add a Program to the Start or Programs Menu

1. Click Start, point to Settings, and then click Taskbar & Start Menu.
2. Click the Start Menu Programs tab.
3. Click Add, and then click Browse.
4. Locate the program you want to add, and then click it.
5. Click Next, and then double-click the menu on which you want the program to appear.
6. Type the name that you want to see on the menu, and then click Finish.
7. If Windows prompts you to choose an icon, click one, and then click Finish.

5.2.17 To Add a New Font to Your Computer

1. Click Start, point to Settings, click Control Panel, and then double-click Fonts.
2. On the File menu, click Install New Font.
3. Click the drive, and then click the folder that contains the fonts you want to add.
4. Click the font you want to add

5.2.18 To Adjust the Playback Volume

1. Open the Multimedia Properties dialog box at the Audio tab.
2. In Playback, click the Volume icon to display Volume Control. Adjust the volume for the appropriate device.

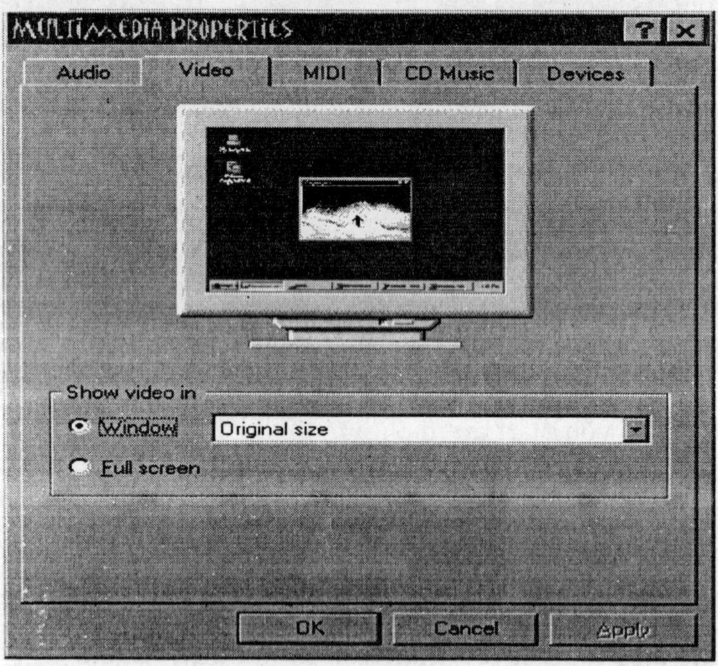

Fig. 5.11 Setting your Multimedia Properties

5.3 STARTING AN APPLICATION (PROGRAM)

Starting an application means, starting a program with which you want to wok. For example, you may like to open internet explorer, MS Word,

MS Access, MS Excel or any other similar program. There are several ways to start an application. Most simple way to start an application is by navigating through Start button. All you have to do is to click on the start button, which is at the left corner of the task bar. When you click on it Task Menu is displayed which contain many pads. Select Program menu which contain all applications including Accessories, Windows Explorer, MS Word, MS Access, MS Excel, MS-DOS prompt and many other applications of windows. You may find several applications on entertainment, system tool, communication, calculator etc in the accessories of program menu. For starting any application, you should first select the application and click on the application by mouse.

There is another faster way to start an application. You may create a short cut of that application and place the short cut on your desktop. This is very helpful for the application, which you run very frequently. All you have to do is to create a short cut, is to move mouse pointer to that application using My Computer or Start button, press right button of mouse, select create short cut. Then you may drag it to the desktop. Many accessories such as Games, Multimedia, Calculator, Paint, Wordpad are provided in windows 95. The folder Games contains many games based on windows. Multimedia has a CD player, Media player and Volume control to operate multimedia programs. In System Tool, Scan disk is a very important utility which enable hard disk to operate smoothly and prevent it from problem. Paint is used for painting with color, Calculator to calculate some mathematical operation and word pad to write a letter or to print a report.

5.4 KNOWING YOUR WINDOW

Windows 98, if you start an application, it will always run in windows. You may run more than one application at a time in Windows 98. This feature of Windows 98 is called multitasking. All the windows you open has the following component. For example when you start Windows explorer application, it will run into a new window which is shown in the figure 5.12

5.4.1 Title Bar

The application executed will run in a window. It displays the title of window on the top. The dark color bar is called title bar. On the right hand side you may see the three boxes which are used to minimize, restore or close the application. Title bar is also used to move a window. Double clicking on title bar either restores or maximizes the

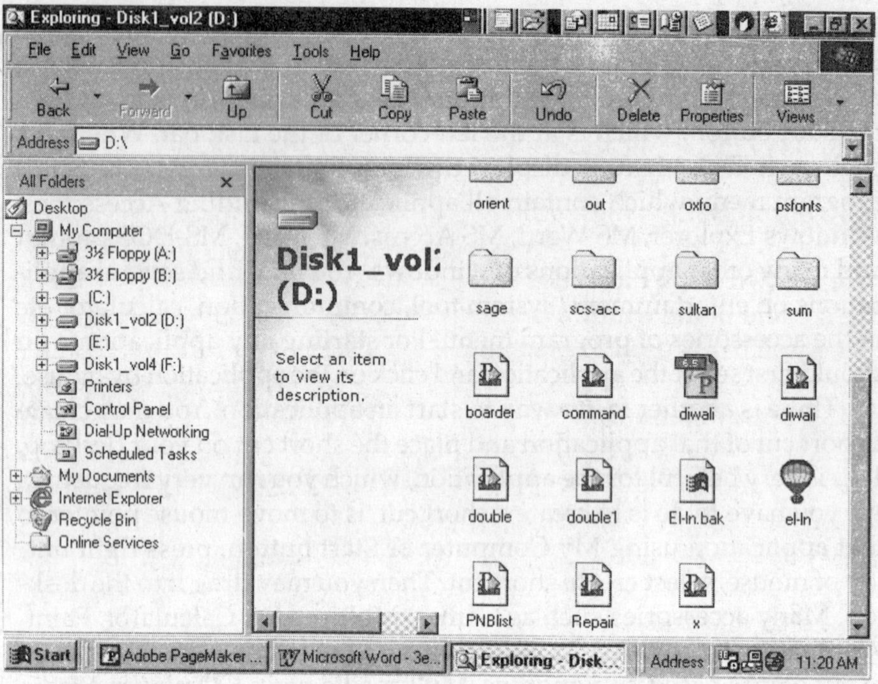

Fig 5.12 Window

window. The left corner icon on the title bar is called control box, which when clicked invokes a Control Menu, used to control the window. If the window is already maximized then the restore button is used to restore the window.

5.4.2 Menu Bar

The next bar below the title bar is Menu bar. This is divided into many menu items such as File, Edit, View, Go, Favorite, Tools and Help. Clicking on any menu item displays a menu list. This list contains several menu Item, clicking on it will issue a command of appropriate nature.

5.4.3 Tool Bar

The bar next to the menu bar is seen with many small buttons. The common commands, which are given through menu bar, can be issued by tool bar. Clicking on any button is sufficient to give a command by tool Bar. In some application such as Microsoft Word. Two-tool bars are sees.

5.4.4 Status Bar

The bar at the bottom of any window is called the status bar. It shows the status of the application.

5.4.5 Scroll Bar

There are two scroll bar called horizontal and vertical which are seen if the content of the window are larger than the window. Small button of the scroll bar is used to navigate in a window.

5.4.6 Control Menu Box

Control Menu appears when the icon of the left side in the title bar is clicked. This Menu is used to control the whole application window to move a window on the desktop, Move is selected. To change the size of application window, Size is clicked. Maximize and Minimize are used to maximize or minimize the application window. The last option is to close which is used to close the application. To activate the control, menu by keyboard press Alt+Space bar keys simultaneously. Use arrow keys to select an option.

5.4.7 How to Close an Application

You may quit the application or close the application in one of the following ways:

1. Click the button on the title bar, which is seen as X on the right corner.
2. Choose the file on menu bar and select exit command from menu bar.
3. Press the Alt + F4 keys simultaneously.
4. Activate the Control Menu of the application window by Clicking on the Control menu icon at left corner in title bar and select Close.

5.4.8 Clip Boards

Clipboard is a utility provided by the Windows 98 to add the process of copying information between the application. It is temporary storage area on which we can clip a small amount of information. This information stays on the clip board unless it is replace or exit windows. Using clip board portion of the text, graphic or sound can be marked in one application and dropped into other.

5.5 HOW TO SWITCH BETWEEN THE VARIOUS APPLICATIONS

By virtue of being a multitasking operating system, windows 98 allows you to run more than one application simultaneously. You may see the status of various applications which are displayed on the status bar. You may click on to the appropriate item on the status bar to switch to that application. Alternatively you may also use alt and tab keys of your keyboard to switch between the applications.

5.6 MANAGING YOUR FILES THROUGH WINDOWS EXPLORER

Windows explorer is a powerful tool of Windows 98, which allows you to manage your files and folders on the disk. You can start windows explorer by navigating through start button then select windows explorer in program files. All the information on your disk is saved in the form of files. This information may be a document, letter, image, video, sound or any other format supported by a specific application. All files in a computer are stored in directory, which is called Folder. A Folder contains many files and folders. Double clicking any folder opens it and lists the contents of it. Windows Explorer is used to copy, move and delete files/folders. Properties of the file can also be seen in the explorer. We can also find the location of a file in the explorer. To move file or folder click on the files/folder and drag it to desired location. To copy/folder to other location click it and drag it to desired location by holding the Control key down. To Create a new file/folder go to file menu on menu bar and select new option. A screen shot of Windows Explorer is shown in the figure.

5.7 STARTING DOS APPLICATION

Although Windows 98 is an operating system yet you may work on Microsoft Disk operating system in the Windows 98. All you have to do to start a DOS application is to click on start button and navigate through program and select MS DOS prompt. By clicking on this item you may start DOS application. The DOS has almost no use in Windows but it is provided only to assist the old users who are familiar with DOS. You will see the DOS prompt on the DOS window and you may issue any DOS command.

5.8 HOW TO SHUT DOWN YOUR COMPUTER

Never switch off your computer when your applications are running. This may corrupt your window file system. It has been recommended to shut down your computer by navigating through shut down on start button. On clicking this item following window will appear. You may select to shut down, restart or restart in MS DOS mode your computer. If you select shut down, then click in the box provided and press OK button. You must wait until the message "It is now safe to turn off your computer" comes on to your screen.

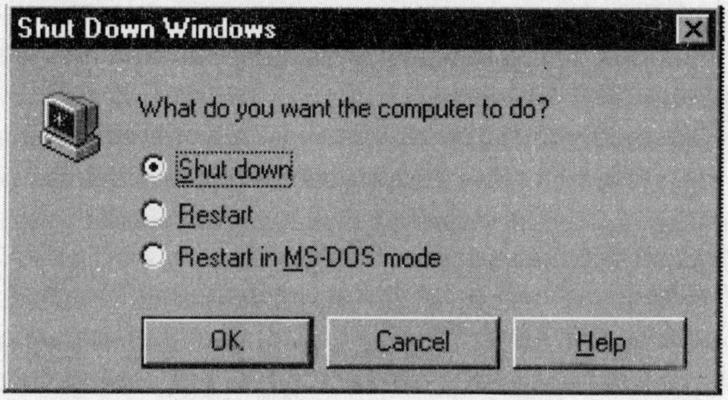

Fig. 5.13 Shut Down Menu

SELECT EXERCISES

Q. 1. What is Desktop? What are other important icons present on your desktop area?

Q. 2. What is the role of Recycle Bin? How does it help to prevent accidental deletes?

Q. 3. What are the contents of My Document Folder?

Q. 4. What is the role of Start Bar? What are the contents of menu item Program and Accessories?

Q. 5. How will you open a folder using Window Explorer?

Q. 6. Explain the purpose and role of Windows Explorer?

Q. 7. Explain the steps to change the background of your screen?

Q. 8. How will you install a screen saver of your choice to your system?

Q. 9. How will you find a file or folder of your interest using Windows Explorer? Explain the process of searching a file/folder.

Q. 10. Give complete History of WINDOWS 1.0 to WINDOWS 98. Distinguish the development with supporting features that advanced version possessed?

Q. 11. Enlist the important functions that WINDOWS 98 has in it?

Q. 12. Give possible reasons that might crash Windows 98 in your computer?

Q. 13. Explain the process of adding your favourite program to Start or Program Menu.

Q. 14. What are the reasons for calling "Windows 98" operating system as Windows?

Q. 15. Explain the process of Shut Down? What happens if you do not shut down the machine properly?

Q. 16. Suppose you have started many applications in Windows. If you want to close some of them, what steps you will take?

Q. 17. Explain the process of switching between the several applications running on Windows.

Q. 18. Explain how many different ways an application may be started in Windows 98.

Q. 19. Explain briefly the important menu item present in Start bar.

Q. 20. Explain how will you do the followings in the Windows.

(a) Copying the file from one to another directories

(b) Changing the attribute of the file.

(c) Create the short cut of an application.

(d) Adjust the rate of cursor blink.

Q. 21. What is Control Panel? How the control panel is used?

Q. 22. How will you close an application?

Q. 23. How will to toggle between various applications running on Windows?

Q. 24. Explain the role of My Computer icon on your Desktop?

6 Introduction to Internet

6.0 INTRODUCTION

Internet is based upon the concept of networking. Networking is the basic need to share the information between two or more computers. The computers may be connected through various media such as lying the cable. The Internet may be thought as a network of various small networks, on which an user can store and share the information. Human beings have seen a lot of advantages of Internet working. By virtue of internet, it has become possible to place the order for shopping, maintaining the bank account, sending and receiving the mails and other information simply by pressing a few buttons.

First event, that has given the way to current Information Technology rise, was an attempt to establish a network by U.S. Defence Agency. Nearly twenty years back, U.S. defence department started a project for information communication among its various computers. Main objective of this project was to prevent its computers from failure that is in case of failure of one computer system, another was ready to take up the job and no information or data content was lost. This event was probably the first step in building of a large network which now has matured enough. Now the reach to this very large network is not limited to scientists or researchers. It is available to common man. This large network is called Internet. Approximately 20 million computers are attached with this network. Communication between these computers is established using telephone lines, fiber optic cable and satellite transmission. Computer and communication are probably the basic ingredient of Internet. Earlier this network was being used for communication between the scientists and researchers but major breakthrough was the launch of the web browser. After the launch of the web browser, it has become possible for common man to use the internet. Web browser can be seen as a tool to view the large information contents stored on different computers worldwide. It has become possible to gather information about any topic of interest on Internet. One can find out a product of his choice, placing order, search for new audio, video, news group, mail to friends and much more.

6.1 NETWORKS

Computer Network refers to the collection of several computing machines, peripheral devices, storage unit. The computer systems may communicate over computer network and share the resources. These networks enable the computer to communicate with a remote computer, where the remote computer may be located at a distance of few meters to several thousand kilometers. The users of a computer system on network are able to share the software resources such as programs, databases, and program utilities. The computer network has been the basic necessity and triggered the development of several applications, which uses the computer objects distributed over a large geographical area. The conventional concept of installing a high performance and large computer system has now been replaced with computer networks where several low cost, low performance computer systems collectively exhibit high performance at a lower cost. The computer network connects several peripheral devices, databases and computer systems.

On the basis of location of the computer connected through network, the Network may be classified into several categories viz. LAN (Local Area Network), WAN (Wide Area Network) etc. LAN stands for Local Area Network. The network of computer installed within a room or a building is called LAN. CAN which stands for Campus Area Network contains the computer spread in the campus which are on network when the connectivity of computers crosses the boundaries of the building and users get the access to a computer located in the city, that network is called MAN, Metropolitan Area Network. When the connectivity of these computers crosses the limits of city/town/state then this type of networking falls under the category of WAN (Wide Area Network). At last, it is also possible to have a network of computers, where computers are spread in the large region such as different countries/continents. This type of network is called Long Haul Network. It should be remembered that purpose of all kinds of network is to share the information available on different computer on network.

The main motivation behind the networks is

- Resource sharing
- Enhanced performance

- Improved reliability and availability
- Modular expendability

The resource sharing implies the sharing of software/program/data of remote computer system. This eliminates the need of replication of resources. The over all performance is increased as data migration and distributed scheduling of the programs or jobs may be done using the computer network. The availability of the components increases as whenever any system or component is down or the other similar resource on the network may be used. It is also possible to add up new computer/disk and other component without any hassle. These factors have initiated all the organizations to establish their network.

6.2 GROWTH OF INTERNET

In the early years of 90's various organizations, corporate offices, government offices started setting up their own computer network within their premises. This was required for faster transfer of data from one desk to another, from one computer to another. Slowly it has become possible to access network of one organization from another organizations network. This gave the birth to Internet, where any computer located worldwide may be accessed from any point in the work over communication channel. In 1983/84, there were only 500-600 computers on internet, but it grew very fast, in 1993 it was 1.2 million, in 1996, it was 15 million and now there are more than 25 million computers on internet.

The internet is not governed by any person or company. However their certain voluntary organizations such Internet Architecture Board (IAB), InterNIC, Internet society (ISOC), a membership organization. Nobody pays for Internet usage but one thing must be remembered that nothing comes at free of cost. There has been a misconception that use of internet is free. These people are completely ignorant of the hidden price paid by them. Users pay to Internet Service Provider (ISP) for getting an access to Internet, telephone line they use. These are called direct cost. However users pay for the hidden cost like advertisements and commercial messages they get every day to their mail accounts. Thus users of internet pay indirectly for the usage of Internet in the form of telephone tariff, fee to Internet Service Providers and indirectly for the advertisement and cost of information hiring to web site. The commercial use of Internet has already started.

6.3 ELECTRONIC MAIL

E-MAIL is one of the most common and widely used service, an user may send letter, message to another user on internet which are delivered almost instantly. The conventional method of communication or sending a message by ordinary mail used to take several days or weeks to get delivered. E-Mail is the most reliable and cheap mailing service to send or receive message. In E-mails, the letters or messages are sent electronically to the recipient similar to ordinary mail, every recipient must have a unique address. The E-mail is delivered to inbox of mail recipient. E-Mail addresses appear to be little complex, but they have simple meaning. E-Mail is now one of the most popular media of communication. This medium is being used to send and receive letters / notes or draft, let it be personal or business. One of the main advantages of this medium is that these mails are delivered almost instantly. Technically, E-Mail is the way of sending documents in electronic form from one computer to another computer. Every recipient of the E-Mail must have an E-Mail address. This mail address is used to send the mail. Earlier E-Mail was considered good for sending and receiving short mails but because of rapid growth in the bandwidth of the channel, it is now possible to send large mail with attachment which may have images, graphics or animation, voices etc.

E-Mail is probably one of the most important services available on internet. It may be used to transfer the letter, text, images etc. over the network. E-Mails are normally delivered almost instantly to the recipient. E-Mail, one of the most common and widely used service on Internet may be used to send letter; greetings, music, message to another user on internet. Because of fact that it provides the instant delivery to the recipient, it has in very short time gained an edge over conventional methods of communications. Conventional methods of communication, which includes ordinary mail normally, takes several days or weeks to get the mail delivered. E-mail is considered as most reliable and cost effective mail service. The letters or message are sent electronically to the recipient over communication channels like telephone links, radio links, satellite etc. E-Mail address is usually divided into two parts, the name of the user and another part is name of the server on which user has address. Following are few examples of E-Mail address.

krishna@hotmail.com
ajayks@cse.iitkgp.ernet.in

vkag@unisa.edu.au
dskushwaha@vsnl.net.in

Syntax for the mail is

Username @ address of Server

In the example, Krishna is the name of the user who has mail account at server hotmail.com, ajaysks and Vkag and DSY are users who have account on cse.iitkgp.ernet.in, unisa.edu.au, vsnl.net.in server. The letter after the dot (.) denote the type of server and their location. Most common of them are

• .com	Commercial	.in	India
• .edu	Educational	.my	Malaysia
• .gov	Government	.uk	U.K.
• .org	Organisation	.de	Germany
• .net	Network	.fr	France
• .ac	Academic	.au	Australia

One may easily come to know that the mail address rkag@unisa.edu.au has user name rkag and is present at university of South Australia (unisa), an educational institution located in Australia.

6.4 UNIFORM RESOURCE LOCATOR (URL)

Each web page on the internet is accessed by providing an address. This unique address is called Uniform Resource Locator or URL in short. In a number of cases, each web page may contain several URLs, as clicking on hypertext you may navigate from one page to another. These all pages are addressed by specifying their addresses. In all the web browsers, you have to specify the URL in the space provided for URL.

Here are some examples of URL

http://www.iitkgp.ernet.in
http://www.unisa.edu.au
gopher://gopher.kent.edu
http://www.wmich.edu/admi/gradapp.htm

Let us analyze the URL http://www.wmich.edu/admi/gradapp.htm. This address contains three parts. First part http specifies the protocol. For this case the HyperText transfer Protocol will be used to transfer the contents of this web site. Second part www.wmich.edu specifies the address of the site. Here edu specifies the domain name, i.e. this is an educational site. WWW, which stands for World Wide Web, specifies that this site is on world wide web. 'wmich' is name of organization, who has hosted this web site. Here, the name of organization is University of West Michigan, which has been against the name 'wmich'. The third part /admi/gradapp.htm the path of the file gradapp.htm which is stored in the directory / admj/.

IP Address

The IP address is an actual address of a node or computer or server on internet. IP addresses are also sometimes called IP number or internet address. These addresses are of following type.

An IP address is divided into four blocks (e.g 144.16.202.19)or numbers each separated by a dot. These numbers uniquely identify the network or location or machine itself. These numbers are provided in consultation with by the Internet Service Provider and InterNIC. InterNIC is an international body for allotment of domain name and addresses. These addresses are given in such a way that no two computers or servers get a single IP address. The Internet is not governed or controlled by any body but there are some bodies who set the rules for internet usage. The popular bodies are InterNIC, Internet Society, an international body for membership, IAB Internet Architecture Board. IAB frames the rules for allocation of addresses on internet.

6.5 WORLD WIDE WEB

The world wide web is a corner of the internet based on on-line documents containing text, image, video, sound. The documents which contain these items are arranged according to need. These documents are written in language called HTML (Hypertext markup language). This language is different from other high level languages (such as C, Pascal etc.).

The HTML document is based upon script and follows standard syntax. Usually various HTML documents provide link to several other HTML documents.HTML is used for creating web pages. Browsers such as Netscape and MS Internet Explorer understand this language and display these pages on the computer screen. World Wide Web is a collection of millions of on-line document/pages written in HTML and they provide a link from one document/page to another page. These pages are called web pages. Hypertext as the name indicates is something more than a simple text. In fact, hype text itself is a source of related pool of information. HTML allows the formatting of the document on the web. The documents are prepared in such a way that they are linked to each other. By simply clicking on the text/object on the screen, it navigates you to desired information pool.

The HTML document is based upon script and follows standard syntax. Usually various HTML documents provide link to several other HTML documents. Now it is time to know about the hypertext. Hypertext as the name indicates is something more than a simple text. For example if you are collecting the information on tourist places of India on the net. You may be provided various destinations on one screen, if you like to know about Taj Mahal or Agra in detail you should click on the text Taj Mahal or Agra to seek more information about Taj Mahal or Agra. Infact, hype text itself is a source of related pool of information. Thus World Wide Web is a collection of millions of online document/pages written in HTML and they provide a link from one document/page to another page. These pages are called web pages.

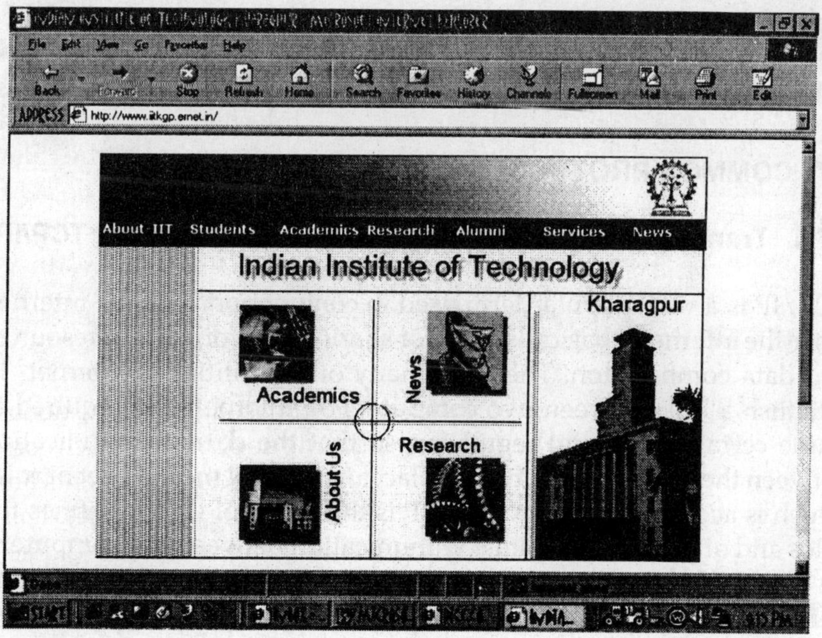

Fig. 6.1

Figure 6.1 shows the home page of site of Indian Institute of Technology (IIT), Kharagpur. The information pertaining to various departments, sections, alumni, research and academics is arranged in a defined format. Upon downloading the page you may click the appropriate block or icon to see more detailed information. For example, you may click to see latest on academics or news to get latest news from IIT Kharagpur.

6.6 WHAT IS A WEB BROWSER?

The web pages can be viewed using web browsers. The web browser are the programs which are used to view the document or page written or coded to HTML. Most popular web browser are MS Explorer and Netscape Nevigator. MS Internet explorer is provided with windows 95/98 operating systems. The browsers window also look like other application window.Web browsers may be of two type, GUI based or text based. GUI based web browsers permit the user to move the mouse and click on to the desired item, selecting a hyper text of choice and tool bar button. When you use web browser for net surfing, it acts as a client and connect you to the desired server after specifying URL address (Universal Resource Locator). It then brings you to the home page of the server. A home page is usually the first page by which you may navigate to the other related pages. Home page provides the link to the other relevant pages available at the server.

6.7 COMMON PROTOCOLS USED IN INTERNET

6.7.1 Transmission Control Protocol/Internet Protocol (TCP/IP)

TCP/IP is a very popular term used in conjunction with the internet. Since the internet is basically used for sharing of information/resources and data combination. There are many other utilities of internet. To establish a link between two computers on internet, it is required to frame certain rules and regulation so that the data communication between the computers may take place. A protocol means a set of rules which is accepted globally. TCP/IP is the protocol which defines the rules and algorithm for data communication between the computers.

To establish a link between two or more computers it is required to define the address of the computer. This address must be unique. Rules and regulations for secure transmission of data over communication channel are also required. TCP/IP is not as such a protocol but it is a collection of various protocols. TCP/IP is divided into two sets of protocols, one is called TCP or Transmission Control Protocol and other is called IP or Internet Protocol.

Transmission Control Protocol deals with packets over networks. The packets are small pieces of data made for effective and safe communication over network. To send a block of data over communication channel, the data is divided into various pieces and these pieces of data are communicated as packets. These packets may have to follow a long path, traversing from one computer or node to another computer. This process is called routing. The data block is divided into packets and size of packets are decided on basis of network capability. The TCP also ensures the safe delivery at the destination and all the packets are assembled to get whole lot of data at destination computers.

Internet Protocol mainly deals with the address of computers. The Internet Protocol decides the address of computer to be labelled on the packet. This allows a computer or intermediate node to read the address of destination and route the packet to destination node.

Transmission Control Protocol and Internet Protocol (TCP/IP) is the most talked about protocol used in Internet. It mainly deals with slicing the data into small sized packets and routing along the communication channel. These packets are routed to destination and pass through node to node and are assembled in order to form the data at the destination.

6.7.2 Simple Mail Transfer Protocol (SMTP)

SMTP is used to deliver of E-Mail. When a E-Mail is to be sent, then Mail Transfer Program contact with the remote machine and forms a TCP connection over which the mail is transferred. Once the connection is established, then Simple Mail Transfer Protocol (SMTP) identifies the sender itself, specifies the recipient of mail and then transfers a E-Mail message. Other features included in the SMTP are that it allows the sender to ask whether a mailbox to whom the mail is directed, does exist on remote computer or not. It also requires the reliable delivery of message such that sender may keep the copy of mail until the mail is actually delivered.

6.7.3 Point to Point Protocol (PPP)

PPP is used when the internet is accessed using a telephone line. Normally, in India, the server of the Internet Service Provider is accessed from the home on telephone line. PPP is the set of rules which specifies how the data will be communicated over telephone line from your computer when the connection with your ISP has been established. This protocol is used in conjunction with Serial Line Internet Protocol (SLIP). This protocol is used when the communication is done over a serial transmission line like telephone line. The protocol allows the user to use GUI based web browsers like Netscape and MS Internet

Explorer. Internet Service provider uses the PPP and SLIP account to view graphics on the internet. These accounts assign a IP address to your computer when a connection is established.

6.8 SERVICES ON THE INTERNET

Nowadays the Internet is being used for multiple purposes. Following are popular services being offered by the Internet.

- E-mail
- Job hunting
- Marketing/Shopping
- Reading books/journals
- Accessing Libraries
- Accessing the information about admission to various universities
- Games and puzzles
- Reading newspapers, magazines
- Movie clips
- Music, audio
- National, international news

You may use it for sending and receiving mail, for finding a job which matches your profile, for sale/purchase of items, movies, chat, magazines, game etc. In the figure 6.2 and figure 6.3, the popular web site www.dice.com and www. Jobserve.com are shown. These are the site popular for the IT jobs in USA and Europe respectively. You may find out a list of jobs upon entering suitable keyword in the search box.

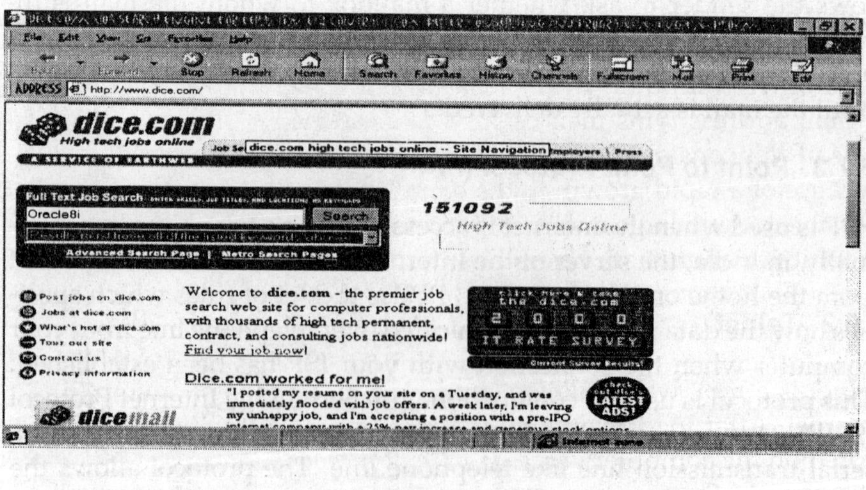

Fig. 6.2

Fig. 6.3

6.9 POPULAR INTERNET SERVICES

6.9.1 E-mail

E-Mail is probably the most important facility on internet; you may transfer the letter, text, images etc. over the network by electronic mail. E-Mail are normally delivered almost immediately to the recipient. E-Mail is now one of the popular medium of communication. This medium is being used to send and receive letters/notes or drafts, let it be personal or business. One of the main advantages of this medium is that these mails are delivered almost instantly. Technically, E-Mail is the way of sending documents in electronic form from one computer to another computer. Every recipient of the E-Mail must have an E-Mail address. This mail address is used to send the mail. Earlier E-Mail was considered good for sending and receiving short mails but because of a rapid growth in the bandwidth of the channel, it is now possible to send large mail with attachments which may have images, graphics or animation, voices etc.

6.9.2 Telnet

Telnet is a tool, which allows you to log on to any computer on the Internet. After log in you may use the software and other programs stored on the computer you logged in. By telnet you can use the computer you had logged in, as if you have full control of that computer. But one should not be confused that Telnet can connect him to any computer on the Internet, as to use Telnet you should have access permission usually in the form of the account and password. Telnet facility is normally used to search an information archive such as public Library or public database. You can also use Internet facility to log on to your machine if you are out of city to read or send your mails.

Telnet is very useful in accessing various services, which are not available on the host computer. For example, if you want to use the GUI developed by any other user then you may log on to remote computer using Telnet and run the desired program and may see the results on your computer. Whenever any person develops any utility or service on his host computer, Telnet may be used to access those service or programs from your computer. Telnet is very similar to the utility called rlogin (Remote Login). It is also called emulation protocol as once the connection between the host computer and remote computer is established, the host computer's commands are executed on the remote computers and results are displayed on the host computer. Following command at prompt may open Telnet session.

> Telnet 144.16.202.14

6.9.3 FTP (File Transfer Protocol)

FTP is an utility for transfer of files from one computer to another. FTP stands for File Transfer Protocol which means the method of transferring files from remote host computer to your computer. On Internet there are thousands of FTP sites from which you may transfer the files to your computer. The word file is used to include all kinds of digital document such as images, text drawing, audio music video files or any software. Any thing which can be stored on the computer may be copied to another destination or vice versa with FTP. Many computers on the Internet have FTP archives, which contain public access file, you may download those files using FTP.

6.9.4 Usenet

Usenet is the international meeting where people gather to meet and discuss on different subjects ranging from business, academics, sport, music, tourism, games etc. Usenet has grown up from where two students wanted to exchange messages in more conventional way. Now there are million of people worldwide talking in thousand of Usenet new groups. The Usenet is a global bulletin board service that uses

Internet as an access point. It is very similar to the Bulletin Board System (BBS) that serves the local users using direct dial up to internet service providers. The Usenet is related with the news groups. The News Group has actually nothing to do with the news but they work as bulletin boards. The person may put the notice, views etc on some topic which may be seen by all the users of news groups. Each message from the users appearing on the Usenet is called article. Each article contains a header just like an E-mail. To read and post the articles, the Usenet news servers are required. The local Internet Service Provider makes available this server.

6.9.5 Gopher

Gopher is a service in the Internet, which allows user to connect resources such as file or text. It is same as World Wide Web but the basic difference is that information is stored in a hierarchical way. Gopher uses internet resources efficiently and allows internet user to locate the information contained in the file. Gopher service is faster in the sense that it contains listing in indexed manner.

The difference between the web browsing and visiting a Gopher space is that in the web browsing, you see thc graphical pictures/text etc. while a Gopher presents you a menu. The web pages are full of hyper text, clicking on to them you may navigate from one pool of resources to another. In Gopher service, the menu is presented before you. This menu is a clickable item and clicking onto them you may go to another menu or the information will be presented in the from of text. To use the Gopher service, you have to use Gopher Protocol. The Gopher service may be accessed by specifying URL as stated below,

Gopher :// gopher.kent.edu

The URL of the site has to access using Gopher protocol like you use Hyper text transfer protocol (http) to access normal web pages.

6.9.6 Archie

Archie is a simple service on the Internet that searches for FTP Archie on the Internet. Archie is a great tool for finding files when part or all the name or the file. Thus Archie is a sort of search program that look through different anonymous FTP sites. Files and other information may be downloaded through FTP tool. Archie is now becoming obsolete as there are many other ways to search FTP sites and tools for file transfers. Archie indexes file names that are available on public FTP servers. If you search for a particular file, then you will be presented a list of FTP sites which contains that file. If the name of the file is not known, Archie will probably not be a choice for the user. Since many of the user friendly softwares are available today which make a quick search for the file. It is the main reason for Archie for loosing users' interest.

6.9.7 Veronica

Veronica is also a search tool like Gopher. The user performs keyword search of Gopher space. The result of search is presented on user's screen as a menu with items leading to more specific information. Veronica is accessed through a gopher server just like gopher itself. Veronica searches for a string or text in the Gopher space only. Once the item is found or searched then a menu is presented before the user to select the item. Here it is important to note that World Wide Web has a number of search engines with which you may search for an item or site on World Wide Web but Gopher space offers only one search engine. The veronica servers may be found at different sites but in fact they execute only one software for search, thus there is no reason to search again on different server. If the search is unsuccessful at one server it will again be unsuccessful at another server.

6.9.8 WWW (World Wide Web)

World Wide Web is one of the most popular servers on the internet. It can be thought of a network of millions of servers, hosts and users. Operations of the web are based on the type text. Hypertext is similar to normal text but has link to another text or page or information content. Hypermedia is an advanced version of hypertext document as it contains sound, image or video apart from text. All the documents on word wide web is accessed through a standard or protocol. This protocol is HTTP (Hype text transfer protocol). Using HTTP you may transfer the hypertext document from host to your computer.

6.10 ISDN (INTEGRATED SERVICE DIGITAL NETWORK)

6.10.1 Introduction

Integrated Service Digital Network is the most powerful tool for various services such as voice, images, video and multimedia data communication over the telephone network. ISDN may be viewed as logical extension to the digitalization of telephone network and has become very common in the western countries. In India too, the various mail network service providers as well as DOT, VSNL and MTNL are providing this service to users. In ISDN, the voice, image, video and multimedia data is transmitted over the telephone line in digital form.

The ISDN works in the following modes.

1. BRI (Basic Rate Interface)
2. PRI (Primary Rate Interface)

User can opt for a BRI connection from local ISP or user can opt for PRI connection in BRI also called, 2B+D, two 64 kbps channel available to the user. The other, PRI is used for ISDN compatible EPABX etc. with the induction of state of the art digital technology in the telecom network in India, these services are being offered by new technology exchanges laid by DOT or MTNL. The ISDN connection is provided at the user's premises located within permissible distance for digital exchange.

6.10.2 Difference in ISDN Line and Analog Telephone Line

In the normal telephone line, the user can make a voice call and the voice data is transmitted in analog form, which is normally vulnerable to the distortions in the voice. In ISDN, the multimedia data i.e. voice data or image graphics is transmitted over the telephone lines in digital form. In ISDN the user may establish two independent calls to other user over the telephone pair of existing telephone line. These simultaneous calls can be of any type image, data or voice. In normal telephony one call is possible at one time. ISDN users may also make a call to other analog telephone subscribers.

6.10.3 Services Offered by ISDN

Mainly following four services are offered by ISDN are dial up basis between any two ISDN subscriber.

- High speed data transmissions at 64 kbps.
- High quality voice transmission at 64 kbps.
- Desk top video conferency using a single ISDN line at 128 kbps (two B channel)
- High quality conferency on dial up basis between any two ISDN user by three ISDN lines (3*128)= 384 kbps.

The advantage of video conferencing is that user may talk to each other at distant places thus saving time and money. This is done by transmission of voice and video images of both user as well as by transmitting images, drawing, text or still produces documents at a high speed. Data files on the PC may also be transmitted at a very high speed of 64 kbps.

6.10.4 ISDN Terminals

Normally when an user wants a ISDN connection at its own premises, DOT OR MTNL provide a NT (Networking Terminal) equipment. The user may also procure the terminal from the open market. The telephone line from electronic exchange is terminated at on NT Box up to 8 ISDN terminal equipment may be terminated to NT Box. This ISDN terminal may be a ISDN telephone set, videophone, fax, personal computer (PC), video conferencing equipment. These equipment must be compatible to ISDN and it is a mandatory requirement to procure a DOT/MTNL certified equipment. Details of the equipment are as follows.

➢ Normal ISDN Phone

It is the ISDN phone in most simple form and contains hand set phone unit and converts the user's voice into digital signal, which may be carried over ISDN line to destination.

➢ Advance ISDN Phone

Advance ISDN phone, in addition to normal ISDN phone the additional keys and functions are as follows.

➢ Display

The ISDN phone contains a Liquid Crystal Display (LCD). The user may dial number, which are displayed on LCD. The calling takes place when button (digit) is pressed. The calling takes when calling user lifts the handset after dialing or calling. In this calling, a recipient of call may see the number of calling user.

➢ Logging

Logging facility provides automatic storing of numbers dialed when the call could not be answered. The calling number may be recalled from the log.

➢ Terminal Adopter

Devices such as 44 fax, answering machine, push button telephone, cordless phone may be connected to ISDN line through a terminal adapter. Any PC with RS232C port (serial port) can be connected to ISDN line. In such case data communication may take place in 9600 kbps. In this communication PC does not require modem.

6.10.5 Video Conferencing

Video conferencing is a process of participation of various users where video and audio from one user to another is sent. The participant on video chat may see and talk to each other.

The video conferencing equipment requires a computer, color monitor, digital camera and other control units. This equipment is connected to telephone network using three ISDN lines. The similar equipment is also required at the other end. The conferencing is established by dial up through network. Moving images are communicated from one point to another. During conversation, it is also possible to send graph, report diagram and still picture through video conferencing equipment. Other control equipment and software help the user to focus zoom on the participant conferencing. The equipment from the Picture Tel is one of the popular options for video conferencing.

6.10.6 Video Phone

This is a subset of video conferencing equipment in video telephony, a user may dial up to another user and the recipient also requires the same unit. The equipment consists of compact screen and camera. This requires only one ISDN line and the moving images are sent at 128 kbps (2B) channel. Videophone could be made available as an add on facility to Personal Computer.

6.11 HOW TO SET UP ISDN CYBER CAFE

In recent days, you may see various cyber cafes at every corner, market and may be at your doorstep. These café are being utilized for sending and receiving mail, video telephony, web browsing, job hunting, finding a course of your choice at university, internet chat and for other internet application. ISDN will allow you to your data digitally on fax, ISDN voice phone and data transfer. DOT, government of India is providing ISDN connection to subscriber in all major cities of India. If you wish to get an ISDN connection, you should contact either DOT or MTNL office. Approximate cost of establishment and rental charges are as follows,

1. **Installation charges**
   Wiring up to network terminal (NT), ISDN handset, TA, fax terminal, ISDN PC card costs approximately Rs. 10,000/=. This expenditure has be borne by the user.
2. **Access charges**

(a) Rental for BRA	Rs. 1000/=
(b) Usage charges for 64 kbps circuit : (Unrestricted)	same as normal tariffs but minimum charges are Rs 5000/=

The actual charges are calculated on the basis of number of calls. These rates are subject to ISDN server provides at your city and on rates as and when calculated by DOT or MTNL.

6.12 HOW TO CHOOSE INTERNET SERVICE PROVIDER

The internet service provider is abbreviated as ISP. They were earlier known also named as internet account provider or internet providers. In India, last few years has intended a rapid growth in the number of ISP and service they are providing. Some of ISPs are VSNL, DOT, MTNL, and Satyam on line and so on. It is not uncommon to have two or more than two internet service providers in your city.

6.12.1 Requirement for Internet Access

Now it is easy to get a connection in India if you can choose a right ISP in your city. To get an access to the internet following are mandatory.

1. A legal account with your local ISP.
2. A computer (486 or above) with required software to access internet.
   - Intel 486 or higher processor
   - Windows 95/98
   - 16 MB RAM
   - 70 MB of disk space (minimum)
   - CD ROM drive
   - Color monitor (preferred)
   - Sound card and speaker (preferred)
3. A Modem (14.4 kbps or above)
4. A telephone connection

Important tips while choosing your local ISP

6.12.2 Cost

Cost of accessing internet is one of the prime factors which should be looked for while selecting an ISP. Generally, different ISP's offer different schemes and they charge Rs. 500-10000 for providing an internet access for hours ranging from 10 hours to 500 hours. This time indicates the maximum number of hours you may use various Internet services through your ISP. There are ISPs, who provide unlimited internet access to you for a fixed duration ranging from one to twelve months at fixed charge. It would be advisable to estimate your internet access hours and decide among the various options by ISP. You should also look for various ISP from time to time.

6.12.3 Connectivity

To get a good and sustainable connectivity of your computer to the ISP, over telephone line is also a prime factor. It is very common that you are disconnected from your ISP. It could have two reasons, one is problem with your telephone or disturbances over your telephone problem at your server of ISP. Before you finalize your ISP you should also enquire about the connectivity from your friends and dear ones who are regularly using internet service.

6.12.4 Modem and Dial up Regions

Modem (modulator/demodulator) is a device by which you may connect your computer to ISP over telephone line. Since our telephone line uses analog communication thus computer or digital data from your computer cannot be transferred over telephone line. Modem is a device, which converts analog data to digital data and vice versa.

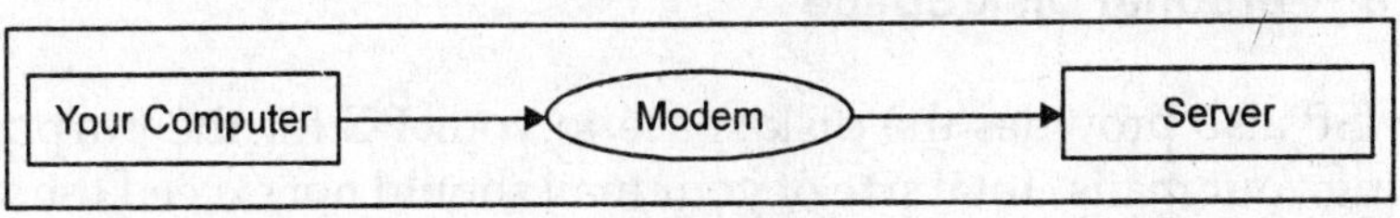

Fig. 6.4

A modem translates the digital data from your computer to analog data and transmits over telephone line. The modems are available in various ratings in the range of 14.4 KBPS to 33.6Kbps and 56 KBPS. To get a faster rate you should get fastest modem subjected to the condition it is suppressed by your ISP. The rating KBPS stands for Kilobytes per second. Thus a 33.6 KBPS modem is capable to transferring 33600 bytes per second.

6.12.5 External and Internal Modem

External modem is a small device which can be connected/installed to your PC easily. GVC and Motorola manufacture modems which are considered to be good and are available in the range of Rs 2000 to Rs 5000. Internet modem comes along with your motherboard and lies under the cabinet of your computer. These modems are cheaper than external modems. Installation of internal modem may be little complex than external modem. If you wish to use your modem on other computer too than external modem is the right choice.

6.12.6 Dial up Region

If you are a frequent traveller across the country/region with your own laptop then you should check for whether your ISP provides the facility for getting an internal access with your account at other cities of the country without charging any additional amount. If an ISP allows you to have an access to your account while yourself on tour then you may think choosing this ISP for your internet service.

6.12.7 Technical Service Offered by ISP

Many ISPs provide a help desk for the benefit for user. In case of any technical trouble you may dial a specific number provided by your ISP. In most of the cases, these systems are IVRS (inter radio voice response system) where you will be asked by computer to press required key on your telephone set. Or you may ask a person for your specific query. Before choosing an ISP you should also enquire about the technical support service of the ISP's available in your city.

6.12.8 Personal Disk Space

Your ISP also provides the disk space to your PC for the purpose of keeping your mails. Total size of your mail should not exceed the space reserved for you in the range of 1MB to 10MB depending on the internet service providers. You should also estimate the size of your mail to be kept in mail account.

6.13 NATURE OF INTERNET ACCOUNTS

At presently VSNL is dominating the internet accesses in India through GIAS (Gateway internet access service) Similarly the DOT (Department of Telecom) provides this service through DOT internet access service. VSNL and DOT primarily provides following types of account for user to internet access.

1. Shell account
2. TCP/IP account

These two services are offered on normal dial up telephone lines available at your work or home. To get an access to either of account, your computer will dial a number through your modem and within 30 sec – 1 min, you will get an massage on your screen about the connection status

➢ Shell account

Using a dial up access, the user may be connected to ISP server with shell account. It is a UNIX based account on an ISP's server. In shell account the user is able to get almost all the services of Internet but limitation of this account is that user cannot get graphics etc. on the screen. Web browser like Nestcable, Navigators or MS internet explorer cannot be used for this account. You will receive only text with shell account thus it imposes restrictions on the service to be offered by Internet. This account is also known as text account, earlier this account was available especially to the students for the sole purpose of sending and receiving text based mails.

➢ TCP /IP account

TCP/IP account is also an option before user which can access through dial up. User can use transmission control protocol (TCP) and internet protocol (IP) to connect to host system and access it. In this mode an user will be able to use graphical web browser like MS internet Explorer and Netscape Navigator. You can also view moving picture; graphics animated design and may hear music or sound. Shell account also imposes restriction on sending and running mail through the account, whose size is limited. But in TCP/IP account, after using web browsers like MS Internet Explorer/Netscape Navigator you may view and attach graphic/animated design. While working on TCP/IP account you can use easily the free E-mail service at yahoo, hotmail, rediffmail and other sites to send and receive the mail to/from your computer.

6.14 BROWSING THE WEB/NET SURFING

Web browsing or Net surfing is the process of viewing and visiting the millions of the web sites present on the web. These web sites may belong to the university college, company, industry, job site, cooking and recipe, fashion, movie, magazines and newspaper etc. There are presence of million of web site on the web. Each web site has unique URL popularly called web site address. The syntax is as below:

WWW. Domain name.Domain suffix
or
http:// www. Domain name. Domain suffix

Domain name specifies the name of site and domain suffix indicates nature of the site. Some of the popular web site addresses are:

- http:// www.timesofindia.com
- http:// www.hot mail.com
- http:// www. Alumni.net
- http:// www.mit.edu
- http:// www.anu.edu.au.
- http:// www.ietlucknow.edu

Consider the first case i.e. http:// www.timesofindia.com, here the domain name or name of website is timesofindia which is registered as commercial (.com)site. This site is accessed through www or world wide web. Http (hyper text transfer protocol) indicates that view and accessing the site using http. Following is the list of some widely used domain suffixes.

- .org organization
- .com commercial
- .edu education
- .gov government
- .mil military
- .net large network
- .ac academic Community

6.15 HOW TO USE WEB BROWSER

Before you type the web site address or URL, you should start internet explorer or you may double click the MS Internet Explorer as follows:

Go to start → program → Internet Explorer
or
Double click the MS Internet Explorer icon on your window desktop you will then be presented by the following screen

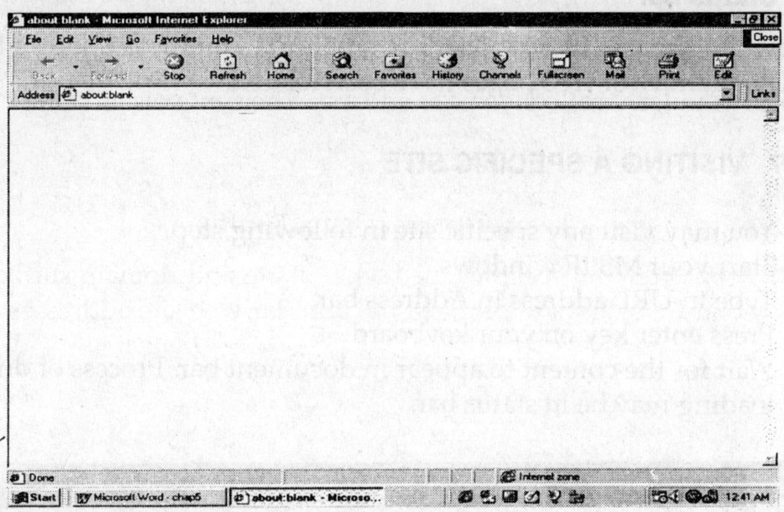

Fig. 6.5

6.16 KNOWING YOUR MS INTERNET EXPLORER

➢ Title bar

It displays the title of the web page, you are viewing currently. At the right side would get the minimize, maximize, and close buttons.

➢ Menu bar

Menu bar contains menu items file, edit, view, go, favourites and help. These are pulldown menu.

➢ Tool bar

This contains various graphical buttons, which are widely used for navigation. The bar is as follows.

➢ Address bar

Contains the address, which has been provided by you. It is a pull down text area containing the history of website accessed by you. You may also pull down and select the website address if you have already visited the site in part.

➢ Document Area

This is the target area and contains the text, graphic, animator etc. for the site you are visiting.

➢ Status bar

Show the process of downloading a page. It graphically shows how much quantity of web pages have been loaded.

6.17 VISITING A SPECIFIC SITE

- You may visit any specific site in following step.
- Start your MS IE windows.
- Type in URL address in Address bar.
- Press enter key on your keyboard.
- Wait for the content to appear in document bar. Process of downloading may be in status bar.

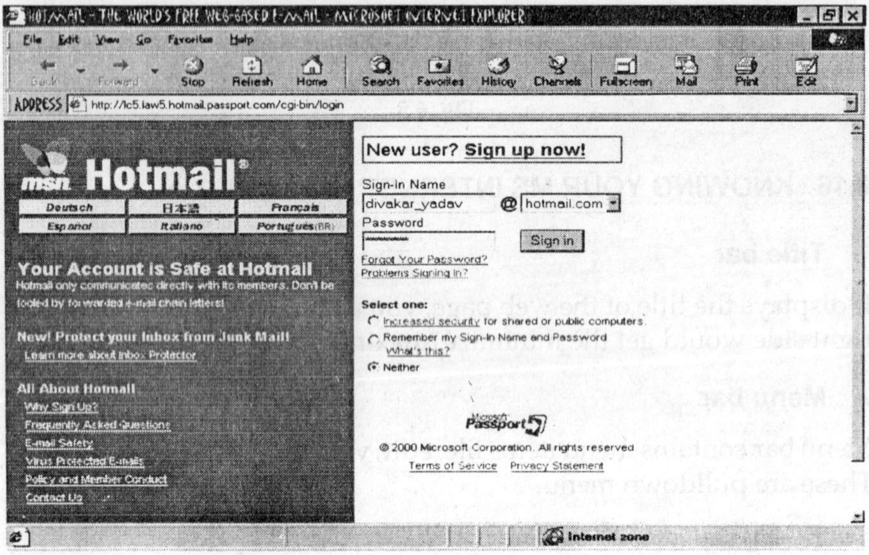

Fig. 6.6

6.18 HOW TO FIND A SITE OF YOUR INTEREST/SEARCH ENGINES

It is usually a great problem for the user to find the appropriate site or site of his/her interest. The solution to this problem is to use the search engine. The search engines are actually web sites and contain the link to the million of web pages. All you have to do is to type in the URL of the search engine and type in the keyword for the document you are searching. The method of putting the keyword varies slightly according to the search engine. After putting the key word in the dialog base for search, when you press the button "search", it will give you a list of hypertext documents which contain the keyword you have entered. Next step is to open those pages by drawing the hypertext and you can get the exact content of that document.

Some of the popular search engines are as follows.

- www.Lycos.com
- www.Allavista.com
- www.Hotbot.com
- www.yahoo.com
- www.webcrawler.com
- www.excite.com

The screen for the first page of search engine yahoo is shown in figure 6.7. You may enter the search string in the text box and start search by pressing search with the mouse.

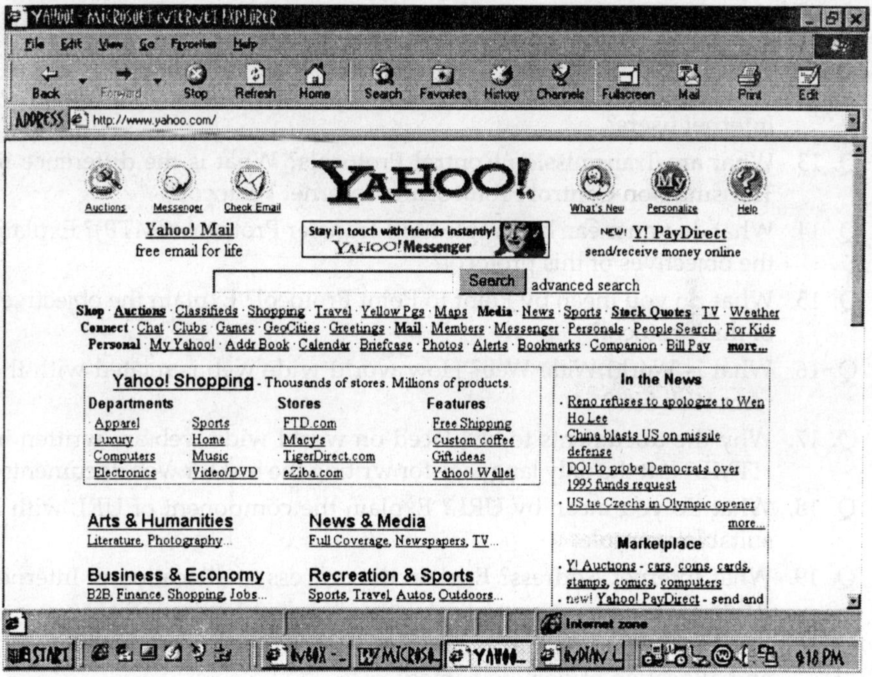

Fig. 6.7

SELECT EXERCISES

Q. 1. Explain with the reasons why the number of computer/computer network added to Internet at an exponential rate.

Q. 2. Explain how E-mails are important? How they are sent?

Q. 3. Explain the various services that are available on internet.

Q. 4. Give full details about ISDN, DOT, VSNL, and MTNL. Give details how ISDN cyber café is established?

Q. 5. Who governs Internet? List various societies who are responsible for laying the guidelines for Internet users.

Q. 6. Why an E-Mail is considered as most important service offered by Internet. Comment on whether an E-Mail is secured?

Q. 7. What do you mean by Local Area Network (LAN)? How it is different from Metropolitan Area Network (MAN)? Explain with a suitable examples.

Q. 8. Give details how the same message through E-mail can be sent to more than one person at a time?

Q. 9. Justify the statement. "Internet is a decentralized network of million of computers".

Q. 10. What are attachment file? Explain the conditions when attachment files are sent. How the attachments are downloaded at recipient end?

Q. 11. Explain the process of E-Mail delivery system. How the mails are delivered to the recipients?

Q. 12. What do you mean by TCP/IP? Why TCP/IP is so important for Internet users?

Q. 13. What are Transmission Control Protocols? What is the difference in Transmission Control Protocol and Internet Protocol?

Q. 14. What do you mean by Simple Mail Transfer Protocol (SMTP)? Explain the objectives of this protocol?

Q. 15. What do you mean by Point to Point Protocol? Explain the objectives of this protocol?

Q. 16. What is World Wide Web? How world wide web is related with the term Web Site?

Q. 17. Why the documents to be placed on world wide web are written in HTML? Is it the only language for writing the text for web documents?

Q. 18. What do you mean by URL? Explain the component of URL with a suitable example.

Q. 19. What Internet Address? Explain the process of allocation of Internet Addressees.

Q. 20. What is domain name? Name the society which governs the usage and allocation of domain names?

Q. 21. What IP address? How are they different from URL? Does there exist one to one correspondence among them?

Q. 22. What are Free E-Mail Service Providers on Web? What are the possible reasons for providing the free servive to the users?

Q. 23. What is address book? How the address book is used ?

Q. 24. How the mails are composed? How will you reply to a mail, you have received?

Q. 25. What are signatures? How will you send the signature with the E-Mail.

Q. 26. List few popular free E-Mail providers on the Web.

Q. 27. Explain the process of opening an E-Mail account on a Web based E-Mail service?

Q. 28. What are the possible advantages of opening a mail account on Web based E-Mail service provider?

Q. 29. What do you mean by Telnet? How a Telnet session is started? Under what circumstances the Telnet is used?

Q. 30. What are Netiquette? List any five important netiquette which you consider important.

Q. 31. Give configuration of a computer that is essential for accessing an Internet?

Q. 32. What are modems. Distinguish between internal and external modem?

Q. 33. Give complete detail about VSNL and also enlist what are services provided by VSNL.

Q. 34. What are search engines? What for the search engines are used? List any two popular search engines.

Q. 35. What do you mean by File Transfer Protocol (FTP)? What are FTP sites? Under what circumstances the FTP is desirable to be used?

Q. 36. Give configuration of a computer that is essential for accessing Internet?

Q. 37. Give complete details about VSNL and also enlist the services provided by VSNL.

Q. 38. What is meant by Browsing the WEB or NET surfing, and how it is performed?

Q. 39. Give details about the search engine and how they are accessed?

Q. 40. What are E-Mails? and How they are sent?

Q. 41. What is Network? What are the differences between LAN, MAN and WAN?

Q. 42. What do you mean by Internet? Give a brief account of growth of Internet.

Q. 43. Give the Syntax of E-Mail address?

Q. 44. What is World Wide Web?

Q. 45. What do you mean by FTP service? Under what circumstances you would like to use FTP?

Q. 46. Explain the Telnet service in brief? What are the major advantage of this service?

Q. 47. What is USENET? Explain in brief.

Q. 48. What are the advantages of ISDN over normal telephone line?

Q. 49. How would you get ISDN connection to your office or home? Give details of expected expenditure.

Q. 50. What is PRI? How it is different than BRI? What advantages you would get if you opt for PRI while applying for ISDN?

Q. 51. What do you mean by the term Video Conferencing? Is there any difference between Video Telephony and Video Conferencing?

Q. 52. What is the role of Internet Service Provider? List any five popular ISPs in your city.

Q. 53. What do you mean by Dial Up region?

Q. 54. What are the differences between the TCP/IP and shell account offered by DOT?

Q. 55. Explain the various components of your Web Browser?

Q. 56. What are Search Engines? How will you search for a good university in US for admission to PG course?

Q. 57. What do mean by URL? How will you visit a specific site?

7 Sending and Receiving E-Mails

7.0 INTRODUCTION

In this chapter, we will discuss the utilities like Outlook Express to manage mails in Windows, PINE and ELM for managing mails in UNIX. Electronic Mail, popularly known as E-Mail has become an important way of communication in this decade. The conventional definition of literacy is now changing. Earlier, a person who was able to express his feelings in writing was known as literate but in present circumstances, a person who cannot express his views in this electronic medium, specially a person who cannot communicate using E-Mail is called illiterate. E-Mail is now the most popular medium of communication. This medium is being used to send and receive letters /notes or drafts, let it be personal or business. One of the main advantages of this medium is that these mails are delivered almost instantly. Technically, E-Mail is the way of sending documents in electronic form from one computer to another computer. Every recipient of the E-Mail must have an E-Mail address. This mail address is used to send the mail. Earlier E-Mail was considered good for sending and receiving short mails but because of a rapid growth in the bandwidth of the channel, it is now possible to send large mails with attachment which may have images, graphics or animation, voices etc.

7.1 HOW E-MAILS ARE SENT?

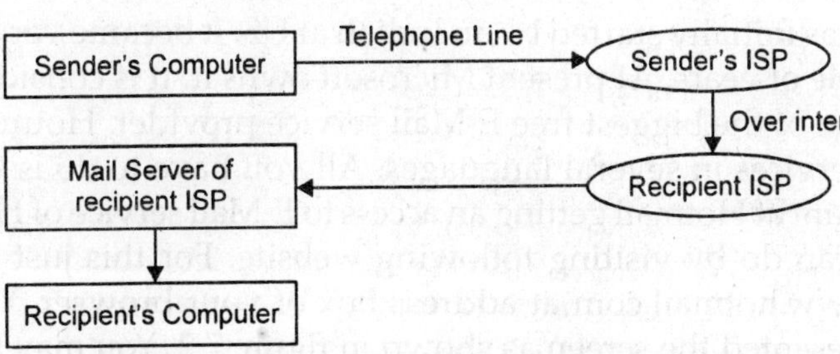

Fig 7.1 Delivery of E-MAIL

Sending and receiving an E-Mail is very simple and this requires a few clicks of mouse. Any person who wishes to use this medium for communication need not know the rigorous details of the computer system.

Figure 7.1 shows the process of sending and receiving E-Mail. Sender has to specify the mail address of every recipient of mail. Before sending a mail, the sender must connect to the local ISP (Internet Service Provider) server (e.g. Satyamonline, Avadhonline, DOT, MTNL etc). When a sender sends the mail, it first gets converted into the analog message by modem and delivered to local ISP server. It then further goes to the recipient ISP and stored in the mail server of recipient's (recipient mail box) ISP. The recipient may receive the mail in its own computer when it connects to its ISP. It is essential to write the correct mail address of the recipient otherwise it will not be delivered to the recipient. Whenever a sender enters incorrect mail address of recipient or if the mail is not delivered to recipient's mail box because of other reasons, in such cases the sender receives the message about non-delivery of the mail. In most of the cases, after sending a mail, the user is informed that his mail has been sent.

7.2 SENDING A MAIL

You may open your mail account with your local internet service provider at the same time you may also open a mail account with free E-mail service providers e.g. Hotmail, Indiatimes.com, rocketmail, yahoo, sify, lycos, rediffmail etc. Advantage of keeping account on global free E-mail service provider like hotmail or yahoo is that these accounts may be accessed by browsing from any place in the world. In the case of dependence on local ISP, it might be little cumbersome as well as costly to connect to your local ISP.

7.2.1 How to Get E-Mail Address at Hotmail?

Hotmail was initially started by an Indian at US. It became very popular in couple of years. At present Microsoft owns it. It is considered as world's one of the biggest free E-Mail service provider. Hotmail provides its services in several languages. All you have to do is to open up an account at Hotmail getting an access to E-Mail service of Hotmail. This you can do by visiting following website. For this just type in http:// www.hotmail.com at address box of your browser. You will then be presented the screen as shown in figure 7.2. You may sign up by clicking at sign up if you are a new user. After this procedure you will get an E-mail address and a password to have an access to your mail box.

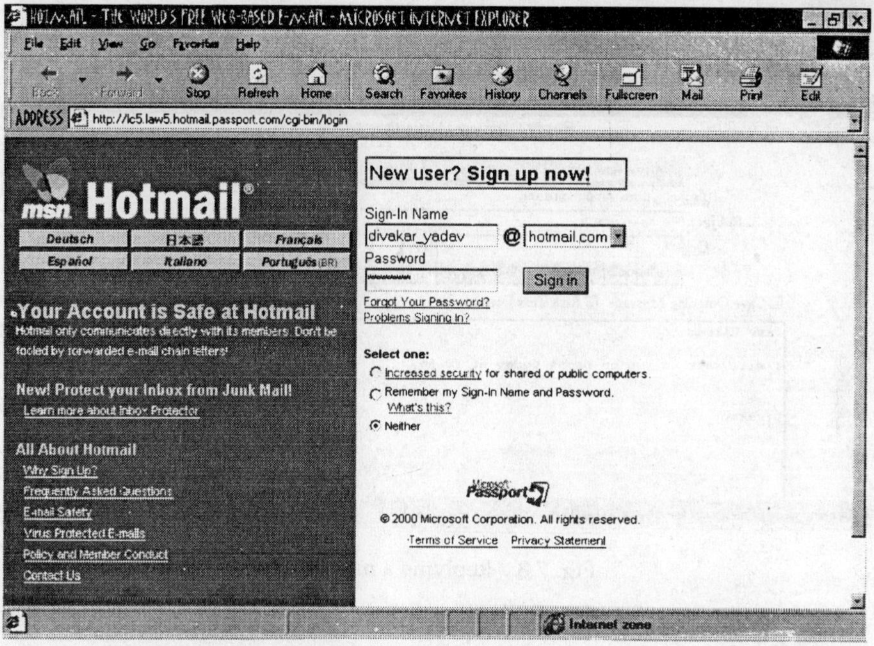

Fig. 7.2 Snap shot of Hotmail, a free E-mail service provider

7.2.2 How to Manage Mails at Hotmail

You may compose the mail, reply and receive a mail, make folders, keep track of addresses on Hotmail. Before sending a new mail, you should compose the mail by clicking compose. After composing the mail, you may send the mail after clicking send. You may also specify the address of all recipients to whom you want to send a copy of this message. Similarly, you may check the spelling, save the draft of out going mail or you may use the dictionary. To send the file attachment to the mail, you have to click on attachment to attach the file you want to send along with the mail. On this you will be presented the screen as shown in figure 7.4. Now you may select the file of your choice from the hard disk or floppy by specifying the drive and file name. It may take few minutes to upload the file to get it attached to mail. If you have received an attachment with the mail, you may click on the attachment to download the file. This process may take few minutes or some more time depending upon the size of file and the band width you are enjoying.

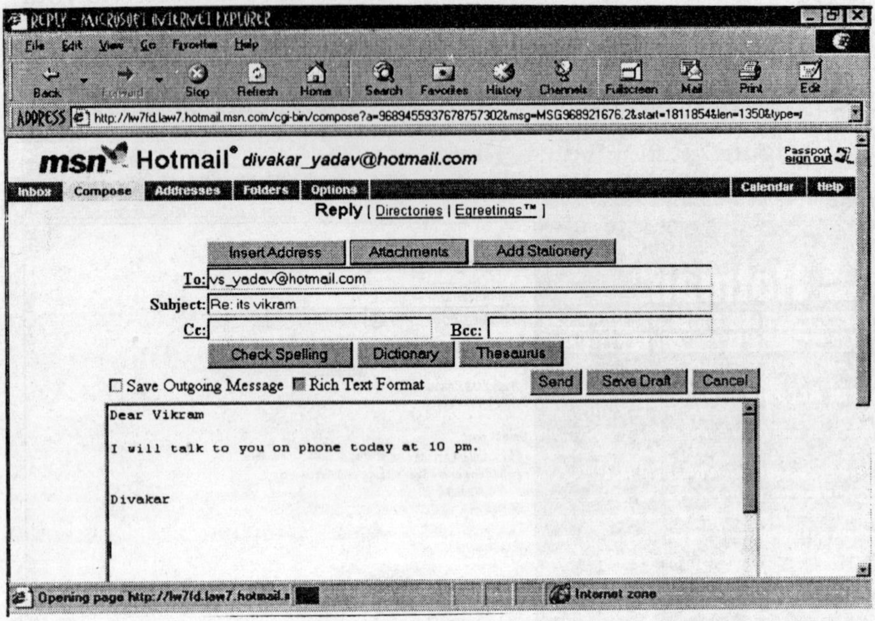

Fig. 7.3 Replying a message

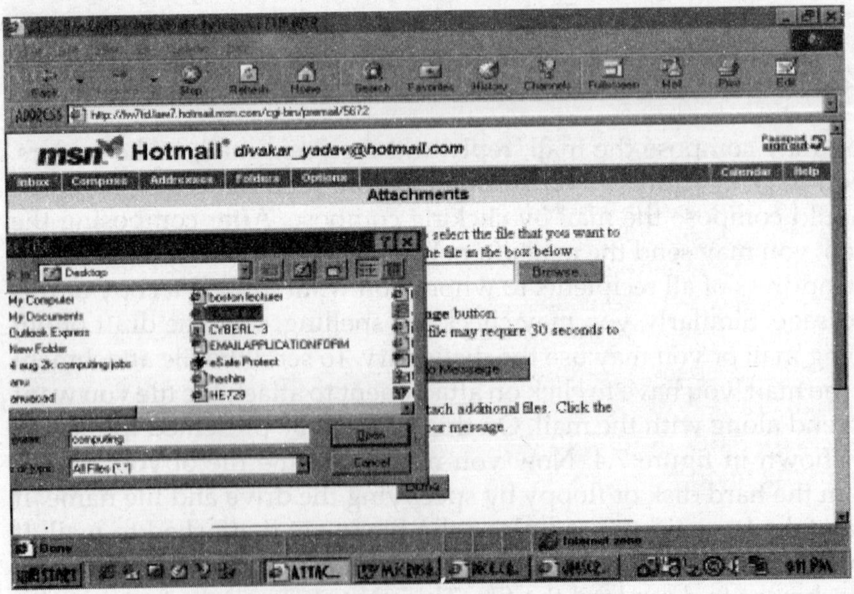

Fig. 7.4 File Attachment to a Mail

7.3 WORKING WITH OUTLOOK EXPRESS

Outlook Express helps you to send and receive E-mails. This keeps the mail items into various folders, namely, Inbox, Outbox, Sent items, Deleted Items and Drafts. It is an user friendly tool for managing your mails. Figure 7.5 shows the Outlook Express.

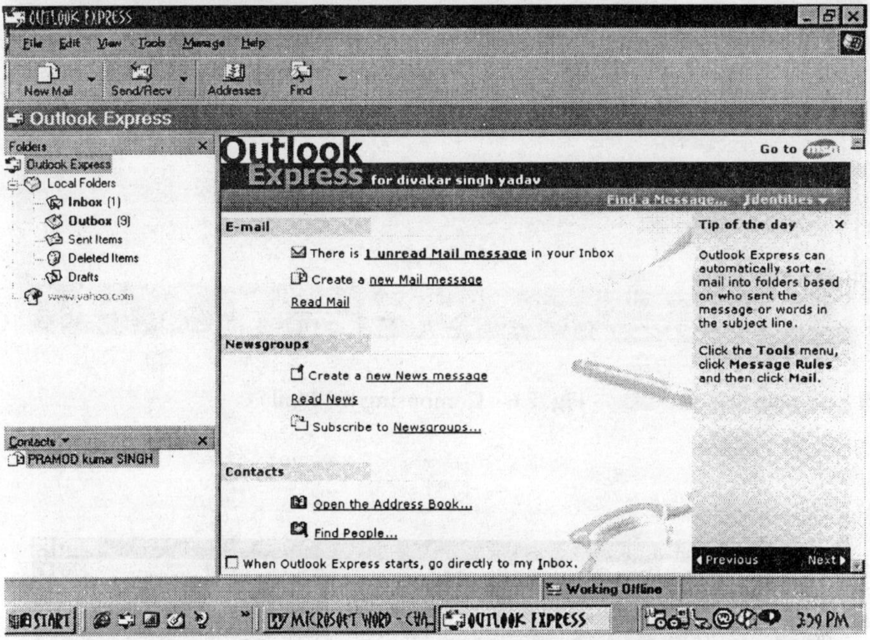

Fig. 7.5 Outlook Express

7.3.1 Composing a Mail

To compose a mail click on, new mail icon at standard tool bar. You will get new screen as shown in the figure 7.6. You may then type recipient's E-mail address, subject of the E-mail and finally type the message in space as shown in the same figure. You should enter the E-mail address of all the recipients whom you want to send a copy of the mail. After putting in the mail text, you may click on the send to send the mail.

7.3.2 Attachment to Mail

You may send the file of your choice as a attachment along with the mail. All you have to do, is to click attach icon on the tool bar. By this process you may attach a file of your interest and send it with the mail as shown in the figure 7.6.

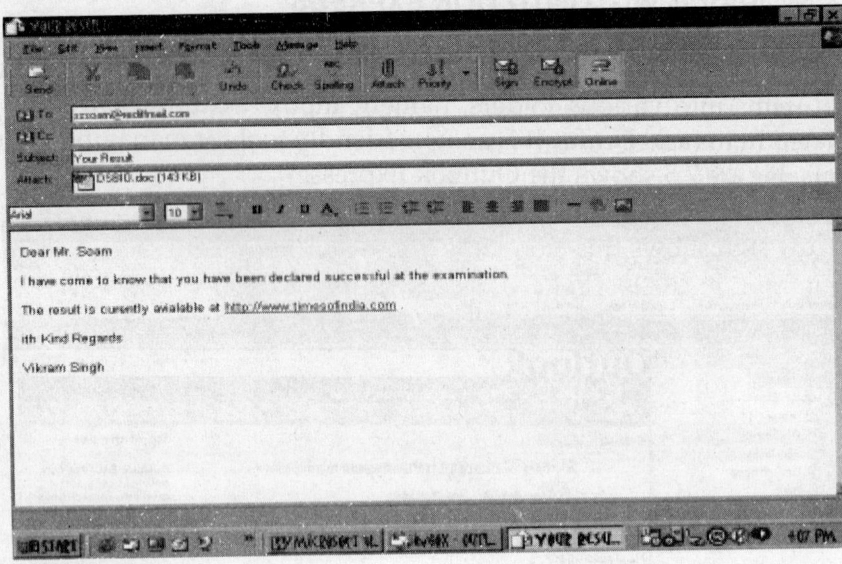

Fig. 7.6 Composing the Mail

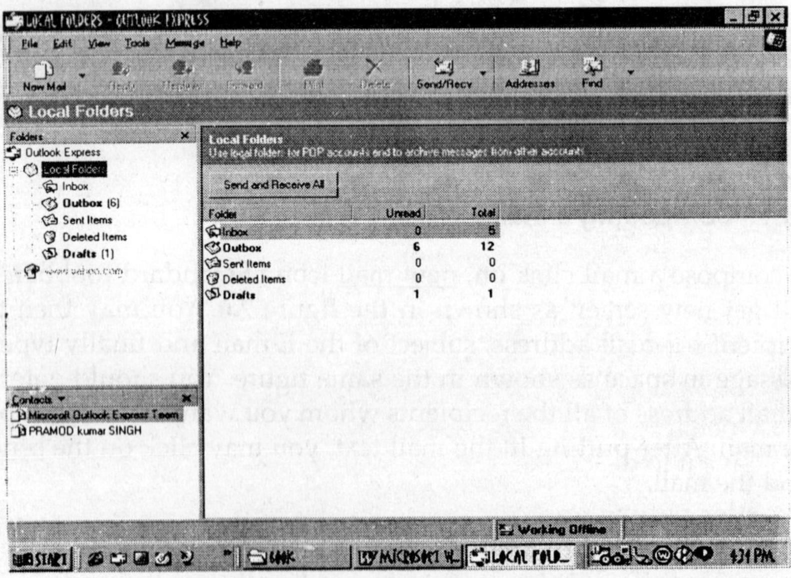

Fig. 7.7 Sending and receiving all mails

7.3.3 Opening the Attachments

You may also receive the attachments sent to you by your friends with the mail. The attachment can be opened before saving it to your disk or you may choose to directly save it to your disk. For viewing the attached files, go to your INBOX and select the mail. Every mail that contains the attached file displays an icon at the lower half of the screen. Arrow sign shows this icon in the following figure 7.8.

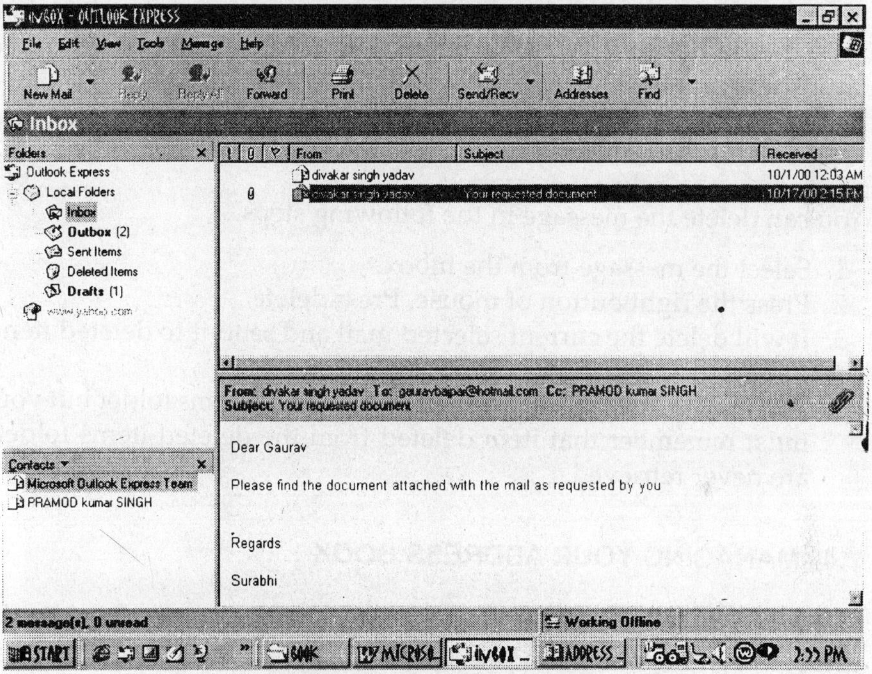

Fig. 7.8 Opening the attachment

You should click to this icon to view the attachment. This will open a dialogue box and will ask you to enter one of the following choices.

1. Open it
2. Save it to disk.

After putting appropriate choice in the dialogue box, you may choose to open the attached file or opt to save it to the disk. If you opt for opening the file, windows will attempt to open the file using the program most suitable for it. If you opt for saving it to your disk then it will ask you to specify the location/path on the disk.

7.3.4 Forwarding a Mail

You can also pass the mail you have received to someone else. This process is called forwarding the mail. This can be done in following two ways.

1. Select the mail to view it. Click forward message icon on the outlook express tool bar.
2. Go to compose and then select forward.

Now you may enter the recipient's address in the address box and send the mail. It is also possible to put your comment at the same time with the contents of the mail forwarded by you.

7.3.5 Deleting a Mail

You can delete the message in the following steps.

1. Select the message from the inbox.
2. Press the right button of mouse. Press delete.
3. It will delete the current selected mail and send it to deleted item folder.
4. You may further delete the mail from deleted items folder but you must remember that item deleted from the deleted items folder are never retrieved.

7.4 MANAGING YOUR ADDRESS BOOK

Outlook Express allows you to enter the details including E-mail addresses of your friends and relatives. In fact address book is like a diary where you may store various attributes of contact address of your friends. You may open the address book by choosing address book option from the tools icon on the menu bar of outlook express. Screen as shown in figure 7.9 will appear.

If you wish to add a new contact to the address book, press the icon New on the tool bar. This opens a screen as shown in figure 7.10 where you may enter the various attributes including his default E-mail address.

You may also opt for entering other attributes e.g. Home, Business, Personal, Other, NetMeeting, Digital Ids by moving on the respective tab page. If you choose to send a mail to a friend whose address is listed in the address book, in that case his name will appear in the address field of compose screen. You may also delete or modify the current contact stored in your address book. Selecting address book from tools menu on outlook express can do this job. You may click to the field which you wish to modify then select properties. It will allow you to modify the contents.

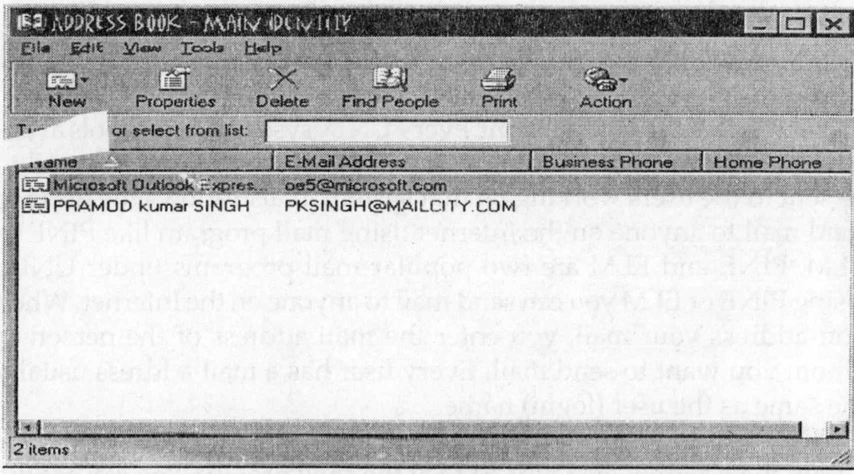

Fig. 7.9 Address Book

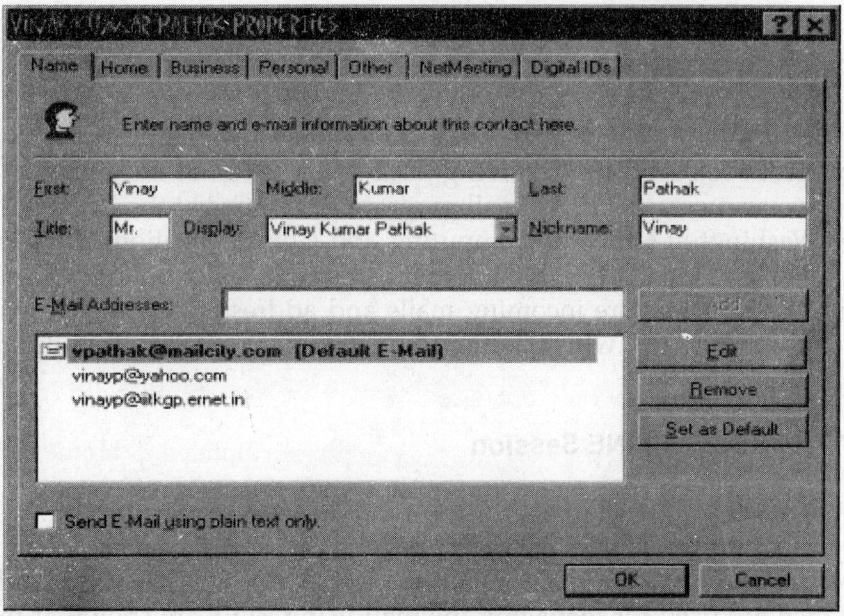

Fig. 7.10 Entering a Mail address in Address Book

7.5 CREATING YOUR SIGNATURE

You may create your own signature in the outlook express. Here signature means your address which will be added to every mail sent automatically. To create the signature go to outlook express menu bar and select stationary. Fill up your address (signature) in the dialogue box. You may also choose to add this signature to all the outgoing mails.

7.6 MANAGING E-MAIL IN UNIX (PINE AND ELM)

Just like Windows environment, every UNIX system has the tools available for sending and receiving mails. UNIX system allows the mail to be sent to the users working on that system. It also allows the users to send mail to anyone on the Internet using mail program like PINE or ELM. PINE and ELM are two popular mail programs under UNIX. Using PINE or ELM you can send mail to anyone on the Internet. When you address your mail, you enter the mail address of the person to whom you want to send mail. Every user has a mail address usually the same as the user (login) name.

ELM is a sophisticated full-screen mail system for interactive use. To run the program, just type ELM at the shell prompt. You can see the 'message index' containing list of your messages. Various commands pertaining to ELM are displayed at the bottom of screen.

7.7 PROGRAM FOR INTERNET NEWS AND E-MAIL (PINE)

PINE is intended to be an easy-to-use full-featured menu-driven mail program for sending, receiving, and filing Internet messages and Netnews messages. It is a mail program developed at the University of Washington Office of Computing and Communications. PINE is available to the world-wide Internet community as a public service. It uses folders to store incoming mails and addresses. It also lets you send attachments, which are non-text files, such as graphics, files or spreadsheets.

7.7.1 Starting PINE Session

Whenever you wish to start using PINE to send or receive mail. Just type in pine on UNIX shell prompt. Upon pressing the enter, you will be presented with a main menu of PINE. List of all the commands which are used for managing the mail using PINE are shown at the bottom of the screen. PINE uses the bottom of the screen to show you what keys you can press to issue commands. The bottom of screen presents only frequently used PINE commands. However, the other related commands may be displayed using other command option. Looking over these commands is very important if you don't know what to do next.

7.7.2 Brief Introduction to PINE Commands

Command	*Description of Command*
➢ ?	➢ Shows the help screen.
➢ C	➢ Composes and sends a message.
➢ P	➢ Selects the next item displayed on the menu.
➢ N	➢ Selects the next item displayed on the menu.
➢ R	➢ Displays release notes, which contain information for using PINE.
➢ K	➢ Locks the keyboard.
➢ G	➢ Goes to a specified folder.
➢ I	➢ Displays messages in the current folder.
➢ L	➢ Selects a folder to view.
➢ A	➢ Creates or modifies address books.
➢ S	➢ Accesses setup options.
➢ Q	➢ Quits PINE.
➢ O	➢ Shows all other available commands.

In the PINE, number of command includes a caret (^) in front of a letter. This indicates that control key (Ctrl) and the desired command letter has to be pressed simultaneously. This is done by holding the control key alongwith pressing letter key. For example, ^C exits the editor when you are composing a message.

Here are some tips on how to use the PINE:

1. Choosing Option 1 (E-Mail) from the VSNL menu will start the PINE E-Mail session.
2. Press the **q** key to quit PINE.
3. You should take the help of the command listed at the bottom of the screen. This will help you to enter the appropriate command.
4. Most of the time, the sender of the mail expects early reply. Therefore, one must make it a point to see and reply the mail as early as possible.
5. It is not desirable to keep the old mails in your mail box. Keeping old mails in the mailbox will unnecessary occupy the space for which you have paid to your ISP. Keep deleting old E-Mail

messages and if you want to keep them for future reference, they may be transferred to other folders on your disk.

7.7.3 How to Enter Pine Command

The bottom two lines of the screen are always used to show the commands you can use. You press the key that is highlighted to give the command. On some screens, there is a command labelled Other Cmds. Selecting this will change the bottom two lines to show you the other commands available. Note that the command does not have to be on the screen for you to use it. This is a nice feature once you memorize the common commands.

On some screens you will see a ^ character next to a highlighted letter. This indicates you must hold down the key while you tap the highlighted letter once. Release the key after you tap the letter. You can use the arrow keys to move up or down a line. Be sure the Num Lock is off to enable the arrow keys on the numeric keypad; otherwise numbers will appear.

The + and – keys are used for moving to the next or previous page. Note that you can also use V and Y to page up and down. You will use these keys often in the message composer. L command may be used to redraw the screen.

7.7.4 Composing Mail in Pine

You may compose the mail using the *Compose Message*. It will invoke the e PINE message composer and allow you to create and send a new message. You will see four lines at the top of your new message: To, CC, Attachment, and Subject. Enter an E-mail address -or- an address book name on the To line. If you want anyone else to get a copy, enter their E-mail addresses (or address book names) on the CC line; otherwise leave this line blank. If you want to send a file with your message, you enter its location here (see view attachments described in the Folder Index section of this Chapter for more info); otherwise leave this line blank. Enter a general one-line overview of your message as the subject. At this point, the cursor has moved into the message area. Essentially, just start typing. As you add text, it automatically wraps as you type past the end of the line, you don't have to hit at the end of each line. To send the message, press X.

7.7.5 How to Abandon the Mail

You will be asked if you are sure that you want to abandon your message. If you reply Y, the message is discarded and not sent and not saved: if you reply N, you are returned to your unsent message.

7.7.6 How to Send the Mail

By entering **X** command, PINE will ask you to confirm that you want the message to be sent. If you answer **N**, you are returned to your unsent message; if you answer **Y**, the message is sent and copied to your sent-mail folder.

7.7.7 Justifying the Text

Justify (J) command reformats the text in the paragraph the cursor is in. Paragraphs are separated by one blank line. This is useful when you have been editing the paragraph and want to make it look 'neat' again.

7.7.8 How to Copy the Text from other File to Your Mail

Read File (R) command allows you to copy text from an existing file into your message. You will be prompted for the name of the file to be inserted into the message. The filename is related to your home directory or must be a full path name. The contents of the entire file are inserted at the cursor location.

(R) command allows you to read files only from the UNIX machine. If your file exists on some other machine it must be copied to UNIX machine before using the PINE (R) command.

7.7.9 How to Search a String

Where (W) is a command that will search the message for a word or phrase. The search does not include the header. The search starts from the cursor and moves down; if found, the cursor is moved to it. The entire document is searched; when the end of the message is reached, the search wraps to the top and continues. To fine the next occurrence, press W and it will use the previous word again.

7.7.10 How to Run Spell Checker

You may call the UNIX spell-checker to check your mail for spelling mistakes. Spell Check (T) tool of PINE invokes the spell checker of the UNIX. This will check the whole mail text but it does not suggest alternative spellings. Because of the sorting, your cursor will move up/

down/sideways as it highlights the unknown word in the message text; don't be concerned with this – it is just showing you the context of the unknown word.

7.7.11 How to Manage the Folders in PINE

Folder is a place similar to the directory where the files may be kept. PINE allows you to store your messages in these folders. Every message has to be in a folder. New messages are automatically kept in your 'INBOX'. Whenever you are reading a message, you can also shift and put them in another folder. You can move messages between folders by highlighting a message and using the Save command. When you choose 'Save' (S), you will be prompted for the name of the folder. You can type the name for a new or existing folder. If the folder does not exist, it will be created for you. You can also press **Ctrl T** to go to a list of your folders. Using folders is an effective way to organize your messages. All the commands for reading, replying to, deleting, and printing messages work in folders. Folders make it easy to organize your messages; for example, you might have a folder for your study group, another for mail from professors, and another for your social correspondence with friends.

After pressing **I**, a screen will appear that displays captions for each message in the currently open folder. It is an important utility, if you want to quickly find a particular message. The current message is always highlighted, and its message number is shown in the status line. To highlight a different message, use the arrow keys. When you press Enter, the highlighted message is brought into the Message Text screen.

7.7.12 Replying or Forwarding a Mail

After reading the mail, you may decide to either reply or forward the mail to other user. Depending upon the choice, you would use reply if you want to get E-mail back to the author of the message (and/or other people who have already seen it). You use forward if you want someone new to see the message.

7.7.13 How to View the Attachment Files

You may receive the attachment with the mail you have received. After viewing the mail text you will like to view the attached files. Attachments are files sent with the message, but not actually shown in the message text. View Attachment (V) command allows you to see the attachment to the mail. Attachments are useful to send large files and especially binary files (programs). If the file is text, you will be able to read it by selecting it and pressing. If the file is not text, you can save it to your home directory and try to across it outside of PINE.

7.7.14 Managing the Mail Folders

If you wish to see the name of all the message folders or wish to delete, rename or add folders. Folder List (L) tool will help and allow you to view, rename, delete and add folders. You can open a different folder by highlighting it (using the arrow keys to move around), and pressing; this will take you to the Folder Index screen.

7.8 MANAGING THE ADDRESS BOOK IN PINE

Address book is the place where you may keep the mail address and other attributes of your near and dears. It will also help you to block the mail. Address Book toll (A) helps you do these jobs in PINE. Blocking the mail means that you will not receive the mail from the person whose address has been blocked. While putting the mail address in the address book, you may specify the short name of the person whose address is this one. After this whenever you wish to send the mail, you need not enter the E-mail address of the person. You may specify the short name of that person in the first column instead of typing in the long E-mail address in the third column. You may take the address from the current message into your address book while reading a message by pressing Ctrl T together. Pressing A will take you to the Address Book management screen. From here, your personal address book(s) may be updated. You can also use it as a shortcut for addressing a new message; if you highlight an address and select C to compose a new message, the address is inserted as the addressee.

Apart from address book maintained by users, a global address books can also be maintained by the system administrator. The global address books are shared, and everyone can see them. You use them like you would use your own address books (except that you cannot make changes in the global address books).

7.8.1 Details of Attributes of Address Book

1. Nickname

Nickname is a short, easy-to-remember name which identifies the user.

You recall the identity of an user by nick name. You can type this in as the address in the Compose Message screen, and it will automatically use the real address associated with the nickname.

2. *Full Name*

Full Name attribute allows you to enter the full name of the user. Relatively a longer field, allows you to keep full name of the person. Usually the full names are put in last name first so they sort nicely. Note that all address books are sorted by the full name. Whatever you put here will appear on the message when it is finally delivered.

3. *Address*

In this field, the E-Mail ID of a person may be stored.

7.8.2 Editing the entries in the Address Book

You may edit or correct or modify the current contents in the address book. Edit (E) command will help you in modifying. To modify an existing entry, you use this command. You can only edit one field of the highlighted entry at a time. You will be asked which field to modify.

7.8.3 Block Sending of Mail

There are several occasions when you would like to send the mail to a large number of persons. For example, you may like to send the festival greeting, invitation etc to your all friends, near and dears. This you can do by Create List (S) command in the PINE. This command allows you to create a distribution list, which is a collection of E-mail addresses. These addresses are related in some way, such as all the persons working in your organization, your relative or all your friends. While sending a message to a distribution list, the message actually gets sent to each address listed in the distribution list. This is a convenient way to send to a group of people.

7.8.4 Creating your Signature (S) IN pine

Normally you enter your name and address at the end of each message that you send it. Doing this job again and again may be little boring. The best option to this problem is defining your signature. You signature will contain all of the possible attributes of your address, e.g, your name, mailing address, E-mail address, URL to your home page, telephone number etc. This job can be done in PINE using signature (S) command. You can make use of the signature option provided. You can store the information that you want to attach at the end of the messages as your signature. Now you can configure your system in such a way that all the out-going messages will have your signature at the end of the message.

The signature can be anything from your name and address, to your URL or contact information.

7.9 HOW TO QUIT PINE

You may quit PINE by entering quit (Q) command. On entering this command you will be asked if you are sure you want to quit if your option is Y, you will exit PINE and return to the UNIX prompt.

7.10 INTRODUCTION TO ELM

ELM is an another utility used in the UNIX systems for sending and receiving the mails. To invoke ELM program enter elm at UNIX prompt sign. You see the 'message index', a nice listing of your messages with one message per line. At the bottom of the screen is a list of the ELM commands you can use.

7.10.1 Sending a Message in ELM

You can send a mail in the following steps. First invoke ELM utility by entering ELM at UNIX prompt.

1. Press M.
2. ELM asks you to enter the mail id of the person whom you want to send the mail. Enter the mail id of the recipient of the mail. Then ELM prompts you for the message subject. Enter one.
3. ELM will also assist you, if you wish to send the copies of the mail to different persons.. You may enter the name of the persons whom you wish to send the copy of mail. You may also enter you own mail id if you want to keep a copy for yourself. Just press 'Enter' if you want to send any copies.
4. VI editor is supported by the ELM. Type your message using VI editor. After completing your message, give the commands to save the completed message and exit the editor.
5. Then ELM will ask you to choose one of the following options.

You may send the message by pressing "S", "H" to edit the header lines, "E" to go back and edit the message some more, "C" to copy a file into the message,, "F" to forget it and abandon the mail message.

To send the message, press S. ELM sends the message and displays the list of messages in your mailbox again.

7.10.2 How to Read the Mail Message in ELM

1. Enter ELM at the shell prompt.
2. Use cursor key to select the message you want to read or open. If the message is off the bottom of the screen (because you have more messages than can fit), press the spacebar to see each subsequent screen of messages or use the cursor keys to scroll through the list. If your cursor keys do not work, press J to move forward and K to move backward.
3. Press Enter to view the message. If the message is too long to fit on-screen, press the spacebar to see more of it.
4. Once you finish reading the message, you may decide whether you want to keep it for future reference or you may decide to delete it. Press D to delete the message and go on to the next one. To keep it, press the up- or down-arrow key (or J and K) to go to preceding or subsequent messages without deleting anything.
5. To stop reading messages, press I to return to the message index.

7.10.3 How to Print a Mail

ELM also allows you to take hard copies of the mail you have received in the form of printouts. The ELM helps you to do this job on the printer connected to your UNIX machine. This process will not work if you are using the dial up utility. In the case of dial up you must save the message to a file, download the file, and then print the downloaded file.

1. Enter ELM to view the message index.
2. Press the cursor keys (J or K) to select the message you want to print.
3. Press P to print the mail.

7.10.4 How to Save a Mail in the ELM

You can use ELM to store messages in a text file. For this you must follow following steps.

1. Press the cursor keys to select the message you want to save.
2. Press S.

3. Type the name of the file in which to save the message or just press enter to save the file with name automatically suggested by ELM.

Your mailbox usually resides in a subdirectory of your home directory called mail. If you precede a filename with an equal sign (=), ELM puts the file in your mail directory. You can save multiple messages into one file; ELM just adds the new messages to the end of the file.

7.10.5 How to Exit ELM

To quit ELM and save any changes you made to your mailbox, such as deleting messages:

1. Press Q.
2. ELM asks whether you want to save the messages you have already read. Press Y or Enter to save them in a file named received, or press N to leave them in your mailbox. Either way, your messages are saved in one place or the other.

To quit ELM without saving changes to your mailbox:

1. Press X.
2. If you make changes, ELM asks whether you really want to exit without saving them.
3. Press Y to exit without saving or N if you change your mind.

7.10.6 Customizing your ELM

You can customize ELM so that it uses the editor you like, displays messages in the order you want, and does other things. To customize, follow these steps:

1. To see your ELM options, press 'O'. ELM displays a list of its options, along with your setting for each one. You should leave most of these settings for each one, alone so that you do not break ELM.
2. To use a different editor for composing messages, press 'E'. Your cursor jumps to the name of the editor that ELM currently runs when you want to send a message. Edit this program name and press Enter. Notice that it is a full pathname; ask your system administrator to tell you the full pathname of the editor you want to use. Then press 'enter'.
3. To change the order, in which messages are displayed in the message index, press 'S'. Then press the spacebar repeatedly until you see the ordering you want. Press 'R' to switch between forward

and reverse orders. You may sort according to Date Mail Sent, sorting from least recent to most recent. Then press' enter'.

4. To change other settings, press the letter that appears in front of the parenthesis at the beginning of its line. Make the changes and then press Enter.
5. When you finish with the options, type > to save your changes. If you think that you may have made a mistake, skip this step.
6. To return to your ELM message index, press I.

7.11 E-MAIL ETHICS/NETIQUETTE

Sending an E-Mail is similar to writing a letter. When you write a letter to some one, personal or business letter, you follow some unwritten rules. Writing a letter is an art and it not only communicates the matter but also the mood and sentiments of the sender. One may like or dislike the way of presenting the matter. These unwritten rules are called ethics. Since E-mail are also letter, the same rules also applies to the E-Mails. The ethics on the internet are called Netiquttee (internet Etiquette). While interacting with some known or unknown, you must follow certain rules. There are few Netiquette listed below.

1. Do not use bold letters. It appears that you are shouting on the net.
2. Do not leave the subject field black. If you leave it blank it appears that you have nothing concrete to say.
3. While communicating to elders or in official mails, do avoid acronyms.
4. Do not forget to check your draft of mail spelling mistakes. It is better you make it a point to use spell checker before you actually send the mail.
5. While writing mail, you must remain cool and use humour while writing the mail.
6. While sending a copy of the mail to someone, please make sure that it is really necessary to send a copy to him. Otherwise it is very embarrassing for the receiver on deciding what to do with the mail.
7. Do not send junk mails. Junk mail is considered as the mail, which was neither expected nor requested by the receiver.
8. Please remember that none of the recipients likes a document with long, boring and broken statements. You must look sharp with clarity.
9. If you have to present certain points, it is always better to break into small pieces of statements and write with number.

10. Try to write your mail offline and read the mail again before sending it.
11. You must see your mail regularly. It is a belief on the net that if answer or confirmation is expected, it would come immediately.

Before sending a mail make sure that it conveys exactly what you want to communicate. You should remember that it is a bullet when fired cannot be taken back.

SELECT EXERCISES

Q. 1. What are E-mails? Explain how they are sent?

Q. 2. Explain in brief the role of Internet Services Provider in delivery of the mails.

Q. 3. What are Free E-Mail service providers? Explain how they manage to impart free E-Mail service to a large number of users.

Q. 4. Which E-mail was developed by an Indian and who owns it now. How this E-mail is important. When any message is sent by this mail, whether it is secured?

Q. 5. Give details how same message through E-mail can be sent to more than one person at a time?

Q. 6. What is Outlook Express? Who developed this utility?

Q. 7. Explain how an attachment may be sent alongwith the mail using Outlook Express?

Q. 8. What are attachment files? How the attachments are downloaded?

Q. 9. Explain the process of reading the mail, sending a mail and sending copies of the mail to different users in Outlook Express.

Q. 10. Explain the process, how the mails are delivered to the recipients?

Q. 11. What is address book? How the address book are used?

Q. 12. How a mail is deleted in outlook express?

Q. 13. How the mails are composed? How will you reply a mail, you have received?

Q. 14. What are signatures? How will you send the signature with the E-mail.

Q. 15. List few popular free E-Mail provider on the Web.

Q. 16. What are Netiquette? List any five important netquettes which you consider important.

Q. 17. Answer following with respect to PINE.

- How will you start PINE
- How will you create and send a message in PINE?
- How will you read your incoming messages in PINE? How will you view attachments?
- How will you reply to a message in PINE?

- Why do you need to forward e-mail? How will you forward a message in PINE?
- How will you print a message in PINE?
- How will you save a message in PINE?
- How will you delete and expunge messages in PINE?
- How will create and delete folders in PINE?
- How will you create a directory of addresses in PINE? How will you use it? How will you add, modify and delete addresses in Address Book?
- What is a signature in E-mail? Why do you need to attach a signature in your E-mail? How will you create and modify a signature in PINE?
- How will you quit PINE?
- How will you change various options in PINE?
- How will you get online help in PINE? What are the other sources from which you can get additional information about PINE?

Q. 18. Answer with respect to ELM.

- How will you start ELM?
- How will you send a message in ELM?
- How will you read your messages in ELM?
- How will you print a message in ELM?
- How will you save a message in ELM?
- How will you exit from ELM?
- How will you change options in ELM?
- How will you get help in ELM?
- Compare PINE and ELM. Which one do you prefer? Why?
- What are the limitations of PINE and ELM? What are their advantages over other UNIX mail utilities available?
- How do PINE and ELM compare with other mail programs under UNIX and Windows?

8 Introduction of EDIT and VI Editors

8.0 INTRODUCTION TO EDITORS

Editors are the programs or utilities provided both in Windows and Unix for creating simple text file. Most of the time these editors are used for writing programs. EDIT is a widely used text editor in DOS environment. Its function is to create and edit simple ASCII text files. The text files in DOS are usually represented with extension.txt. EDIT is a graphic-interface editor which is easy to use, full screen editor. This editor make is easy to create, edit and modify the contents of a text file. You may also print the contents, may use the scroll bar to view the contents etc. Advantage of EDIT editor over other word processor is that most of other word processor use non ASCII character as per their formats. You may have to use other means to create a ASCII to remove formatting with that document. Like other word processors, EDIT allows you to use the mouse, keyboard, it possesses a complete help to guide you. You may cut, copy and paste the text on the clip board. It also allows you to interact with graphical construct like access menu, dialog boxes.

8.1 HOW TO START EDIT IN WINDOWS 98

You may start EDIT editor in one of the following ways in Windows 98 environment.

1. Double click the MS DOS icon on your desktop or
2. Go to START-> PROGRAM and click MS DOS.
3. At the DOS prompt, write edit and press enter.

After doing as above a full screen will appear containing the menu item as given below.

8.2 CREATING A TEXT FILE

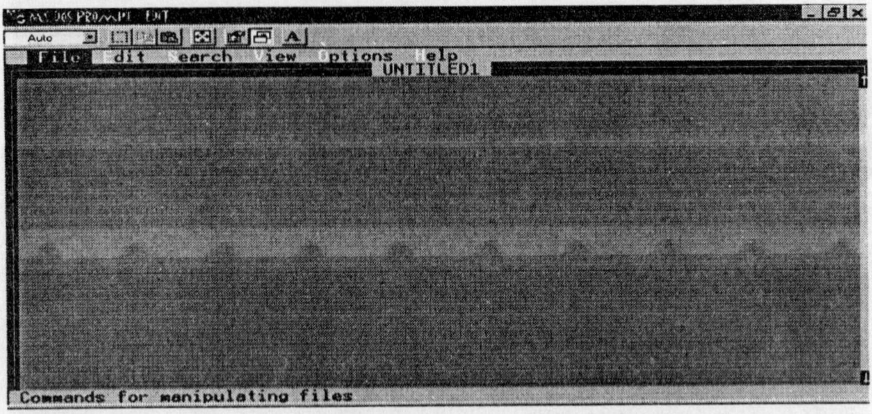

Fig. 8.1

You may create the text file in two ways. One option is to enter following command while you start EDIT editor.

EDIT filename

This command will start a EDIT editor with file name provided by you. If the file exists then it will open that file and if the file does not exist then it will create a file for you with the file name provided by you.

Another option is to start this editor without mentioning the file name and you may enter the text for the file in the editing area of the EDIT. After putting your text you may choose to save it from the menu item FILE -> SAVE.

8.3 CURSOR MOVEMENT KEYS

8.3.1 Cursor Movement Commands

To move the cursor on the editing area, you may use following the commands along with the normal cursor movement keys.

➤ Home	Move to the start of the current line.
➤ End	Move to the end of the current line.
➤ Ctrl+Up	Scroll up one line.
➤ Ctrl+Down	Scroll down one line.
➤ PageUp	Scroll up one screen.

- PageDown — Scroll down one screen.
- Ctrl+PgUp — Scroll left one screen.
- Ctrl+PgDn — Scroll right one screen.
- Ctrl+Home — Scroll to the start of the document.
- Ctrl+End — Scroll to the end of the document.
- Ctrl+Left — Move left one word.
- Ctrl+Right — Move right one word.

8.3.2 Editing Commands

You may edit the text by inserting, deleting, copying, pasting the text/lines. In the following table, you may find the command, which are used to edit the text in the edit area.

- Enter — Start a new line.
- Delete — Delete the character that the cursor is on.
- Backspace — Delete the character to the left of the cursor.
- Tab — Move the cursor to next tab stop.
- Insert — Switch between insert and overwrite modes.
- Ctrl+Y — Delete the current line.
- Ctrl+V — Paste buffer contents into file.
- Ctrl+P — Allows special characters to be inserted.

8.3.3 Commands for Working with Selected Regions

Following table contains the list of commands, which allows you to work with the selected regions.

- Shift — Use the shift key in conjunction with the cursor movement functions to select regions.
- Ctrl+C — Copy the current selection to buffer.
- Ctrl+X — Delete the current selection and copy it to buffer.
- Delete — Delete the current selection.
- Tab — Indent the selected lines.
- Shift+Tab — Unindent the selected lines.

8.3.4 Commands for Finding and Replacing Text

Using the command given in the following table you may search for the text in the file. If you wish so you may also replace all the occurrences of the text with another text.

➢ Ctrl+Q+F	Find text.
➢ Ctrl+Q+A	Find text and replace it.
➢ F3	Repeat the last search.

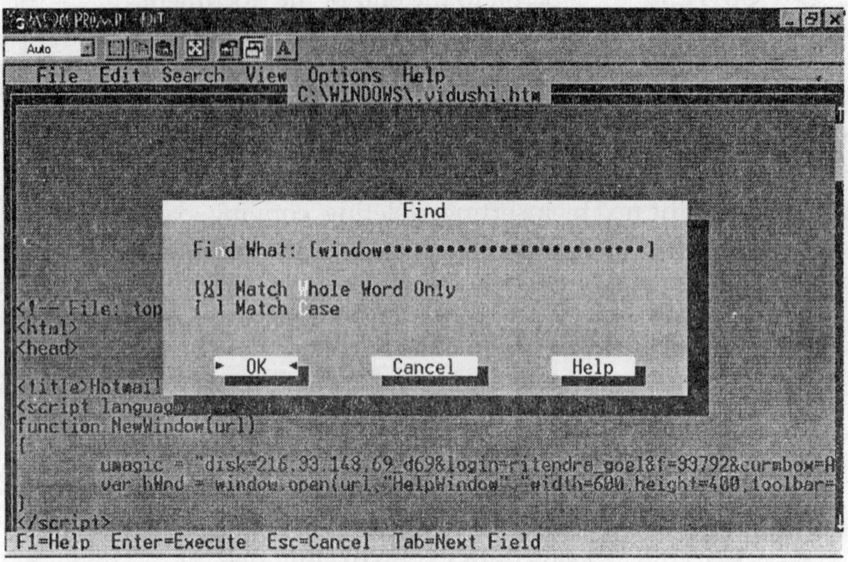

Fig. 8.2

You may also use the search menu item from the menu bat in EDIT command window as shown. With this tool you may search the string/ text and replace with the text of your choice.

8.3.5 Window Management Commands

➢ F6	Switch to next edit window.
➢ F8	Switch to next file you are working on.
➢ Ctrl+F6	Open second edit window.
➢ Ctrl+F4	Close second edit window.
➢ Ctrl+F8	Resize edit windows.

8.4 MOVING A BLOCK OF TEXT TO ANOTHER LOCATION

8.4.1 Copying the Block

- Select a block of text using the mouse
- Choose the EDIT-> COPY menu item from the menu bar

- Move cursor to desired location
- Choose the EDIT -> PASTE menu item from the menu bar

8.4.2 Moving a Block

- Select a block of text.
- Choose the EDIT-> CUT menu item from the menu bar
- Move cursor to the desired location
- Choose the EDIT -> PASTE menu item from the menu bar

8.5 INTRODUCTION TO VI EDITOR

'VI' is an editor used in UNIX environment. It is a powerful user friendly text editor available with UNIX. Other editors which are also used under UNIX environment are 'ED', a line editor, 'EX' an editor which combines screen and line editing facilities, 'SED' a non-interactive text editor. VI is an screen oriented editor and you may use several commands to move forward, append, insert, character handling etc. This editor is just like any other editor and mostly used to write the programs and other utilities in the UNIX. It is also used in the similar operating systems like XENIX/LINUX etc.

8.6 STARTING VI EDITOR

VI Editor may be started using following commands at UNIX prompt.

$ vi filename

Here 'filename' specifies the name of the file you want to edit. If the file has not been created in the past, it will create a new file with the name 'filename' and allows you to enter the text or data. If the file has been created in the past, it will open the file 'filename' and allow you to edit the text or data.

8.7 ARROWS KEY IN VI EDITOR

In some cases, you may not use the arrows key provided on your keyboard to move the cursor on the screen. You may use following keys for this purpose.

- K UP
- H LEFT

- I RIGHT
- J DOWN

You may switch from 'append' or 'insert' mode to the 'command' mode by pressing the 'ESC' key at the keyboard. In the command mode you may enter the command specific to the VI Editor. In the 'append' or 'insert' mode, it allows you to write the text. While entering the text, you may move to down, up, left or right by pressing the K,H,I, and J key as defined above.

8.8 HOW TO QUIT VI EDITOR

When your job gets over, you would like to quit the editor. You may do it by entering following command to return to UNIX shell command prompt.

:q <enter>

8.9 HOW TO ENTER THE TEXT IN VI EDITOR

While working with the VI Editor, an user will be either of the two modes, namely, insert mode or command mode. When a user starts VI editor, he enters into command mode. At this point he may enter the commands. To enter the text, user may enter any of the following commands. After entering any of the commands i.e. "I" or "a", the user will enter into the insert mode.

"i"	insert	text will be entered before the current position of the cursor.
"a"	append	text will be entered after the place of the cursor.
"o"		text will be inserted after the line in which the cursor is placed.

8.10 HOW TO SAVE THE WORK

When you are entering the text or data to your file, you work in the insert mode. To save the changes in your text or data to your file, you must change to the command mode. This you may do by pressing the "ESC" key of your keyboard. After entering into the command mode you may save the changes before you quit or you may quit without saving. A list of commands is given in the following table.

" :q! " <enter>	quit without saving
" :w " <enter>	write to the file and continue
" :x " < enter >	save and quit

8.11 OTHER OPERATIONS PERFORMED IN VI EDITOR

8.11.1 Deleting a Character

If you want to delete a character, then you position cursor on it and press "x". It will delete this character and whole line will be moved to one character towards left.

8.11.2 Deleting a Word

You may delete a word, which may be separated by space, punctuation mark or tabs. All you have to do is to place a cursor on the first character of the word and press "dw" (delete word).

8.11.3 Positioning in the File

Apart from using cursor movement key H, I, J, K, you may use following commands for positioning in the file. These commands are given below

- ➢ Ctrl D for moving half screen downward in the file.
- ➢ Ctrl U for moving half screen upward in the file.
- ➢ Ctrl B for moving full screen upward in the file.
- ➢ Ctrl F for moving full screen downward in the file.

There are some useful commands also.

- ➢ W to move forward a single word
- ➢ B to move backward by a single word
- ➢ $ to go to the end of the line
- ➢ ^ to go to the beginning of the file.

8.11.4 Searching for a String

You may search for a string in the text. This can be done in two ways, namely, forward search and backward search. This command is given in command mode. All you have to do is to write the string after "/ " in the command mode. (e.g. /string). This will search for the "string" in the text and will place the cursor at the starting of "string". Next occurrence may be searched by pressing "N". If you wish to search in backward mode, then you must enter the string after "?". (e.g.? string). After doing the first backward search, you may go to the next occurrence by pressing "N".

8.11.5 More on Delete

For the editing purpose, you may use the following commands in the command mode. It will make editing of your file easier.

- "x" delete current character
- "dw" delete current word.
- "db" delete previous word
- "dd" delete current line.
- "d$" delete rest of the line from the current place.

These commands may be used in conjunction with the integer. For example 4x will delete next four character and 7dw will delete next seven words.

8.11.6 How to Undo the Change

If you feel that the last change you have made incorrect, you may undo the change by entering "u" command. It will undo the effect of last command and produce the text before the change.

8.11.7 Command Summary for VI Editor

Command	Action
➢ "l"	➢ Move cursor right
➢ "h"	➢ Move cursor left
➢ "k"	➢ Move cursor up
➢ "j"	➢ Move cursor down
➢ "I"	➢ Insert
➢ "a"	➢ Append
➢ "x"	➢ Delete a character
➢ "dd"	➢ Delete a line
➢ "dw"	➢ Delete a word
➢ "r"	➢ Replace a text
➢ "u"	➢ Undo the last change
➢ ":n"	➢ Go to the line number n
➢ "/string"	➢ Search for the string "string"
➢ "?string "	➢ Search for a "string " backward"
➢ "n"	➢ Next occurrence in search
➢ "ctrl D"	➢ Scroll down half page
➢ "ctrl U"	➢ Scroll up half page
➢ "$"	➢ Go to the end of line
➢ ":q!"	➢ Quit without saving

➢ ":w"	➢ Save and continue
➢ ":wq"	➢ Save and quit
➢ ":x"	➢ Save and quit

SELECT EXERCISES

Q. 1. What do you mean by Editors? When they are used? How will you start EDIT editor under Windows 98?

Q. 2. Compare the EDIT tool with its counterpart and list the advantages/ disadvantages?

Q. 3. Exlain the process of creating a text file in EDIT editor.

Q. 4. Explain the purpose and use of cursor movement keys in EDIT editor?

Q. 5. Explain how a string may be searched in a text file using EDIT?

Q. 6. List the commands of EDIT to work in selected regions.

Q. 7. How a block of text may be moved from one place to another using EDIT?

Q. 8. How will you cut and paste a selected block of text in EDIT editor?

Q. 9. How a line is deleted in EDIT?

Q. 10. What is VI Editor? How will you start VI editor in UNIX?

Q. 11. How VI is different from 'ED' editor?

Q. 12. How to search for a string in EDIT and VI editor? Can you replace all the instances of a string in a text by another string? If yes, How?

Q. 13. How to undo the change you have made in VI editor?

Q. 14. How a cursor movement takes place in VI editor?

Q. 15. List and explain commands used in VI for positioning in the file.

Q. 16. Discuss various file saving options of VI editor.

Q. 17. Give the command summary of VI and EDIT.

9 Introduction to UNIX

9.0 INTRODUCTION

The UNIX operating system is not a single large program, but a combination of a small kernel, which does low-level jobs, a shell and the file system. The kernel does not execute all the jobs itself but uses the other software tools or utilities that do all the peripheral work. The shell plays the role of an interpreter. We must communicate with the shell in order to have our requests processed. The files are classified and organized in a tree structure. UNIX, an operating system, manages the computer's resources (the CPU, main memory, input and output channels, and so on) and makes these resources usable by programmers. This operating system was mainly used by mainframe but today it is being used by different kinds of computing machine may it be microcomputers, workstations, and mainframes. One of the main feature of this operating system is portability and it is being used on microcomputers, workstations, and mainframes. The other attributes are the fact that it supports multiple users at a given time (unlike DOS) and supports multiprogramming. Many of the commercial popular operating systems e.g. Linux, Xenix, HP UNIX, SUN OS etc has inherited its main feature. UNIX was written in the programming language C at AT&T Bell laboratories.

9.1 HISTORY OF UNIX

UNIX operating system was derived from MULTICS. MULTICS was an early OS created as a test platform in 1964. MULTICS was a large, multiple-user, time-sharing system that did not gain much acceptance outside its development environment. MULTICS was a collaborative effort of Massachusetts Institute of Technology (MIT), AT&T, and General Electric USA. Subsequently AT&T eventually dropped out of the collaborative efforts. MULTICS is historically recognised as the first

OS to implement most of the multitasking features. When AT&T has been pulled out from MULTICS project, Ken Thompson has started putting effort towards development of UNIX in assembly language at AT&T which was a small version of MULTICS. Dennis Ritchie soon joined hands in this project, and UNIX was rewritten in the C language. UNIX and C have been joined since their beginnings at AT&T. UNIX OS was developed at AT&T Bell Laboratories, USA, by Ken Thompson and Dennis Ritchie in 1969 and the early 1970s. The original versions were designed to run on DEC PDP-11 16-bit computers and VAX 32-bit computers. Bell Labs completely rewrote UNIX in the C programming language in 1973. This made UNIX highly portable, and it now contains system components written in a common, well-known programming language that are easily recompiled to work on a variety of systems. The UNIX system was developed internally at AT&T, but because of legal constraints, AT&T could not market it. Starting in 1974, UNIX was licensed to universities. Around 1975, AT&T made the OS available on an open basis to universities and colleges for use in research projects and computer science programs.

Linux is another free UNIX-like OS that runs on a variety of platforms, including Intel, SPARC, PowerPC, and DEC Alpha processors as well as multiprocessing systems. Linux is a "user-developed" product, meaning that users around the world who ran the OS for their own use have developed many of its components and drivers. Linux Torvalds developed the original OS as a college product. It is now well-supported and gaining ground as a respectable OS despite its home-grown roots.

9.2 CHARACTERISTICS OF UNIX OPERATING SYSTEM

UNIX is a multi-user/multitasking system that supports networking and distributed file systems. Conventional operating systems consist of a small kernel that runs processes such as user applications and services. The UNIX kernel is a large monolithic kernel that changes little from system to system. The design approach followed in this operating system makes it easy for the user to add new services or remove unwanted services. It also makes upgrades easier since the entire OS does not need to be recompiled.

In this operating system all the users interact through a shell. Shell is a process that accepts user input and performs various tasks. Shell in the UNIX is of following types.

1. Bourne shell,
2. C shell, and
3. Korn shell.

In the new versions of UNIX, transmission control protocols and internet protocols are closely associated. Every UNIX implementation now includes TCP/IP and support for internet. In addition, Sun Microsystems uses common distributed file-sharing system included with UNIX. Thus, UNIX provides in one package the ability to install a powerful operating system on a computer that lets users share files and run programs on other users' computers.

9.3 UNIX ARCHITECTURE

The UNIX is written largely in a language called 'C' which is not processor dependent. Part of the UNIX operating systems is also written on assembler. Since UNIX has been written in a language, which is not machine dependent it implies that UNIX is portable and it can run on various processors with small modifications.

In the next sections we will emphasize the architectural differences between conventional Operating Systems and UNIX. The major functions of an operating system are command interpretation, I/O control, communications etc. To perform these tasks, a large number of programs are required. Conventionally, all of these programs are combined together to form a larger monolithic kernel. Therefore, major drawback of any operating system was that it occupies a large amount of memory and response was very slow. UNIX has different architecture and it has basically following parts.

- **Kernel**—A main functional unit, interacts with the hardware.
- **Shell**—An outermost unit, interacts with the user to perform functions submitted by an user.
- **The file system**—The idea was to keep the units related but still separate so that the entire program did not park itself in the memory and slow down the system.

9.4 UNIX KERNEL

The core unit is called the Kernel. Its tasks include CPU scheduling, allocating the necessary hardware, controlling I/O operations, etc. It is very interesting to see how it allots the CPU to various processes. A *process* is a running program. UNIX is a multi-user, multitasking OS. It means several users can work on the system at the same time and each user can submit several jobs for execution at the same time. Since there are several jobs submitted and running simultaneously, the kernel gives them a tag or identification. The simplest form of identification for the kernel is an integer. So, for every job initiated, the kernel assigns an identification number called PID (*Process ID*). The kernel maintains a table called '*Process Table*', which describes every running process. When a process is initiated the kernel creates an entry in the process table and discards the entry when the process is completely halted.

We see that the UNIX system is able to respond to so many users simultaneously, but this is not the reality. When several users initiate several jobs at the same time, every process likes to be serviced first. But the kernel keeps track of every process initiated or running. The entry of each process in the Process Table also indicates the process priority. The *process priority* is a measure of the importance of the process. The kernel refers to the priority of the processes when allotting the CPU to it. Once the CPU is allotted to a job it runs for an interval and then the CPU is allotted to another job. An interval is a small amount of time for which a process runs. This ensures that all the processes get a chance to run. A process can be halted for any of the following reasons:

- The process exhausts its interval.
- The process cannot go any further.
- The process has to wait for an event to occur.
- Another process assumes higher priority and the CPU is allotted to this new process.

The allocation and reallocation is done at an amazing speed and the users all along think that the system is responding to all of them simultaneously.

9.4.1 Swapping

Just like the CPU time, the memory space is also a valuable resource. As always, a valuable resource has so many users and too little of it is available. Memory is used by the operating system, by the program and by the data, which has to be processed. With a number of users working on the system, the memory space available at any point of time will be less than the space required. A good OS should be able to handle this. If a process has to be executed, all parts of the process have to be in the memory. If one process is running, logically the other process need not be present in the memory. The kernel, therefore, moves the waiting process to the secondary storage i.e., the hard disk, whereby the currently running process gets all the memory space it needs. This is called *swapping*. This process takes place at a dazzling speed.

9.4.2 Context Switching

The kernel does its work in two modes. One is the *User Mode* and the other is the *Kernel Mode,* which are also known as *Unrestricted Mode* and *Restricted Mode* respectively. When the kernel processes a program it works in the user mode. If there is a need to create a file in the program then the kernel switches to the kernel mode to create the file. Once this is done, the kernel automatically switches its context to the user mode to execute the next statement. This is called *context switching*. This is illustrated in next section about the login procedure.

9.4.3 Unix Shell

The outer unit, which interacts with the user, is called *shell*. It acts like an interpreter between you and the kernel. The commands that you type are interpreted by the shell and passed on to the kernel for execution. The result, if any, is the output by the shell in a form which the user can understand.

Presently, there are several shells available on the UNIX OS. Some of these are the Bourne Shell, 'C' Shell, the Korn Shell, etc. The most popular of the shells are the Bourne and the 'C' shell.

The shell interprets the commands following some basic rules, which are as follows:

The first 'word' (A set of character(s) ending with a space) is interpreted as the command. If the second word is preceded by a minus (–) then it is treated as an option of the command. The words following this are arguments to the command. The shell also recognises some special characters. For example,

wc –l games

This command performs a word count on the file games. The '–l' option specifies that only the number of lines to be output.

At the end of the command when you press the Enter key, the shell begins to evaluate the command. It recognises the first word as the command and the second word as the option of the command. Now since the command 'wc' is to be executed, it has to be loaded in the memory. The shell then searches through all your directories to see if the file 'wc' is present. If it is present, then the shell will proceed to the next step, i.e., read the next word of the command. It reads the next word as 'games' and understands it to be an argument to the command, i.e., 'games' is the name of the file on which it has to act. It will then search the directory in which you are working to see if the file 'games' is available. If it is, it will pass the command, the options and the argument to the kernel for execution. In case the file 'wc' is not found it will display the message *wc not found*. If the file 'games' is not found, it will display a message *file not found*. After execution, the shell passes on the output given by the kernel to the user in a form in which the user can understand it. Some of the utilities and their functions are described below.

Utility	Function
➢ Ls	➢ directory listing
➢ Rm	➢ remove file
➢ Cp	➢ copy a file
➢ Mv	➢ rename a file
➢ Mkdir	➢ make new directory
➢ Rmdir	➢ remove directory
➢ Pwd	➢ print working directory
➢ Chmod	➢ change file attributes
➢ Chgrp	➢ change group
➢ Chown	➢ change owner
➢ Mkfs	➢ make file system
➢ Mount	➢ mount file system
➢ umount	➢ unmount file system
➢ date	➢ display system date
➢ cal	➢ display calendar
➢ sort	➢ sort a file
➢ awk	➢ pattern matching
➢ cat	➢ display or concatenate files
➢ pg	➢ display page-wise
➢ man	➢ online help
➢ find	➢ locate a file

UNIX Shell Commands

9.5 UNIX COMMAND INTERPRETER

UNIX handles user commands through a command interpreter, a special interface program that processes commands entered at the keyboard. After you log in, a command prompt (a symbol that indicates the interpreter is ready for a command to be entered) will be shown, which may look like this:

```
%
```

or

```
machine %
```

where 'machine' is the name of this particular UNIX system. Note though, that the command prompt may be different. There are three command interpreters. These are the C *shell*, the *Bourne shell*, and the *Korn shell*. If the C shell is not already active, typing the command csh may start it.

After the command prompt appears, the system is waiting for a command to be typed. Commands usually result in the system doing some work and printing the results on the screen. Unless otherwise noted, when the term 'print' is used, it means output shown on the screen, not a printer; sending output to the printer will be discussed later. After typing a command, press the Enter key.

Don't expect that the shell will be able to understand anything that you type as a command. The shell expects you to follow a very strict discipline in terms of syntax. If the commands that you type in are incorrect, the system will either perform the unintended activity or inform you that you have entered an unknown command. However, the shell does permit you to write your own command syntax. As a programmer, you can write shell scripts which will let other users use some easily understood syntax rather than the condensed syntax understood by UNIX.

9.5.1 Special Keys

When typing commands and running programs in UNIX, you must be able to deal with typing mistakes and to interrupt executing programs. There are special keystrokes for handling these operations. They can be set by the user, and therefore may vary in different environments. Each of the three basic operations is associated with a character. With their most common association, they are:

- The *kill* character (**Ctrl U**), which removes the current command
- The *erase* character (**Ctrl H**), which backs up one space in the current command
- The *interrupt* character (**Ctrl C**), which stops the execution of a running program.

To control the associations of keys and operations, the 'ssty' command is used. Typing it will show the current setting for a terminal. For example, to change the interrupt character to control-Q and the erase character to control-N, the command is:

```
stty intr ^Q erase ^N
```

where the caret(^) character represents the unprintable control key on the screen. Some common control characters are given in Table 5.2.

^U	Kill current line
^H	Erase one character
^C	Interrupt running program
^S	Stop scrolling
^Q	Resume scrolling

9.5.2 Common Control Characters in UNIX

This line typically is inserted into the '.cshrc' file, which is located in the user's home directory. '.cshrc' stores user preferences and other system commands that customise the user's working environment.

There are two keystrokes for controlling the scrolling of information on the screen. Ctrl S stops it, and Ctrl Q resumes it. Some terminals react slowly to these commands or may send information to the screen in such a large chunk that the command is too late to have the desired effect. If you press Ctrl S remember that Ctrl Q must be typed to undo it, even if the scrolling is finished. A terminal can appear 'hung' if this is forgotten.

9.6 LOGGING IN AND OUT

UNIX, like other mainframe and workstation operating systems but unlike most personal computer operating systems, requires that users obtain access privileges through the system administrator. An identification name and a password must be entered in order to gain access to the system and identify a UNIX account.

9.6.1 Login

When you switch on your UNIX system a message comes on, asking you to login i.e., to enter your username and password. Before you begin your 'hands-on' session on the UNIX system you have to first log in. The login procedure involves two pieces of information: a username and a password. The system administrator may have already done the necessary homework that will let you log in. The system administrator assigns the username while creating an account on a UNIX system. The username is usually associated with the user's name, but it may contain extra information also. Note that UNIX commands are case-sensitive, and input is normally expected in lower case; this is probably true for most usernames. The system administrator may also assign the password at first, perhaps to some generic string like 'newuser'. The system administrator will tell you your login name and password. You can change your password after you log in.

To log in to a UNIX system, the login prompt must be visible on your screen:

login:

You now have to enter your login name or user id. Login name or user id is the name by which the UNIX system will identify you. Type your user id on the login line and press the Enter key. The system will now prompt you to enter your password. The following line should appear:

Password:

Type your password and press the Enter key. The password's characters will not appear on the screen when they are typed, since the password is supposed to be a secret. After you have entered your password the UNIX system checks the username and password internally to see if it is correct. The system would verify your username etc. If it is matched, you are permitted in. If you do not enter the password correctly, it finds a problem, an error message is printed. The system will ask you to 'login' once again and you can try again. Typing mistakes are common, especially on the password, so do not give up. If, after several attempts, you are still unsuccessful, talk to your system administrator for help. If the login is successful, some standard system messages may be printed along with the message of the day. The former does not usually change, but later often contains important and timely new information for users.

The UNIX OS consists of a large number of small individual programs, which are invoked and loaded into the memory only when required. An example is the login process. When you switch on the system, you see a message prompting you to enter username. You enter your username and your password, if necessary, and you log on. This sounds very simple from the outside. But internally, when you power on the system, the firmware loads the /unix file in the memory and executes it. The /unix file contains the kernel which sets up the necessary processes to let you log in.

1. A process table is created. The kernel itself being the first process gets a PID 0. The kernel process ends only when the system is halted.
2. The kernel invokes the 'init' process by executing the '/etc/init' file. This process is responsible for the initiation of all other processes. It has a PID 1 and halts only when the system is halted. But unlike the kernel it does not interact with the hardware and it is fully dependent on the kernel for such interactions.

3. Once the 'init' process is on, it in turn invokes the '/etc/inittab' file. The 'inittab' file informs 'init', as to which terminal can be used and which terminal is ready and is in a position to accept the login message. The 'inittab' process exits and 'getty' process starts.
4. Again the 'init' process starts. 'init' then invokes the '/etc/getty'. This file has various parameters for communication between the terminal and the computer. Using these parameters the login prompt is displayed.
5. When you enter your login name the '/login' program takes over. If you have a password for your account the '/login' program prompts you to enter your password. Once you enter your password correctly, it will inform you that you have successfully logged in.

The above explanation was to illustrate how the UNIX system works using the software programs as tools rather than including them in the main body of the OS. Each program is invoked when necessary and is discarded when the required function is completed.

At the first login, you should change your password to a secret word. In general, passwords are from six to eight characters long and may contain special characters such as question marks or parentheses. For security reasons, it is a good idea to use one or more special characters in a password. Don't use something easy and obvious—a spouse's name or the digits of date of birth, as unscrupulous outsiders trying to gain illegal access to your system may guess these. On the other hand, a password must be remembered, so random characters are not a good idea. You may use the beginning words of some English saying.

To change your password, type the command **passwd** at the command prompt. The system will respond by prompting for the current password, then for the new password, and finally to repeat the new password as a check. If all is successful, the new password will be enforced at the next login.

9.6.2 Logout

To end a login session, type 'logout' at the command prompt. This will cause the login prompt to appear on the screen again. When you use a GUI such as Open Windows a login session is probably inside a window. In this case, the logout command may cause the error message 'Not a login shell' to appear. Then the proper command is **exit**.

9.7 BASIC UNIX COMMANDS

9.7.1 Home

As you login, after giving your password, the system will automatically put you onto your Home directory. When the super user gives you an account, he will allot a directory for you to work in. Each user will have a unique directory. This is called the Home directory.

Your home directory is that directory under /usr which has been assigned to you. This is the directory in which you will work as soon as you log in. Your login directory or home directory will be recorded in the /etc/passwd file. If you type echo $HOME the name of your login directory is displayed. This is the starting point from where you will begin to move around the UNIX system. However, as you continue to work, you will soon find yourself working in other directories too.

Who command

To see the list of users who are working presently on the system. The command is given as

$ who

The system outputs as follows

You tty 2 May 23 09:40
rishi tty 4 May 23 10:00

9.7.2 pwd (present working directory)

In order to ascertain your exact location within the UNIX system use the **pwd** command. Typing **pwd** (and press **Enter**) will let you know which directory you are in. The command **pwd** displays the directory you are working in. Initially it shows the directory that is a subdirectory of *usr*, which is a directory under *root*.

9.7.3 ls (list)

To see what files you have in your directory type **ls** and press **Enter**. ls command gets the system to display the list of files in the directory you are referring to. If no directory is specified, the default directory is your current directory. If your system does not display anything, and another '$' prompt comes on, it means that there are no files in your directory. This is in case of a new account. You may often have to take a listing of files in your directory.

To see the list of files in the directory

$ ls

After execution of this command the list of files will be presented to the user. Following table shows the various option with list command.

Option	Action
➢ Ls –a	➢ lists all directories including '.' entries
➢ ls –I	➢ lists files with i node numbers
➢ ls –l	➢ lists in long form
➢ ls –r	➢ lists files in reverse order
➢ ls –t	➢ lists files sorted by last modified time
➢ ls –u	➢ lists files sorted by last access time
➢ ls –lt	➢ lists files in long form sorted by last modified time
➢ ls -R	➢ recursive list of all files in all subdirectories

9.7.4 Cat (concatenate)

A file can be created using any of the editors available under UNIX or by simply using cat command. Remember that UNIX is case-sensitive, i.e. A and a are treated as different characters. After you type cat file1 and press Enter, the cursor will jump to the next line and wait for your command. Enter the matter that you want to. Press Ctrl D to save the file and to bring you back to the system prompt. Now you have a file by name file1 in your directory.

To get the contents of a file or terminal give following command:

$ cat file-name

Where file-name is the name of file whose contents are to be seen. The system will display the contents of file on terminal.

9.7.5 cp (copy)

The syntax of this command for copying file(s) is cp [{source file} {target file}]. For example, cp file1 file2. Now we have two files, namely file1 and file2.

To make copy of one file in another file give following command

$ cp source-file dest-file

Where source-file is the name of file whose copy is to be made and dest-file is the name of file by which new copy will be made.

Example:

$ cp test1 test2

This will copy the contents of test1 into a file named test2. cp can be thought of as a short form of copy.

9.7.6 Changing the name of a file

To change the name of a file give following command

$ mv old-file-name new-file-name

Where old-file-name is the name of file whose name you want to change and new-file-name is the name which you want to give to the file.

Example:

$ mv test1.txt test2.txt

This command will change the name of file test1.txt to test2.txt

9.7.7 Deleting a file

To delete a file from the system use following command

$ rm file-name

Where file-name is name of file which is to be deleted.

Example:

$ rm test

Now the file test will be removed from system. If you list files now, it will not be seen.

9.8 ADDITIONAL FEATURES OF UNIX FILE

Any UNIX file is seen as a stream of bytes by the operating system no matter whether it is a directory, text file or a file containing program instructions. One byte will represent one character for text data, one digit for numeric data and the byte itself for binary data.

This requires a very simple file structure but something more is needed to keep track of the file and its contents. In any computer system files are stored in a secondary storage media called disk. In UNIX OS, at the time of creation of file an I-node entry is created on a part of the disk set aside for this purpose called I-node area.

9.8.1 I-Nodes

The I-node is there one for each file existing in the file system. It contains the location of disk where actual data of file is starting, the size of file, last access and updating times and access permission of the file (about which we will see later), who owns the file. Any file name given by the user is first translated to its unique I-node number and then onwards, this becomes reference point for the system. Only things missing in i-node is the name of file and its contents. The name is stored as part of the contents of the directory file to which this file belongs. The i-node number of the file is also kept with its name in the contents of the directory which is again a file for Unix Operating System. The I-node number of Root directory (/) is known to the system at the time of starting up.

If you want to set the i-node number given to a file use following command:

$ ls -l file-name

9.9 TYPE OF UNIX FILES

Any Unix can be one of the following types:

- Directory
- Data file or ordinary file
- Block device file
- Character device file.

We have already seen, in brief, the first two types of files. The other two are those files that correspond to a device. The contents of these files do not reside on the disk but on any other device. In case of these type of files the i-node contains the characteristics of device in place of starting address and size. A block device is capable of reading and writing data in terms of blocks while a character device always reads/ writes one character at a time.

9.9.1 File Naming Conventions

Any file in Unix can be 14 characters long. The characters can be all printable characters of computer character set. Difference is made between upper case and lower case characters unlike DOS. Character/ cannot be used in making name of file.

Following are examples of valid file names:

cd13
A12
A%&bcA$#12
a12

Here A12 and a12 are different files.
Following are invalid file names

1/2 : It means file 2 of directory 1
ABCDEFGHIJK123 : more than 14 characters.

9.9.2 Directory Files

These are the files that represent directory. As we have seen earlier directories are also seen as a special file by the operating system. The contents of these files are as follows:

Name of file which is under that directory
Number of I-node of that file

9.9.3 Accessing Files

In UNIX, any file is accessed by giving absolute or relative path name. On receiving the request, operating system passes the component of pathname. If it is starting with a / then it assumes the path to be absolute, otherwise it is treated as relative.

If absolute pathname is given then it goes to the content of the root file whose I-node is known to the system. If it is relative, then it goes to the content of current working directory whose I-node is also known to system.

Now the next name is taken from path and searched into current directory file. If found then I-node number is picked up and the process goes on till full path name is scanned or there is a failure to find the next name in current directory.

If the full pathname was scanned then final I-node number at hand is the I-node number of the asked file, otherwise system reports absence of file.

9.9.4 Using Devices as Files

Unlike other operating systems, in UNIX, all devices are seen as a special file of the file system. This gives a uniformity of operations over different types of devices of the file system. Every device available is given a file name under the system. So this name will go in some directory and I-node will be allocated. No data area is allocated on the disk for such files.

Normally such files are kept in /dev directory. In the I-node of such files we do not have start of data and file size as we do not have any data on the disk of these files. The files associated with a device as indicated by a b or c in the file type byte in I-node. So if we see the directory of the /dev directory we will see:

```
$ls-l/dev
crw-w-w- 1 root          0,0 jan 13:01 console
brw-r-r— 1 root          7,0 jan 8 11:57 dsk
crw-w-w- 1 root          1,2 jan 9 11:51 tty01
crw-w-w- 1 ankita        1,3 jan 10 10:30 tty02
```

As we see that all the file entries are having c or b in first column which tells the system whether it is a character device (from which data comes character by character like keyboard, console, printer etc.) or a block device (from which data can be read/written in blocks like disks, tapes etc.).

In I-nodes of these files, we have a pair of number in place of start address and size. The major identifies the type of device and minor number specifies individual unit of that type. Device names like ttynm are the names of our terminal devices. For ordinary files the read/write operations takes place on the disk itself while for device files these operations are performed by a Set of kernal routines which are called device drivers.

9.10 IDENTIFICATION AND ROLE OF VARIOUS USERS

9.10.1 User-id

As we have seen already, to enter into the system one has to give an identification name and password. The identification name is called user-id. A numeric number is also given to each identification name by the system internally. This number is also called user-id.

9.10.2 Group-id

The administrator of the system may put related users in a group by telling the system the list of user-ids constituting this group. The group is given a name and this name is called group-id.

9.10.3 Process-id

In UNIX operating system any program that is running is called a Process. Every process of the system is identified by a unique number given by the operating system. This number is called process-id of the process.

9.10.4 Super-User

The users of Unix system can be classified in two categories. First those who are allowed to use the system for their own use. These users may not be allowed to do certain operations like:

-Creating new user-ids
-Accessing files of some important directory
-Boot the system

Second are those users who are authorized to do anything on the system which it can do. These are called super-user.

9.11 MANAGING DIRECTORIES AND FILES IN UNIX

In Unix operating system, the files are organized in the form of a tree. In a tree there is a root, branches, sub-branches and finally leaves. Similarly in Unix file system there is a root directory, sub-directories and files. In this scheme every file is assigned to a directory.

A directory is a specialized form of file that maintains a list of all the files in it. Moreover, a file in a directory can be a directory in itself, it would be called a sub-directory of the original. Each user of the system is assigned a home directory, which is called his root-working directory. From that point he can make his own structure of files and directories.

The root directory which is named/, is the prime directory and starting point of the file system. All the files and directories will emerge from this point.

The tree scheme makes it easy to organize files. You can create a sub-director for C programs, under which one for pay-roll and other for financial accounting etc.

When you tell the system, name of any file then it assumes it to be the current working directory. At the time of login, user's home directory, which is fixed by the administrator, becomes the current working directory. At any time to know the name of current working directory give the following command, as we have seen in the last chapter.

$ pwd

Pathname

The full specification of a file/directory in Unix is given by preceding the name of file with a list of all directories leading to it separated by

/, starting from root directory. Such a specification is called pathname of file/directory.

For example suppose root(/) directory has following sub-directories.

usr bin etc

Directory usr has following sub-directories or files

raman	*sub-directory*
ajay	*sub-directory*
Test	*file*

Directory raman has following directories and files

a.c.	b.c	as files
finac		as subdirectory

Now the full name of file a.c. would be

/usr/raman/a.c.

While full name of file test would be

/usr/test

These pathnames are also called absolute path names.

If a file is existing in a directory which is a descendent of current working directory then it can be specified by a relative pathname which is given by preceding the name of file with a list of all directories leading to it starting from current directory.

For example in above case if /usr is current working directory then a.c. could be specified as

raman/a.c.

The current working directory is also denoted by .(dot), while the directory to which current working directory belongs is called parent directory and is denoted by ..(double dot). These special names can be used in specifying when /usr/abhay is current directory, as

../test

Moreover in above case for working directory /usr/raman

../.. and/are equivalent

Because while reading pathnames, operating system goes on changing its working directory temporarily. So second.. will refer to the parent directory of /usr/raman.

When you log-in into the system then the directory in which you are left is called your home directory. This is fixed by system administrator.

9.11.1 How to Change Current Working Directory

Current working directory can be changed by cd command as follows:

$ cd name-of-directory

If name of directory, which is optional, is not given then home directory becomes current working directory of the user.

For example if /usr/raman is current working directory then to makr/usr/rishi as working directory following command should be given.

$ cd /usr/rishi

or

$ cd../rishi

9.11.2 How to Create and delete directories

To create any directory at any place the command is mkdir. To create a directory, follow this command with name of directory with absolute or relative pathname. For example, to create a directory cfiles under the directory /usr/raman we should give command:

$ mkdir /usr/raman/cfiles

or

$ md /usr/raman/cfiles

or

$ cd /usr/raman
$ mkdir cfiles

But while giving the name of directory make sure that all other directories which occur in the pathname of the directory to be created are already created. To remove a directory the first condition is that there should not be any entry of file remaining under that directory and you should not be working in that directory. The command is rmdir or rm -r. This should be followed by name of directory to be removed. In any computer system files are stored in a secondary storage media called disk. In Unix OS, at the time of creation of file an i-node entry is created on a part of the disk set aside for this purpose called I-node area. The i-node is there one for each file existing in the file system. It contains the location of disk where actual data of file, starting size of file, last access and updation times and access permission of the file, who owns the file. Any file name given by the user is first translated to its unique i-node number and then onwards, this becomes reference point for the system. Only things missing in I-node is the name of file and its contents. The name is stored as part of the contents of the directory file system which this file belongs. The i-node number of the file is also kept with its name in the contents of the directory, which is again a file for Unix operating system. The I-node number of Root directory (/) is known to the system at the time of starting up.

If you want to set i-node number given to a file use following command:

```
$ ls -l file-name
```

To see the details of any file kept in i-node give following command:

```
$ ls -l
$ mkdir/usr/raman/cfiles
```

or

```
$md/usr/raman/cfiles
```

or

```
$cd/usr/raman
$mkdir cfiles
```

but while giving thc name of directory make sure that all other directories which occur in the pathname of the directory to be created are already created.

To remove a directory the first condition is that there should not be any entry of file remaining under that directory and you should not be working in that directory.

The command is rmdir or rm -r. This should be followed by name of directory to be removed.

To remove the directory which was created earlier, give following command.

```
$cd/usr/raman
$4rmdir/usr/abhay/cfiles
```

or

```
$rm -r cfiles
```

9.12 SECURITY FEATURES IN UNIX

UNIX provides the facility to specify who can and who cannot use your file and in which manner. The system divides the domain of its users as the user (you), members of your group (those whose group name has been given same as that of you) and others. As we have already seen the group formulation is job of system administrator. For each of these 3 divisions the system keeps track of 3 kinds of permission to read, write and execute for each file. Read permissions means one can see contents of a file. Write permissions allow updation of contents of file. Execute permission lets one run a file which is supposed to contain an executable program. We can see these permissions through ls-l command

```
$ls-l test.c
-rw-r-r— 1 test.c 2451 jan 16 12:32 raman
```

information about permission is kept as a 10 character structure which is shown in the beginning. We will not care about first character which we have seen so far as indicating file type. Character - implies an ordinary file. Next nine characters are for total nine permissions (read, write, execute) for owner, group members and others.

First three (rw-) tells permissions for user about read, write, execute permissions sequentially. Here it says that user can read, write but cannot execute it. Similarly next three are for group members and further next three are for other users, a- at a place says that permission is not granted. Meaning of characters is

r read
w write
x execute

The command for changing these permissions is chmod. To use it you follow the command with an instruction string by name of file. The instructions string basically has three parts.

The first three parts contain one or more letters indicating groups affected after change (u for user, g for group, o for others).

The second part consists of a + or -, indicating whether permission is to be set to yes or no respectively.

Finally a string of one or more characters indicating type of permission that are not affected (r for read, w for write and x for execute).

A general instruction string could be a combination of such basic strings. For example, to allow write permissions for group members for file test.c, we have to say

```
$ chmod g+w test.c
```

If you want to set the permission so that nobody should be able to read or write the file except you, then give the command

```
$ chmod go-rw test.c
```

9.13 GETTING HELP

The command line prompt environment of UNIX is not very user-friendly. There are two basic commands to get help though. The first, 'man' prints the manual page (often referred to simply as the 'man page') for a specific command. For example,

man passwd

This will tell how to use the password command. A manual page can be quite long, containing more than one screenful of information. If so, one screenful will be displayed at a time and the system will wait for you to press the space bar to get another screenful, d to scroll forward one-half page, Enter for one more line, b to scroll backwards one screenful, or q to quit. Note that it is not necessary to press the Enter key after the space, d, b or q.

The information in a manual page is complete for a given command, but it is not always easy or ready to understand and remember, and it is assumed that its information can be placed in context—not something that a beginning user can always do. In addition, it is assumed that you know the command itself, so questions like 'How do I see what files are in this directory?' are not directly answerable.

The second help command is 'apropos'. It also needs a word to work with but the word need not be an actual command. For example,

apropos file

will print a list of all commands that deal with files. It is then upto the user to find the specific command. This again may not be all that helpful—a common UNIX word like 'file' can produce dozens of lines on files, few of which will be useful or even understandable to a beginner. This state of affairs keeps UNIX guidebook authors busy.

Some systems now offer other methods of obtaining help. For example, GNU's 'info' command offers a menu-based help utility, and commercial versions of UNIX often have proprietary help utilities.

9.14 INTRODUCTION TO SHELL PROGRAMMING

9.14.1 Introduction to Shell

Shell, a facility in UNIX, provides the environment for an user to execute his commands. Shell is a program that interprets the request made by an user to run his program. It is the most important program for Unix users. By using Shell efficiently most of the works can be accomplished without much hard work or programming in a conventional languages like C. In other words, we can say that Shell is utility or tool provided by the UNIX to users to run the commands, execute programs without much of efforts. There are basically three types of Shell available in Unix Environment.

- C-Shell
- V-Shell
- Bash

Program Shell and C-Shell are the most popular among such programs. The basic theme of both the programs is same. Most of the Linux users prefer to use Bash Shell.

9.14.2 Command Execution in UNIX

The simplest command of Unix is a single word, usually naming a file for execution (later we will see some other type of commands). The examples are

```
$cat pawan.c
$ ls -ls
$ pwd
```

It is also possible to give multiple command in a same line. The semicolon is used as a deleminator. You may enter more than one command separated by semicolon, these commands will be executed one after another. A command usually ends with a new line (carriage return) but semicolon ; is also used as command terminator. For example:

```
$ who;
```

But it is not necessary to give each command on a fresh line; we can give multiple separated by; as follows:

```
$ who ; pwd
$ date ; who
```

Here first the date command will be executed, followed by execution of who commands as follows:

```
$ date ; who
Wed May 23 09:43:17 EDT 1990
you      tty2      May 23 09:55
ajay     tty4      May 23 10:00
$
```

You may note that output of second command follows immediately the output of the first command, without giving even the prompt. The prompt is given at last. Here the execution of commands is sequential. Although it is a command terminator but even now final new line character has to be given; until that Shell will not proceed with the command line. About redirection and pipes we have already learnt. These facilities are provided by Shell only. Now look at following:

```
$ date ; who | wc
Wed May 23 09:43:17 EDT 1990
2       10      60
$
```

wc is a command which counts and writes number of lines, words & characters in its standard input. So as we mentioned above, output of the date was given on the terminal but that of who was piped to wc. So pipe doesn't combine the output of all previous commands. It gives rise to concept of precedence to such symbols in the manner as desired. So in above case if output of date and who both is to be piped to wc then we can say

```
$ (date; who) | wc
3       16      89
```

9.14.3 Executing Commands in Background

Since UNIX is multiprocessing Operating System, it provides the facility of executing two or more programs/commands to be executed simultaneously. You may enter a command or execute the program which will run in background. The word background means that it will run in isolation and may take time to complete execution. Another command terminator is ampersand &. Syntactically it is exactly similar to the semicolon or newline; except that it tells the Shell not to wait for the command to complete and let it run in background. Normally this is used with commands, which run for a long time and do not interact with user during execution. The command terminated with & is activated by the shell and it displays the process-id of this background process before returning to the prompt. It may be used in combination of ; but precedence of & is higher than that of ; So a command line like

```
$ ls -ls ; a.out ;
```

will print the directory list and a.out will execute the program in the background which may take time but the command prompt will be made available to user or Shell is ready to execute other commands to be given by user. The command execution will also return the process identification number (process id) of program under background execution. The completion of a background command could be known by ps command because we know the process-id of the background process. This could also be known by printing a diagnostic message as follows

$(cp lfile1 lfile2 ; echo copy process is completed) & 3876

In this case cp and echo command both will be executed in background mode in sequence. 3876 is the process-id of the process of cp command. After the copy operation is complete following message is given by echo command on terminal

Copy process is completed

Most commands accept arguments in command line such as name of file in cp. command. These arguments could be

- Name of files to act upon
- General words
- Options

In Unix it is a command practice to represent option with a leading minus sign, but it is not mandatory. The various special character interpreted by the shell, such as < > ; and & are not argument to the programs, instead they control the way Shell executes the programs. Following is order of precedence in decreasing order of the symbol used by shell in interpreting the command. (>< | & ;). But by use of parenthesis the desired control can be achieved.

9.14.4 How to Create the Command of Your Own Command?

Shell provides the facility to create the command of your desire. These are called user defined commands. New commands are created by Shell by using older ones. This is most powerful facility of Shell. Let us see following command

$ cp ajay.c temp.c

Above command will copy contents of ajay.c to temp.c. If this process is to be done again and again, we can replace this command by s shorter command, i.e. if we like to get a handy command, the first step is to produce a normal file containing the command

$ cp ajay.c temp.c It can be done by following process. This we can easily do as
$ echo ' $ cp ajay.c temp.c ' > handy

Here command echo will be outputting the sequence $ cp ajay.c temp.c into a handy file. The quotes are essential. Now if we issue the command

$ sh handy

Then the result would be counting of uses. Command sh takes input line of standard input or of given file as command and executes them. We can make the 'handy' itself as a command by specifying that 'handy' contains some commands and such files are called Shell files All you have to do is to change mode of 'handy' as executable

$ chmod +x handy

and after that you may enter the following only to copy the file.

$ handy

So in this fashion any new command can be generated by putting the already available commands in desired fashion in a file and making the file executable by changing the mode of that file.

9.14.5 Command with Arguments and Parameters

The argument of any Shell command line can be referred as follows, after invoking the command line:

$0	for name of command
$1	for 1st argument
$2	for 2nd argument
$9	for 9th argument
$*	for all argument

Using this notion we can make a command for setting the mode of any given file as executable. The command could be known as cx

$ echo 'chmod + x1' >cx

Now file cx contains

chmod + x $1

if we enter

$sh cx cx

then the Shell is having two arguments

$0	as	cx
$1	as	cx

Here sh itself is not taken as command name so the command in cx file which is *chmod +x $1* will be executed as.

chmod +x cx

After parameter substitution; which will make cx as executable Now type the command

$cx nu

Since cx has been made a file so now

$0	as	cx
$1	as	nu

Therefore mode of nu will be made executable.

Moreover we can make a command which will make all files executable given on command line as follows

$echo 'chmod +x$*' >cx

And given the command

$sh cx cx

Will make cx as executable. Now if command

$cx file1 file2 file3

is given then it will make all file executable because $* will argument except the command itself.

9.14.6 Shell Variables

Every Shell has a set of variables. In Borne shell there are two sets of variables as

(i) User created variable
(ii) System Shell variable

The Shell variable can be used at any place where a word could be used as

$ Variableid

When such names are encountered, they are substituted by their given values. Any variable in Bourne shell can be assigned a value by Variableid = value.

for example

$name= pawan
$echo $name
pawan

It may be noted that variable name must begin with $ sign. For example $echo name will give 'name' at screen.

So to get the value of any Shell variable we must precede name of variable by $ sign

The set command, on its own, print list of Shell variable and their values.

Local Shell Variables

In general, a shell variable is a local variable. That is, it is known to the Shell, which created it. When you start a new Shell (by running a Shell script or by typing sh command) then this shell is ignorant of the variable created by previous Shell. If this new Shell creates any variable then after the execution of this shell the variable would also vanish.

```
$name=pawan          name is local shell variable
$ echo $name
pawan
```

Now create a new shell by issuing the following command.

```
$sh                  A new shell is created
$echo $ name
```

At this command, Shell will not recognize variable 'name' as its declaration is not known to new Shell. You may return to earlier Shell by doing

```
$ctrl D
```

then issue

```
$ echo $name
pawan
```

The previous Shell remembers the values of the variable declared locally to them. Then the command will be executed.

Global Shell Variable

Sometimes we want the new Shell to know the old Shell variables. Then we can use export command. Any Shell variable used as an argument of this command will exit in child Shells also. Exported variables are made global to only child shells and to parent shells. For example:

```
$export variableid
$variableid = kharagpur
```

```
$echo $variableid
kharagpur
$sh
$echo $variableid
kharagpur
$variablaid = europe
$echo $variableid
europe
$control D
$echo $variableid
kharagpur
```

To find out the variable, already exported just give the command export without any arguments. As we can see above, export causes the old Shell to give a copy of the variable to the new one. This copy has the same value as in original Shell. Subsequently value of copy can be changed but when new Shell dies, old one recovers the value of original variable.

9.15 CONTROL STRUCTURES IN SHELL PROGRAMMING

Just like conventional programming, in the Shell Programming also, one have to come across the situation when the programmer needs the control structures/statement. In the Shell, use of if-then-else, for loop etc are allowed to use.

9.15.1 If Statement

Syntax of If statement is as follows,

If condition
then Commands
fi

Following example illustrates the use of If statement. Write following Shell script in a file "ram".

```
if [ $1= shayam ]
then
        echo " Hello $1"
fi
```

Change the file "ram" into a executable file and run it at UNIX prompt.

```
$ ram shyam
Hello shyam
```

If the following command is executed at prompt,

```
$ ram kishan
$
```

The script will check whether the $1 is equal to "shyam". If the condition is satisfied then the command inside the then clause will be executed.

The same statement may be used with the else clause. The full syntax of if-then-else statement is given below.

```
If condition
then commands
else commands
fi
```

9.15.2 For Loop

The general syntax of for loop is given below,

```
for [ identifier ] in [ values ]
do
        commands
done
```

Just type in following script in to the file "example".

```
for I in 1 2 3 4
do
        echo $I
done
```

Make the file "example" executable and run following command at Unix prompt.

```
$ example
   1
   2
   3
   4
$
```

SELECT EXERCISES

Q. 1. Why the password is not displayed on the screen? Explain why UNIX always asks for a User Name before logging on to system?

Q. 2. What is a Shell? How many types of Shell UNIX provides? Explain the main features of these.

Q. 3. Explain the UNIX architecture in brief. What is the role of Kernal? How the commands are interpreted in UNIX?

Q. 4. Give brief description on UNIX, LINUX, and describe which of them should be used and when?

Q. 5. What do you mean by the process of Swapping?

Q. 6. What do you mean by Context Switching? How much time is required to do context switching among the process? Is it possible to measure this time?

Q. 7. How a variable can be exported to its parent shell?

Q. 8. Write a shell script to copy one file to another. The script should prompt the user to enter the source and destination file.

Q. 9. Write a shell script to rename the file. Do not use MV command in the script.

Q. 10. Write a script to locate a word in a group of files. The program must stop execution when it encounters the given word.

Q. 11. How a message is sent from one user to another in UNIX system?

Q. 12. Write a shell script which can find and delete a file, which contains the string "fine".

Q. 13. What is UNIX? Give its historical developments along with its characteristics.

Q. 14. What do you understand by system prompt? What is the symbol used for displaying system prompt at your UNIX installation?

Q. 15. Give complete description of UNIX shell. What are the basic rules that it follows to interpret the commands. Give at least 10 utilities with its functions that it interprets?

Q. 16. What information is presented when one enters date command?

Q. 17. What happens when you try to execute an erroneous command?

Q. 18. What is the use of who command?

Q. 19. What is a user-id?

Q. 20. What is difference between a normal user and super user?

Q. 21. Why super user is required on UNIX operating system?

Q. 22. What is a process and process-id?

Q. 23. How the commands are executed in the background?

Q. 24. How can you create a command of your own using Shell?

Q. 25. How will you change the mode of your file?

Q. 26. What do you mean by Local and Global Shell Variable?

10 Elements of Programming in C

10.0 INTRODUCTION TO PROGRAMMING LANGUAGE & C

Program is set of well-defined instructions written in the programming language, which a computer understands. These instructions are executed sequentially i.e. one after another. A Programming Language is essentially the neat & clean description of set of rules in which real world problems may be submitted to computer. Till date many programming languages has been developed for various specific & general-purpose problem domains. Essentially we may classify the programming language in to three sets called Machine Languages, Assembly Language and Higher Level Programming Languages. In early days, programmer used to write the program in the machine language which were very much hardware dependent and programming in that language was a tough & complex job. In assembly language, programs are written in mnemonic and writing programs in assembly language are convenient to programmers. Program written in the assembly language is converted/translated in to machine level program by a translator called Assembler. Writing programs in the higher level language are most convenient to the programmers. Programs written in Higher Level Languages are translated by a translator called Compiler.

Till date many general purpose programming languages have been developed. FORTRAN, BASIC, PASCAL, LISP, ADA, PROLOG, COBOL, APL & PL/1 are the popular examples. C programming languages is a distinguished programming language, which is being widely used by the scientific community. C is a versatile language programming language in the sense that you may write program from any problem domain. Program written in C is portable in the sense that it may be executed on different computing environment.

10.1 BODY OF PROGRAM IN C

Program written in C contains one or more functions. The program must contain a function called main and program begins with main function. Every function contains, a function heading, a list of argument declaration and a set of statements. You may also put the comments for your ready reference or for any other purpose in the C Program. A compiler omit the comments when it translate the program. The comment must be bounded by /* comments */.

Let us write the first program, which will displays a statement " Welcome to C World".

Program 1

```
/* This is the first program in C */
# include <stdio.h>
main ( )
{
printf(" Welcome to C World");
}
```

In the program 1, first line contains the remark " This is first program in C ". Second line #include <stdio.h> is preprocessor directive which ensures reading an header file stdio.h . A preprocessor directive is a command to the preprocessor pass of compilation to perform a specific task. Third line contains the beginning of the main function. Immediately after this within curly parenthesis, the statement of the C program are included. This statement print a line on the standard output (your monitor). Basic block structure of the C program is as follows. It may contain one or more section as defined below.

- Comment Lines
- Link section
- Definition section
- Global declaration section
- Main()
- {
- declarative statements;
- executable statements;
- }

Here comment lines consists of set of comment lines containing the name of author, date of program, purpose of program etc or any other thing which a programmer wish to attach with the program. Link section contains instructions to compiler to include the system function from the C library. In the definition section defines all symbolic constants and global declaration section contains the declaration of variable which will be used in the program. Main body of program contains declaration of variables etc and executable statements of the program.

10.2 DATA TYPES

10.2.1 Character Set

The number of characters which may be used in the C programming language may be grouped in the following four categories namely letters, digits, special character, white spaces. Any variable, statement, constant may consist of the character from the character set.

- Letters
  Lowercase Letter a to z
  Uppercase Letter A to Z
- Digit 0 to 9
- Special Character !,@,#,$,%,^,&,*,(,),+ etc.
- White Spaces
  Blank space
  Tabs
  Return
  New line

10.2.2 Identifiers

Identifiers are the word or names used to refer to the variable, constant, function name etc. Theses are user-defined name which consist as a string of character from character set. There are also a list of key word which have a fixed meaning in the C. const, case, if, then, else, while, do etc are the key words. Programmer to define any variable or constant can not use the key word.

10.2.3 Constant

Constant in the C may be classified in to four categories namely Integer constant, real constant, character constant and string constants.

Integer Constant : Integer constant refer to the sequence of digit. It must not have any character except digit, however an integer constant may be preceded by '+' or '-'.

Example

153, -876, 3543, 0, 2, -998, + 118 are the valid integer constant.

11,435, $ 4000, Rs 5000, 7500/- are invalid constant.

Real Constant : A real constant in the C is numeric constant with a sign of decimal point or exponent or a combination. Following is an example showing the list of invalid & valid real constant.

Example :

34.789, 0.0001, 9.0, 3e-9, +247.0, 4e-3, 2.58e+3, 315. are the valid real constant.

2, 2,000.00, .34e+12.67, are invalid real constants.

Character Constant : A character constant is any symbol or value that is the part of valid character set. An valid character constant must be enclosed within the single quotes.

Example :

```
Char c;      /* define the character c */
c= ' B';     /* assigns character 'B' to the variable c of character
                type. */
```

String Constant : String constant is the sequence of the one or more characters from the defined character set i.e. Following are the example of valid string constants.

"Fine", "27863", " @#$%&* ", "b" are the valid string constants.

10.2.4 Variables

A variable is the meaningful name assigned represent a data object. The value of the variable may change during the execution of the program. There are few rules for declaring the variable name. They are as follows

- Variable name must start with a letter (a-z or A to Z)
- Variable name can not begin with the digit.
- Variable name can not contain punctuation mark, math symbol or other special symbols.
- ANSI (American National Standard Institute) restrict variable to be of 32 characters.
- Reserved words name can not be used a variable name.

'tax', 'value', 'intrate' 'a123' are the valid variable name. '-vi', ' static', '+value' are the example of invalid variable names.

Assigning Value to Variable

Variables are created to store the value of data object in the program. Result of an computational statement may be may be assigned to a variable.

Program 2

```
/* This program print result of addition of two numbers */
#include <stdio.h>
main ( )
{
int  number1;
int number2;
int result;
number1=50;
number2=100;
result= number1+number2;
printf( " Result of addition is ", result );
}
```

Output of the program is as follows

Result of addition is 150

In the Program 2, addition to number 1 & number 2 is assigned to variable result.

10.2.5 Relational Operator

Relational operators are used to compare the value of two variable for various conditions such as greater, less than or equal etc. All relational operator returns the result in either 'True' or 'False'. Following are some widely used relational operator in C.

- < less than
- <= less than or equal to
- > greater than
- >= greater than or equal to
- == equal to
- != not equal to

Following is the example showing result of some relational expressions.

12 !=15	True
12==12	True
46 >= 47	False
2.88 <= 3.10	True

10.2.6 Logical Operator

An expression, which combines two or more relational expression, is called logical expression. Just similar to the relational expression, an logical expression results in either true or false.

Following are the logical operators used in the C program.

&&	Logical AND
||	Logical OR
!	Logical NOT

A table showing the result of two relational expression A & B is shown below.

A	B	A &&B	A||B
True	True	True	True
True	False	False	True
False	True	False	True
False	False	False	False

Example

Suppose
int a=10
float b = 2.5
char c = 'a'

Then the following relational expression yields true or false as follows.

Expression	Boolean Value
a < 15	true
((a > 5)&&(c=='a'))	true
((a< 5) && (c=='a'))	false
(c != 'd') || ((a+b)< 15)	true
(c =='d')|| ((a -b)== 6)	false
! ((a > (b+2))	false
c >= 100 * (a+b)	false

10.2.7 Conditional Operator

Conditional operators are used in place of inf-then-else construct. An expression, which uses the conditional operator, is called conditional expression. This type of expression is used in place of if-then-else statement. General format of this expression is as follows.

E1 ? E2 : E3 , here E1,E2,E3 are expressions.

In such cases the E1 is evaluated first. If its value is found to be true then E2 is evaluated . If the E1 is evaluated to be false then expression E3 is evaluated. For example consider the following statements.

```
I= 5;
J= 10
Val = ( I > J ) ? I : J;
```

In this example the, Val is evaluated as follows.

If (I > J) then Val = I

Else Val = J

10.2.8 Library Functions

C allows some mathematical functions also. These functions are called mathematical functions. The compiler evaluates these functions. Following table presents some widely used library functions.

Function	Explanation
sqrt (x)	Square root of x
exp(x)	'e' to the power 'x'
pow(X,Y)	X to power Y
log (x)	Log of x with base e
abs(x)	Absolute value of x
rand()	Generate positive random number
ceil(x)	Rounds the value of x to nearest integer
sin(x)	sin x, where x be in radian.
cos(x)	cos x, "
tan(x)	tan x, "
tolower(x)	Return lower case value of character
toupper	Converts to uppercase
toascii(x)	Returns ASCII value of character x
getchar ()	Enters a character from the keyboard
putchar(c)	Prints a character to output device
rand(0	Returns a positive random number

These library functions are not the part of the language but these are supplied with the C. In order to use these library function it is necessary to use header file. The header files are the logical collection of various functions. For example the functions which are used to carry out standard input/output operation, functions for character handling, mathematical functions are bundled in the appropriate header file. If you do not include the appropriate header file in the program, these function will not be available for use. The vendor as a part of C compiler supplies these library or header files. The name of these header files are supplied by individual C compil ɔr vendor, but some of the common header files are stdio.h, conio.h, math.h etc. These gheader files are included to your program using preprocessor directive as give below.

```
#include <stdio.h>
#include < conio.h >
#include <math.h>
```

10.2.9 Basic Input and Output instructions

scanf: This function is used to input a set of values. The general format of the scanf function is as follows.

scanf (FS, List of arguments)

Here FS is known as format string & list of argument contains the variable in to which the value or data from standard input will be stored. Format string is a string with characters indicating the format of the variables. Each format must start with % sign . Each numeric variable must be preceded by & sign.

Example

scanf("%d", & number);

This statement will store a decimal type of integer data in to the variable number from the input.

scanf ("%s %d %f ", code, &quantity, & rate)

This statement will store a string to variable code, decimal type integer data to quantity and floating point value to rate from the standard input .

printf : This function is used to print any combination of string, number or character to the standard output (monitor of your computer). The format of the printf statement is given below.

printf ("FS", List of arguments);

Here format string contains the format characters for the corresponding variables. It must be preceded by the % sign.

Example

printf (" sum= %f Number1= %d Number2= %d \n", sum,number1,number2);

This statement prints the value of floating variable sum and integer value of number1 & number2 variables.

10.2.10 Single Character Input / Output Statement

Single character may be entered from the standard input using the standard I/O library function getchar(). It when executed, expects a character from the standard input e.g. keyboard. Single character may be displayed to the dtandard output e..g. monitor using standard input /output library function putchar () .

Example

char I;	declares I as character variable
I= getchar();	assign input from keyboard to I
putchar (I)	displays or send the value of I to monitor.

Program 3

```
/*THIS PROGRAM CONVERTS A BINARY NUMBER TO DECI-
   MAL*/
#include <conio.h>
#include <stdio.h>
#include <math.h>
#define M 15
main()
{
int n,a[M],count=0,p,i,sum=0,temp;
clrscr();
printf ("\n GIVE THE NUMBER IN THE BINARY FORM (only 1
   & 0 are allowed)\n");
scanf("%d",&n);
p=n;
do
{
a[count]=n%10;
count++;
n=n/10;
}while(n>0);
for(i=0;i<count;i++)
{
temp=a[i]*pow(2,i);
sum=sum+temp;
}
printf("\n\nTHE DECIMAL EQUIVELENT OF %d IS :
   %d",p,sum);
getch();
}
```

10.2.11 Assignment Statement & Shorthand Operator

Assignment operators are used to assign the result of computational statements. C also provides the use of short hand operators for the purpose of assignments.

The assignment statement A O = E; where A is the variable and O is the operator and E is the expression.

This statement is equivalent to

A= A O E;

Example :

X+=3;	is equivalent to	x=x+3;
A-=3;	is equivalent to	A=A-3;
A/=B+C;	is equivalent to	A=A/(B+C);
A*=A	is equivalent to	A=A*A

Increment & Decrement Operators :

C provides to operator for the purpose of increment & decrement. These operators are ++ and — . First operator adds one to the value of variable and other decrement the value of variable by one. These operator may be used in two way i.e. it may precede or succeed the variable name.

Example

++a, a++, a—, —a are the valid statements. ++a and a++ increase the value of a by one and a—, —a decrement the value of a by 1. The difference in the mode is given in the following example. A prefix operator first adds one to the operand and then result is assigned to the variable on the left hand side. A post fix operator first assign the value to the variable on left then increment the operand.

Example

Consider following statements .

A=1;
B=++A;

After the execution of the second statement value of A & B would be 2.

Consider following statements,

A=1;
B=A++;

In this case value of B would be 1 and value of A would be 2.

Program 4

```
/* This program illustrate the usage of short hand operator */
# include <stdio.h>
main( )
{
int a,b,c;
a=2;b=3;c=4;
a*=b+c;
printf ("%d %d %d ", a,b,c );
```

```
c++;
printf ("%d %d %d ", a,b,c );
}
```

Output of this program after first print statement
A=14,b=3,c=4
Output of this program after first print statement
A=14,b=3,c=5

Program 5

```
/* This program computes the gross pay
gross pay= basic pay + basic pay * Dearness Allowance */
#include <stdio.h>
main ( )
{
int basic_pay, da;
float gross_pay;
printf (" enter the basic pay & dearness allowance);
scanf(" %d %d ", & basic_pay, & da);
gross_pay= basic_pay + ( basic_pay * da);
printf(" Gross pay = %f\n", gross_pay)
}
```

10.3 CONTROL STRUCTURES IN C

Decision making and looping is the one of the basic construct of any programming language. These constructs are also provided in the C Programming language.

10.3.1 If Then Else Statement

Decision making in the C programming language is provided through if -then -else statements. There are several instances when a decision is required subject to the fulfillment of a specified condition. The syntax of this statement is given below.

```
If ( Condition Expresssion)
{
statement set1;
}
else
{
statement set2;
}
```

In this statement, the expression given as condition expression is evaluated as true or false. If the condition expression is evaluated to true, the statements given in the statement set1 are executed . if the condition expression is evaluated to be false, then the statements given in the statement set 2 are executed. For example, in the given program, if the value of "a" is grater than "b", first printf() is executed. This will print the statement " A is greater than B" otherwise if the value of a is less than or equal, the second printf() statement is printed. This will print that " A is less than or equal to B".

```
If ( a>b )
printf ( " A is greater than B ");
Else
printf ( " A is less than or equal to B);
```

Program 6

```
/* This program finds the Largest of the three numbers */
#include <stdio.h>
main ( )
{
int p,q,r;
printf("enter all the three number\n");
scanf (" %d %d %d ", &p, &q, &r);
if (p>q)
{
if (p<r)
{
printf ( " Largest  number is %d\n", p);
}
else
{
printf(" Largest Number is %d \n", r);
}
}
else
{
   if (r>q)
         {
                  printf("Largest Number is %d \n",r);
         }
   else
         {
                  printf (" Largest Number is %d \n ",q);
         }
}
}
```

10.3.2 While Statement

One of the mostly used control structure for repeated execution of statement is while statement. When a large numbers of statements are to be executed sequentially for numbers of time or subject to the fulfillment of certain condition the WHILE statement is frequently used. Syntax of this statement is given below.

```
While ( condition expression )
{
statement1;
statement2;
.
.
statement n;
}
```

In this statement, the condition expression is evaluated before the execution of the statements. If the condition is found to be true, then statements given in the statement set are executed. These statement are executed in the sequential manner till the condition is evaluated to be true.

Program 7

```
/* This program calculate m to the power n */
#include<stdio.h>
main ()
{
int m,n, count;
printf ( " enter the value of m & n ");
count=1;
while ( count < n)
{
m*=m;
count++;
}
}
```

Program 8

```
/* This program reverses a string        */
#include<conio.h>
#include<stdio.h>
#include<string.h>
main()
```

```
{
int i,counter=0;
char str[20],str2[20];
clrscr();
printf("THIS IS A PROGRAM OF REVERSING THE STRING
    ORDER");
printf("\nenter your desire string");
scanf("%s",str);
/counter= strlen(str);
for(i=0;str[i]!='\0';i++)
counter++;
for(i=0;i<=counter;i++)
str2[i]=str[i];
printf("\nthe reverse string-\n");
for(i=counter;i>=0;i—)
printf("%c",str2[i]);
printf("\nthe length of string=  %d",counter);
getch();
}
```

10.3.3 Do Statement

This statement is similar to while statement with little difference. Syntax of this statement is given below.

```
Do
{
statement 1;
statement 2;
statement n;
}
while ( condition expression )
```

In this statement the while condition is tested after the statements execution. Next time the statement will be executed If the condition is evaluated to be true again.

Program 9

```
/* This program print a table Fahrenheit, Celsius for the tempera-
    ture
given from 1 F  to 100 F in a step of 2 */
#include <stdio.h)
main()
(
```

```
float fahr, celc;
fahr=1.0;
do
{
celc= ( fahr-32.0)/1.8;
printf ( "%f %f \n",fahr,celc)
fahr=fahr+2.0;
}
while ( fahr<=100.0);
)
```

Program 10

```
/*THIS PROGRAM CONVERT A DECIMAL NUMBER INTO
    BINARY*/
#include<conio.h>
#include<stdio.h>
#define M 15
void main()
{ int n, a[M],i=0,j,p;
clrscr();
printf("Enter the decimal number\n");
scanf("%d",&n);
p=n;
do
{
a[i]=n%2;
i++;
n=n/2;
//i++;
}while(n>0);
printf("\nTHE BINARY EQUIVELENT OF %d IS ::   ",p);
for(j=i-1;j>=0;j—)
printf("%d",a[j]);
getch();
}
```

Program 11

```
/*THIS PROGRAM IS FOR FIBONACCI SERIES */
#include <conio.h>
#include <stdio.h>
#define M 20
main()
```

```
{
int i,n,a[M],sum=0;
char ch;
clrscr();
printf("\n Enter a number of term you wants in your series ?(less
    than %d)\n",M);
scanf("%d",&n);
a[0]=0;
a[1]=1;
for(i=2;i<n;i++)
a[i]=a[i-1]+a[i-2];
printf("\nTHE FABONACCI SERIES OF %d TERM",n);
for(i=0;i<n;i++)
printf("   %d",a[i]);
printf("\n\nDO YOU WANT THE SUMMATION OF THIS SE-
    RIES (y/n)");
ch=getch();
if(ch=='Y'||ch=='y')
{
for (i=0;i<n;i++)
sum=sum+a[i];
printf("\n\n THE SUM OF FIBONACCI  SERIES IS  %d ",sum);
}
else
exit(1);
getch();
}
```

10.3.4 For Statement

For statement is also a widely used statement in the C programming language. Syntax of the for statement is given below.

```
for ( expression1; expression2; expression3)
{
statements;
}
```

In this statement, expresssion1 is normally used to initialize the variables that controls th e loop. The expression2 is the test condition that determines whether the next round of execution of the statement is possible. Expression 3 provides the steps under which the value of the variable should change.

Program 12

```
/* This program prints the number from 1 to 10 */
#include <stdio.h>
main ( )
{
int a;
for (a=1;a<=10;a++)
{
printf ("%d\n",a)
}
}
```

Program 13

```
/*This program  generate table for any given number */
#include<conio.h>
#include<stdio.h>
void main()
{
int n,i;
clrscr();
/*printf("\n ENTER THE NUMBER WHOSE TABLE IS
    REQUIRED :  ");
scanf("%d",&n);*/
printf("\n\nTHE TABLE UPTO 10 IS AS \n\n");
for (i=1;i<=10;i++)
{
for(n=1;n<=10;n++)
{
printf(" %5d", n*i);
}
printf("\n");
}
getch();
}
```

Program 14

```
/*THE PROGRAM FOR FINDING THE FACTORIAL OF ANY
    GIVEN NUMBER GREATER THAN 1*/
#include<conio.h>
#include<stdio.h>
main()
{
```

```
int i,n;
long f=1;
clrscr();
printf(" /*THE PROGRAM FOR FINDING THE FACTORIAL OF
    ANY GIVEN NUMBER GREATER THAN 1*/ ");
printf("\n\n GIVE THE NUMBER WHOSE FACTORIAL IS RE-
    QUIRED (LESS THAN 16)");
scanf("%d",&n);
if(n==0)
f=1;
else if(n==1)
f=1;
else{
for(i=1;i<=n;i++)
f=f*i;
}
printf("\nTHE FACTORIAL OF %d IS  ::  %ld",n,f);
getch();
}
```

10.3.5 Switch Statement

If then else statement is a nice construct to when one of many alternatives are to be selected. Use of nested IF construct become little complex when the selection is to be made out of many alternatives. Switch - Case statement is a feature of C programming language, which provide multiple branch selection. It checks for the value of an expression against a list of integer or character constant. If the match is successful, the group of statement associated with that constant are executed. The SWITCH statement test for the value of a given expression against a list of CASE values. When the match is found, group of statement associated with that CASE statement are executed. The general form of SWITCH CASE statement is given below.

```
switch ( Expression )
{
case        constant 1 :
            group of statement 1;
            break;
case        constant 2 :
            group of statement 2;
break;
. . . . . . . . . . .
```

```
..........
default :
            group of statement 3;
}
```

The switch statement check for the equality with the constant, whereas as IF THEN ELSE statement may evaluate the relational or logical expression. It is also not possible for the two case statements to have same value. These are some of the restrictions with the Switch - Case statements.

Following program calculate the final velocity (v) using different Newton's Law of motion.

Program 15

```
/* THIS PROGRAM IS TO CALCULATE FINAL VELOCITY, DIS-
   TANCE USING DIFFERENT  NEWTON'S LAW */
#include <conio.h>
#include <stdio.h>
#include <math.h>
main()
{
int n;
float u,v,a,t,s;
clrscr();
printf("\n   THE THREE FUNDAMENTAL NEWTON'S EQUA-
   TIONS ARE\n\n");
printf("\n 1.  v = u + a*t \n 2.  s = u*t + (1/2) a*t*t");
printf("\n 3.  v = sqrt(u*u + 2*a*s)");
printf("\n\n\n WHERE    u = intial velocity\t v = final velocity");
printf("\t a = accelartion\t\t  s = displacement\t t= time");
printf("\n\n\n THE EQUATION WHICH YOU REQUIRE TO USE
   : ");
scanf ("%d",&n);
switch(n){
   case 1:
         printf ("\n\n Enter the value of intial velocity(u)");
         scanf ("%f ",&u);
         printf ("\n\n Enter the value of accelartion(a)");
         scanf ("%f ",&a);
         printf ("\n\n Enter the value of time(t)");
         scanf ("%f ",&t);
         v=u+a*t;
         printf("\n\n THE FINAL VELOCITY IS v = %f m/sec",v);
         break;
```

```
    case 2:
        printf ("\n\n Enter the value of intial velocity(u),
        accelaration(a),time(t)");
        scanf ("%f %f %f",&u,&a,&t);
        s=u*t+(1/2)*a*t*t;
        printf("\n\n THE TOTAL DISPLACEMENT IS s = %f
        m",s);
        break;
    case 3:
        printf ("\n\n Enter the value of intial velocity(u),
        accelaration(a),displacement(s)");
        scanf ("%f %f %f",&u,&a,&s);
        v=sqrt(u*u+2*a*s);
        printf("\n\nTHE FINAL VELOCITY IS v = %f m/sec",v);
        break;
    default:
        printf("\n\n !!!  SORRY YOU HAVE ENTERED THE
        WRONG CHOICE");
        break;
    }
getch();
}
```

Program 16

```
/*THIS PROGRAM IS TO FIND THE ROOTS OF A QUADRATIC
   EQUATION */
#include<conio.h>
#include<stdio.h>
#include<math.h>
void main()
{
float a,b,c,d,r1,r2;
float real,img,p;
clrscr();
printf("\n\n PROGRAM TO FIND THE ROOTS OF A QUA-
   DRATIC EQUATION");
printf("\n\n THE GENERAL FORM OF QUADRATIC EQUA-
   TION IS : ");
printf("\n\n\t ax^2 + bx + c ");
printf("\n\n Enter the values of 'a', 'b', 'c' of your equation\n ");
scanf("%f %f %f",&a,&b,&c);
d=b*b-4*a*c;
```

```
if(d==0)
  {
  printf("\n\n THE ROOTS ARE EQUAL");
  r1=(-b)/(2*a);
  r2=r1;
  printf("\n\n THE ROOTS ARE r1 = r2 = %f ",r1);
  }
 if(d>0)
  {
  printf("\n\n THE ROOTS ARE DISTINCT");
  r1=((-b)+sqrt(d))/(2*a);
  r2=((-b)-sqrt(d))/(2*a);
  printf("\n\n THE ROOTS ARE \n\tr1 = %f \n\tr2 = %f ",r1,r2);
  }
 if(d<0)
  {
  p=sqrt(-d);
  real=((-b)/(2*a));
  img=p/2;
  printf("\n\nTHE ROOTS ARE IMAGINARY");
  printf("\n\n THE ROOTS ARE :");
  printf("\n\n\tr1  = %f +  %f i ",real,img);
  printf("\n\tr1  = %f -  %f i ",real,img);
  }
 getch();
 }
```

10.3.6 Break & Goto statements

The Break & Goto statements are used to change the flow of execution. The goto statement is considered to be hazardous statement and is not preferred by rich programmers. Goto statement is rarely used but still it may be useful in certain circumstances. This statement requires a label and control is transferred to that label whenever goto statement is executed. Following is the genera syntax of this statement.

```
        Goto LABEL;
        Statements;
Label : Statement;
```

The break statement is used in conjunction with SWITCH-CASE statement. However this statement may be used to discontinue the loop e.g. for loop, while loop. Whenever, the break statement is encountered within the loop, execution of further statements of that loop is abandoned and program control comes out of the loop. For example,

```
# include <stdio.h>
main( )
{
int I=1;
while ( I< 100)
{
printf (" Number = %d \n", I );
I++
if (I==20)  break;
}
```

The above program segment will print the number up to 20 and when ever value of I becomes 20 the loop will be forced to terminated without reaching the while condition.

Program 17

```
/* PROGRAM TO CHECK WHEATHER THE GIVEN NUMBER
   IS PRIME OR NOT*/
#include<conio.h>
#include<stdio.h>
#include<math.h>
void main()
{
int n,p,i;
clrscr();
printf("\nENTER THE NUMBER TO BE CHECKED   ");
scanf("%d",&n);
p=sqrt(n)+1;
i=2;
while(i<=p)
{
if(n%i==0)
{
printf("\n\n THE GIVE NUMBER %d IS NOT PRIME",n);
break;
}
i++;
}
if(i==p+1)
printf("\n\nTHE GIVEN NUMBER %d IS PRIME",n);
```

```
getch();
}
```

10.4 ARRAYS

An ARRAY is a collection of variables of same type that are represented by a common name. A specific element of an array is accessed by an index. For example, In a class of 50 students, an array 'height' may be defined to represent the height of all 50 students. Thus array 'height' may be used to access on or more values pertaining to get the height of a student. Each array element is accessed by specifying a array name followed by subscript. Each subscript must be a non negative number. Following figure shows the logical representation of array of height of 50 students.

Student

191	152	--------	-------	-------	178
student[0]	**student[1]**	--------	-------		**student[49]**

Here in this example, **student[1]** represent the value stored in the array student at the index 1. Similarly **student [n]** refers to the n th element in the array students. It must be remembered that size of an array must be specified at the time of declaration of an array. For an array of size n, the indexes begins with 0 to n-1.

The number of the subscripts defines the dimension of the array. In the previous example, the student array is one dimensional array because this uses one sub script. In the similar way, A [I] [j] refers to the an element in a two dimensional array. This items exist at j th element of I th row. Following is the representation of an two dimensional array.

A[M][N] : **Array of Size M X N**

A[1][1]	A[1][2]	A[1][3]			A[1][N]
A[2][1]	A[2][2]	A[2][3]			A[2][N]
- -	- -	- -	- -	- -	- -
- -	- -	- -	- -	- -	- -
- -	- -	- -	- -	- -	- -
A[M][1]	A[M][2]	A[M][3]			A[M][N]

Thus increasing number of subscripts means increasing the dimension of an array. A[I][j][k] indicate that array A is an three dimensional array. An n dimensional array will use n subscript to represent an item. Array having n subscript It must be remembered that array is collection of homogeneous items. The values stored in an array must be of same type. Every array has a base type and all the entries to an array must be of the base type.

10.4.1 Declaration of Array

Arrays are defined in the way similar to that of defining a other variable. It can be thought of declaring another variable with an index or sub script. A one dimensional array is defined by defining its type followed by an identifier with a expression in the bracket. This expression must be evaluated to positive integer value. This is called the size of an array. For example, declaring a array of to store the height of the students for a class of 50 students.

```
Int  student[50];
```

This statement will define a array student, whose base type is integer and size of array is 50. Index of this array start with 0 and last index, which may be accessed, is 49.

It is always a good strategy to define the size of an array as a symbolic constant. For example,

```
# define     M    50
int          student[M];
```

Following are the example of array definitions.

```
int          Salary [10] ;
char         name[25] ;
float        amount[100] ;
float        Matrix [10][10];
char         Value [5][10][10];
```

10.4.2 Initialization of Array

As indicated above the elements of an array can be initialised as the other variables at the time of declaration. Base type of an array can of Int, Char, float etc. The syntax of the initialization of array can be defied as below.

```
Static data_ type   array_name[size]  = { list of elements };
```

Here 'static' is a keyword, data_type is the base type of the elements, array_name is the identifier which requires an meaningful name to an array, size is the size of an array which represents the number of elements to be stored in an array, list of elements is the actual list of elements which requires to be stored in an array.

Following are the examples of the array initialization.

Static int height[5] = { 178, 162, 153, 169, 171 };
Static char name [7] = {'S', 'U', 'R', 'A', 'B', 'H', 'I'};
Static float price[4] ={ 2.50, 5.30, 4.10, 0.45 };

First statement declares the one-dimensional array of size 5 and initializes the values as follows. This statement declares the array of size five and its entries are represented as height[0], height[1] ....height[4].

Height[0]	178
Height[1]	162
Height[2]	153
Height[3]	169
Height[4]	171

Similarly second and third statement declares the one-dimensional array as follows.

Second statement declares its entries to be represented as name[0], name[1] ....name[6] and third statement declares its entries to be declared as price[0], price[1].. price[4].

Name[0]	S
Name[1]	U
Name[2]	R
Name[3]	A
Name[4]	B
Name[5]	H
Name[6]	I

Price[0]	2.50
Price[1]	5.30
Price[2]	4.10
Price[3]	0.45

10.4.3 Dynamic Arrays

All the arrays declaration define the maximum size of an array thus they are called static arrays. 'C' also provide an flexibility not to define the size of an array explicitly. A programmer may leave the size of an array unspecified. The total number of the entries specified in the list of values define the maximum size of an array. This type of an arrays are called dynamic arrays. Following are the examples of dynamic arrays.

```
int student_age [ ] = { 12, 8, 9, 10, 14 };
float price [ ] = { 2.50, 4.20, 3.0 };
char name [ ] = { 'A', 'K', 'K', 'U'};
```

In the above three examples the size of an array is determined by the 'C' compiler it self. First declaration defines the size of an array to be five as there are five entries in the list of values. Similarly second & third array declaration defines the array size to be fixed at three and four receptively.

10.4.4 Initialization of Multi Dimensional Array

In the one-dimensional arrays the value to be stored are simple. Multidimensional array may have multiple size indices. Following are the examples of declaration of multidimensional array.

```
int marks [3][5];    /* Two dimensional Array */
float values [5][5][5]   /*Declaration of three dimensional array */
```

Similar to previous examples, it is also possible to mention the list of entries in the multidimensional arrays. Following are the examples.

```
static int marks [3][4] ={ 34, 56, 56, 57, 12, 34, 23, 23, 45, 43, 24, 23 };
static int value[2][3] ={ 2,4,3,4,5,3};
```

This example initializes the elements of the first row as (2,4,3) and second row as (4,5,3). The same initialization may be done as under where the braces surround elements of rows.

```
static int value [2][3] ={ {2,4,3}, { 4,5,3} };
```

There may exist situation that one may require putting the table in an array. For example the marks obtained in four subjects in a class of five students. Following table shows this situations.

Student	Subject 1	Subject 2	Subject 3	Subject 4
1	54	76	67	76
2	56	87	65	71
3	56	76	86	87
4	76	78	55	76
5	65	76	55	56

All of the entries in this table are contained in the five rows and four columns. Each rows represents the students number and each column represents the subject number. If we represent above table as matrix, then element '54' in first row & first column represents the marks obtained by the first student in the first subject. Thus if this matrix is represented by A, then A[I][j] represents I th row and j th column.

This array may be declared and initialized by putting the values inside the array declaration. But a good strategy is to read the values from the standard input using 'scanf' statements.

Program 18

```
/* This program reads the height of  ten students and print their
    average */
# Include <stdio.h>
main ( )
{
   int I
   float  sum, height [10];

   for (I=0;I<10;I++) /* This statement reads height of 10 students
     to array */
   {
   printf (" Enter the height of the  student No=%d  \n", I+1);
   scanf ("%d", height[I] );
   }
   for (I=0;I<10;I++)  /* This statement computes the sum of height
     of 10 students */
   {
   sum= sum + height[I];
   }
   printf (" Average Height of the Class =  %d \n", sum/10.0 )
}
```

10.4.5 Processing an Array

As shown in the previous example that it is not possible to process an array in a single shot. If an operation is to be carried out on array, it must be done on element basis. This is usually done using a control structure like For Loop, Do While Loop etc on element basis until end of array is achieved. Suppose the element or the values stored in the two array has to be processed (e.g. addition, multiplication etc), then element of both the arrays are read from the respective indices and in each pass of the loop the appropriate action is carried out. This process is done until the computation is completed. Following is the program which read the element of two one-dimensional array and storing the sum and multiplication of elements in another array.

Program 19

```
/* This program read the values to two arrays (A & B ) and stores
     addition & multiplication of elements in to array C & D.   */
# include <stdio.h>
main ( )
{
int I, j, a[5], b[5], c[5], d[5];
printf (" Enter the elements of array A \n");
for ( I=0 ; I<5; I++)
{
scanf (" %d", & a[I] );
}
printf (" Enter the elements of array B \n");
for ( I=0 ; I<5; I++)
{
scanf (" %d", & b[I] );
}
/* This segment computes addition & multiplication */
for ( I=0 ; I<5; I++)
{
c[I]= a[I] +b[I];
d[I]=a[I] * b[I];
}
/* This segment prints the elements of array C & D  */
for (I=0; I<5; I++)
{
printf ( "  %d      %d \n", c[I],d[I] );
}
```

The two & multidimensional arrays can be processed in the same way. Following is the program for addition of two matrices. Each matrix is represented as an two dimensional array. Addition of the receptive elements is done in almost the same way as in one dimensional array.

Program 20

```
/*THE PROGRAM  FOR ADDITION OF TWO MATRIX */
#include<conio.h>
#include<stdio.h>
#define M 5
main()
{
```

```
int i,j,p,q;
int a[M][M],b[M][M],sum[M][M];
clrscr();
printf("FOR ADDITION OF TWO MATRIX THEIR ORDER
    SHOULD BE SAME ");
printf ("\n\n Give the order of first & second matrix");
printf("\n\n  ENTER THE NUMBER  OF ROWS ");
scanf("%d",&p);
printf("\n\n ENTER THE  NUMBER  OF COLUMN  ");
scanf("%d",&q);
/* THIS SEGMENT  ENTER  THE ELEMENTS OF FIRST MATRIX
    */
for(i=0;i<p;i++)
  {
  for(j=0;j<q;j++)
    {
    // printf("\n ENTER THE ROW NO %d COLUMN NO %d's
    ELEMENT :: ", i+1,j+1);
    scanf("%d",&a[i][j]);
    }
  }
/* THIS SEGMENT READS THE  ELEMENTS OF SECOND MA-
    TRIX */
for(i=0;i<p;i++)
  {
  for(j=0;j<q;j++)
    {
    // printf("\n ENTER THE ROW NO %d COLUMN NO %d's
    ELEMENT :: ", i+1,j+1);
    scanf("%d",&b[i][j]);
    }
  }
for(i=0;i<p;i++)
  {
  for(j=0;j<q;j++)
    {
    sum[i][j]=a[i][j]+b[i][j];
    }
  }
printf("\n THE FIRST MATRICES IS AS ::\n\n");
for(i=0;i<p;i++)
  {
```

```
  for(j=0;j<q;j++)
    {
    printf("%5d", a[i][j]);
    }
    printf("\n");
  }
printf("\n THE SECOND MATRICES IS AS ::\n\n");
for(i=0;i<p;i++)
  {
  for(j=0;j<q;j++)
    {
    printf("%5d", b[i][j]);
    }
    printf("\n");
  }
printf("\n THE SUM OF TWO MATRICES IS THE GIVEN
    MATRIX\n\n");
for(i=0;i<p;i++)
  {
  for(j=0;j<q;j++)
    {
    printf("%5d", sum[i][j]);
    }
    printf("\n");
  }
getch();
}
```

Following program computes the exponential series
.e^ x = ? x^n / n ! where 0<x<1 .

Program 21

```
/*To compute exponential series    e^x ( e to power x)*/
#include <conio.h>
#include <stdio.h>
#define M 30
main()
{
float x, t[M], sum=0;
int n=5,i;
clrscr();
printf("THE GENERAL FORM OF SERIES IS AS ::");
printf("\n\n Enter the value of  x :  ");
```

```
scanf("%f",&x);
t[0]=1;
t[1]=x;
for (i=2;i<=n;i++)
t[i]=t[i-1]*(x/n);
for (i=0;i<=n;i++)
sum=sum+t[i];
printf("\n\n THE SUMMATION OF e^x  i.e. e^%f  IS :: %f
    ",x,sum);
getch();
}
```

Program 22

```
/*THE PROGRAM FOR ADDITION OF TWO MATRIX*/
#include<conio.h>
#include<stdio.h>
#define M 5
void main()
{
int i,j,p,q;
int a[M][M],b[M][M],sum[M][M];
clrscr();
printf("FOR ADDITION OF TWO MATRIX THEIR ORDER
    SHOULD BE SAME(genarally both of (3 * 3) order)  ");
printf ("\n\ngive the order of first & second matrix");
printf("\n\nTHE NO OF ROWS IN FIRST & SECOND MATRIX
    IS ");
scanf("%d",&p);
printf("\nTHE NO OF COLUMN IN FIRST & SECOND MATRIX
    IS ");
scanf("%d",&q);
printf("\nGIVE THE ELEMENTS OF FIRST MATRIX\n ");
for(i=0;i<p;i++)
  {
  for(j=0;j<q;j++)
    {
     // printf("\n THE ROW NO %d COLUMN NO %d's ELE-
    MENT IS:: ", i+1,j+1);
    scanf("%d",&a[i][j]);
    }
  }
printf("\nGIVE THE ELEMENTS OF SECOND MATRIX\n ");
```

```
for(i=0;i<p;i++)
  {
  for(j=0;j<q;j++)
    {
     // printf("\n THE ROW NO %d COLUMN NO %d's ELE-
    MENT IS:: ", i+1,j+1);
    scanf("%d",&b[i][j]);
    }
  }
for(i=0;i<p;i++)
  {
  for(j=0;j<q;j++)
    {
    sum[i][j]=a[i][j]+b[i][j];
    }
  }
printf("\n THE FIRST MATRICES IS AS ::\n\n");
for(i=0;i<p;i++)
  {
  for(j=0;j<q;j++)
    {
    printf("%5d", a[i][j]);
    }
    printf("\n");
  }
printf("\n THE SECOND MATRICES IS AS ::\n\n");
for(i=0;i<p;i++)
  {
  for(j=0;j<q;j++)
    {
    printf("%5d", b[i][j]);
    }
    printf("\n");
  }
printf("\n THE SUM OF TWO MATRICES IS THE GIVEN
    MATRIX\n\n");
for(i=0;i<p;i++)
  {
  for(j=0;j<q;j++)
    {
    printf("%5d", sum[i][j]);
    }
```

```
    printf("\n");
    }
  getch();
  }
```

Program 23

```
/*THE PROGRAM FOR SUBTRACTION OF TWO MATRIX*/
#include<conio.h>
#include<stdio.h>
#define M 5
void main()
{
int i,j,p,q;
int a[M][M],b[M][M],sub[M][M];
clrscr();
printf("\nTHE NO OF ROWS IN FIRST & SECOND MATRIX IS
   ");
scanf("%d",&p);
printf("\nTHE NO OF COLUMN IN FIRST & SECOND MATRIX
   IS ");
scanf("%d",&q);
printf("\nGIVE THE ELEMENTS OF FIRST MATRIX\n ");
for(i=0;i<p;i++)
  {
  for(j=0;j<q;j++)
    {
/printf("\n ENTER THE %d ROW  %d COLUMN ELEMENT IS::
   ", p,q);
   scanf("%d",&a[i][j]);
   }
  }
printf("\nGIVE THE ELEMENTS OF SECOND MATRIX\n ");
for(i=0;i<p;i++)
  {
  for(j=0;j<q;j++)
    {
    //printf("\n THE %d ROW  %d COLUMN ELEMENT IS:: ",
   p,q);
   scanf("%d",&b[i][j]);
   }
  }
for(i=0;i<p;i++)
```

```
  {
  for(j=0;j<q;j++)
    {
    sub[i][j]=a[i][j]-b[i][j];
    }
  }
printf("\n THE FIRST MATRICES IS AS ::\n\n");
for(i=0;i<p;i++)
  {
  for(j=0;j<q;j++)
    {
    printf("%5d", a[i][j]);
    }
    printf("\n");
  }
printf("\n THE SECOND MATRICES IS AS ::\n\n");
for(i=0;i<p;i++)
  {
  for(j=0;j<q;j++)
    {
    printf("%5d", b[i][j]);
    }
    printf("\n");
  }
printf("\n THE DIFFERENCE OF TWO MATRICES IS THE GIVEN
    MATRIX\n\n");
for(i=0;i<p;i++)
  {
  for(j=0;j<q;j++)
    {
    printf("%5d", sub[i][j]);
    }
    printf("\n");
  }
getch();
}
```

Program 24

```
/*THE PROGRAM FOR MULIPLICATION OF TWO MATRIX*/
#include<conio.h>
#include<stdio.h>
#define M 5
```

```
void main()
{
int i,j,p,q,r,s,x;
int a[M][M],b[M][M],mul[M][M];
clrscr();
printf("FOR MULTIPLICATION OF TWO MATRIX ");
printf("\nTHE COLUMN OF FIRST MATRIX SHOULD BE
    EQUAL TO ROWS OF SECOND MATRIX");
printf("\nTHE NO OF ROWS IN FIRST MATRIX IS ");
scanf("%d",&p);
printf("\nTHE NO OF COLUMN IN FIRST MATRIX IS ");
scanf("%d",&q);
printf("\nGIVE THE ELEMENTS OF FIRST MATRIX\n ");
for(i=0;i<p;i++)
  {
  for(j=0;j<q;j++)
    {
    //printf("\n THE %d ROW  %d COLUMN ELEMENT IS:: ",
   i,j);
    scanf("%d",&a[i][j]);
    }
  }
printf("\nTHE NO OF ROWS IN SECOND MATRIX IS ");
scanf("%d",&r);
printf("\nTHE NO OF COLUMN IN SECOND MATRIX IS ");
scanf("%d",&s);
printf("\nGIVE THE ELEMENTS OF SECOND MATRIX\n ");
for(i=0;i<r;i++)
  {
  for(j=0;j<s;j++)
    {
    //printf("\n THE %d ROW  %d COLUMN ELEMENT IS:: ",
   i,j);
    scanf("%d",&b[i][j]);
    }
  }
printf("\n THE FIRST MATRICES IS AS ::\n\n");
for(i=0;i<p;i++)
  {
  for(j=0;j<q;j++)
    {
    printf("%5d", a[i][j]);
    }
```

```
    printf("\n");
   }
printf("\n THE SECOND MATRICES IS AS ::\n\n");
for(i=0;i<r;i++)
   {
   for(j=0;j<s;j++)
     {
     printf("%5d", b[i][j]);
     }
     printf("\n");
   }
if(q==r)
{
for(i=0;i<p;i++)
   { // mul[i][j]=0;
   for(j=0;j<s;j++)
    {
    mul[i][j]=0;
    for(x=0;x<r;x++)
    {
    mul[i][j]=mul[i][j]+a[i][j]*b[i][j];
    }
     }
   }
printf("\n THE PRODUCT OF TWO MATRICES IS THE GIVEN
    MATRIX\n\n");
for(i=0;i<p;i++)
   {
   for(j=0;j<s;j++)
     {
     printf("%5d", mul[i][j]);
     }
     printf("\n");
    }
 }
 else
 printf("\n\n!!! SORRY !!! MULTIPICATION IS NOT POSSIBLE");
 getch();
 }
```

Program 25

```
/*THE PROGRAM FOR FINDING THE FACTORIAL OF ANY
    GIVEN NUMBER GREATER THAN 1*/
#include<conio.h>
#include<stdio.h>
void main()
{
int i,f=1,n,a;
int facto(int p);
clrscr();
printf(" /*THE PROGRAM FOR FINDING THE FACTORIAL OF
    ANY GIVEN NUMBER GREATER THAN 1*/ ");
printf("\n\n GIVE THE NUMBER WHOSE FACTORIAL IS RE-
    QUIRED ");
scanf("%d",&n);
a=n;
if(n==0)
f=1;
else
f=facto(n);
printf("\n\n THE FACTORAIL OF  %d!  IS %d ",a,f);
getch();
}
int facto(int p)
{
 int s;
if(p==1)
 return(1);
else
s=p*facto(p-1);
return s;
}
```

Exercises

This section presents the solution to some of the selected exercises as par the Question Bank.

Program 26

```
/*
#include<conio.h>
#include<stdio.h>
#include<string.h>
void main()
```

```
{
 int i,counter=0;
 char str[20],str2[20];
 clrscr();
  printf("THIS IS A PROGRAM OF REVERSING THE STRING
   ORDER");
 printf("\nenter your desire string");
 scanf("%s",str);
// counter= strlen(str);
 for(i=0;str[i]!='\0';i++)
   counter++;
 for(i=0;i<=counter;i++)
 str2[i]=str[i];
 printf("\nthe reverse string-\n");
 for(i=counter;i>=0;i—)
  printf("%c",str2[i]);
 printf("\nthe length of string=   %d",counter);
 getch();
 }
```

Program 27

```
/* This program adds the digits of a given number */
#include<stdio.h>
#include<conio.h>
#define max 12
void main()
{
  int i=0,num,sum=0;
  int rem[max];
  clrscr();
  printf("\nTHIS IS A PROGRAM OF ADDITION OF DIGITS OF
    A NUMBER\n ");
  printf("\nenter the number which u want\n");
  scanf("%d",&num);
  do
  { rem[i]=num%10;
    sum=sum+rem[i];
    num=num/10;
        i++;
   }
  while(num>0);
  printf("the sum of digit your desire number=%d",sum);
```

```
  getch();
 }
```

Program 28

```
/* Program to accept two string at input & find length of greatest
    common substring */
#include<conio.h>
#include<stdio.h>
#include<string.h>
void main()
{
char str1[10],str2[10],str3[10];
int i,j,len1,len2,count=0;
clrscr();
printf("\n Enter the first string ");
scanf("%s",str1);
printf("\n Enter the second string ");
scanf("%s",str2);
len1=strlen(str1);
len2=strlen(str2);
for(i=0;i<=len1;i++)
 {
 for(j=0;j<=len2;j++)
   {
  if(str1[i]==str2[j])
  {
  str3[count]=str1[i];
  count++;
   // break;
//       delete str1[i];
  }
  //break;
  }
  }
printf("%d %d \n ", len1,len2);
printf("%s  %s  %s",str1,str2,str3);
getch();
}
```

Program 29

```
/* THE PROGRAM IN C TO FIND THE SUM OF ODD & EVEN
    NUMBER FROM 1 TO 100*/
```

```
#include<conio.h>
#include<stdio.h>
void main()
{
int num,i,j;
int evensum=0,sumodd=0;
clrscr();
printf("\n The sum of odd numbers is  \n");
printf("0");
for(i=1;i<=99;i=i+2)
{
sumodd=sumodd+i;
printf("+ %d",i);
}
printf( "= %d\n\n\n",sumodd);
printf("The sum of even number\n\n");
printf("0");
for(i=2;i<=100;i=i+2)
{
evensum=evensum+i;
printf("+ %d",i);
}
printf( "= %d",evensum);
getch();
}
```

Program 30

```
/* Program to calculate the compound interest for a given princi-
   pal amonut */
#include<conio.h>
#include<stdio.h>
void main()
{
float principal_amount,original_amount;
float rate_interest;
int i, no_of_year;
float simple_interest,compound_interest;
clrscr();
printf("\nEnter the principal amount");
scanf("%f",&principal_amount);
original_amount=principal_amount;
printf("\nEnter the rate of interest");
```

```
scanf("%f",&rate_interest);
printf("\nEnter the number of year");
scanf("%d",&no_of_year);
simple_interest=principal_amount * rate_interest * no_of_year/100;
printf("\n Simple interest =  %f",simple_interest);
for( i=1;i<=no_of_year;i++);
{
simple_interest=principal_amount * rate_interest * i/100;
 principal_amount=principal_amount+simple_interest;
 }
compound_interest=principal_amount-original_amount;
printf("\n compound interest = %f ",compound_interest);
getch();
}
```

Program 31

```
/* Program to print 'a' ...'z' and digit '0'...'9' and their ASCII
   interger value in Decimal  */
#include <conio.h>
#include <stdio.h>
void main()
{
char ch='a';
int i;
clrscr();
printf("\n The ASCII value of \n");
for(i=0;i<26;i++)
{
printf("\n%c = %d",ch,ch);
ch=ch+1;
}
ch='0';
printf("\n");
for(i=0;i<=9;++i)
{
printf("\n%c = %d",ch,ch);
ch=ch+1;
}
getch();
}
```

Program 32

```
/* Program to convert upper case to Lower case letter */
#include<conio.h>
#include<stdio.h>
void main()
{
char ch;
clrscr();
printf("\nEnter a letter");
scanf("%c",&ch);
printf("\n%c\t%c",ch,ch+32);
getch();
}
```

Program 33

```
/* Write a program to Evaluate the Polynomial 3*x*x*x - 5*x*x +6
   for x=2.25 */
#include<conio.h>
#include<stdio.h>
#include<string.h>
void main()
{
float x,Z;
clrscr();
printf("Z= 3*x*x*x -5*x*x+6");
printf("\n Enter the value of x ");
scanf("%f",&x);
Z= 3*x*x*x -5*x*x+6;
printf("\nZ= %f",Z);
getch();
}
```

Program 34

```
/* Program to Convert millimeter to meters, centimenetrs */
#include<conio.h>
#include<stdio.h>
#include<string.h>
void main()
{
float mtr,mm,cm;
clrscr();
printf("\n Enter a Quantity in Millimeters ");
```

```
scanf("%f",&mm);
cm=mm/10;
mtr=mm/1000;
printf("\n%7.3f  millimeter = %7.3f cm\n\n %7.3f millimeter =
    %7.3f mtr",mm,cm,mm,mtr);
getch();
}
```

Program 35

```
/* Write program to evaluate Z for values of x & y varying from -2
    to 2 step 1 */
#include<conio.h>
#include<stdio.h>
void main()
{
int Z,x,y;
clrscr();
printf("\n\n The required expression is");
printf("\n\nZ=x*x*x - 2*x*y*y + 3*x*y + y - 2*y*y*y");
for(x=-2;x<=2;x++)
{
  for(y=-2;y<=2;y++)
  {
   Z=x*x*x - 2*x*y*y + 3*x*y + y - 2*y*y*y;
   printf( "\nfor x= %3d and y=%3d value of Z is : %3d  ",x,y,Z);
  }
  printf("\n");
 }
getch();
}
```

Program 36

```
/* Write program to calculate Cosine values for angle 0 to 180 */
#include<conio.h>
#include<stdio.h>
#include<math.h>
#define PI 3.1416
void main()
{
int i;
float angle;
clrscr();
```

```
printf("\n The cosine of different angle");
printf("\n\n angle \t COS(angle)\n\n");
for(i=0;i<=180;i=i+10)
{
angle=(PI/180) *i;
printf("\n %3d\t %7.5f",i,cos(angle));
}
getch();
}
```

Program 37

```
57
/* Program to find numbers of integers & sum of integers greater
    than 100 and less then 200 that are divisible by 7 */
#include<conio.h>
#include<stdio.h>
void main()
{
int num[20],sum=0,count=0,i;
clrscr();
for(i=100;i<=200;i++)
{
if(i%7==0)
{
 num[count]=i;
 count++;
 sum=sum+i;
 }}
 printf("\n The numbers are :-\n");
 for(i=0;i<count;i++)
 {
 printf("\t%d",num[i]);
 }
 printf("\nThe total number is   %d\n The sum of these numbers
     are   %d",count,sum);
 getch();
 }
```

Program 38

```
/* Program to process the application of students and list eligible
    candidate subject to following eligibility criteria
Maths Marks >=60, Physics Marks >= 50, Chemistry Marks >=10,
```

```
    Total >= 200  */
#include<conio.h>
#include<stdio.h>
void main()
{
int maths,phy,che,total;
clrscr();
printf("\nEnter the marks of Maths");
scanf("%d",&maths);
printf("\nEnter the marks of physics");
scanf("%d",&phy);
printf("\nEnter the marks of Chemistry");
scanf("%d",&che);
total=maths+phy+che;
if((maths>=60 && phy>=50 &&che>=10&&total>=200) ||
    ((maths+phy)>=150))
        printf("\n Your are  an eligible Candidate");
else
printf("\nSORRY !! SORRY !!");
getch();
}
```

Program 39

```
/*Cost of operation of unit consisting of two components C1 & C2
    can be expressed as function of a parameter p as follows
C1=30-8P ;C2= 10 + P*P; The parameter ranges from 0 to 10. Write
    program in C which determine C1 & C2 with different values
    of I */
#include<stdio.h>
#include<conio.h>
void main()
{
float C1,C2,p;
int i;
clrscr();
printf("\nThe Expressions are \n C1= 30 - 8*p \nC2 =10+p*p\n");
/*printf("Enter the value of p:");
C1 =30 - 8*p;
C2 =10+p*p;   */
printf("\nThe value of C1 and C2 for different range of values of p
    from 0 to 10");
for(i=0;i<=10;I=i++)
```

```
{
C1= 30 - 8*i;
C2 =10+i*i;
printf( "\nfor i=%2d the C1 = %7.2f and C2 = %7.2f ",i,C1,C2);
}
getch();
}
```

Program 40

```
/* Write program to evaluate equation V=P(1+r)n for various com-
   bination of P, r and n
P=1000,2000,.......10000; r=.10,.11,.12.......... .20; n=1,2,3, 10;
#include<conio.h>
#include<stdio.h>
#include<math.h>
void main()
{
int i,j,k, count=0;
float v[30],p,r,n;
clrscr();
printf("\n ");
for(i=1;i<=3;i++)
 {
  p=1000*i;
  for(j=1;j<=3;j++)
  {
        r=0.10+i*0.01;
        for(k=1;k<=3;k++)
        {
        n=k;
        v[count]=p*pow((1+r),n);
        count++;
        }

   }
  }
  for(i=0;i<count;i++)
 printf("\n %f ",v[i]);
 getch();
 }
```

Program 41

```
/*THIS PROGRAM IS TO FIND THE ROOTS OF A QUADRATIC
    EQUATION */
#include<conio.h>
#include<stdio.h>
#include<math.h>
void main()
{
float a,b,c,d,r1,r2;
float real,img,p;
clrscr();
printf("\n\n PROGRAM TO FIND THE ROOTS OF A QUA-
    DRATIC EQUATION");
printf("\n\n THE GENERAL FORM OF QUADRATIC EQUA-
    TION IS : ");
printf("\n\n\t ax^2 + bx + c ");
printf("\n\n Enter the values of 'a', 'b', 'c' of your equation\n ");
scanf("%f %f %f",&a,&b,&c);
d=b*b-4*a*c;
if(d==0)
  {
  printf("\n\n THE ROOTS ARE EQUAL");
  r1=(-b)/(2*a);
  r2=r1;
  printf("\n\n THE ROOTS ARE r1 = r2 = %f ",r1);
  }
if(d>0)
  {
  printf("\n\n THE ROOTS ARE DISTINCT");
  r1=((-b)+sqrt(d))/(2*a);
  r2=((-b)-sqrt(d))/(2*a);
  printf("\n\n THE ROOTS ARE \n\tr1 = %f \n\tr2 = %f ",r1,r2);
  }
if(d<0)
  {
  p=sqrt(-d);
  real=((-b)/(2*a));
  img=p/2;
  printf("\n\nTHE ROOTS ARE IMAGINARY");
  printf("\n\n THE ROOTS ARE :");
  printf("\n\n\tr1  = %f +  %f i ",real,img);
  printf("\n\tr1  = %f -  %f i ",real,img);
```

```
 }
getch();
 }
```

SELECT EXERCISES

Q. 1. Define the overall structure of a C program. Explain in brief the role of the comment lines.

Q. 2. What are the Data Type ? List the various categories from which the Character Set of C is formed.

Q. 3. What are Constants ? How they are declared in the Program. Discuss various types of constant declared in C.

Q. 4. What are variables ? How the value are assigned to variables.

Q. 5. Which of the following are invalid constant and why ?

0.234 4 * 566 "2xbr[illegible]f%" -12.34 0.00001

Q. 6. What is the difference between Relational operator & Logical operator ? Explain with a suitable example.

Q. 7. What are Library function ? How are they used ?

Q. 8. What is a String ? Write statement in C to read five names from the input.

Q. 9. What are Short Hand operator ?

Q. 10. State with the example, the difference between postfix operator & prefix operators .

Q. 11. Write a program in C to evaluate following expressions.

V = U + A*T

S = U*T + 1/2 A* T^2

Q. 12. Write a program in C to find the root of Quadratic Equation.

Q. 13. Write a prgram to convert Pounds & Ounces to Kilogram & Grams.

Q. 14. Consider following code

```
Int I=10, J=11,K=13;
I += J += K += 7;
```

Write a equivalent statement that is fully parenthesized.

Q. 15. What are control structure ? What is a nested If Statement ?

Q. 16. What is advantage of CASE Statement ? Can it be a replacement for IF statement ? If not Justify your answer.

Q. 17. What is the use of Continue statement in C language ?

Q. 18. Why the use of GOTO statement is discouraged ? Give reason why break statement is considered Harmful.

Q. 19. Give the syntax of following control structure

For statement

While Statement

Do While Statement

Q. 20. What do you mean by formatted output ? Give the frequently used format symbol to output a floating number.

Q. 21. Distinguish between the Local & Global Variables.

Q. 22. What are Identifiers ? How a user defined identifier different from a keyword ?

Q. 23. Why is C called a Structured Programming Language ?

Q. 24. Discuss the role of qualifiers, Constant and Volatile.

Q. 25. Write a formatted input statement for following input data.

"s52"

12.345

101

Q. 26. Write a C program to read a string and print it in a reverse order.

Q. 27. Write a iterative program to compute the factorial of a number.

Q. 28. Write a program to read a statement and print the total number of character in it .

Q. 29. Write program in C to convert all lower case letter to upper case.

Q. 30. What is the condition to be satisfied by the all element of an array ?

Q. 31. What are subscripts ? How they are written ?

Q. 32. What is the advantage of declaring an array size in terms of symbolic constant over fixed integer quantity ?

Q. 33. How are arrays processed in C ? Can entire array be processed with single instruction without repetition ?

Q. 34. How are multidimensional arrays defined ? How is the values to the multidimensional arrays are assigned ?

Q. 35. What values are assigned to array when they are not initialized ?

11 Functions in C

11.0 INTRODUCTION

We have discussed the Library functions in the previous chapter. The C vendor as a package supplies these functions. These functions when used require the programmer to include appropriate header file or package that contains the function definition. C provides the facility to create the function of your requirement, which may be used repeatedly whenever required. These functions are called user-defined function. Normally these functions are crated and defined when set of instruction is to be used repeatedly. User defined function are called from the main program. The use of these functions allows a great flexibility to the programmer as a programmer may write code for different modules and may call it to the main program as and when required. This programming approach is called Modular Programming. In this programming methodology, the whole program is broken in to the pieces that are smaller and self contained. There are number of advantages of modular programming over writing a large monolithic program. At may times programmer wants that a group of statements be executed at different places in the main program. Theses statements may be grouped and defined under single function. At every place, where the group of statement needs to be executed then appropriate function is accessed. At the time of decomposition of large program in to a collection of small programs, logical clarity and self sufficiency should not be sacrificed. If functions has been written keeping this constraint in the mind, then debugging of that programs becomes easier. Programmer or user may also create a library of his own defined functions. Each routine or module may be programmed as special function and may be stored in a header file. This avoids repetitive programming and makes the program more portable.

Consider a case of evaluation of power series where a factorial of numbers is to be used repeatedly. It will be very cumbersome for the programmer to write a group of statement that calculates the factorial of that numbers and using it again and again. It would be better strategy, if programmer write a function that returns the value of factorial whenever the value for factorial is needed. Consider the following syntax,

```
# include <stdio.h>
main ( )
{
...................
...................        |   Main Program
...................        |
Value = Factorial (n);  <----  Call for Function
...................        |
}
int Factorial (n)
{
............   |
............   |
............   |        User Defined Function
.............  |
}
```

In this example, Factorial (n) invoke the function. It then computes the factorial of n written separately. After the computation, the function passes the value of factorial of n to main program which is then assigned to the variable Value.

11.1 SCOPE OF THE USER DEFINED FUNCTION

C programming language recognizes 'main' as a very special function. Every program written in C ought to have 'main' function. It is the function, code pertaining to that is executed first. As discussed before, modular programming approach require dividing the main program logic in to various modules. These modules may be written independently leading to multiple functions. Each function complete the task (sub task) associated with it and passes the value to the calling environment. The function may be invoked from the ' main ' function or from another function. Thus a function may call another function. The function is also called black box as once it is written it does the specific task by receiving the argument list from the calling environment and return the value (result) to the calling environment. The calling environment does not know details written inside the functions. It is also possible to write the whole code within the ' main ' function but it leads to several problem like debugging, testing and program becomes complex. Let as try to understand how the functions are called.

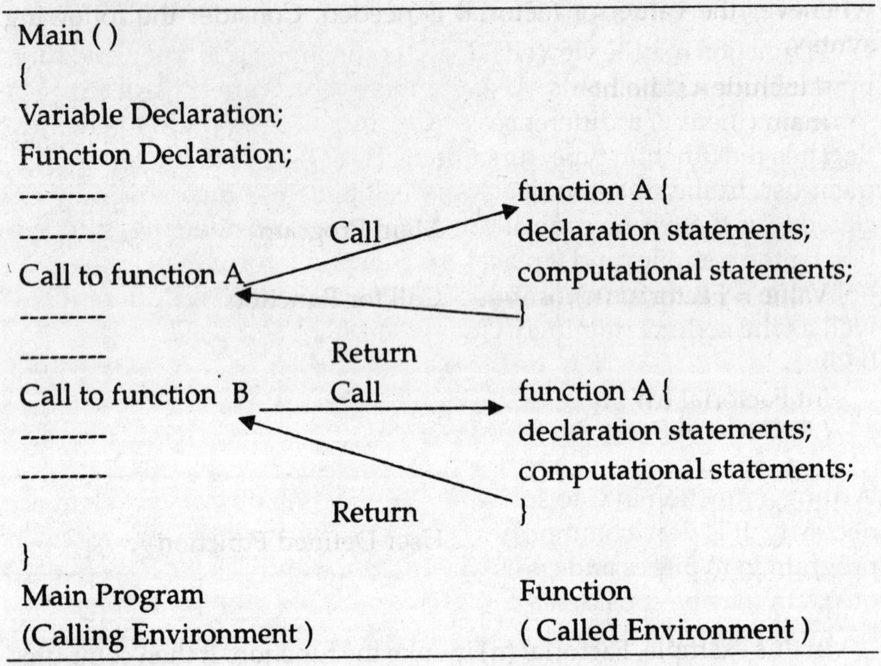

11.2 GENERAL SYNTAX OF THE USER DEFINED FUNCTION

The general syntax of the function is given below.

```
Base_Type   Function_ Identifier ( Parameter List )
{
Body of the function;
}
```

the base type denote the type of the data or value that a function returns. A function may return any type of the data except the array. Function identifier is the meaningful name given to the function. For example, the function doing multiplication may be given the name ' mult '. The parameter list contains the list of variables and their types. Variable included in the list of parameter are used to receive the values when a function is called. It is not mandatory to have to parameter list i.e. parameter list may be blank. A blank parameter list indicate that there is no values to be passed from the calling environment but it must be specified . Following are the example of function parameter declaration.

```
Mult ( int a, int b, int c );
Power ( int a, float b );
Max (int a, int b );
```

A function may be viewed has either function declaration and function definition statements. Usually these words are considered to be same but there is a difference in it. A function definition statement declares the function type, function name & list of parameter or argument list. In the function declaration statement, function is only declared thus there is no code allotted to it. This considered as information by the compiler and it places the function information in the symbol table. A function definition contains the function declaration as well as the code pertaining to the function. This is called as function body.

11.2.1 General Program Structure

Writing a function in C to solve any complex or intricate problem is a necessity. It is very common and advisable to break the logic of main program in to pieces and code then independently. In such cases a 'C' program may be considered to have a collection of various functions. Each function is designed to do a specific task. The 'C, program is developed by creating different function and then put them together. The General structure of a 'C ' program would be as follows,

```
Documentation statement
Link Statement
Definition statement
Global variable declaration statement
main ( )
{
local declaration;
computational statements;
}
Function Definitions
```

As described earlier, documentation statement are normally the comment line which describe the program written. It may contain the other detail pertaining to the program. The Link statement is a set of statement which link to the library functions. Definition statement includes the constant declarations. Every program written in C must 'main' function. The main function can be instantiated only once. It consists of local declaration and computational statements that do the main computational work as par the logic. At the last function code is written. It is also known as sub program. It contains all the computational statement which does the sub task in totality. This sub program returns the value to the main program whenever they are invoked. The values or arguments for which the function is to be executed receives it from the main program or from the function they are called.

11.2.2 Global & Local Variable

In C, you may declare the variable whose presence is global i.e. they need not be declared in the sub program or function separately. Consider the following example,

```
#include <stdio.h>
int I;
float j;
main ( )
{
int k;
int l;
____
____
l= max ( )
}
max ( )
{
int k;
______
______
}
```

In the above example, the variable declared out side the scope of any function are i & j . These variables are recognized by all the function of the program without their further declaration in the function where they will be used. Thus these variable have their global presence & recognition. These variables are called Global Variable or External Variable.

Consider the variable k & l, which are declared in the main function. These variable are not known to other functions as they are visible to the function, in which they have been declared. These variables are called Local Variables. Similarly, the variables declared inside the max () function is 'k'. It may be noted that 'k' has been declared in the main also. Value of ' k' does not conflict as they are considered as different entity by the compiler. The value of 'k' keeps modified independently, therefore changing the value of 'k' in one function will not affect the value of 'k' in another function.

Consider the following example to understand global & local variable.

Program 1

```
/* Illustration of Local & Global Variable */
#include <stdio.h>
int a= 4;  ←———————— Global Variable
int b= 6;
main ()
{
a=10;
multiply ( );
}
void multiply ( )
{
int mult;  ←———————— Local Variable
mult = a*b;
printf ("multiplication of a & b = %d \n",mult);
}
```

11.3 STORAGE CLASSES

Every variable in the 'C' programming language is defined by two characteristics, namely, Type & Storage Class. Type of variable defines the basic type of variable e.g. int, float, Char etc. Its storage class indicates the acceptability or recognition of the variable inside or outside the function where they have been declared. In particular, the storage class specifies the life & scope of the variables in the function or program. These classes are named as auto, extern, register & static.

There are four type of storage class in 'C'. These are listed below.

1. Auto
2. Static
3. Extern
4. Register

11.3.1 Automatic (Auto) Variable

It is not mandatory to mention the storage class of a variable. If the storage class of a variable is not specified then it is taken as 'auto' storage class variable. Declaration of the variable inside the function is 'auto' and remain confined to the function. Inside the function these variables are considered to be local to that function. Whenever that function is invoked, memory space for that block is kept reserved. Whenever, the function call is over, the computer releases the memory that was kept reserved for that variable. Thus after the exit, these variables are not available to any other function. Whenever the function is again invoked, the system does the memory allocation again and the values stored to variable earlier are lost. To understand the scope of 'auto' variable, consider the following example.

Program 2

```
/* Understanding Automatic Variables */
#include <stdio.h>
main ( )
{
auto int a;
fun_call (a);
printf ("b=%d\n",b);
}
void fun_call(a)
int a;
{
int b;
b=a*a;
}
```

In the a bove program, the 'a' is declared as 'auto' integer variable. Note that 'b' is declared in the function 'fun_call' . This program, when compiled, will give an error that undeclared/ unrecognized variable in function 'main'. This happens because, variable 'b' is defined in the function and the scope is limited to function. The memory space for the 'b' will be allotted when the function is called. When the function call is completed, the space reserved for the 'b' is released. Therefore the 'b' will not be available to the 'main' function.

11.3.2 Static Variable

Static variables are permanent within the function they are declared. They work in the similar way as 'auto' variable but they retain the latest value in such a way that whenever the function is invoked again, previous value allotted is available. This all happens because system does not release the memory space allotted to static variable whenever the call to the function is completed. In the case of re-invocation of that function, the previous value of that variable is made amiable. There are two type of static variable available in 'C' namely, internal static and external static. Internal static variables are defined inside the function and there scope id limited to the function where they have been declared. Whereas, the external static variables are declared outside the function and their scope are lies in the remainder of the program.

11.3.3 External Variables

Variables declared as external are similar to the global variable. The variables declared before the 'main' function are available to the rest of program & all the functions. The variable declared as 'extern' are similar to the global variables. By vitue of being declared as 'extern', these variables scope lies with entire program & all the functions, although they are declared in the function.

Example : extern int salary;

11.3.4 Register Variables

The registers are considered as the fastest storage. Thus keeping a value in the register will be accessed with minimum time. The variables, which are used and accessed frequently, are kept in the register, provided they have been declared as of 'register' type. Advantage of declaring a variable as 'register' that it will improve the performance and program will be executed in lesser amount of time i.e. faster execution. There are certain rule to be followed when a variable is declared as 'register' type. Only a limited number of variable can be declared as 'register'. It is not possible to access the address of register because they are not kept in the memory. Type of 'register' must be of int, float or pointer type.

Example : register int salary;

11.4 PASSING PARAMETER TO FUNCTION

As explained in the previous section that a function body is executed only when it is called from the calling environment. At the invocation of the function, a list of arguments is passed to the function, which receives the values of parameter or argument and does the computation based on it. This process is called parameter passing. There could be are several ways the parameter may be passed. When a single value is passed to the function using argument, value of actual parameter is copied to the function . This procedure of coping the value is called as passing by value. In this case the value of the argument from the calling environment is passed to the function by copying the argument. The function may change or modify or alter the value of the argument but the value of argument the main function will remain same. Let us consider following program segment,

Program 3

```
/* This program computes the square of integer by calling a func-
   tion */
# include < stdio.h>
main ()
{
int x, y;
void  square (int x );
x= 5;
printf (" At first print statement value of X=%d\n", x);
square (x );
printf (" At second  print statement value of X=%d\n", x);
}
void  square (int x)
{
x= x*x;
printf (" At third  print statement value of X=%d\n", x);
Return;
}
```

In this program, it is important to note that in the calling environment (Main function) when 'square (x) ' is executed, function square (X) is invoked. The value of argument x (x=5) is passed to function by copying . The function square(x) computes the square of 5 . In the first print statement, value of x will be printed as '5'. After a call to function, print statement (third print statement) written in the function will print the value of x as '25' i.e. after computing square of 'x' . When the program control is returned back to calling environment after the 'return' statement, the second print statement will print the value of x as '5'. Thus the program shows the output as follows,

```
At first print statement value of X= 5
At third  print statement value of X= 25
At second print statement value of X= 5
```

Thus it is evident that the function may modify or alter the value of argument but value of actual argument (declared in main) within the calling environment will not change.

Consider following program, which has a function to compute the square and the computed value may be returned to the calling environment. This value may be used for further computation in the calling environment. Following is the program, which computes the area of a circle.

Program 4

```
/* writing a function to compute the area of circle */
# define        PI    3.14
main( )
{
float radius;
float  area ( float radius );         /* Protoype declaration */
radius = 5.0;
m= area ( radius );
printf (" First time —area of circle is = %f \n", m);
}
float  area ( float r )               /* Prototype Definition */
{
float a;
a = PI * r * r;                       /* Area of circle */
printf ("Second time ——area of circle is = %f \n", a );
return (a);
}
```

In this program, a prototype declaration & prototype definition of a function 'area' is used. When a function is called from the calling environment, it is not mandatory to have the same names of arguments given in the declaration that of actual arguments. It is also not mandatory to have the same data type in actual argument and name given in the declaration.

The variable 'a' has been defined as a local variable in the function definition. 'radius' has been defined in the main program, when a call to function is invoked at statement 'm=area(radius) ' the value of radius (= 5.0) is passed to function and variable 'r' in the function definition is initialized at '5.0'. Function thus computes the area of circle and assigns this value to variable 'a'. Finally at the last statement ' return(a)' statement return this value to calling environment and variable 'm' get the value equal to area of circle. Thus both the print statement print the area as 94.985.

Thus the above example present both the type of function, one which returns a value, secondly which returns nothing. It must be remembered that A function may or may not return a value. If at all it returns a value, it is always single. 'Actual ' argument list should b e contained in the function call. Actual and format argument must have the same data types. By default, the functions return integer value. If function return the value other than the integer ten its type must be defined in the function header. A function without the return statement will not return any value but a global variable will retain (if modified) its value for the future use.

11.5 CALL BY VALUE & CALL BY REFERENCE

The functions are invoked by their name and passing the list of parameter to the function. These parameters or arguments must be of same type & number in the function definitions. All the arguments passes the value to the function when the function is invoked. This mechanism is called Call by Value. Here it must be noted that the value is passed to function not the parameter it self. In such cases, the value of variable in the calling environment will be not be changed, however the called environment or function may change the value of variable. The value passed must be assigned to a local variable declared inside the function. Consider the following example,

Program 5

/* illustration of concept of *Call by Value* parameter passing */

```
# include < stdio.h>
int mult ( int m, int n );
main ()
{
int m,n, result;
printf (" Enter the value of M  & N \n");
scanf("%d %d ", &m, &n );
printf ("Value of M & N before the call to function = %d   %d\n",
     m, n);
result = mult (m,n );
printf ("Value of Multiplication  = %d \n ", result);
printf ("Value of M & N after  the call to function = %d  %d\n", m,
     n);
}
int mult (int m, int n )
{
int result=0; temp;
/* swaping the values of m & n */
temp= m;
```

```
m=n;
n= temp;
result= m * n;
return (result);
}
```

In the above program, suppose you enter following values to m & n
m=4, n= 2
The value of m & n before the function call : m=4, n=2
At the function call mult (m,n), the values of m & n will be copied to function.
Function swaps the values of m & n : thus m= 2, n=4
Function passes the result of product : result=8
In the Main function, value of result will be printed as : result =8;
Next print statement will print the values of m & n as : m=4, n=2

Thus you may see that although the values of m & n has been altered in the function call, but it remained unchanged in the main function. This happened because the variable itself has not been passed but the values has been passed. This "Call by Value " parameter mechanism is strictly followed in 'C'.

"Call by Reference" is another mechanism of parameter passing. Several other language provides this mechanism. As you have seen in previous example that in the case of "Call by Value" mechanism, the values of the parameters in the calling environment remains unchanged. "Call by Reference" is the mechanism in which the values of variables are changed in the calling environment as par the changes in the functions. This mechanism may be accomplished in the 'C' using pointers. When the function is called the . addresses of variables (through pointers) must be passed as argument. Since the address of the variable is passed as value, then changes in the variable value takes into effect. Following example show this mechanism.

Program 6

```
/* Illustration of concept of Call by Reference parameter passing .
   This example swaps the value of two variables */
#include <stdio.h>
swap ( int *, int *);
main( )
{
int m,n;
printf (" Enter the value of M & N \n");
scanf("%d %d ", &m, &n );
printf("Values of M & N before the swap m=%d n=%d\n",m,n);
```

```
swap (&m,&n);
printf("Values of M & N after the swap m=%d  n=%d\n",m,n);
}
void swap ( int *a, int *b )
{
int temp;
temp = *a;
*a=*b;
*q = temp;
}
```

The above example swaps the values of m & n. Suppose you enter following values for m & n, M=1, N=2

The values of m & n before the call to swap( ) function are: M=1, N=2
The values of m & n after the call to swap () function are : M=2, N=1

Thus it may be noted that using pointers, it is possible to change the values of variable in the calling environment in accordance with the changes made by the function. This process of parameter passing is defined as "Call by Reference ".

Program 7

```
/*THE RECURSIVE PROGRAM FOR FINDING THE FACTO-
    RIAL*/
#include<conio.h>
#include<stdio.h>
void main()
{
int i,f=1,n,a;
int facto(int p);
clrscr();
printf(" /*THE PROGRAM FOR FINDING THE FACTORIAL OF
    ANY GIVEN NUMBER GREATER THAN 1*/ ");
printf("\n\n GIVE THE NUMBER WHOSE FACTORIAL IS RE-
    QUIRED ");
scanf("%d",&n);
a=n;
if(n==0)
f=1;
else
f=facto(n);
printf("\n\n THE FACTORAIL OF  %d! IS %d ",a,f);
getch();
```

```
}
int facto(int p)
{
 int s;
if(p==1)
  return(1);
else
s=p*facto(p-1);
return s;
}
```

11.6 RECURSION

The process of calling a function by itself is called Recursion. This process is continued until a particular condition is satisfied. This process is used for the repetitive computations in which each function call return a value, for which the function needs be invoked again. As shown in the previous program, the function 'Fact' is called until the condition for call is satisfied. Logic for the factorial computation by recursion may be understood as given below.

n! = n * (n-1)!   And 1!=1

To calculate 5! Following steps are taken.

Step 1	5! = 5 * 4!	Compute 4!
Step 2	4! = 4 * 3!	Compute 3!
Step 3	3! =3 * 2!	Compute 2!
Step 4	2! = 2 * 1!	1!=1

In this case the function 'fact' must be called four times, one each for 4!, 3!,2!, & 1!. Thereafter the values from each function called are passed back to previous one. Thus after four returns the value of !5 is computed. This is made possible by using the stack (First in Last out) structure. When the function calls are made, the recursive function calls are not executed immediately. These calls are placed on the stack until the termination condition is achieved.

There are several function which needs be represented recursively. For example, the each term in Fibnocci Series may defined as follows,

F(1)= 1;
F(2)=1;
F(n) = F (n-1) + F(n-2);

Where the F(n) denotes the n th term of Fibnocci Series. Few of the terms of Fibnocci Series are as under.

1, 1, 2, 3, 5, 8, 13, 21, 34

Program 8

```
/* Write a Recursive Program / Function to compute nth term of
     Fibonaci Series */
#include <stdio.h>
int term ( int n)
int sum (int  m )
main( )
{
int n;
printf ("\n Enter the term \n");
scanf ("%d", &n );
printf ("\n Enter the Term number to which the sum is to be com-
     puted \n");
scanf ("%d", & m );
printf (" n th term of Fibonacci series is  = %d\n", term (n) );
printf ( " Summation of all terms up to n th term is  = %d\n", sum
     (m ) );
}
int term ( int n )
{
if (n<=2 )
return (1);
else
return ( term(n-1) + term(n-2) )
}
int sum ( int  m)
{
int I;
int result =0;
for (I=1; I<=m;I++)
{
result= result + term (l);
}
return(result);
}
```

Program 9

```
/* Write a function to compute the x to power n */
#include<stdio.h>
#include<conio.h>
void main()
{
```

```
int n;
float x,y;
char ch;
float power(float, int);
clrscr();
do{
printf("\nEnter the number(in fraction) of which power is to be
    calculated\n");
scanf("%f",&x);
printf("\nEnter the power upto which the value is to be
    calculated\n");
scanf("%d",&n);
y=power(x,n);
printf("\n The computed value is : %f",y);
getch();
printf("\n Do you wish to calculate for another(y/n): ");
fflush(stdin);
scanf("%c",&ch);
}while(ch=='y');
}
//******************************
float power(float a, int b)
{ int i;
float c=1.0;
float d;
d=a;
for(i=1;i<=b;i++)
c=c*d;
return(c);
}
```

Program 10

```
/* Write function to compute the GCD of two numbers */
#include<stdio.h>
#include<conio.h>
#include<process.h>
int a,b;
void main()
{
printf("\nEnter the two numbers of which gcd is to be calculated
    \n");
scanf("%d \n %d",&a,&b);
```

```
gcd();
}
void gcd()
{
if(a==b)
{
printf("\ngcd of the two no. is %d",a);
getch();
exit(0);
}
else if(a<b)
{
b=b-a;
gcd();
}
else{
a=a-b;
gcd();
}
}
```

Program 11

```
/* Write functions to compute the multiplication & summation of
    terms of series x,x**2,x**3,....for x<1 */
#include<stdio.h>                              r
#include<conio.h>
#include<stdlib.h>
void main()
{
 int n,i,j,m;
 float x;
 char ch;
 void multi(float, int);
 void addition(float, int);
 clrscr();
 printf("\n Program to compute the multiplication and addition
    of series x,x**2,x**3,....for x<1");
 do{
 printf("\n\n Enter the power upto which manipulations are to
    be taken into account\n");
 scanf("%d",&n);
 printf("\n Enter the value of which power is to be calculated\n");
```

```
scanf("%f",&x);
if(x>=1)
{
printf("\n Program terminated\nx should be less than 1");
getch();
exit(0);
}
printf("\n Main Menu");
printf("\n1. Multiplication of Series");
printf("\n2. Addition of Series");
printf("\n3. exit");
printf("\n\nEnter your choice");
scanf("%d",&m);
switch(m)
{
case 1:multi(x,n);
  break;
case 2:addition(x,n);
  break;
case 3:printf("\nexiting from the program");
  exit(0);
}
printf("\nDo u wish to calculate for another(y/n):");
fflush(stdin);
scanf("%c",&ch);
}while(ch=='y');
}
//************************************
void multi(float a, int b)
{
int c;
float mul=1;
int i,j=0;
float d,arr[10];
d=a;
for(c=1;c<=b;c++)
{
 arr[j]=d;
 d=d*a;
 j+=1;
}
for(i=0;i<b;i++)
```

```
{
mul =mul * arr[i];
}
printf("\n The multiplicated value of series is\n");
printf("%f",mul);
return;
}
//**********************************************
void addition(float a, int b)
{
 int i,c;
 float arr[10],d;
 float add=0;
int j=0;
d=a;
 for(c=1;c<=b;c++)
{
arr[j]=d;
d=d*a;
j+=1;
}
for(i=0;i<b;i++)
{
 add = add + arr[i];
}
printf("\n The calculated value of series after addition is\n");
printf("%f",add);
return;
}
```

Program 12

```
/* Write a function to checjk if a number is prime or not */
#include<stdio.h>
#include<conio.h>
#include<math.h>
void main()
{
int n;
char ch;
void prime(int);
clrscr();
do
```

```
{
printf("Program to check the given no. for prime\n");
printf("Enter the no.\n");
scanf("%d",&n);
prime(n);
printf("\nDo you wish to check another number(y/n)\n");
fflush(stdin);
scanf("%c",&ch);
}while(ch=='y');
}
void prime(int n)
{
 int a,b,c;
  a =(int) sqrt(n);
  for(b=2;b<=a+1;b++)
  {
   c = n % b;
   if(c==0)
   {
    printf("\nGiven no. is not prime\n");
    break;
   }
   else if(c!=0 && b<(a+1))
    continue;
   else if(c!=0 && b==(a+1))
   {
    printf("\nGiven no. is prime number");
    break;
   }
  }
}
```

Program 13

```
/* Write a recursive call to evaluate the following series.
F(x) = x  - x^3/3! +  x^5/ 5!  - x^7 / 7! + ......
*/
# include <stdio.h>
# include <conio.h>
# include <math.h>
void main()
{ float power(float,int);
 long int fact(int);
```

```
float x,sig,term,sum=0,sine;
int i,n,j;
clrscr();
printf("Enter the value of x:");
scanf("%f",&x);
printf("Enter the number of terms:");
scanf("%d",&n);
for(i=0;i<n;i++)
{ j=2*i+1;
  sig=power(-1,i);
  term=sig*(power(x,j)/fact(j));
  sum=sum+term;
}
sine=sin(x);
printf("\nThe sine of %f is %f",x,sine);
printf("\nThe value of sum is %f",sum);
getch();
}
float power(float a,int b)
{ int m;
  float val=1;
  for(m=1;m<=b;m++)
  { val=val*a;
  }
  return(val);
}
long int fact(int num)
{ int p;
  long int f=1;
  for(p=1;p<=num;p++)
  { f=f*p;
  }
  return(f);
}
```

SELECT EXERCISES

Q. 1. What are Function ? Why dividing the main logic of a problem in to the pieces is considered to be good programming strategy.

Q. 2. What is the difference between standard library function and user defined function ? state with suitable example.

Q. 3. Give the general syntax of User Defined Functions.

Q. 4. What do you mean by a Call to a function ? Can a function call another function in C ?

Q. 5. What are Global variable ? State the scope of Global Variables ? How are they declared ?

Q. 6. What are Local Variable ? State the scope of local variables.

Q. 7. What do you mean by the Storage Class ?

Q. 8. Explain the key difference between Auto, Static, External & Register Variable.

Q. 9. How and When Register Variable are declared and used.

Q. 10. What to you mean by Parameter Passing ?

Q. 11. Explain the "Call by Value" parameter passing .

Q. 12. Is it possible to have "Call by Reference" parameter passing mechanism in C ?

Q. 13. What do you mean by Recursion? How it is different than Iteration?

Q. 14. Write a function which return a maximum of three integers.

Q. 15. Write a program in C that prints the lower case letter and digit "0....9" and returns their ASCII value .

Q. 16. What is the purpose of return statement ?

Q. 17. What are function prototypes ? What is the purpose of function prototypes ?

Q. 18. What are the differences between actual argument & formal argument ?

Q. 19. How the local variable declared inside a function are interpreted when there is a recursive call ?

Q. 20. List some of the advantages of using recursion.

12 Advanced Features in C

STRUCTURE, POINTER AND DYNAMIC MEMORY ALLOCATION

12.0 INTRODUCTION TO STRUCTURE

Structure is a collection of variables defined under single name. These variables need not be of same type. Thus, Structure provides the convenient way of bundling the related information. The Structure is convenient tool for handling a group of .logically related data items. The variables that contribute to make an Structure are called members. Consider a database of student of a class where the individual record of their Roll No, Name, Father Name, Marks etc has to be maintained. All of this information may be put and used as Structure. We may define following structure,

```
struct Student
{
int        Roll_Number ;
char       name[25];
char       Fname [25];
int        Marks;
float      Weight;
};
```

In the above example, the structure Student have been declared to hold a group of five data items. These data item and their type are defined within the braces separated by semi colon. Here the data items are Roll Number, Name, Father Name, Marks and Weight of the student. These data items are called the structure element or the members. There is no restriction on any members for data type. Every member may have different data type. Student is the name of the structure and is called Structure Tag.

Structure help to organize the complex data in more meaningful way. It gives lot of freedom & flexibility to the programmer to write a code in C.

12.1 DECLARATION OF STRUCTURE

The structure provides the mechanism to group the data of different type, which grouped together presents a information. We may declare a structure 'employee' with the attributes employee name, Department, Designation, Basic Pay, Gross Pay, DA, HRA. Following is the 'C' program segment, which declare the structure.

```
struct Employee
{
char    emp_Code[5];
char    emp_name[50];
char    department[50];
char    designation[30];
float   basic_pay;
float   gross_pay;
float   da;
float   hra;
};
```

Following is the template, which will be used to describe information.

Emp_code	Array of Five Character
Emp_name	Array of fifty Character
Department	Array of fifty Character
Designation	Array of thirty Character
Basic_Pay	Float
Gross_pay	Float
DA	Float
HRA	Float

Consider the structure 'student' defined above, We may declare the structure variable using the tag name. 'C' segment to declare the structure variable student1, student2 is as follows.

```
struct Student
{
int         Roll_Number ;
char        name[25];
char        Fname [25];
int         Marks;
float       Weight;
};
Struct student student1,student2;
```

It must be noted that use of tag name is not mandatory. The above declaration alongwith the structure variable as shown below is also valid.

```
struct
{
int         Roll_Number ;
char        name[25];
char        Fname [25];
int         Marks;
float       Weight;
} student1, student2;
```

The structure definition appears at the beginning of the program, normally before declaration of any other variable. They may also appear before the 'main', in such cases the definition is global and may be used by any function.

12.2 INITIALIZATION OF VALUES TO MEMBERS OF STRUCTURE

The following program segment assign the values to members of structure variable student.

```
Main()
{
Static Struct
{
int         Roll_Number;
char        name[25];
char        Fname [25];
int         Marks;
float       Weight;
};
student = {111, "Yogendra Yadav ", "P P Yadav", 29, 51.8 };
```

This assigns the values as

```
Student. Roll_number  = 111
Student. Name         = "Yogendra Yadav"
Student. Fname        = "P P Yadav"
Stdent.Marks          = 29
Student.weight        = 51.8
```

The link between the variable and member is established by a dot

Another way of assigning values to members of structure is as follows.

```
Struct Student
{
int          Roll_Number;
char         name[25];
char         Fname [25];
int          Marks;
float        Weight;
} student1;
```

we may assign the values to the members of structure variable Student1 as shown below.

```
Student1.roll_number = 111;
Strcpy(student1.name, "Yogendra Yadav");
Strcpy ( student1.fname, "P P Yadav");
Student1.marks      = 29
Student1.weight     = 51.8;
```

It is also possible to use the 'scanf' statement to input the record from the standard input e.g. Key board.

Following program reads the values from the input and assign it to the members of structure variable.

Program 1

```
/* Program to read value using 'Scanf' assigning it to member of
    structure */
Struct Student
{
int          Roll_Number;
char         name[25];
char         Fname [25];
int          Marks;
float        Weight;
};
```

```
main ()
{
struct student student1;
printf(" Enter the values \n");
scanf (" %d   %s   %s   %d    %f", & student1.roll_number,
student1.name, student1.fname, &student1.marks, &student1.weight);
printf (" Printing the record \n");
printf (" %d   %s   %s   %d    %f\n", student1.roll_number,
student1.name, student1.fname, student1.marks, student1.weight);
}
```

12.3 ARRAYS OF STRUCTURE

Use of structure is not limited to just a collection of heterogeneous type variable. As we have seen that a student entity may be represented as structure and its attributes may be represented as members. It is also possible to crate an array of structure. For example, if we have to represent the class of fifty students, each student's attribute may be stored and processes by declaring the class as an array of structure. This is done by doing following.

```
Struct Class student[50];
```

This statement defines an array of structure called Class. Each element of this array is an struct type. We can initialize the members of all the fifty student by doing following. Following is the example, which initialize the members of only three students.

```
struct Student
{
int        Roll_Number ;
char       name[25];
char       Fname [25];
int        Marks;
float      Weight;
};
main( )
{
static struct student class[4] = { {111, "Ritendra Goel", "P P Yadav", 29,
51.8 }, {112, "S S Soam", "O S Soam", 55, 71.8}, {113, "Tanvir Tahir", "Y
M Tahir", 53, 99.9 }, {114, "Ankita Singh", "D S Yadav",33,23.6}};
}
```

This program segment declares class as an array of four element class[0],class[1],class[2],class[3] and initializes the values as following.

```
Class[0].roll_number      = 111;
Class[0].name             = "Ritendra Goel"
Class[0]. Fname           ="P P Yadav"
______
______
class[3].rollnumber       = 114
class[3].name             = "Ankita Singh"
Class[3].fname            = "D S Yadav"
Class[3].marks            = 33
Class[3].weight           = 23.6
```

In case of large data required to initialize the member, it is advisable to read the data from standard input. This can be done using 'scanf' statement. Following program read the student data from the input. This program prints the complete record of student who have obtained maximum marks.

Program 2

```
/* Program to find the student who have obtained maximum marks
   */
Struct Student
{
int       Roll_Number;
char      name[25];
char      Fname [25];
int       Marks;
float     Weight;
};
main ()
{
int n, index, max
struct student class[50];
For (n=0; n<50; n++)
{
printf("Enter the record of %d student \n", n+1);
scanf ("%d  %s  %s  %d   %f", & class[n].roll_number,
    class[n].name,   class[n].fname,   &class[n].marks,
    &class[n].weight);
}
Max= 0;
for (n=0; n<50; n++)
{
if ( Max <  class[n].marks)
```

```
index =n;
}
printf ("Printing the record of student obtained maximum marks
    \n");
printf ("%d   %s   %s   %d    %f\n", class[index].roll_number,
    class[index].name, class[index].fname, class[index].marks,
    class[index].weight);
}
```

12.4 POINTERS

Pointers are probably the most important feature of C programming language. Pointer is a powerful tool to efficiently access the data by indirect reference because it holds the address of data item in question. Pointer are very efficient in writing the program which requires handling with the table. Real power of C lies with efficiently using the pointers.

Typically the pointer is integer variable which holds the address of the another variable. The pointer always contains the memory address. Here memory address refers to the memory location where the a variable has been allotted space to hold the value. If out of two variable, one variable holds or contain the address of another variable, the first is said to point to second variable.

For example the following statement declares & initialize the variable amount,

Int amount = 100;

This statement prompt the system to allot the space for this variable in the memory. The Value 100 is stored in that memory location and is called the content of that memory location. Suppose the system has allotted the memory location 1000 to the variable amount.

Memory Address	Content of Memory	Logical Name
0		
1		

999		
1000	100	amount
1001		
1002		

In the above figure, you may observe the continuous memory location. System may allot any memory location to the variable. Every memory location may be thought to composed of its address and contents. This memory location may be addressed by giving the logical name as declared in the program . Here 'amount' is allotted memory location whose address is '1000' and value of amount '100' is pushed to memory location. Now, the value '100' may be accessed in two ways, one by logical name 'amount', secondly by address '1000'. Memory address are always integer and they may be assigned to any integer variable which can also be stored in the memory just like any other variable. These variable are called pointer, because hold the memory address of another variable.

Suppose the variable 'ptr' holds the memory address of variable 'amount' i.e. '1000'. The 'ptr' is called the pointer (variable) and it points to 'amount'. It may be represented as following,

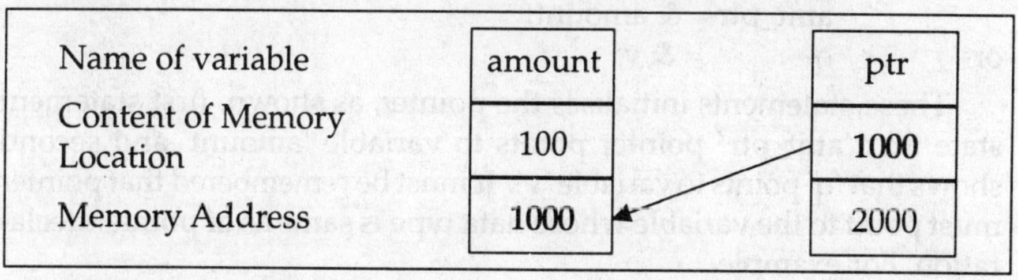

Here you may note that 'ptr' is a pointer to 'amount' as contents of 'ptr' are the memory address of 'amount'. However, the memory address of 'ptr' variable is '2000'.

The memory allocation for a variable is done on 'run time', therefore the address of the variable is not known immediately. However, the address of the variable may be determined using '&' operator. For example,

```
ptr = & amount;
```

this statement will returns the address of variable 'amount' and initialize to 'ptr'. The '&' operator may be used in conjunction with any variable or array element. Consider the following array declaration.

Int Marks[10];

This statement initializes an array 'Marks'.

I = & Marks[1]; statement returns the address of 1st element of 'Marks' array and assigns to 'I'.

12.5 DECLARATION & INITIALIZATION OF POINTERS

The pointer contains the address of variable and variable may be of any data type. The general declaration syntax of pointer is as shown below,

```
Data Type    * name;
```

Here the Data Type indicate the type of variable to which this pointer points . "*" shows that the variable 'name' is pointer. 'Name' is the name of pointer variable. Following are some example of pointer declaration.

```
int *amt_ptr;
float *q;
```

First declaration scalares 'amt_ptr' as pointer variable which points to variable of 'int' data type. Second statement shows that 'q' is pointer variable which point to variable of 'float' data type. After the declaration of pointer variable, it can be initialised to point to a particular variable. For example,

```
      amt_ptr = & amount;
or    q       = & v;
```

These statements initialises the pointer, as shown, first statement state that 'amt_ptr' pointer points to variable 'amount' and second shows that 'q' points to variable 'v'. It must be remembered that pointer must point to the variable whose data type is same as of pointer declaration. For example,

```
int *amt_ptr
float amount;
amt_ptr = & amount;
```

These statement are in correct, as 'amt_ptr' has been declared to point to the variable of type ' int' . But the variable 'amount' has been declared as 'float'. Thus these statement will result in to incorrect.

12.6 POINTER ARITHMETIC

It would be advisable initially to understand the meaning of "*" and "&" as following.

' * '   Contents of Memory Location
'&'   Address of memory location.

For example consider the following set of statement.

```
int  *amt_ptr;
int next, amount=100;
amt_ptr = & amount;
next    = *amt_ptr;
```

First statement declares 'amt_ptr' as a pointer, second declares 'next' & 'amount' variable of 'int' data type. Third statement declares the 'amt_ptr' as pointer to variable 'amount' by putting the address of variable 'amount' in to 'amt_ptr'. Fourth statement, returns the contents of memory location whose address is stored at 'amt_ptr', which is equal to '100'. Thus 'next' would be initialized as '100'. Thus it may be noted that following two statements

```
amt_ptr = & amount;
next    = *amt_ptr;
```

may be written as

```
next = *& amount; which is equivalent to following statement
next = amount;
```

The pointer may be used in the expression just like any other variable. The 'a', 'b' & 'c' are the pointers then following expression are valid.

```
Interest = amount * (*b);
*a = *b * *c ;
amount = *b / *c + *a * *b;
a++;
amount *= *c;
- - c;
```

12.7 ACCESSING AN ARRAY USING POINTER

At the time of declaration of array, the contiguous memory locations are allotted to each element of an array . consider following array declaration statement.

```
Int Marks [3];
```

This will allot the contiguous memory location for each element of array 'Marks' as shown below.

Element of array	Marks[0]	Marks[1]	Marks[2]
Address	2500	2502	2504

It may be noted that each integer takes two bytes to store an integer, therefore every element of array will take two byte to store single value. We may declare 'ptr' pointer to pint the array 'marks' as shown below,

```
int *ptr;
ptr= marks;
```

First statement declare the 'ptr' as pointer and second makes the pointer to point to array 'marks'. Immediately after second statement 'ptr' will contain the address of memory location marks[0] i.e. ptr =& marks[0]. Now to access other element of array 'ptr' may be incremented by one each time.

Following program uses pointers to access an array.

Program 3

```
/* This program finds largest number in the array using pointer
    */
# include < stdio.h>
main( )
{
int *ptr, max, n;
int Marks[50];
max=0;
ptr=marks;
printf ( "Enter the numbers \n");
for ( n=0; n<50; n++ )
{
scanf("Enter number :: %d \n", &Marks[n];
}
n=0;
while ( n<50 )
{
if ( max > *ptr )
max= *ptr;
n++; ptr ++
}
printf (" Largest number = %d \n", max );
}
```

12.8 DYNAMIC MEMORY ALLOCATION

When a program written in 'C' is executed the various structures like Variables, Array etc are allotted memory space as par the requirement. This memory allocation requirement is normally 'static' in nature. For example, following array declaration

Int amount[50];

Reserves the memory location required to store '50' interger values. In many cases, the array requirement is over estimated by the programmer. This allocation is done as par the programmer wish and a whole lot of memory is reserved before the start of execution of program. This type of memory allocation is called static memory allocation. In short, in the case of static memory allocation, size of memory may be required for the coputation work before the execution. In the case of Dynamic Memory Allocation, the size of memory is determined and allotted at the time of execution. The Dynamic Memory allocation has many advantages over static memory allocation.

Consider a case of array of structures, whose declaration is given below.

```
Struct Student
{
int        Roll_Number ;
char       name[25];
char       Fname [25];
int        Marks;
float      Weight;
};
struct student class[1000];
```

In the above declaration, the memory space for storing the '1000' element of 'struct' type is allotted statically. But the at run time, it might be the case that only '400' students record is to be entered. In such cases, the memory worth storing '600' such record is wasted. Secondly, if it is required to change the size of memory (e.g. entering '2000' student record in this case) will leads to an error. This is because the size reserved for the array is lower than the actual requirement. In this case, you have to change the code of your program. Both of the cases are not desirable. Thus the preferred strategy is to allot the memory whenever required at the run. This concept is known as Dynamic Memory Allocation and supported by the 'C' Programming Language.

Allocating the Memory

Malloc() function is used in 'C' programming language to allocate the memory dynamically. This function reserves the memory and returns a pointer which point to the memory where it has been reserved. Consider the following statement,

```
ptr = ( int * ) malloc (10 * size of (int) );
```

This function (malloc) reserves the block of memory location whose size the 10 times the size required to store one integer. This function returns a pointer to an integer ('ptr') which points to the beginning of the memory block.

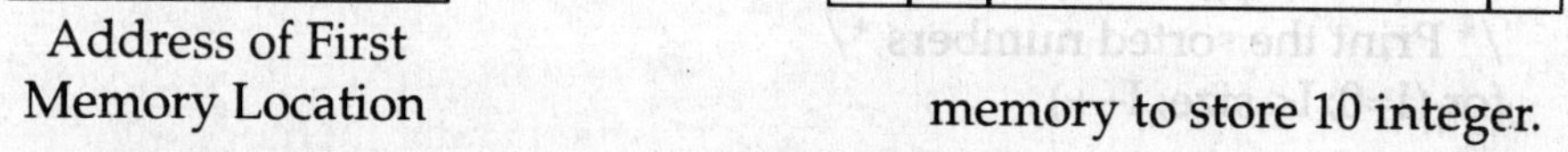

Address of First Memory Location

memory to store 10 integer.

Similarly the statement,

ptr = (char *) malloc(100);

reserves the memory to store 100 character and return a pointer to character ('ptr') which points to the first memory location, in other words, the address of the first memory location is assigned to ptr.

Similarly it is also possible to allocate the memory block for 'structure' . For example,

ptr = (struct student *) malloc (size of (struct student));

reserves the memory location to store the record of student (struct 'student' has been defined in structure section) and return a pointer. If the system fails to allocate the memory then it returns 'NULL'.

Consider following program, which uses Dynamic Memory Allocation to create a array of integer and sort the numbers entered in increasing order.

Program 4

```
/* This program create an table of numbers using dynamic memory
    allocation and sorts the number in increasing order */
#include <stdio.h>
#include <stdlib.h>
# define NULL 0
void sort ( int size, int * q);
main ( )
{
int *q;
int I, size;
printf (" Enter the number of entries to be entered \n");
scanf ("%d", &size);
/* Allocate the memory to store the integer whose number is 'size'
*/
q= (int * ) malloc (size * sizeof (int));
/* Read the entries */
printf ( "please enter total %d entries ", size );
for (I= 0; I < size; I++)
{
printf (" Enter %d number ", I+1 );
scanf ("%d", q + I );
}
/* Function to sort the number */
sort ( size, q );
/* Print the sorted numbers */
for (I=0; I< size; I++)
```

```
{
printf( " position = %d      value = %d \n", I+1, *(size + I ));
}
}
void sort (int size, int *q )
{
int I, item, temp;
for (item=0; item < size; item ++ )
{
for ( I= item + 1;I < size; I++)
{
if ( *(q+I ) < *(q+item))
{
temp = *(q+item);
*(q+item) = *(q+I);
*(q+I) = temp;
}}}
return;
}
```

Program 5

```
/* Write a program to find number of character in a line */
#include<stdio.h>
#include<conio.h>
void main()
{
char ch;
int count=0;
clrscr();
printf("\n\t\tProgram to find number of characters in a line\n");
printf("\t\t*********************************************\n");
printf("Enter the character string\n");
do{
ch=getc(stdin);
count++;
} while(ch!='\n');
count—;
printf("\n Number of characters in the line are\n");
printf(":%d",count);
getch();
}
```

Program 6

```
/* Write a program using pointer to concatenate two strings */
#include<stdio.h>
#include<conio.h>
void main()
{
 char *str1,*str2,*str3;
 int i,j;
 clrscr();
 printf("\n\t\tProgram to concatenate two strings");
 printf("\n\t\t**********************************\n");
 printf("\n Enter string1:");
 gets(str1);
 printf("\n Enter string2:");
 gets(str2);
 for(i=0;str1[i]!='\0';i++)
 str3[i]=str1[i];
 str3[i]=' ';
 for(j=0;str2[j]!='\0';j++)
 str3[i+j+1]=str2[j];
 str3[i+j+1]='\0';
 printf("\n The concatenated string is:\n %s",str3);
 getch();
 }
```

Program 7

```
/* Wrute a program to  find number of words in a statement.  */
#include<stdio.h>
#include<conio.h>
void main()
{
 char *str,ch;
 int count=0;
 clrscr();
 printf("\n\t\tProgram to find number of words in a statement");
 printf("\n\t\t*******************************************\n");
 printf("\n Enter the character string:\n");
 fflush(stdin);
 //gets(str);
 do{
 ch= getc(stdin);
 if(ch==' ')
```

```
count++;
}while(ch!='\n');
count++;
printf("\n The number of words in the string are: %d",count);
getch();
}
```

Program 8

```
/* Write a program to sort the name in Alphabetical Order using
    Pointers */
#include<stdio.h>
#include<conio.h>
#include<string.h>
void main()
{
 char *str[10];
 char *temp;
 int i,n;
 clrscr();
 printf("\n\t\tProgram to sort names in alphabetical order");
 printf("\n\t\t*******************************************\n");
 printf("\n Enter how many names do u want to sort:");
 scanf("%d",&n);
 printf("\n Enter %d names one by one:",n);
 for(i=0;i<n;i++)
 {
 printf("\n Name[%d]: ",i);
 gets(str[i]);
 }
 for(i=1;i<n;i++)
 {
 for(j=1;j<=n-i;j++)
 {
  if(strcmp(str[j-1], str[j])>0)
  {
  strcpy(temp,str[j-1]);
  strcpy(str[j-1],str[j]);
  strcpy(str[j],temp);
  }
  }
  printf("\n The names in sorted order are:\n");
  for(i=0;i<n;i++)
```

```
{
 printf("%s  ",str[i]);
}
getch();
}
```

Program 9

/* Write a program using pointers to prepare salary slip of the employee . The program is written with Dynamic Memory Allocation. An employee record contain Employee Code, Employee Name, Designation, Basic Pay, DA, HRA, PPF, GPF, Net Pay. DA is computed as 45% of Basic pay HRA is 10, PPF is 5% and GPF is 10% of basic Pay. Gross Pay is computed as sum of Basic Pay, DA, HRA and Net Pay is computed by deducting PPF & GPF contribution from Gross Pay*/

```
#include<stdio.h>
#include<conio.h>
#include<string.h>
#include<alloc.h>
struct employee
{
 char emp_code[10];
 char emp_name[20];
 char designation[20];
 float basic_pay;
 float da;
 float hra;
 float ppf;
 float gpf;
 float netpay;
 struct employee *next;
 };
void get_data(struct employee **);
void net_pay(struct employee **);
void main()
{
 struct employee *p=NULL;
 int choice;
 while(1)
 {
 clrscr();
 printf("\n\tMain Menu");
 printf("\n\t1. Enter the record of employee:");
```

```
printf("\n\t2. Salary slip of employee");
printf("\n\t3. Exit");
printf("\n\nEnter your choice:(1,2,3)");
scanf("%c",&choice);
switch(choice)
{
case 1:get_data(&p);
  break;
case 2:net_pay(&p);
  break;
case 3:exit(1);
  break;
default:printf("\nError!!!!");
  printf("\nWrong choice entered.....");
  getch();
  break;
}
}
}
//**************************
void get_data(struct employee **p)
{
struct employee *q=*p;
struct employee *r,*s;
char choice;
char emp_code[10];
char emp_name[20];
char designation[20];
float basic_pay;
do{
q=*p;
r=(struct employee *) malloc (sizeof(struct employee));
printf("\n\t\tEmployee Record");
printf("\n\t Employee id: ");
fflush(stdin);
gets(emp_code);
strcpy(r->emp_code,emp_code);
printf("\n\t Employee Name: ");
fflush(stdin);
gets(emp_name);
strcpy(r->emp_name,emp_name);
printf("\n\t Designation: ");
```

```
fflush(stdin);
gets(designation);
strcpy(r->designation,designation);
printf("\n\t Employee's basic pay: ");
scanf("%f",&basic_pay);
r->basic_pay=basic_pay;
r->next=NULL;
if(*p=NULL)
*p=r;
else
{
 while(q!=NULL)
 {
 s=q;
 q=q->next;
 }
 if(q==*p)
 {
 r->next=q;
 *p=r;
 }
 else
 {
 r->next=q;
 s->next=r;
 }
 }
 printf("\n Do you want to add more employee records(y/n): ");
 fflush(stdin);
 scanf("%c",&choice);
 }while(choice=='y' | | choice=='Y');
 }
 //*******************************************
  void net_pay(struct employee **p)
  {
   struct employee *q = *p;
   if(q==NULL)
   printf("\n No data currently stored");
   else
   {
    q->da = .45 * q->basic_pay;
    q->hra = .10 * q->basic_pay;
```

```
q->ppf = .05 * q->basic_pay;
q->gpf = .10 * q->basic_pay;
 q->netpay = (q->basic_pay + q->da + q->hra) -( q->ppf + q-
>gpf);
printf("\nThe employee's salary is: %d",q->netpay);
}
}
```

Exercise

Write a program in C using structures which maintains the records of students (roll_no, name, hostel_no, physics marks, chemistry marks, math marks). Write functions which computes the following.

1. Find the student who scored the maximum marks (Topper)
2. Find average marks in Physics
3. Find Average marks in Chemistry
4. Find Average Marks in Mathematics
5. Find students who lives in a particular Hostel.
6. To add 10% bonus marks to all the students in individual subject.

Program 10

```
#include<stdio.h>
#include<conio.h>
#include<alloc.h>
#include<process.h>
#include<string.h>
#define NULL 0
struct student
 {
  int roll_number;
  char name[30];
  int hostel_no;
  float physics;
  float chemistry;
  float maths;
  struct student *next;
 };
void get_data(struct student **);
void maximum(struct student **);
void average(struct student **,char *);
void hostel(struct student **);
void bonus(struct student **);
void main()
```

```
{
 struct student *p=NULL;
 int choice;
 while(1)
  {
  clrscr();
  printf("\n\t1. ENTER RECORD OF STUDENT");
  printf("\n\t2. MAX MARKS OF TOPPER");
  printf("\n\t3. AV_MARKS_PHYSICS");
  printf("\n\t4. AV_MARKS_MATHS");
  printf("\n\t5. AV_MARKS_CHEMISTRY");
  printf("\n\t6. DISPLAY RECORD OF STUDENT ACCORDING
    TO HOSTEL NO.");
  printf("\n\t7. ADD BONUS MARKS");
  printf("\n\t8. EXIT");
  printf("\n\tENTER YOUR CHOICE(1,2,3,4,5,6,7,8):");
  scanf("%d",&choice);
  switch(choice)
   {
   case 1:  get_data(&p);
            break;
   case 2:  maximum(&p);
            break;
   case 3:  average(&p,"PHYSICS");
            break;
   case 4:  average(&p,"MATHS");
            break;
   case 5:  average(&p,"CHEMISTRY");
            break;
   case 6:  hostel(&p);
            break;
   case 7:  bonus(&p);
            break;
   case 8:  exit(1);
            break;
   default:printf("\n\tERROR!!!!!");
            printf("\n\tWRONG CHOICE ENTERED....");
            getch();
            break;
   }/*end of switch-case*/
  }/*end of while*/
 }/*end of main*/
```

```
void get_data(struct student **p)
{
 struct student *q = *p;
 struct student *r,*s;
 char choice;
 int roll_number;
 char name[30];
 int hostel_no;
 float physics;
 float chemistry;
 float maths;
 do
 {
 q=*p;
 r = (struct student*)malloc(sizeof(struct student));
 printf("\n\t******STUDENT RECORD*****");
 printf("\n\tNAME : ");
 fflush(stdin);
 gets(name);
 strcpy(r->name,name);
 printf("\n\tROLL NUMBER : ");
 scanf("%d",&roll_number);
 r->roll_number = roll_number;
 printf("\n\tHOSTEL NO. : ");
 scanf("%d",&hostel_no);
 r->hostel_no = hostel_no;
 printf("\n\tPHYSICS MARKS : ");
 scanf("%f",&physics);
 r->physics = physics;
 printf("\n\tCHEMISTRY MARKS :" );
 scanf("%f",&chemistry);
 r->chemistry = chemistry;
 printf("\n\tMATHS MARKS :");
 scanf("%f",&maths);
 r->maths = maths;
 r->next = NULL;
 if(*p==NULL)
  *p=r;
 else
  {
  while(((r->physics + r->maths + r->chemistry)<=(q->physics +
   q->maths + q->chemistry))&&q!=NULL)
```

```
    {
     s=q;
     q=q->next;
    }
   if(q==*p)
    {
     r->next=q;
     *p=r;
    }
   else
    {
     r->next=q;
     s->next=r;
    }
   }
  printf("\n\tDO YOU WANT TO ADD MORE RECORDS(Y/N):
    ");
  fflush(stdin);
  scanf("%c",&choice);
  }while(choice=='y' || choice=='Y');
 }
void maximum(struct student **p)
 {
  struct student *q = *p;
  if(q==NULL)
   printf("\n\tNO RECORDS CURRENTLY STORED");
  else
   {
   printf("\n\t******MAXIMUM MARKS OF TOPPER*******");
   printf("\n\tPHYSICS : %f",q->physics);
   printf("\n\tCHEMISTRY : %f",q->chemistry);
   printf("\n\tMATHS : %f",q->maths);
     printf("\n\tTOTAL : %f",(q->physics + q->chemistry + q-
    >maths));
   }
  getch();
 }
void average(struct student **p,char *c)
 {
  struct student *q=*p;
  int i=0;
  float total = 0;
  if(q==NULL)
```

```
printf("\n\tNO RECORDS CURRENTLY STORED");
if(strcmpi("physics",c))
{
 while(q!=NULL)
 {
  total = total + q->physics;
  i++;
  q = q->next;
 }
}
else
{
 if(strcmpi("chemistry",c))
 {
  while(q!=NULL)
 {
 total = total + q->physics;
 i++;
 q = q->next;
 }
 }
 else
 {
  if(strcmpi("physics",c))
 {
 while(q!=NULL)
 {
  total = total + q->physics;
  i++;
  q = q->next;
 }
 }
 }
}
printf("\n\tAVERAGE MARKS IN %s : %f",c,(total/i));
getch();
}
void hostel(struct student **p)
{
 struct student *r=*p;
 int n;
 if(r==NULL)
```

```
 printf("\n\tNO RECORDS CURRENTLY STORED");
else
 {
 printf("\n\tENTER THE HOSTEL NO. :");
 scanf("%d",&n);
 printf("\n\t******STUDENT RECORD*****");
 while(r!=NULL)
  {
  if(r->hostel_no==n)
 {
 printf("\n\tNAME : %s",r->name);
 printf("\n\tROLL NUMBER : %d",r->roll_number);
 printf("\n\tPHYSICS MARKS : %f",r->physics);
 printf("\n\tCHEMISTRY MARKS : %f",r->chemistry);
 printf("\n\tMATHS MARKS : %f\n",r->maths);
 }
  r=r->next;
  }
 }
getch();
}
void bonus(struct student **p)
{
 struct student *q = *p;
 int n;
 if(q==NULL)
 printf("\n\tNO RECORDS CURRENTLY STORED");
 else
 {
 printf("\n\tENTER THE STUDENT ROLL NUMBER :");
 scanf("%d",&n);
 while(q!=NULL && q->roll_number!=n)
  q=q->next;
 if(q->roll_number==n)
  {
  q->physics = q->physics + (0.10 * q->physics);
  q->chemistry = q->chemistry + (0.10 * q->chemistry);
  q->maths = q->maths + (0.10 * q->maths);
  }
 else
  {
  printf("\n\tNO RECORD CORRESPONDING TO THIS ROLL
  NUMBER EXISTS");
```

```
        getch();
        }
    }
}
```

OUPUT

```
1. ENTER RECORD OF STUDENT
2. MAX MARKS OF TOPPER
3. AV_MARKS_PHYSICS
4. AV_MARKS_MATHS
5. AV_MARKS_CHEMISTRY
6. DISPLAY RECORD OF STUDENT ACCORDING TO HOSTEL NO.
7. ADD BONUS MARKS
8. EXIT
   ENTER YOUR CHOICE(1,2,3,4,5,6,7,8): 1
   ******STUDENT RECORD*****
   NAME : Shyam
   ROLL NUMBER : 1
   HOSTEL NO. : 5
   PHYSICS MARKS : 97
   CHEMISTRY MARKS : 95
   MATHS MARKS : 98
   DO YOU WANT TO ADD MORE RECORDS(Y/N): y
   ******STUDENT RECORD*****
   NAME : Gaurav
   ROLL NUMBER : 3
   HOSTEL NO. : 3
   PHYSICS MARKS : 96
   CHEMISTRY MARKS : 86
   MATHS MARKS : 92
   DO YOU WANT TO ADD MORE RECORDS(Y/N): n
   MAXIMUM MARKS OF THE TOPPER
1. ENTER RECORD OF STUDENT
2. MAX MARKS OF TOPPER
3. AV_MARKS_PHYSICS
4. AV_MARKS_MATHS
5. AV_MARKS_CHEMISTRY
6. DISPLAY RECORD OF STUDENT ACCORDING TO HOSTEL NO.
7. ADD BONUS MARKS
8. EXIT
   ENTER YOUR CHOICE(1,2,3,4,5,6,7,8): 2
```

```
******MAXIMUM MARKS OF TOPPER********
PHYSICS : 97.000000
CHEMISTRY : 95.000000
MATHS : 98.000000
TOTAL : 290.000000

AVERAGE MARKS IN VARIOUS SUBJECTS
1. ENTER RECORD OF STUDENT
2. MAX MARKS OF TOPPER
3. AV_MARKS_PHYSICS
4. AV_MARKS_MATHS
5. AV_MARKS_CHEMISTRY
6. DISPLAY RECORD OF STUDENT ACCORDING TO HOSTEL NO.
7. ADD BONUS MARKS
8. EXIT
ENTER YOUR CHOICE(1,2,3,4,5,6,7,8): 3
AVERAGE MARKS IN PHYSICS : 96.000000
```

SELECT EXERCISES

Q. 1. What do you mean by Static Memory Allocation? What are the disadvantages of it?

Q. 2. What is Dynamic Memory Allocation? Discuss the main advantage of Dynamic Memory Allocation.

Q. 3. What are the difference between an array & structure?

Q. 4. Give the general syntax for the declaration of structure? it is possible to define an member of structure as a structure it self?

Q. 5. What are structure variable ? How are the they initialized?

Q. 6. What do you understand by array of structure? How the array of structures are declared and initialized?

Q. 7. Define an structure that contain following three members.
Character array with length of 50. (Name)
Floating point quantity (Age)
Structure containing two integer (phone numbers)

Q. 8. Is it possible to pass entire structure to a function? if yes then How?

Q. 9. How can an individual member of an structure be accessed by pointer.

Q. 10. What are pointers and how are they initialized?

Q. 11. List the different kind of object that can be associated with pointer variable?

Q. 12. Is it possible to pass an part of an array to function? if yes then how?

Q. 13. Describe the two different ways to specify the address of array element?

Q. 14. How can a multidimensional array defined in terms of a pointer to collection of contiguous array?

Q. 15. Give different way to initialize the values to member of an structure.

Q. 16. What are memory locations? Who determines the memory requirement after the declaration of an array?

Q. 17. What do you mean by pointer arithmetic?

Q. 18. How the memory is allocated using 'malloc' statement?

Q. 19. Discuss various preprocessor directives?

Q. 20. While declaring an array of integers, how the address of all the memory locations are determined to be used by pointers ?

13 Introduction to Web Technologies

13.1 OBJECT ORIENTED PROGRAMMING

The Object Oriented Design is relatively a new paradigm for software design. Object Oriented Design concept is entirely different than the traditional function oriented approach. Initially the program or code written used to be small and their complexity were also small. During early programming days, every programmer use to have its own programming approach and code were written in adhoc style. This type of programming is known as Exploratory Style of Programming. When the size and complexity increased with the time, this programming approach was proved to be inefficient and control structure based programming was introduced. It was realized that a good control flow through flow charting technique are required to deal efficiently with the increasing size and complexity of code. JSP, Jackson Structured Programming proposed that three construct sequence, selection & iteration are sufficient to express the large problem. Gradually, Data Structure base programming technique & Data flow oriented techniques were evolved to solve the large & complex problems. With further advancement in the field, the data flow oriented techniques evolved in to Object Oriented Design techniques.

All the computer programs or software deal primarily with two elements: code and data. A program can be conceptually organized around its code or around its data. The first approach is called the process-oriented and characterizes a program as a series of operations on data. In other word it may be thought of a code acting on data. Procedural languages such as Basic, COBOL, Pascal and C are based on this approach.

With increasing complexity & size of code, the other second approach, called object-oriented programming was evolved. Object–oriented programming organize a program around its data and a set of well –defined interface to that data. An object-oriented program can be characterized as data controlling access to code.

Large & Complex programs are prone to errors and becomes a expensive affair because of debugging & modification in the code. Object-oriented programming offers a new and powerful way to cope with this complexity. Its goal is clear, more reliable, more easy, more maintained programs.

Object Oriented Programming involves concepts of hiding, encapsulation, & polymorphism which are at the heart of object – oriented programming, are relatively new to the conventional programmer who works with C, COBOL, PASCAL, BASIC etc..

13.1.1 Procedural vs Object Oriented Languages

In the procedural programming language, the programming language like Pascal, C, Basic, Fortran give thrust on the construct which are suited for sequence, selection and iteration. In this programming environment, the code or program is written first which act on the set of data i.e. each statement in the language tells the computer to do some operation on data such as input data, arithmetic & logical operation on data and finally print the processed data. When programs become larger, a single list of instructions becomes unwieldy. Few programmers can comprehend a program of more than a few hundred statements unless it is broken down into small units. The idea of braking a program into functions can be further extended by grouping a number of functions together into a larger entity called a module, but the principle is similar: a grouping of components that carry out specific tasks. Programming with dividing a program into functions & modules is called structured programming. In the object-oriented approach the fundamental idea behind object-oriented language is to combine into a single unit both data and the functions that operate on that data. Such unit is called an object. An object's functions called member functions in C++ and Java. C++, JAVA are pure object oriented programming language, provides the feature for code reusability.

13.1.2 Drawbacks of Conventional Programming Approach

As programs grow ever larger & more complex, even the structured programming approach begins to slow signs of strain. It is evident from the experiences of software indsutry that as the project's complexity grows, the schedule slips, more programmers are added, complexity increases, costs skyrocket, the schedule slips further and many more problems. In procedural language, the emphasis is on doing things- read the keyboard, invert the vector, check for error, &so on. The subdivision of a program into functions continues this emphasis. Data is, after all, the reason for a program's existence. The important part of an inventory program isn't a function that displays the data, or a function that checks for correct input; it's the inventory data itself. Yet data is given second-class status in the organization of procedural languages.Now suppose a new programmer is hired to write a function to analyze this inventory data in a certain way. Unfamiliar with the subtleties of the program, the programmer creates a function that accidentally corrupts the data. This is easy to do because every function has complete accesses to the data. It's like leaving your personal papers in the lobby of your apartment building: any one can change or destroy them. In the same way, global data can be corrupted by function that have no business changing it. Another problem is that, since many functions access the same data, the way the data is stored becomes critical. The arrangement of data can not be changed without modifying all the function that access it.if you add new data items, for example, you will need to modify all the function that access the data so that they can also access these new items. It will be hard to find all such functions, add even harder to modify all them correctly. So to overcome this problem the second approach object-oriented is used.

The object-oriented approach is based on to combine both data and the functions that operate on that data. Such unit is called an object. An object's functions called member functions in C++ and Java. Typically provide the only way to access the data. If you want to read the data items in an object, you call a member function in the object. it will read the item and return the value to you. You can't access the data directly. The data is hidden, so it is safe from accidental alteration. Data and its function are said to be is said to be a single entity. Data encapsulation & data hidings are key terms in the description of object oriented languages. If you want to modify the data in an object, you know exactly what functions interact with it: the member functions in the object. No other functions can access the data. This simplifies writing, debugging and maintaining the program.. It may be emphasized that object- oriented programming is not primarily concerned with the details of program.

Most individual programs statements in C++ and Java are similar to statements in procedural functions in C. it is only look at the larger context that you can determine whether a statement or a functions is part of a procedural C program or object-orient C++ or Java program

13.1.3 Principles of Object Oriented Programming

All object oriented programming languages provide mechanisms that help you implement the object-oriented model. They are encapsulation, inheritance and polymorphism. These are explained below.

13.1.4 Encapsulation

Encapsulation is the mechanism that binds the code and the data manipulates and keeps both safe from interference and misuse. One way to think about encapsulation is a protective wrapper that prevent the code and data from being arbitrarily access by other code defined outside the wrapper. Access to the code and their data inside the wrapper is tightly control through a well-defined interface. In Java, the basis of encapsulation is the class. A class defines the structure and behavior that will be shared by a set of objects. Since the purpose of the class is to hide complexity of the implementation inside the class. Each method or variable may be declared private or public. In C++ and Java the basis of encapsulation is the class a class defines the structure and behavior (Data and code) that will be shared by a set of objects. Each object of a given class contains the structure and behavior defined by the class, as if it were stamped out by a mold in the safe of the class. For this reason, objects are sometimes referred to as instance of the class. Thus a class is a logical construct: an object is a physical reality.

13.1.5 Inheritance

Inheritance is a process by which one object acquires the properties of another object. This is important because it supports the concepts of hierarical classifications mentioned earlier, most knowledge is made manageable by hierarchical classifications. It supports the concept of hierarchical classification. It is the inheritance mechanism that makes it possible for one object to be specific instance of a more general case. Inheritance interacts with encapsulation as well. If a class encapsulates some attributes, then any subclass will have the same attributes plus any that it adds as part of its specialization. Most people naturally view the world as made up of objects that are related to each other in a hierarchical way. Inheritance interacts with encapsulation as well. If a given class encapsulates some attributes, then any subclass will have the same attributes plus any that it adds as part of its specialization. This is a key concepts, which lets object-oriented programs grow in complexity linearly than geometrically. a new subclass inherits all of the attributes of all its ancestors.

13.1.6 Polymorphism

Polymorphism is a feature that allows one interface to be used for a general class of actions. The specific action is determined by the exact nature of situation. More generally, the concept of polymorphism is often expressed by the phrase "one interface, multiple methods." This means that it is possible to determine a generic interface to a group of related activities. This helps reduce complexity by allowing the same interface to be used to specify a general class of action. It is the compiler's job to select the specific action as it applies to each situation. Polymorphism is a feature that allows one interface to be used for a general class of actions. The specific action is determined by the exact nature of the situation. consider a stack. This means that it is possible to design a generic interface to a group of related activities. This means that it is possible to design interface to be used to specify a general class of action. it is the compiler's job to select the specific action as it applies to each situation.

13.2 INTRODUCTION TO JAVA

13.2.1 Introduction

JAVA being introduced as Object Oriented Language, was initially considered to be simply "Internet version of C++". Java is related to C++, which is direct descent of C. Because of the similarities between Java & C. initially impetus for Java was not the Internet. Instead the primary motivation was the need for an architecture neutral language or platform independent that could be used to create software to be embedded application in various consumer electronic devices, such as microwave ovens & remote controls. One other point is that Java was not designed to replace C++, it was simply designed to solve a certain set of problems while C++ was designed keeping different views in mind.

13.2.2 Java Byte Code

The thing that makes Java secure & portable is that the output of Java compiler is not an executable code, rather it is bytecode. Bytecode is a highly optimized set of instructions designed to be executed by a virtual machine that the Java runtime system emulates.

Because Java programs are interpreted rather than compiled, it is much easier to run them in a wide variety of environments. The fact that Java is interpreted also helps to make it secure. Because the execution of every Java program is under the control of the run time system, the run time system can contain the program and prevent it from generating side effects.

13.2.3 Advantages with Java

OOP organizes a program around its objects and a set of well defined interfaces to that data. OOP is at the core of Java. Infact, all Java programs are object oriented. An essential element of object oriented programming is abstraction. Object oriented concepts form the heart of Java just as they form the basis for human understanding. All object oriented programming languages provide mechanisms the help to implement the object-oriented model.Following are the JAVA advantages. The popularity and general acceptability of JAVA code lies behind the following characteristics.

- **Java is Simple**
  Java system was built as closely to C++ as possible in order to make the system more comprehensible. Java omits many rarely used, poorly understood, confusing features of C++ that bring more grief than benefit.
- **Java is Secure**
  Java is intended to be used in networked/distributed environments. So, keeping that view in mind a lot of emphasis is given on security. It enables the construction of virus free tamper-free systems.
- **Java is Portable**
  As already discussed, Java is compiled to bytecode which is platform independent, this provides portability to Java. The sizes of primitive data types are specified, as is the behavior of arithmetic on them.

- **Java is Object-Oriented**
  The object-oriented facilities of Java are essential those of C++. Object-oriented design is a technique for programming that focuses on the data and on the interfaces to that object. To make an analogy with the carpentry, an "object-oriented" carpenter would be mostly concerned with the table he was building, and secondarily with the tools used to make it; a "non object-oriented" carpenter would think primarily of his tools.
- **Java is Robust**
  Java is intended for writing programs that must be reliable in a variety of ways. This feature is also very useful. The Java compiler detects many problems that in other languages would only show up, at run time. As for the second point, for a programmer chasing memory corruption caused by a pointer bug will be very happy with this feature of Java.
- **Java is Multithreaded**
  Java provides an easier way of multi threading than any other language. Multithreaded programming allows writing programs that can do many things at once. Threads in Java also have the capacity to take the advantage of multiprocessor systems if the base operating system does so. Nonetheless, the ease of multithreading is one of the main reasons why Java is such an appealing language for server side development.
- **Java is Architecture-Neutral**
  A central issue for Java designers was "write once, run anywhere, any time, forever". Due to operating system upgrades, processor upgrades, and changes in core system resources there was no guarantee that if you write a program today, it will run tomorrow even on the same machine. The Java designers made many hard decisions to provide platform independence and to a great extent this goal was accomplished.
- **Java is Interpreted**
  The Java interpreter can execute Java bytecode directly on any machine to which the interpreter has been ported. But on the other hand, it provides disappointment by being quite slow.
- **Java provides High Performance**
  While the performance of interpreted bytecode is usually more than adequate, there are situations where high performance is required. The bytecode can be translated on the fly (at run time) into machine codes for the particular CPU the application is running on.

- **Java is Distributed**
  Java has extensive library routines for copying with TCP/IP protocols like HTTP and FTP. Java applications can open and access objects across the net via URLs with the same ease as when accessing a local file system.
- **Java is Dynamic**
  Java was designed to adapt to an evolving environment. Libraries can add freely new methods and instance variables without any affect on their clients. So in that way, Java is more dynamic than C++.

13.2.4 A Simple Java Program

```
public class Sample
    {
     public static void main(String args[])
    {
     System.out.println(" Its easy to use JAVA");
    }
    }
```

The file name of the source code is named same as the name of the public class itself with the extension '.java', so name of the above file should be Sample.java, keep in mind that it is case sensitive. Now the program is compiled on dos prompt as follows

C:/javac Sample.java

After the compilation is over and no error is present, it creates.class file. It is executed on dos prompt as follows:

C:/java Sample

This produces the desired output as follows

' Its easy to use JAVA'

13.3 HYPER TEXT MARKUP LANGUAGE (HTML)

13.3.1 Introduction

HTML and the web were first conceived in 1989 by a researcher named Tim Berners Lee who worked for CERN, the European laboratory for practical physics in Geneva, Switzerland. CERN researchers developed the first World Wide Web programs in 1990 and began releasing programs and specification to internet users in 1991. Contrary to its name, HTML does not qualify as a language. It is actually follows a script pattern where you may enter text, table, link, image, graphics etc and may produced on web browser in a desired format. Now we will explain what each of this word means Hypertext Markup Language.

Hypertext

It is ordinary text that has been dressed with extra features, such as formatting, images, multimedia, and links to other documents. Thus it is more than a simple text. Usually, those who have visited the net are familiar that on certain text or line or work, clicking on to it opens new page of information relating to text. Thus it is called Hyper Text.

Markup

It can be called as process of taking ordinary text and adding extra symbols.each of the symbol used for markup in HTML is a command that tells a browser how to display the text.

Language

It is actually a key point to remember about HTML. Markup languages are a special type of computer language because they are solely concerned with classifying the parts of a document according there function.In other words,HTML is used to define the different parts of your document.

Thus HTML is not really a programming language. Instead, HTML is markup language that has different goal than creating a program. The important thing to remember is that HTML is designed to work on a wide variety of platforms, such that you should be able to trust that your document will be attractively and correctly displayed by any browser on any computer any in the world. HTML has several inherent advantages including Flexibility to work, Price and independence of machine or platform. At present may versions of HTML e.g HTML, HTML+,HTML 2.0, HTML 3.0, HTML 3.2, HTML 4.0 are available

13.3.2 Basic Structure Elements of HTML

Basic element in the HTML is the 'tag'. You may write text, include table, image, audio, graphic etc within the tag. Tag defines the way of presentation of combination of all component on the web browser. Following is simple code written in HTML which displays information (few text line) about Computer Science Department of Institute of Engineering And Technology.

```
<html>
<head>
```

```
<title> INSTITUTE OF ENGINEERING & TECHNOLOGY</title>
</head>
<body>
<h1> <b>Welcome To The Department of Computer Science and
Engineering</b></h1>
<h2><b>COURSES UNDERTAKEN</b></h2>
<ol>
<li>B.Tech. (Computer Science and Engg.)</li>
<li>B.Tech (Information Technology.)</li>
<li>MCA.</li>
</ol>
<h4> To view the course structures click <a href="syllabus.html"
>here</a>
</body>
</html>
```

It my be observed from the code written above that general html document contains two parts namely Head and Body.

HEAD describes the elements that define certain information about an HTML document for example what is the title of page. In above example the title is defined using <title> </title> tags which is "Institute of Engineering and Technology".

BODY describes the real code for the display of the web page to be developed. Whole of the html document is wrapped within the <body> and </body> tags.

Following section explain the main building block called the HTML Tags. The Tags are used in Body section, belongs to two categories called Block Level Tags and Text Level Tags

13.3.3 Block-Level Tags

They include tags that position text on the page, set heading levels and create lists. Commonly used block-level elements and their tags are listed below.

- : <p> and </p>
- Heading levels: <h1> and </h1>,<h2> and </h2>..........<h7> and</h7>.
- Horizontal rule: <hr>.
- Centering: <center> </center>.

13.3.4 Text Level Elements

They are used to markup bits of texts, including changing text appearance or creating hyperlinks. Some commonly used text-level elements are:

- bold: <b> and </b>
- italic: <I> and </I>
- line break -:
- link-anchor <a href="url">and</a>
- image: <img src="url">

13.4 INTRODUCTION TO JAVA APPLETS

13.4.1 What is an Applet?

JAVA program that work on Web pages are called Applets. It is embedded in HTML files. To use an applet one need to have JAVA enabled Web Browser, which interprets the Bytecode. Applets can also be used to add buttons and input fields to a Web page. In general when user downloads applet, it works much like embedding an image in a Web page. The applets become part of the page and text flows around the space used for the applet. Here the striking feature is that the image is live. It reacts to user command, changes its appearance and sends the data between the computer and the computer serving it.

Applets like application program can do many things. It can perform arithmetic operations, display graphics, play grounds etc. In order to locate and load applets on Web we must know its address on the Web. This address is known as URL (Uniform Resource Locator) and must be supplied in applet's HTML document.

13.4.2 Difference Between an Application and an Applet

- Applets don't use the main() method to initiate execution.
- Applets can't be run independently it can only be run in a Web page.
- Applets can neither read nor write to files of local computer.
- Applets can't communicate with other server on the network.
- Applets can't run any program from the local computer.
- Applets are not allowed to use libraries from other languages such as C/C++.

All this is possible because applets are interpreted by Java Virtual Machine and not directly execu :d by CPU on the user's computer. Actually applets are generally used to add something dynamic in the display of Web page and to have some flash output. Following are the Steps taken to write and embed an applet in Web page

- Building an applet source file (.java file)
- Creating an executable applet (.class file)
- Preparing an <APPLET> tag.
- Incorporating <APPLET> tag into Web page.
- Creating HTML file.
- Testing the applet inside browser.

13.4.3 Applet Life Cycle

In applet life cycle applet contains a set of default behavior from the Applet class. When applet is loaded, it run through different states. The different states are given below.

1. Born or Initialization state
2. Running state
3. Idle state
4. Dead or destroyed state

13.4.3.1 Born or Initialization State

Applet enter the initialization state when it is first loaded. The is achieved by calling the init() method of Applet class. The applet is born. At this stage, we may do the following if required.

- Create Objects needed by the applet.
- Set up initial values
- Load images or fonts
- Set up colors

We can initialize the applet using int(), as given below.

```
Public void init()
{
.......................
(actions)
......................
}
```

13.4.3.2 Running State

Applet enters the running state when the system calls the start() method of Applet class. This occour automatically after the applet is initialized. Starting can also occour if the applet is already in "stopped"(idle)state.

For example,we may leave the web page containing the applet temporarily to another page and return to back page.Like as,

```
Public void start()
{
......................
...................(action)
....................
}
```

13.4.3.3 Idle State

An applet becomes idle when it is stopped from running. Stopping occurs automatically when we leave the page containing the currently running applet. we can also do so by calling the stop() method explicitly. Like as,

```
Public void stop()
{
.................
................. (action)
................
}
```

13.4.3.4 Dead Destroyed State

An applet is said to be dead when it is removed from memory. The dead state can be invoked by using destroy( ). This stage occurs only once in the applet's life cycle.

```
Public void destroy()
{
......................
...................... (action)
......................
}
```

13.4.4 Writing Code for Applet : An Example

Now we see the code of a typical applet.

```
// Creation of an applet
import java.awt.*;
import java.applet.*;
public class pise_muk extends Applet
{
 public void paint ( Graphics g )
```

```
{
g.drawstring( " PISE & MUKHERJEE ",20,150);
}
}
```

This was code of an applet. Now we'll incorporate this code into Web page that is HTML file.

```
<HTML>
<! THIS FILE EMBEDS APPLET >
 <HEAD >
 <TITLE>
THIS IS APPLET EXAMPLE
</TITLE>
</HEAD>
<BODY>
<CENTER>
WELCOME TO APPLET
</CENTRE>
 <CENTER>
<APPLET
CODE =pise_muk.class
WIDTH=200
HEIGHT=200>
</CENTER>
</BODY>
</HTML>
```

13.5 WIRELESS APPLICATION PROTOCOL (WAP)

13.5.1 Introduction

WAP or Wireless Application Protocol is the latest buzzword in IT industry. The beginning of WAP is said to have started when Ericsson began work on a protocol known as ITTP, or Intelligent Terminal Transfer Protocol, with the intent of making it easy to add services to mobile telephony platforms. During 1996 and 1997, Nokia began work on a concept called Smart Messaging, and Unwired Planet created HDML. The Handheld Device Markup Language was a markup language similar to HTML, but optimized for devices with small screens such as phones and PDAs. Realizing that these competing protocols could fragment and possibly destroy the potential market, in December of 1997, Ericsson, Motorola, Nokia, and Unwired Planet (now known as Phone.com) joined forces to launch the WAP Forum.

Wireless Application Protocol is a new set of standards designed to extend Internet services to the mobile telephony environment that includes, mobile phones, pagers and Personal Digital Assistants (PDAs). WAP is a method of letting a wireless device, usually a mobile phone where WAP is enabled, to view very simple Internet pages, through the existing wireless networks. The web site has to be specially designed for the WAP phone, and the pages have to be fairly small as the data speed on mobile phones is a lot slower than a domestic modem. Also, all the phones will have different shape and size screens, so pages will look different depending on the phone your are using.

13.5.2 Motivation for WAP

WAP was designed to meet the constraints of a wireless environment. Both limitations in the network and client are taken into consideration. WAP was created to address three main issues related to data communications across wireless networks:

- Low Bandwidth
- High Latency
- Connectivity

WAP adapts to the Wireless Device. WAP is targeted at handheld devices of various kinds. Services should be accessible from a Handheld PC as well as from a small phone. WAP address this fact by taking into consideration the of following

- Small Displays
- Limited Input Facilities
- Limited Memory & Slow CPU
- Limited Battery Power.

13.5.3 WAP Advantages

Using WAP technology to deliver internet content and applications to mobile phones offers great potential benefits to both organizations and the end user. In the near future it is likely that a well written and maintained WAP site will be as important for a company's profile as its current Web site. Their relatively low cost, ease of use and small size means that WAP enabled phones offer some distinct advantages over portable computers. At present, limited screen size and resolution mean that WAP phones may not be used to surf the Internet in the same way that people use the standard PC Web browsers. As the technology grows, so will the scope of the applications offered.

WAP must provide independence across air interfaces and device. The majority of WAP solutions that have already surfaced in the marketplace must support several forms of independence. Those forms of independence are air interface independence, device independence, and full interoperability. The word air Interface Independence means that WAP solutions are to be designed to work optimally with all air interfaces. This allows the largest number of mobile service providers, software developers and handset manufacturers to create solutions for a unified specification. Device Independence suggest that WAP solutions must also be independent of any particular wireless device. Interoperability enforce that any solution component built to be compliant with the WAP specification can interoperate with any other WAP-compliant component

13.5.4 WAP Specification

The WAP specification defines an open, standard architecture and set of protocols for implementing wireless Internet access. The key elements of the WAP specification are:

- A prcgramming model based heavily on the existing WWW programming model. Much like a web browser, a WAP device engages in a series of request/response transactions with content servers that deliver both static and dynamic content.
- A markup language adhering to XML standards. The language used to write applications, the Wireless Markup Language (WML), has a limited number of XML elements (called tags in HTML) and is designed to work with small screen displays. Much like HTML, WML focuses on presenting formatted content and limited execution options for users.
- The WMLScript scripting language designed to add computational capabilities to WML.
- A specification for a microbrowser to control the user interface. An analogy can be made with a standard web browser. This specification defines how WML and WMLScript should be interpreted in the handset and presented to the user. It also defines the minimum functionality and basic user interface a WAP device must have.

13.6 WML : A LANGUAGE FOR WAP

WML, similar to HTML, is a tag - based document language. In particular, it is an application of a generalized markup language. WML shares a heritage with the WWW's HTML and handheld device markup language HDML2. WML is specified as an XML document type. it is optimized for specifying presentation and user interaction on limited capability devices such as telephones and other wireless mobile terminals.

WML and its supporting environment were desingned with certain small narrow Band device constraints in mind including small displays, limited user input facilities,narrowband network connections,limited memory resources and limited computational resources given the wide and varying range of terminals targeted by WAP.

13.6.1 Salient Features of WML

Support for user input
WML includes a small set of input controls to receive the users input. WML includes a text entry control that supports text and password entry.text entry fields can be masked preventing the end user from entering incorrect character types. WML include san option selection control that allov' the author to Present the user with a list of options that can setdata, navigate cards. WML also includes task invocation controls.

Support for Navigation and history stack
WML allows several navigation mechanisms using URLs. it also exposes a first class history mechanism. Navigation includes HTML style hyperlink, inter card navigation's well as history navigation elements.

Support for text and images:
WML provides the authors with means to specify text and images to be presented to the user. This may include layout and presentation similar to other mark up languages. WML requires the author to specify the Presentation in very general terms and gives the user agents a great deal of freedom to determine exactly how the information is presented to the end user. WML provides a set of text mark-up elements including various emphasis elements. Another WML advantages is that its character set is UNICODE and this allows presentation of most languages and dialects.

13.7 INTRODUCTION TO VB SCRIPT

13.7.1 Introduction

VBScript, or the Microsoft Visual Basic Scripting Edition language, is a simplified version of the Visual Basic programming language. It is a powerful & easy to learn tool that can be used to add interaction to the web pages. VBScript is a powerful, light-weight scripting language for creating interactive, multimedia-rich, and ActiveX-enhanced Web applications. Before scripting languages such as VBScript, dynamic Web pages were created by server-side CGI applications. In some cases, the execution of server-side CGI applications is unnecessarily resource intensive. VBScript can be used in such cases to create dynamic content without any interaction with the Web server. If you are using Internet Information Server 3.0 or later, VBScript can also be used to develop server-side Web applications in the form of Active Server Web. Basically scripts make a Web page alive. A script tells the elements, on a page, how to behave & interact with one another. VBScript is more precisely a "scripting environment", which can enhance HTML Web pages by making them active, as compared to a simple static display. A script is a series of commands that are executed by the host environment, which is either the client or the server. VBScript can be written to run at either end.

13.7.2 Tools Required to Write VBScript

1. A Text-Editor. Any word-processor or Notepad, Word pad or any HTML editor.
2. An Internet Browser that supports VBScript like IE 3.0 or above.

VBScript is a scripting language. It means that it does not really do anything on its own, it is dependent on a Web Page.

13.7.3 VBScript Advantages

- VBScript is a powerful
- Lightweight, easy-to-use
- Freely available
- Cross-platform
- Cross-language scripting language for the Internet

13.7.4 Sample VBScript Code

All the Web page Editor provide the mechanism to include the VBScript with HTML. However, the embedding of VBScript in to HTML document may be done using any editor such as Notepad etc. In an ASP page, VBScript code is included within <% and %>. Following is an example.

```
<HTML>
<HEAD><TITLE> ASP with VBScript </TITLE></HEAD>
<BODY>
This is a
<% For I= 1 To 10 %>
Very,
<% Next %>
simple example of VBScript. The current time is <% = NOW() %>
</BODY>
</HTML>
```

When a Web browser displays this ASP, output is:

This is a Very, Very, Very, Very, Very, Very, Very, Very, Very, Very simple example of VBScript.

13.8 INTRODUCTION TO JAVASCRIPT

13.8.1 JavaScript

JavaScript was developed by Netscape Communications Corporation, the makers of the popular Netscape Navigator Web browser. JavaScript was the first Web scripting language to be introduced, and it is by far the most popular. JavaScript is almost as easy to learn as HTML, and it can be included directly in HTML documents. Here are a few of things you can do with JavaScript:

- Add scrolling or changing messages to the browser's status line.
- Validate the contents of a form and make calculations
- Display messages to the user, either as part of a Web page or in alert boxes.
- Animate images or create images that change when you move the mouse over them.
- Detect the browser in use and display different content for different browsers.
- Detect installed plug-ins and notify the user if a plug-in is required.

JavaScript is a kind of scripts which provides a set of instructions for browser to perform. Web script provides the same type of instructions for the browser. HTML is one of the computer languages that browses understands. Since HTML is a simple text markup language, it can't respond to the user, make decision, or automate repetitive tasks. Interactive tasks like these more complex languages: a programming language, or a scripting language.While many programming languages are complex, scripting languages are generally simple. They have simple syntax, can perform tasks with minimum of commands, and are easy to learn. Web scripting language allow you to combine scripting with HTML to create interactive Web pages.

13.8.2 JavaScript vs. Java

It's a matter of common misunderstanding that JavaScript & Java are same or one is extension of another. In fact, Java & JavaScript shares the name only. Both of them are entirely different languages. Java is a programming language developed by Sun Microsystems that can be used to create applets, or programs that execute within a Web page. Java is a compiled language, but the compiler produces code for virtual machine rather than a real computer. The virtual code is then interpreted by a Web browser. This allows the same Java applet to execute the same way on PCs, Macintoshes, and UNIX machines, and on different browsers-at least in theory.

JavaScript and Java are entirely different languages. Here are a few of the most differences :

- Java uses simple text commands, which can be include Java applets, are compiled into class files to be used on a Web page but JavaScript in HTML document itself.
- Java applets are generally displayed in a box within the Web document; JavaScript scripts can affect any part of the Web document itself.
- While JavaScript is best suited to simple applications and adding interactive features to Web pages, Java can be used for incredibly complex applications.

There are many differences but the important thing to remember is that JavaScript and Java are separate languages. They are both useful for different things; in fact, they can be used together to combine their advantages.

13.8.3 Platform to Create JavaScript

JavaScript scripts are stored in simple text files, usually as part of HTML documents. Any editor that can store ASCII text files will work. Like for Windows computers some of the recommended editors are:

- Microsoft FrontPage 2000
- NetObjects Script Builder
- Editpad

13.8.4 How JavaScript Fits into a Web Page

HTML i.e Hypertext Markup Language is the language we use to create Web documents. This document consists of a header within the <head> tag and the body of the page within the <body> tags. To add JavaScript to a page, we use a similar tag : <script>.The script tag tells the browser to start treating the text as a script & the </script tag returns to the regularly scheduled HTML. There are actually four different places where we might use scripts in an HTML document:

- In the body of the page in this case the output of the script is displayed as part of the HTML document when the browser loads the page.
- In the header of the page between the <head> tags. Scripts in the header are not executed immediately, but can be referred to by other scripts.
- Within an HTML tag. Thus is called an *event handler* and allows the script to work with HTML elements.
- In a separate file entirely. JavaScript supports the use of files with the. is extension containing scripts: these can be included by specifying a file in the <script> tag.

13.8.5 Displaying the JavaScript on Web Browser

Like HTML, JavaScript requires a Web browser to be displayed, and different browsers may display it differently. Unlike HTML, the results of browser incompatibility with JavaScript are more drastic: rather than simply displaying your text incorrectly, the script may not execute at all, may display an error message, or may even crash the browser. How ever since the JavaScript language was developed by Netscape, the newest features of the language are supported only under Netscape Navigator. Internet Explorer does support the basic JavaScript commands, and newer version may implement all of the new features.

13.9 INTRODUCTION TO JAVA SERVER PAGES (JSP)

13.9.1 Introduction

JavaServer Pages technology allows web developers and designers to rapidly develop and easily maintain, information-rich, dynamic web pages that leverage existing business systems. As part of the JavaTM family, JSP technology enables rapid development of web-based applications that are platform independent. JavaServer Pages technology separates the user interface from content generation enabling designers to change the overall page layout without altering the underlying dynamic content. JSP is a server-side technology that allows developers to create Web-based applications that can make use of components that are developed in the Java programming language, according to the JavaBeans specification. In some respects, it can be compared to server-side scripting languages such as ASP and PHP. JSP is similar to PHP in the C-style syntax of the Java language, but JSP was also designed to be extendable using components like ASP.

Java Server Pages allows you to mix regular, static HTML with dynamically-generated HTML. Many Web pages that are built by CGI programs are mostly static, with the dynamic part limited to a few small locations. But most CGI variations, including servlets, make you generate the entire page via your program, even though most of it is always the same. JSP lets you create the two parts separately. You normally give your file a. jsp extension. The JSP page just gets converted to a normal servlet, with the static HTML simply being printed to the output stream associated with the servlet's service method.

13.9.2 JSP Building Blocks

Following are the main JSP construct to create JSP documents. These are

1. Scripting elements.
2. Directives.
3. Actions.

Scripting elements let you specify Java code that will become part of the resultant servlet, directives let you control the overall structure of the servlet, and actions let you specify existing components that should be used, and otherwise control the behavior of the JSP engine. JavaServer Pages technology uses XML-like tags and scriptlets written in the Java programming language to encapsulate the logic that generates the content for the page. Java Server Pages technology is an extension of the Java Servlet technology. JSP technology and servlets provide an attractive alternative to other types of dynamic web scripting/programming that offers platform independence, enhanced performance, separation of logic from display, ease of administration, extensibility into the enterprise and most importantly, ease of use.

JSP pages share the "Write Once, Run Anywhere" characteristics of Java technology. JSP technology is a key component in the Java 2 Platform, Enterprise Edition, Sun's highly scalable architecture for enterprise applications.

13.9.3 Pros & Cons of JSP

Advantages of JSP

- Extremely fast.
- Platform independent.
- Highly scaleable with built-in support for distributed processing
- compatible with all major Web servers.
- Portable to non-Microsoft Web servers.
- It is more powerful and easier to use.
- Extensibility into the enterprise

Disadvantages of JSP

1. Java Code Required.
   JSP actually demand putting Java code in the page.
2. JSP technology is far complex than the counterpart to learn.
3. Lousy Looping.
4. JSP page syntax errors can cause surprisingly odd and useless error messages. This is due to the fact the page is transformed into a servlet and then compiled.
5. Needs a Compiler.
6. Requires More Space.

   JSP consumes extra hard drive space and extra memory space.

13.10 AN INTRODUCTION TO ENTERPRISE JAVA BEANS (EJB)

13.10.1 Introduction

Enterprise Java Beans is a specification model for server side computing.

Which is used in distributed application environment. The Enterprise JavaBeans specification is a dramatic step forward in the

Standardization and simplification of distributed object computing. It is a major piece of the Java 2 Enterprise Edition (J2EE) platform and is receiving much support from the distributed object community. Many tools are currently available or will be available in the near future to help accelerate the development of EJB components.

Suppose you need to develop a multi-tiered application to view and update records in a database through a Web interface. You can write a database application using JDBC, a Web interface using JSP/servlets, and a distributed system using CORBA/RMI. But what extra considerations must you make when developing a distributed object system rather than just knowing API's? Here are the issues:

Performance

The distributed objects you create must perform well, as they could potentially service many clients at a time. You'll need to use optimization techniques such as caching as well as pooling resources like database connections. You'll also have to manage the lifecycle of your distributed objects.

Scalability

The distributed objects must also be scalable. Scalability in a distributed application means that the number of instances of your distributed objects can be increased and moved onto additional machines without modifying any code.

Security

A distributed object must often manage the authorization of the clients that access it. Ideally, you can add new users and roles to it without recompilation.

Distributed Transactions

A distributed object should be able to reference distributed transactions transparently. For example, if you are working with two separated databases, you should be able to update them simultaneously within the same transaction and roll them both back if a certain criteria is not met.

Reusability

The ideal distributed object can be effortlessly moved onto another vendors' application server. It would be nice if you could resell a distributed object component without making special modifications, or buy someone else's component and use it without having to recompile or rewrite it.

Availability

If one of the machines in the system goes down, clients should automatically fail-over to backup copies of the objects running on other machines.

These considerations, in addition the business problem that you set out to solve, can make for a daunting development project. However, all the issues except for your business problem are redundant—solutions must be reinvented for every distributed business application. Sun, along with other leading distributed object vendors, realized that sooner or later every development team would be reinventing these particular solutions, so they created the Enterprise JavaBeans specification (EJB). EJB describes a server-side component model that tackles all of the considerations mentioned above using a standard approach that allows developers to create business components called EJBs that are isolated from low-level "plumbing" code and that focus solely on providing business logic. Because EJB's are defined in a standard way, they can vendor independent.

13.10.2 Java Beans vs. EJBs

Because of the similarity in names, there is much confusion about the relationship between the JavaBeans component model and the Enterprise JavaBeans specification. While both the JavaBeans and Enterprise JavaBeans specifications share the same objectives in promoting reuse and portability of Java code between development and deployment tools with the use of standard design patterns, the motives behind each specification are geared to solve different problems. The standards defined in the JavaBeans component model are designed for creating reusable components that are typically used in IDE development tools and are commonly, although not exclusively, visual components. The Enterprise JavaBeans specification defines a component model for developing server side java code. Because EJBs can potentially run on many different server-side platforms—including mainframes that do not have visual displays—An EJB cannot make use of graphical libraries such as AWT or Swing.

The EJB specification The Enterprise JavaBeans specification describes a server-side component model. It defines six roles that are used to perform the tasks in development and deployment as well as defining the components of the system. These roles are used in the development, deployment and running of a distributed system. Vendors, administrators and developers play the various roles, to allow the partitioning of technical and domain knowledge. The vendor provides a technically sound framework and the developers create domain-specific components; for example, an "accounting" component. The same party can perform one or many roles. The roles defined in the EJB specification are summarized as following:

13.10.3 Types of EJB

The Enterprise JavaBeans specification defines different types of EJBs that have different characteristics and behaviors. Two categories of EJBs have been defined in the specification: Session Beans and Entity Beans, and each category has variations.

13.10.3.1 Session Beans

Session Beans are used to represent Use-Cases or Workflow on behalf of a client. They represent operations on persistent data, but not the persistent data itself. There are two types of Session Beans, Stateless and Stateful. All Session Beans must implement the *javax.ejb.SessionBean* interface. The EJB Container governs the life of a Session Bean.

Stateless Session Beans are the simplest type of EJB component to implement. They do not maintain any conversational state with clients between method invocations so they are easily reusable on the server side and because they can be cached, they scale well on demand. When using Stateless Session Beans, all state must be stored outside of the EJB.

Stateful Session Beans maintain state between invocations. They have a one-to-one logical mapping to a client and can maintain state within themselves. The EJB Container is responsible for pooling and caching of Stateful Session Beans, which is achieved through Passivation and Activation. If the EJB Container crashes, data for all Stateful Session Beans could be lost. Some high-end EJB Containers provide recovery for Stateful Session Beans.

13.10.3.2 Entity Beans

Entity Beans are components that represent persistent data and behavior of this data. Entity Beans can be shared among multiple clients, the same way that data in a database can be shared. The EJB Container is responsible for caching Entity Beans and for maintaining the integrity of the Entity Beans. The life of an Entity Bean outlives the EJB Container, so if an EJB Container crashes, the Entity Bean is still expected to be available when the EJB Container again becomes available.

There are two types of Entity Beans: those with Container Managed persistence and those with Bean-Managed persistence. A Container

Managed Persistence (CMP) Entity Bean has its persistence implemented on its behalf by the EJB Container. Through attributes specified in the deployment descriptor, the EJB Container will map the Entity Bean's attributes to some persistent store (usually—but not always—a database). CMP reduces the development time for the EJB, as well as dramatically reducing the amount of code required.

A Bean Managed Persistence (BMP) Entity Bean has its persistence implemented by the Enterprise Bean Provider. The Enterprise Bean Provider is responsible for implementing the logic required to create a new EJB, update some attributes of the EJBS, delete an EJB and find an EJB from persistent store. This usually involves writing JDBC code to interact with a database or other persistent store. With BMP, the developer is in full control of how the Entity Bean persistence is managed. BMP also gives flexibility where a CMP implementation may not be available. For example, if you wanted to create an EJB that wrapped some code on an existing mainframe system, you could write your persistence using CORBA.

13.11 XML : An Introduction to Extensible Markup Language

13.11.1 Introduction to XML

HTML still considered to be most favorite markup Language and millions of web pages have been written using HTML. Now people have started realizing the inherent limitations with HTML and a swing towards XML is being felt. Following are some of the limitations of HTML which have been reported.

— HTML lacks syntactic checking ie. Validation of HTML code
— HTML is not content aware.
— HTML is not suitable for data interchange.
— HTML lacks a robust linking mechanism.

- HTML is not extensible.
- Above all HTML defines and uses its fixed set of Tags. XML solves this problem with limited flexibility.

XML is derived from SGML. SGML (Standered Generalized Markup Language) is a meta language . or a language for describing markup languages. HTML is one such markup language and is therefore called an SGML application. XML uses the features of SGML that it needs and tries to incorporate the lessons learned from HTML.

— XML can be used with existing Web protocols(such as HTTP and MIME) and mechanisms(such as URLs),and it does not impose any additional requirements.

- XML supports a wide variety of applications. It is difficult to support a lot of applications with just HTML; hence, the growth of scripting language.
- It is easy to write programs that process XML documents.
- The number of optional features in XML has been kept to an absolute minimum.
- XML documents are reasonably clear to the layperson.
- The design of XML is formal and concise.
- XML documents are easy to create.

XML is commonly called a subset of SGML but actually it is an application profile *of* SGML; whereas HTML uses SGML and is an application of SGML, XML is just SGML on a smaller scale. From HTML, XML inherits the use of webaddress(URLs)to point to other Objects.

13.11.2 Application Areas of XML

XML is being considered so powerful and flexible that many people are considering it for sevarl other puposes other than just a markup language. XML best suited for the applications which,

- XML may be used to describe metacontent regarding document or on line resources.
- To Publish and exchange Database Contents.
- As a messaging format for communication between application progams.

13.11.3 XML Advantages

Modularity

HTML possesses an implied DTD(Document Type Definition), hard-wired into Web browsers. SGML has a limitless number of DTDs, but only one can be used for one document. XML enables you to leave out the DTD altogether or combine separate DTD into one compound instance.

Extensibility:

XML's powerful linking mechanisms allow you to link to material without requiring the link target to be physically present in the object.

Distribution

XML introduces composite documents i.e. that documents composed of fragments of other documents that are automatically assembled to form what is displayed at a particular moment.

International Character Dealing

Both HTML and SGML rely heavily on ASCII, which makes using foreign characters very difficult. XML is based on Unicode and requires all XML Soft ware to support Unicode as well.

Data orientation

XML operates on data orientation rather than readability by humans.

Question Papers for B.Tech First Semester Examination U P Technical University, Lucknow

B.Tech
First Semester Examination 2000-2001
COMPUTER & LANGUAGES

Time : 2½ Hrs *Max. Marks : 100*

Note *(1) The question paper contains four questions*
(2) Attempt all the questions

1. Attempt any four parts 3*4 = 12
   (a) Draw a block diagram showing all the functional unit of a digital computer. Explain the function and role of each unit in brief.
   (b) Differentiate between Computer Hardware & Computer Software. What is BIOS? State whether BIOS is a hardware or a software? Justify your answer.
   (c) What do you mean by Internal DOS command & External DOS command? Write DOS command to do the following task :-
      (i) Create a directory "ABC" at root
      (ii) Change your present working directory to "ABC".
      (iii) Copy all the files of floppy disk to "ABC".
      (iv) Display list of files in such a way that it pauses after each screen full of information
      (v) Delete "ABC" directory.
   (d) What is an Operating System? Explain the major functions of an operating system in brief .Explain the salient features of the following Operating Systems :-
      (i) Multiprogramming Operating System
      (ii) Multitasking Operating System
   (e) What are the advantages of using Window 95/98 over DOS? Explain the role of following objects of Windows 95/98.
      (i) The Desktop
      (ii) My Computer
      (iii) Recycle Bin

(f) (i) What are I/O devices? Give two examples of each.
(ii) What is Hard disk drive (HDD)? What are ranges of storage capacity of currently available HDD? List any two-performance parameter of HDD.
(iii) What is a printer? Name the different type of the printer available. Explain any one of them.

2. Attempt any four parts 3*4=12

(a)
(i) What are major UNIX Operating System that has made it popular? Discuss the salient feature of UNIX Architecture in brief
(ii) What is an UNIX Kernal? Explain the Explain the process of swapping in brief.

(b) Write steps to perform the following operation in vi editor :-
(i) To search a string "Ramanuja "and then change it to "Ramayan".
(ii) Revert to the last saved version of a file.
(iii) Delete a word.
(iv) Insertion of the text into a file .

(c) (i) List the popular Internet Services available . Explain any one on brief.
(ii) What is a Web Browser? Explain in brief, how you will visit a Website with a given URL.
(iii) Give full form of the following terms:-
(a) WWW
(b) HTML
(c) HTTP
(d) FTP
(e) XML
(iv) Explain the meaning of the following Domain Identifier :
(a) .edu
(b) .ac
(c) .gov
(d) .av
(e) .de

(d) (i) What are search Engines ? List any two popular search engines
(ii) What are e-mail? How are they sent? Explain the composition of any email address.
(iii) What is URL? Give the syntax of an URL by a suitable example.
(iv) What are Netiguette or E-mail Ethics ? List any two of them.

(e) What are PINE ? Write the steps to perform the following operation in PINE:-
   (i) Message Composition
   (ii) Replaying or forwarding a mail.
   (iii) To view Attachment Files
   (iv) To run spell checker.

(f) Write short note any One of the following :-
   (i) ISDN
   (ii) Telnet

3. Attempt any four parts:- 3*4=12

(a) What do you mean by Computer Languages ? Differentiate among High Level, Assembly and Machine Languages.

(b) State the fundamental data type and their size used in 'C' Language. Explain the difference between Prefix and Postfix increment and show how it affects the result of an expression.

(c) Give the structure of a complete "C" Program. List the different type of preprocessor directive available with "C" Language.

(d) Analyze the following program segments and determine how many times the body of each loop will be executed

(i)
```
x = 3
y = 60
while (x < = y)
{
x = y / x
}
```

(ii)
```
int i;
for(i = 1; i< =10; i = i + 3/ 4 )
{
   ............
   ............
}
```

(iii)
```
int m=10;
int n=7;
while (m%n>=0)
{
m=m+1;
n=n+2;
}
```

(e) Determine the value of each of the following logical expressions if a=5,b=10,c=6.
   (i) a>b & & a<c
   (ii) (a>=b | | (b=c)

(iii) a==c | | b>a
(iv) ((b>15) && (c<0 | | a>0))

(f) Attempt any one of the following :
   (i) Write a program in "C" that accepts a floating-point value as input represents a temperature in degree Celsius and returns its Fahrenheit equivalent.
   (ii) Write a recursive program to compute factorial of n.

4. Attempt any two of the following : 7*2=14

(a) The Fibonacci numbers are defined recursively as follows:

F1=1;
F2=1;
Fn=Fn-1+Fn-2, n>2

Write a function in 'C' that will generate and print n Fibonacci numbers and print sum of these numbers.

(b)
   (i) What are pointers in C ? How is a pointer initialized ? Explain with suitable example.
   (ii) Using pointer, write a function that receives a character string and character as argument and deletes all occurrences of this character in the string . Function should return the corrected with no holes .

(c) Consider the following structure :

Struct Employee
{
int Emp_no;
char name;
float salary;
}

Write a program in 'C' to do the following :
   (I) To read 20 (twenty) employee -records from keyboard and display employee -record on employee name.
   (II) Raise the salary of all employees by 25%
   (III) Calculate the average salary of all employees whose salaries is Rs. 5000
   or above.

SOLUTION

Ans. 1.

(a) The basic functional units of the Digital Computer are
   (i) Input Devices
   (ii) Output Devices

(iii) Central Processing Unit(CPU)
(iv) Memory unit

(See Chapter 1)

(i) **Input Devices** - The Input Devices allows user to submit data from outside world and transfer them to CPU for processing. e.g. Keyboard, Mouse, Scanner etc..

(ii) **Output Devices** -The final processed result is communicated by them to user. e.g. Monitor, Printer etc..

(iii) **Central Processing Unit** - Accept data from input devices and process them according to the instructions .Its main parts are ALU (Arithmetic and Logical Unit), Control Unit and Registers.

(iv) **Memory Unit** - It is used to holds the data that needs to be processed, as well as the intermediate result of the computation. It also plays the role of channel for communication between the Microprocessor and peripheral devices. E.g. Main Memory, RAM, ROM, Auxiliary memory.

(b) Computer H/W are the physical component of the computers, which can be physically feel, touch .It is the Skeleton of Computer system.

Where Computer S/W are the programs that cannot physically touch

BIOS - It stand for "Basic Input Output System"

The BIOS serves as a link between the H/W and S/W of computer. It cannot be classified as either S/W or H/W, it is both. Like S/W it is a set of instruction to the CPU. Sometime it is coded on to the chip gives it the H/W classifications. In fact the correct term something like the BIOS is firmware.

(See Chapter 4)

(c) **Internal Dos command** - These command are contains in the file "command .com ". This file is loaded into the memory when one boots his system. One can't see these command when you list directory on Dos disk. E.g. dir., date, time, copy etc.

External DOS Command - These commands are not contained in the file "command.com" These commands are contained in the separate files which usually have extension ". com" or ".exe" or ".bat" . When one see the directory these files are listed with the command name and followed by their extension. E.g. tree, xcopy, diskcopy, doskey etc.

(i) c:\ mkdir ABC
(ii) c:\ cd ABC
(iii) c:\ copy a/*.* ABC

(iv) c:\ dir/p
(v) c:\ rmdir ABC

(See Chapter 3)

(d) **Operating System** - An OS may be viewed as an organized collection of software extension of hardware, consisting of control for operating a computer and for providing an environment for execution of programs.

The major function of OS

- Allocation of resource
- Memory management
- Process Management
- Control I/O devices
- Security

Multiprogramming operating systems -multiprogramming is the concurrent execution of two or more processes. Multiprogramming OS are fairly sophisticated compare to batch OS. Multiprogramming has a significant potential for improving system throughput and resource utilization with very minor differences.

Multitasking Operating System - It allow more than one program / task to run concurrently e.g. In case of SPOOLING, DOS is not multitasking OS . The general multitasking environment is UNIX, LINUX, and WINDOWS

There is two basic type of multitasking

- Pre-emptive
- Co-operative

(See Chapter 5)

(e) Advantages of using WINDOWS 95/98 over DOS

- It provide GUI(Graphical User Interface)
- It is multitasking, multiprogramming
- It is quite efficient in networking
- It provide better security

(i) **The Desktop** - Total visible area on the screen which you get immediately after turning on your computer .It is provided with different icons, folders, shortcuts to run the most frequently used programs

(ii) **My Computer** - It is used to see everything stored on ones computer .It is one of the important icon provided at the desktop. The different folder it has is different drives, control panel, printer etc.

(iii) **Recycle Bin**- After deleting any object it is not actually deleted but it is sent to the Recycle Bin. This avoids the possibility of accidental deletes.

(See Chapter 2)

(f)

(i) **Input /Output Device** - I/O devices enable interaction with the computer they allows the user to submit data from outside world & display the out put to out side world . They serve as the medium of communication between the user and the computer.
Example for Input devices - Keyboard, mouse etc.
Example for Output devices - Monitor, printer etc.

(ii) **Hard disk drive**- The hard disk store and provides relatively quick access to large amount of data on and Electro-magnetically charge surface or set of surfaces. A head record (writes) or read the information on the tracks. Two heads, one on each side of a disk, read or write the data as the disk spins.
Ranges stored capacity of currently available HDD
From 2.3 GB - 40 GB
Performance parameter of HDD
(a) Rotation speed -Spin rate are typically 5400 -7200 rpm
(b) Seek Time - The amount of time it takes for the read/ write head to move one - third of the way across the disk. It range from 8-12 milli-seconds

(iii) **Printer** - Printer are output devices that produce the hard copy (on paper) of the result, which you wise to procure for long time. The
Different types of printers available are -

(a) Dot Matrix Printers

The Dot Matrix printer has a ribbon that is coated with ink. A moving pin strikes it, and its impact on the ribbon, transfers the ink onto the paper behind the ribbon. All the characters printed by dot matrix printer are made up of various vertical dot patterns, hence the name. Some printers pass the print head (the pin), over the paper a second time, slightly offset from the first print. This improves the quality of the output. The noise made while printing is very loud, but with advances in technology, manufacturers have tried coming up with quieter, faster and smaller Dot Matrix printers.

(b) Color Ink-Jet Printer

These printers are smaller in size compared to the Dot Matrix printers. The noise level is much lower and almost non-existent in the color ink jet printers. The working is very much similar to the Dot matrix printer. The Ink-Jet printer also has a printer head that moves over the page, printing an entire line with each pass. The only difference is that the head spews out the ink onto the paper, making it a non-impact printer. The print head contains four ink cartridges (one each for cyan, magenta, yellow and black).

(c) **Laser Printer**

Laser Printers are most popular printers in the offices and employ a sequence of actions to produce flawless output. Though it makes a louder sound than the Ink-Jet, the quality of the printing is supreme, and detailed. They are most commonly found in large offices. The prohibitive costs involved deter their wide usage.

(See Chapter 8)

Ans. 2.

(a) (i) The major features of UNIX are -

(a) UNIX is a multi-user, multitasking system that support networking and distributed file systems.
(b) It is easier to be upgraded since the entire OS does not need to be recompiled
(c) In this OS all the users are interacted through a shell
(d) Every UNIX implementation now includes TCP/IP and support for Internet.
(e) Large selection of Powerful UNIX supplied Programs.
(f) Communication & E Mail.

Salient feature of UNIX architecture -

(a) It is written largely in C language.
(b) Some part of it is also written on assembler
(c) It is portable
(d) Parts of UNIX architecture- Kernel, Shell, The file system.

(ii) **UNIX Kernel** - The core unit is called Kernel. Its task includes CPU Scheduling, allocating the necessary hardware, controlling I/O operation etc. Since there are several jobs submitted and running simultaneously, the Kernel gives them tag or identification.

Swapping - The kernel moves the waiting process to secondary storage (HDD) where by the currently running process gets all the memory space it need. This is called swapping.

(see Chapter 6)

(c) (i) Popular Internet Services

- E-MAIL
- Telnet
- FTP

- Usenet
- Gopher
- Archie
- Veronica
- WWW

(ii) **Web Browser-** Web Browsers are the programs which are used to view the document or page written or coded to HTML. The web pages can be viewed using web browsers E.g. MS - Explorer, Netscape Navigator.

When you use web browser for net surfing, you are connected to the desired server after specifying URL address. It then brings the home page of the server.

(iii) Full forms

- WWW - World Wide Web
- HTML - Hyper Text Markup Language
- HTTP - Hyper Text Transfer Protocol
- FTP - File Transfer Protocol
- XML - Extensible Markup Language

(iv) Meaning of following domain identifier

- .edu-education
- .ac-academic community
- .gov-government
- .au-australia
- .de-germany

(d) (i) **Search Engine** - The Search Engine is actually the web site and contain the link to the million of the web page . It usually a great problem for the user to find the appropriate site or the site of interest. Its solution is search engine.

E.g. of popular search engine -

- www.yahoo.com
- www.exite.com

(ii) **E-mails** - Electronic Mail, popularly known, as E-mail has become an important mean of communication. This medium is being used to send & receive letter / notes or draft. Technically it is the way of sending document in electronic form from one computer to another. E-mail are sent through the computer using Mail tools like MS Outllok, PINE, ELM etc. You may also log on to free E Mail provider website (Yahoo, hotmail, rediffmail etc) to get mail service on the net.

Syntax for the mail address is

Username@addressof server

E.g. krishan@hotmail.com

(iii) URL-Uniform Resource Locator.
When you use web browser for net surfing, you are connected to the desired server after specifying URL address. It then brings the home page of the server. It is also known as the address of the website.

(iii) E-mail Ethics / Netiquiette
- Don't use bold letter
- Don't leave the subject field blank
- Proper Salutations

(See Chapter 9)

(e) PINE- Program for Internet News and E-mail
It is easy to use full feature menu driven mail program for sending receiving and filling Internet message and net news message. It is made available to the worldwide Internet community as a public service.
'C' command is used to compose and send Emails.
How to send the Mail ?

When you press X, you will be asked to confirm that you want the message to be sent. If you answer N, you are returned to your unsent message; if you answer Y, the message is sent and copied to your sent-mail folder.

How to see Attached File ?

Attachments are files sent with the message, but not actually shown in the message text. View Attachment (V) command allows you to see the attachment to the mail. Attachments are useful to send large files and especially binary files (programs).

How to run Spell Checker ?

You may call the UNIX spell checker to check your mail for spelling mistakes. Spell Check (T) tool of PINE invokes the spell checker of the UNIX. This will check whole mail text but it does not suggest alternative spellings

(See Chapter 6)

(f) (i) **ISDN**- Integrated Service Digital Network. It is the most powerful tool for various services such as voices images video and multimedia data communication over the telephone network. It is the logical extension to the digitalization of telephone network. It works in following two modes
- BRI (Basic Rate Interface)
- PRI (Primary Rate Interface)

(ii) **Telnet** -It is a tool, which allows you to log on to any computer on the Internet. After log in you may use the software and other programs stored on the computer you logged in and you have full control over that computer.

(See Chapter 11)

Ans. 3

(a) **Computer Language**

Programming language is essentially the neat and clean description of set of rules in which real world problems may be submitted to the computer.

High level language-writing programs in high level language are most convenient to the programmers. Program written in higher a translator translates level languages called interpreter or compiler. E.g. -Java, C++ etc.

Assembly level language-In this language programs are written in mnemonic and writing programs in this language is convenient to programmers. Programs written in this language is converted/ translated into machine level program by a translator called assembler. E.g. 8085

Machine level language-programs written in this language are very much H/W dependent and programming in this language is tough and complex job.

(b) The fundamental data types & their ranges are as follows:

- char : -128 to 127
- int : -32768 to 32767
- float : 3.4e-38 to 3.4e+38
- double : 1.7e-308 to 1.7e+308

Prefix increment operator: It first adds one to the operand and then result is assigned to the variable on the left-hand side.

For example: Consider A=1;

B= ++A;

After the execution of the second statement value of A & B will be 2.

Postfix increment operator: It first assigns the value to the variable on the left then increment the operand.

For example: Consider A=1;

B=A++;

In this case value of B would be 1 and that of A would be 2.

(c) The basic block structure of complete C program is as follows. It may contain one or more sections as defined below:

Comment lines
Line section
Definition section

Global declaration section
Main ()
{
declarative statements;
executable statements;
}

Different types of Preprocessor directives are as follows:

- #include
- #define
- #ifdef
- #if #else

Ans. 3

(i) Infinity
(ii) Infinity
(iii) Infinity

(e)

(i) False
(ii) False
(iii) True
(iv) False

(See chapter 11 & 12)

Ans. 3

(f)

(i)

```
#include<stdio.h>
#include<conio.h>
void main()
{
float cel,fahr;
clrscr();
printf("\nTHIS IS A PROGRAM OF CONVERSION OF CEL-
SIUS INTO FAHRENHEIT\n");
printf("\nenter the value of temperature in celsious");
scanf("%f",&cel);
 fahr=32+(cel*9/5);
 printf("\nthe temperature in fahrenheit=%f  F",fahr);
 getch();
}
```

(ii)

```
/*THE RECURSIVE PROGRAM FOR FINDING THE FAC-
TORIAL */
```

```
#include<conio.h>
#include<stdio.h>
void main()
{
int i,f=1,n,a;
int facto(int p);
clrscr();
printf(" /*THE PROGRAM FOR FINDING THE FACTORIAL
OF ANY GIVEN NUMBER GREATER THAN 1*/ ");
printf("\n\n GIVE THE NUMBER WHOSE FACTORIAL IS
REQUIRED ");
scanf("%d",&n);
a=n;
if(n==0)
f=1;
else
f=facto(n);
printf("\n\n THE FACTORAIL OF  %d!  IS %d ",a,f);
getch();
}
int facto(int p)
{
 int s;
if(p==1)
 return(1);
else
s=p*facto(p-1);
return s;
}
```

Ans. 4.
(a)

```
/*THIS PROGRAM IS FOR FIBONACCI SERIES */
#include <conio.h>
#include <stdio.h>
#define M 20
void main()
{
int i,n,a[M],sum=0;
char ch;
clrscr();
printf("\n Enter a number of term you wants in your series ?(less
```

```
than %d)\n",M);
scanf("%d",&n);
a[0]=0;
a[1]=1;
for(i=2;i<n;i++)
  a[i]=a[i-1]+a[i-2];
printf("\nTHE FABONACCI SERIES OF  %d  TERM",n);
for(i=0;i<n;i++)
  printf("  %d",a[i]);
printf("\n\nDO YOU WANT THE SUMMATION OF THIS SE-
RIES (y/n)");
ch=getch();
if(ch=='Y' || ch=='y')
{
for (i=0;i<n;i++)
  sum=sum+a[i];
printf("\n\n THE SUM OF FIBONACCI  SERIES IS  %d ",sum);
}
else
  exit(1);
getch();
}
```

(b) (i) **Pointer** -Pointer are the variable, which stores the address of another variable .In C every variable must be declared for its type. Since pointer variable contains address that belongs to a separate data type, they must be used as pointer before we use them.

Initialization - data type *pt_name;
int *p; -
p is a pointer variable to an integer data type

(ii)

```
#include<conio.h>
#include<stdio.h>
#include<string.h>
void main()
{
char* fun(char*,char);
char a,s[10],re[5],*r;
clrscr();
printf("\n Enter the string");
gets(s);
fflush(stdin);
```

```
printf("\n Enter the char");
scanf("%c",&a);
r=fun(s,a);
printf("\n result   %s ",r);
getch();
}
char* fun(char *p,char q)
{
int i,l,j;
l=strlen(p);
for(i=0;i<l;i++)
{
if(p[i]==q)
{
p[i]='1';
}
}
i=0;
while(p[i]!='\0'){
for(j=i;j<l;j++)
{
if(p[j]=='1')
do{
p[j]=p[j+1];
j++;
} while(p[j]!='\0');
}
p[j]='\0';
i++;
}
return p;
}
```

(c)

```
#include<conio.h>
//#include<stdlib.h>
#include<stdio.h>
#define max 20
struct emp{
  int emp_no;
  char name[15];
  int sal;
  }e[max];
```

```
void main()
{
int i,count=0,total=0;
static float increased_sal[max],average;
clrscr();
for(i=1;i<max;i++)
{
printf("  \n Employee No ");
scanf("%d",&e[i].emp_no);
//fflush();
printf("\nNAME of %d employee ",e[i].emp_no);
scanf("%s",e[i].name);
printf ("\n Salary of the employee");
scanf("%d",&e[i].sal);
increased_sal[i]= e[i].sal+(0.25*e[i].sal);
if(e[i].sal>=5000)
{
total=total+e[i].sal;
count++;
}
}
average=total/count;
  printf("\NEMPLOYEE NO    \t EMPLOYEE NAME\t
SALARY\tINCREASED SALARY\n");
for (i=1;i<max; i++)
printf("\n                              %d\t\t%s\t\t%d\t%f
",e[i].emp_no,e[i].name,e[i].sal,increased_sal[i]);
printf("\n\n The average  == %f  ",average);
getch();
}
```

B.Tech

First Semester Examination 2001-2002

COMPUTER & LANGUAGES

Time : 2 Hrs *Max. Marks : 50*

Note (1) Attempt all questions

1. Attempt any *Four* parts of the following:— 3×4=12

(a) Explain the following in context of Computer:—

(i) Secondary Memory

(ii) Cache Memory

(iii) Main Memory

(b) What are advantages of WINDOWS 95/98 over DOS? Explain the following terms related with WINDOWS:

(i) My Document

(ii) Recycle Bin

(c) What do you mean by Multitasking System? How is it different from Multiprocessing System?

(d) Write DOS Commands to do the following:—

(i) Create directory "ABC" at root.

(ii) Copy file "Read me.Txt" from root to "ABC" directory.

(iii) Delete directory "ABC" with all of its subdirectories and files.

(e) Write steps to do the following in WINDOWS 95/98:—

(i) Create a folder in My Document.

(ii) Copy a file from one folder "X" to another folder "Y".

(iii) Send a file from folder "X" to Recycle Bin.

(f) What are output devices used in Digital computer? Discuss any two of them.

2. Attempt any *Four* parts of the following:— 3×4=12

(a) List any two major features of UNIX Operating system. What is the difference between absolute and relative path names of a UNIX file?

(b) What is Web Browser? Explain in brief.

(c) What are Search Engines? List any two popular Search Engines.

(d) What are E-mails? How are they sent? Explain how an attachment is made to the mail.

(e) Explain the following with respect to DOS Editor, EDIT:

(i) List the different menu options and explain any one.

(ii) How do you set colours?

(f) Explain the salient features of PINE or ELM.

3. Attempt any *Four* parts of the following:— 3½×4=14
   (a) State the fundamental data types and their size used in 'C' Language. Explain the difference between Postfix and Prefix increment operators. Show how it affects the result of an Expression.
   (b) Write a 'C' program to sort an array of integers in ascending order.
   (c) Write a 'C' program to find the sum of the series—
   $$1 + X + X^2 + X^3 + \ldots\ldots\ldots\ldots\ldots\ldots\ X^n$$
   (d) What are pointers in 'C'? How is a pointer initialized? Explain with a suitable example.
   (e) Write a program in 'C' to calculate sine & cosine values of the angles 9, 10°, 20°, ... 180° and print the result in tabular form.
   (f) What are functions? Explain the difference between iterative and recursive function calls.

4. Attempt any *Two* parts of the following: 6×2=12
   (a) (i) Write a program to accept the element of the structure; EMP_NO, BASIC_PAY, NAME. Display the same structure along with DA, CCA and GROSS_SALARY. DA & CCA are to be calculated as follows:—
   DA = 51% of basic pay
   CCA = Rs. 100=00 consolidated
   (b) Using pointer, write a function that receives a character string and a character as argument and deletes all occurrences of this character in this string. Function should return the corrected string without space.
   (c (i) What are arrays? How are they declared in 'C'?
   (ii) Write a program in 'C' to transpose a matrix of size N × N.

SOLUTION

1. (a) Explain the following in the context of computer.
   (i) Secondary Memory
   (ii) Cache Memory
   (iii) Main Memory

   (i) Secondary Memory or Auxiliary Memory is the place where the data and programs may be kept for future use. These memory devices are cheaper and provide high amount of storage capacity.

(ii) Cache memory is the fastest and most costly form of storage. Size of cache is small and it is placed between Main Memory and CPU. The processing speed of CPU is much higher than main memory therefore most frequently accessed data are placed in cache so that they can be accessed by the CPU without time delays.

(iii) Main Memory is directly accessed by the CPU. The data to be processed is brought in the main memory and CPU fetches the data from main memory for processing. This memory is also known as scratch pad memory.

1. (b) What are the advantages of Windows 95/98 over DOS? Explain the following terms
   (i) My Document
   (ii) Recycle Bin

Windows 95/98 is based on Graphical User Interface (GUI) while DOS provides textual interface. Different tasks may be accomplished by clicking to certain icons in windows, while DOS requires the users to enter the textual command. It is very easy for a user to work on Windows in comparison to DOS.

My Document is a system managed folder in Windows. Any work done by the users is saved in the form of files in this folder by default. The icon for this folder appears on Desk Top.

Recycle Bin is a System managed folder. It keeps the deleted file. If a user decides to delete a file, it first goes to this folder. Permanent removal of file from the computer system takes place only if files are removed from the recycle bin. This facility prevents the users from accidental deletes.

(c) What do you mean by Multitasking Systems? How are they different from Multiprocessing System?

Multitasking Systems are those where two or more than two tasks (jobs) can be done simultaneously. While multiprocessing systems are those where multiple processors are linked together in a coordinated system.

1. (d) Write DOS command to do the following.
   (i) Create directory "ABC" at root.
   (ii) Copy File Readme.txt from root to "ABC"
   (iii) Delete directory "ABC" with all of its subdirectories and files.

DOS command to do these tasks are given below.

(1) C:\> md abc or C:\>mkdir abc

(2) C:\> copy readme.txt c:\abc

(3) C:\> deltree abc

1. (f) What are output devices used in digital computers? Discuss any two of them.

Output devices are used in the digital computer for presenting the result of processing to users. VDU, Printers, Plotters etc are example of output devices. VDU or monitor is used to display the result, commands etc on the screen, while printers are used for taking permanent hard copy of the result. The plotters are most suited for taking the printout for map, design, drawings etc.

2. (a) List any two major features of UNIX operating system. What are difference between absolute and relative path names of a UNIX files.

Important features of UNIX OS are listed below.

1. Multi-user Operating System
2. Multitasking
3. Time sharing
4. Portability

Absolute path starts from root to the file in directory tree. it includes all the subdirectories and denotes the location of file respect to root.

Relative path locates a file with respect to the current working directory. It shows the file location relative to working directory.

2. (b) What is a Web Browser ? Explain in brief

Web Browser is a software tool used to view the HTML document. Web Browser allows the user to enter the URL of a web site and explore\display the contents to the user. It is also known as client program which a user can use to access the internet. MS Internet Explorer, Netscape Navigator are examples of web browsers.

2. (c) What are search engines? List any two popular search engines.

Search Engines are web sites which allows the user to find the actual \relevant websites. The user may search for a web site by entering few keywords for the search and search engines then presents a list of sites or link to the subject. All search engines use their own syntax for specifying the keywords. Following are popular search engines.

1. www.google.com
2. www.altvista.com
3. www.excite.com
4. www.yahoo.com

2. (d) What are E Mails? How are they sent? Explain how an attachment is made to the mail?

E mail is a service in which a user may send the document\, letter\message to another user electronically. The messages are delivered over the internet to another user almost instantly. Every E Mail user must have an E Mail address which usually has following form,

User id@address of server

An attachment to the mail may be made by the attachment option provided in the mail tools. Any file containing text, audio, graphics etc may be attached with the mail which will be delivered to the recipient over the internet.

2. (e) Explain the following with respect to DOS editor EDIT,
   (i) List the different menu options and explain any one of them.
   (ii) How do you set the colors.

EDIT is a tool used in DOS environment for creating text files. Different menu options available are File, Edit, Search, Option and Help. Options menus, Display option allows you to set the foreground and background colors.

2. (f) Explain the salient features of PINE or ELM.

PINE (Program for Internet News and E mail) is an easy to use full featured and menu driven mail program for sending and receiving mails, internet messages and net news messages. PINE is easy to remember single character has a menu interface which displays options available at every point. It also allows you to manage address book, attachments etc. ELM is a sophisticated full screen mail system for interactive use. It is also used for sending and receiving E Mails.

3. (a) State the fundamental data types and their size used in C language. Explain the prefix and post fix increment operator. Show how it affects the result of the computations.

Four fundamental data types are shown below.

int	Integer	2 bytes
float	Floating point	4 bytes
char	single character	1 byte
double	double precision	8 bytes

Post Fix increment operator assigns the value to the variable on left and then increment the operand E.g.

```
A=1;
B=A ++;
```

Value of B=1, A=2 after the execution of statement.
Prefix increment operator first add one to the operand and then assigns the value to the left. E.g

```
A=1;
B= ++A;
```

Value of B=2, A=2 after the execution of both statement.

3. (b) Write a C program to sort an array of integers in ascending order.

```
/* Program to sort the integer in ascending order */
# include <stdio.h>
void main ()
{
int i, j, n, temp;
int a [50];
print f ("Enter the number to data values to sort");
scanf ("%d", &n);
for (i=1; i<=n; i++)
scanf ("%d", &a [i]);
for (i=1; i<=n;i++)
{
for (j=1; j< n; j++)
{
    if (a[j] <=a [j+1])
    {
    temp=a[j];
    a[j]=a[j+1];
    a[j+a]=temp;
    }
}
}
for (i=1; i<=n; i++)
printf {"%d", a[i] );
getch ();
}
```

3. (c) Write a C program to find the sum of the series-

```
void main ()
{
int n,x,i,
int sum, term;
printf ("Enter the value of X");
scanf ("%d", &x);
printf ("Enter the number of terms");
```

```
scanf ("%d", & n);
sum=0;
term=1;
for (i=1; i<=n; i++)
{
sum = sum + term;
term = term *x;
}
printf (" The sum of series = %d", sum);
getch();
}
```

3. (d) What are Pointers in C? How a pointer initialized? Explain with a suitable example.

A pointer is a integer variable that contains the address of another variable. It may be noted that actual value (location) of a variable in the memory is system dependent therefore the address of the variable is not known immediately.

e.g p = & qty;

this statement assigns the address of location of variable "qty" to variable "p".

Pointer's are initialized as follows,

```
int *amt_ptr,a,b;
amt_ptr = &a;
B = *amt_ptr;
```

3. (e) Write a program in C to calculate sine and cosine values of the angle 0, 10, 20,...180 and print result in tabular form.

```
# include <stdio.h>
# define PI 3.17
void main ()
{
int i;
float angle;
for (i=0; i<=180; i=i+10)
{
angle = (PI/180)*i;
printf ("\n%3d\t %7.5f %7.5f",i, cos(angle), sin(angle));
}
getch()
}
```

3. (f) What are functions? Explain the difference between iterative and recursive function calls.

A function is a self-contained block of codes that perform a particular task. Once a function has been designed and packed it then may be considered as a black box which takes certain values and returns the values. Recursion is a process where a function calls itself.

4. (a) (i) Differentiate between the Structures and Union.

A structure definition creates a format that may be used to declare structure variable. Keyword struct declares a structure to hold the details of the members. All the members of Union uses same location. A union may contain many members of different types, it can handle only one member at a time.

(ii)

```
/* This programs calculate the Gross salary of Employee */
#include <stdio.h>
#include <conio.h>
struct employee {
                int emp_no;
                int basic_pay;
                char name[40];
                float da, cca, gross_salary;
            };
void main ()
{
struct employee emp[50];
int i,j,n;
printf ("enter the number of the employee");
scanf ("%d", & n);
for (i=1 ; i<=n ; i=i++)
{
printf (" Enter the record of %d th employee\n", i);
scanf ("%d %d %s ", & emp[I].emp_no, &emp[I]. basic_pay,
emp[I}.name);
emp[I].da= .51 * emp[I}.basic_pay;
emp{I}.cca = 100.00;
emp{I}.gross_salary= emp{I}.basic_pay + emp[I}.da
+emp[I}.cca;
}
printf ("Printing of employee name and gross salary\n");
for (i=1 ; i<=n ; i=i++)
{
```

```
printf ("%d %d %s \n ", I, & emp{I}.emp_no, emp{I}.name,
emp{I}.gross_salary);
}
```

4. (b)

```
char *delele_char (char *str, char a)
   {
      int i,j,length;
      length = strlen (str);
      for (i=1 ; i<=length ; i=i++)
      {
         if (x != str[I};
         {
         for (j=I, j<length ; j++)
         str[j] = str[j+1];
         length–;
      }
      }
      return str;
   }
```

4. (c) What are arrays? How are they declared in C?
Array is collection of similar type of data or element. They are declared as shown below,

```
Int A[10];
Float sal [50],
Int a[10] [10];
```